# The Gift of Beauty and the Passion of Being

# VERITAS

## Series Introduction

"... the truth will set you free" (John 8:32)

In much contemporary discourse, Pilate's question has been taken to mark the absolute boundary of human thought. Beyond this boundary, it is often suggested, is an intellectual hinterland into which we must not venture. This terrain is an agnosticism of thought: because truth cannot be possessed, it must not be spoken. Thus, it is argued that the defenders of "truth" in our day are often traffickers in ideology, merchants of counterfeits, or anti-liberal. They are, because it is somewhat taken for granted that Nietzsche's word is final: truth is the domain of tyranny.

Is this indeed the case, or might another vision of truth offer itself? The ancient Greeks named the love of wisdom as *philia*, or friendship. The one who would become wise, they argued, would be a "friend of truth." For both philosophy and theology might be conceived as schools in the friendship of truth, as a kind of relation. For like friendship, truth is as much discovered as it is made. If truth is then so elusive, if its domain is *terra incognita*, perhaps this is because it arrives to us—unannounced—as gift, as a person, and not some thing.

The aim of the Veritas book series is to publish incisive and original current scholarly work that inhabits "the between" and "the beyond" of theology and philosophy. These volumes will all share a common aspiration to transcend the institutional divorce in which these two disciplines often find themselves, and to engage questions of pressing concern to both philosophers and theologians in such a way as to reinvigorate both disciplines with a kind of interdisciplinary desire, often so absent in contemporary academe. In a word, these volumes represent collective efforts in the befriending of truth, doing so beyond the simulacra of pretend tolerance, the violent, yet insipid reasoning of liberalism that asks with Pilate, "What is truth?"—expecting a consensus of non-commitment; one that encourages the commodification of the mind, now sedated by the civil service of career, ministered by the frightened patrons of position.

The series will therefore consist of two "wings": (1) original monographs; and (2) essay collections on a range of topics in theology and philosophy. The latter will principally be the products of the annual conferences of the Centre of Theology and Philosophy (www.theologyphilosophycentre.co.uk).

Conor Cunningham and Eric Austin Lee, *Series editors*

# The Gift of Beauty and the Passion of Being

## On the Threshold between the Aesthetic and the Religious

WILLIAM DESMOND

CASCADE *Books* • Eugene, Oregon

THE GIFT OF BEAUTY AND THE PASSION OF BEING
On the Threshold between the Aesthetic and the Religious

Veritas 30



Cascade Books
An Imprint of Wipf and Stock Publishers
199 W. 8th Ave., Suite 3
Eugene, OR 97401

www.wipfandstock.com

PAPERBACK ISBN: 978-1-5326-1710-2
HARDCOVER ISBN: 978-1-4982-4155-7
EBOOK ISBN: 978-1-4982-4154-0

*Cataloguing-in-Publication data:*

Names: Desmond, William, 1951–, author.

Title: The gift of beauty and the passion of being : on the threshold between the aesthetic and the religious / William Desmond.

Description: Eugene, OR: Cascade Books, 2018 | Series: Veritas 30 | Includes bibliographical references and index.

Identifiers: ISBN 978-1-5326-1710-2 (paperback) | ISBN 978-1-4982-4155-7 (hardcover) | ISBN 978-1-4982-4154-0 (ebook)

Subjects: LCSH: Metaphysics | Aesthetics | Aesthetics—Religious aspects | Art—Philosophy | Philosophy and religion | Transcendence (Philosophy)

Classification: BH39 D43 2018 (print) | BH39 (ebook)

JULY 2, 2018

περὶ δὲ κάλλους, ὥσπερ εἴπομεν, μετ᾽ ἐκείνων τε ἔλαμπεν ὄν, δεῦρό τ᾽ ἐλθόντες κατειλήφαμεν αὐτὸ διὰ τῆς ἐναργεστάτης αἰσθήσεως τῶν ἡμετέρων στίλβον ἐναργέστατα. ὄψις γὰρ ἡμῖν ὀξυτάτη τῶν διὰ τοῦ σώματος ἔρχεται αἰσθήσεων, ᾗ φρόνησις οὐχ ὁρᾶται—δεινοὺς γὰρ ἂν παρεῖχεν ἔρωτας, εἴ τι τοιοῦτον ἑαυτῆς ἐναργὲς εἴδωλον παρείχετο εἰς ὄψιν ἰόν— τἆλλα ὅσα ἐραστά:νῦν δὲ κάλλος μόνον ταύτην ἔσχε μοῖραν, ὥστ᾽ ἐκφανέστατον εἶναι καὶ ἐρασμιώτατον.

But beauty, as I said before, shone in brilliance among those visions; and since we came to earth we have found it shining most clearly through the clearest of our senses; for sight is the sharpest of the physical senses, though wisdom is not seen by it, for wisdom would arouse terrible love, if such a clear image of it were granted as would come through sight, and the same is true of the other lovely realities; but beauty alone has this privilege, and therefore it is most clearly seen and loveliest.

PLATO, *PHAEDRUS* 250D-E

My way is this: --

In all nice and ticklish discussions, -- (of which, heaven knows, there are but too many in my book) -- where I find I cannot take a step without the danger of having either their worships or their reverences upon my back -- I write one half *full*, -- and t'other *fasting*; ---- or write it all full, -- and correct it fasting; -- or write it fasting, -- and correct it full, for they all come to the same thing: -- . . . .

Now, when I write full, -- I write as if I was never to write fasting again as long as I live; ---- that is, I write free from the cares, as well as the terrors of the world. ---- I count not the number of my scars, -- nor does my fancy go forth into dark entries and bye corners to antedate my stabs. ---- In a word, my pen takes its course; and I write on as much from the fullness of my heart, as my stomach. ----

But when, an' please your honours, I indite fasting, 'tis a different history. ---- I pay the world all possible attention and respect, -- and have as great a share (whilst it lasts) of that understrapping virtue of discretion, as the best of you. ---- So that betwixt both, I write a careless kind of a civil, nonsensical, good humoured *Shandean* book, which will do all your hearts good ----

---- And all your heads too, -- provided you understand it.

LAURENCE STERN, *THE LIFE AND OPINIONS OF TRISTRAM SHANDY, GENTLEMAN*, VOLUME VI, CHAPTER XVII

With gratitude to the companioning power

# Table of Contents

# Acknowledgements

VERSIONS OF SOME OF the chapters in this book appeared in earlier publications. They have been revisited and revised for current publication. Chapters 5 and 7 appear here in longer versions. I wish to thank the publishers for permission to use my work.

- Chapter 2 as: "On the Surface of Things: Transient Life and Beauty in Passing." *Radical Orthodoxy: Theology, Philosophy, Politics*, Vol. 1, Numbers 1 & 2 (2012) 20–54.
- Chapter 3 as: "Soul Music and Soul-less Selving." In *The Resounding Soul: Reflections on the Metaphysics and Vivacity of the Human Person*, edited by Eric Lee and Samuel Kimbriel, 352–89. Eugene, OR: Cascade, 2016.
- Chapter 5 as: "Schopenhauer's Philosophy of the Dark Origin." In *The Blackwell Companion to Schopenhauer*, edited by Bart Vandenabeele, 89–104. Oxford: Blackwell, 2012.
- Chapter 6 as: "Creativity and the Dunamis." In *The Philosophy of Paul Weiss: Library of Living Philosophers*, edited by L. Hahn, 543–57. Chicago: Open Court, 1995.
- Chapter 7 as: "A Second Primavera: Cavell, German Philosophy and Romanticism." In *Stanley Cavell*, edited by R. Eldridge, 143–71. Cambridge: Cambridge University Press, 2003.
- Chapter 8 as: "The Theater of the *Metaxu*: Staging the Between." In *Topoi: An International Review of Philosophy*, Vol. 30, Number 2 (2011) 113–24.

- The Appendix, Steven Knepper: "'Intimate Intertwining': An Interview with William Desmond on Art and Religion." *Religion & Literature* 49.1 (2017).

I want to thank Ryan Duns for generously reading all the chapters and helping me with proof reading. My thanks also to Maria Kelly and William Desmond for welcome help with proof reading. My warm thanks also to Robin Parry for his much appreciated editorial work on this volume in bringing it to its final shape.

# Introduction

## I

THERE IS HARDLY A book I have written, from *Art and the Absolute* to *The Intimate Universal*, in which aesthetic matters and art are not of great significance.[1] They are of significance for themselves, and for philosophical reflection. There is also a relation to our being religious, which has a like importance. Art, religion, and philosophy: all honor to Hegel for placing these at the highest level of absolute spirit. I agree with the imputation of ultimate importance, but disagree with the way Hegel relates them. I will come to how I see that relation again, but I speak of matters aesthetic and art, since I take aesthetic matters to root us firmly in the flesh of being, and in our own being incarnate. I do not agree with Hegel's claim that art is higher than natural beauty, if this means a downgrading of flesh and our participation in the aesthetics of happening. I would rather a view that allows an ontology of incarnation where the wording of flesh is prior to and beyond our tendency to bifurcate the natural and the cultural. We are often still secretly Cartesian even when we protest to the contrary.

Beyond the confines of already published works I have continued to ruminate on the richness of aesthetic matters and art. I hold there is a metaxological intermediation among art, religion, and philosophy rather than a dialectical sublation, as Hegel held. The metaxological intermediations of the spaces between art, religion, and philosophy are plurivocal rather than univocal, or even simply dialectical. There can be intermediations between philosophy and the aesthetic, as there can be between

1. Desmond, *Art and the Absolute: A Study of Hegel's Aesthetics* (1986); Desmond, *The Intimate Universal: The Hidden Porosity among Religion, Art, Philosophy, and Politics* (2016).

philosophy and our being religious. What of the intermediations between the aesthetic and the religious? I see this book as diversely responding to this question. If *Art, Origins, Otherness* answers the intermediations of art and philosophy, and if *Is There a Sabbath for Thought?* responds to the intermediations of religion and philosophy, this book responds to perplexities arising in the intermediations between the aesthetic and the religious.[2]

## II

In a first pass, and to come directly to the aesthetic matters to be considered, let me offer a taste of my central concerns in advance of their fuller development in particular chapters. In a second pass, I will try to situate this work in relation to some of my other books and the philosophical outlook marking my work overall.

In my *opening chapter*, I reflect on the gift of beauty and the passion of being, and since this sets the tone of the work as a whole a slightly longer précis might help. My reflections depart from the fact that today we often meet an ambiguous attitude to beauty among some who proclaim their advanced aesthetic authenticity. Beauty seems bland and lacks the more visceral thrill of the ugly, indeed the excremental. We crave what disrupts and provokes us, not what gives delight or even consoles. The "really real" is the disturbing, even the revolting. Bland beauty is the death of originality. If this is our attitude, how are we to be open at all to beauty as gift? Granted, we need not, indeed cannot, avoid the ugly, yet something is lacking if our primary emphasis on it makes it impossible for us to be honest and true to beauty. The fact is that we often are disturbed paradoxically by beauty: both taken out of ourselves, hence disquieted, yet awakened to our being at home with beauty, hence enchanted and enlivened. Beauty arouses engimatic joy in us, and we enjoy an elemental rapport with it as other. Surprised by beauty, our breath is taken away, we are more truly there with the beautiful, yet taken outside of ourselves: both at home with ourselves and not being at home, in being beyond ourselves. We are first receivers of the gift of surprise and only then perceivers and conceivers. My attention to the passion of being stresses a patience, a receptivity to what is other. What happens is not

2. Desmond, *Art, Origins, Otherness: Between Art and Philosophy*; Desmond, *Is There a Sabbath for Thought? Between Religion and Philosophy*.

first our construction. There is something given, something awakening, something delighting, something energizing, something of invitation to transcendence.

Our being disarmed by the beautiful I hold to be in tune with our being as marked most deeply by what I call *a primal porosity to being*. Beauty sensuously communicates in and through this awakened porosity. We are a patience of being before we are an endeavor to be. Our *passio essendi* is on the boundary between receiving and responding—responding that may itself become creative in attempting to bring into being works of art in communication, secretly or more openly, with the originating reception. I grant that in modern aesthetics and culture, originating receptivity tends to be downplayed as a depreciation of our claims to creative power. The predominant stress often falls on human autonomy and self-determination. We love only what we construct ourselves, not what we receive. We worry that what is given is a curb or threat or occasion of resistance to our constructive *conatus*. A guarded attitude to beauty as given must follow; a guarded attitude also to the surprise of beauty, for we cannot construct true surprise. By contrast, I would say there is something of the godsend in what is truly beautiful. This might be a way of talking that is not fashionable, but the vocation of the philosopher is not to be fashionable but to be true.

When I speak of beauty and the erotics of being, I am interested in the *directionality* of eros: whether it is an ascending movement that mysteriously is moved towards what is superior to us, or a descending movement that searches below ground into more infernal regions where beauty is hated as a reminder of a heaven lost or an earth rejected. If we circle around the ugly as more thrilling, are we circling around our own lack, becoming ourselves the evil eye whose look on things sees nothing lovely, whose evil eye only blights beauty while blaming it? I found myself at the end of these thoughts in an unanticipated séance with hell.

In *chapter 2*, there is a turn to the *surface* where my exploration dwells on the significance of the surface of things, in connection with life and transient beauty. I explore how different conceptions of life seem to fall between two extremes: the more objectifying conception and the more subjectifying. In the first, the risk is a reductive understanding where life as living and lived seems to evaporate in our determination to comprehend it as "objective." In the second, the immanent self-relation of the living being, while to be granted, can pass over, or distort in intimate life itself, what passes beyond an entirely immanent self-relation.

Life as transient passes but also passes beyond itself as an immanent self-relation. I take seriously what I see as philosophy's vocation to be true to the surface of things, in the transience of life. There is something entirely positive about surfaces as intermediating transient life. Beauty has immense importance in fostering mindfulness of the rich surfaces of things. Beauty intermediates what cannot be completely objectified and what exceeds every self-relation of the subject. It is intimately related to this transience of the interim of life. I want to show how beauty communicates something of surplus significance on the surface of things, beyond the objectifying approach and the subjectifying. An affirming appreciation of the excess of life itself can emerge, even granting that it surfaces as a fugitive passing.

In attending to the shine on things in *chapter 3*, I pay attention to how, generally, scientistic attitudes towards the order of creation tend towards the *reductive*, while postmodern attitudes tend towards the *deconstructive*. The given order of beauty tends to be made problematic. The surface of things is often invested with an equivocity that, whether reductively or deconstructively, we can only approach with epistemic-ontological suspicion. My reflections focus on the connection between given beauty and the order of creation. Beauty itself is inseparable from some sense of formed wholeness, though the closure of this wholeness or its openness is at issue here, with respect to the notion of an open whole (already touched on in chapter 1). My query is about a givenness to beauty in nature that belies the (postmodern) claim that order is just an imposition of (our) power on flux. The notion of creation is inseparable from the origination of order, but the order *comes to be*, arises from originating sources that allow forms of beauty to be that are more than our determination or self-determination. Something marvelously original comes to be, comes to shine. There is a shine on things. But what shines on things when we come to appreciate their given beauty? Is it just *our* shine on things, as if *we* were the sole source of light? Is it the shine *of* things, as if the things were luminescent in their own being there? Is it a shine *on* things, such that the source of the light was not just ours, nor indeed to be confined to the thing of beauty?

In *chapter 4*, I ask why, in our time, there is such a thing as "soul music" but there is no such thing as "self music." Why is this? What is the difference between the two? The language of "self" is all pervasive in our cultures, while the language of "soul" seems to have gone into eclipse. Again why is this? What might be at issue in the music of the soul in soul music, and the music-less self without soul? I take these questions as a challenge to rethink the nature of soul, and connect this with the more primal porosity of our being and the *passio essendi* as more original than the *conatus essendi*. Despite the all-pervasiveness of talk about the self, the fact that there is soul music and not self music tells us of something recessed in intellectual discourse, though not, it would appear, in popular culture. We need to pay attention to what this reveals about something neglected in theory, though unavoidably animating our very existence. I explore the modern stress on the determinability of being which has tended to recess what is not so determinable or open to our self-determination. We need to reflect on soul as naming an animating source more original than determinate and self-determinate being. If we give unquestioning privilege to the language of self we end in a tuneless modality of being, hearing nothing of beauty, and singing nothing of soul. I ask, in a more constructive mood, if we can relate soul and self in a manner that also restores to selving something of its soul, something too of its music. One is led to wonder if there a music of soul that spreads itself abroad more universally and soulfully than our soul music and in which this participates.

Schopenhauer's philosophy has many fascinating aspects, but it raises a crucial issue for any affirmation of beauty and its gift: how to reconcile this affirmation with the evil of being? This is my theme in *chapter 5*. Schopenhauer, in advance of Nietzsche, often gave his imprimatur to the "wisdom" of the Silenus, companion of Dionysus: "Best not to be at all." One finds him invoking Dante's hell, not to endorse it straightforwardly but to *exceed* it: *this world itself is a hell* surpassing Dante's vision, and every man is a devil to every other. The evil of being is felt by Schopenhauer in the flesh itself: instead of the glory of the human body, we are hapless victims of desire and especially the sexual urge. How is anything like the gift of beauty then possible, given the metaphysical terms of his system? Rather than a primal porosity of being and a *passio essendi*, Schopenhauer's metaphysics foregrounds a vehement will to life. This might be seen as a certain *conatus essendi* universalized, inflected now to bring to the fore the judgment that all life shows itself as a constant suffering. The passion of being is pain only, suffering and suffering alone. Originally my reflection focused on Schopenhauer's philosophy of the dark origin, but as I thought about it, there emerged for me a deep tension between his metaphysics of the will and what he sees as the Sabbath of the will that he claims is offered by art. How possible at all is such a Sabbath, how possible at all our release from *eros tyrannos*?

Schopenhauer adds a twist to the reversal of Platonism before that reversal became fashionable with Nietzsche and Heidegger, and even though his admiration for Plato is second behind only his adulation of Kant. Schopenhauer's thinking suggests, in fact, going deeper underground rather than going up above into the higher and purer air above the underground, above ground. I am not sure if he grasped fully the implications of his philosophy of the will on this score; or the implications of his view of the ultimate will, as a kind of tyrannical eros, on the other side of the principle of sufficient reason. Going down in this fashion has been characteristic of much philosophy and culture since Hegel. It reverses the triumphant ascent of speculative *Vernunft* to the heights of thought thinking itself, such as Hegel offered us. Down below the surface of everyday appearances, down deeper than the cavernous darkness of the underground soul, there is monstrous will. And with this monstrous will there are complications for human eros; complications for the mutation of our *passio essendi* (passion of being) and *conatus essendi* (endeavor to be); complications for an adequate philosophical understanding of the porosity of being and the metaxological communication with the origin that is granted most originally in the porosity. Again, on these terms, how is it possible to talk at all about the gift of beauty? That this gift is offered is undoubtedly true, and it is undoubtedly true that Schopenhauer was appreciative of it, even granting his evil eye for given being. And yet the appreciation that would grant beauty given as gift is coupled with a metaphysics that evacuates every kind of gift of the generosity of being that it communicates most tenderly.

Paul Weiss was a great defender of metaphysics against the positivistic and scientistic currents common in much Anglo-American philosophy in the middle of the twentieth century. My reflection in *chapter 6* is a companioning one, since his example as a metaphysician gave witness to an impulse sickening or almost dead at that time, and not only in analytic philosophy. We still seek iron in the blood to restore to spiritual health the anemic body of (post-metaphysical) thought. Weiss shows us respect for ultimate questions and universal considerations, coupled with attentive intellectual care for the diverse domains of human significance. One of his major engagements was with understanding the nature of creative ventures, and not in abstraction from the fundamental considerations of metaphysics. The adventuring spirit of the human being, the being of the human as a venture, is at stake in its intertwining with our creative potential. To venture is to make an attempt, to undertake a risk and strike out into the unknown and the possibly new. We find ourselves participating in, and involved with, a certain energy of creative transcendence.

Here the theme of "creativity" comes to appearance in Weiss, not only as particularized in the arts, not alone as pluralized in a host of human ventures, such as art, mathematics, science, leadership, and so on, but as an ontological principle ingredient in the constitution of all concrete realities. The creativity evident in human venturing is not a human creation simply but invokes "creativity" itself as something to which we must appeal to understand the nature of all being. This is especially clear if we wish to do justice to the dynamic and original dimensions of reality as in process of becoming. The creative becoming of the human being cannot be abstracted from the becoming of creativity in all being. There is no understanding of human transcendence apart from an understanding of the energy of transcendence at work in all being, and singularized in unique and often astonishing ways in the human being. This will be central in my thoughts here: the ontology of creativity as suggesting something other to the human being, yet other in a way that in it the human being participates intimately. There is something intimate and other about creativity. And while, in Weiss's case, we cannot call either creativity or the dynamis by names derived from the sacred, yet it remains a question whether humanistic names are true to the matter also. Is human creativity companioned by a power other than the human? Is Weiss's dynamis a name for this other-power? If so, how so? If not, why not, and how are we to think otherwise of this other-power? One of my main concerns is how Weiss explores a teleology of self-realizing creativity, not an archeology of giving inspiring power. He deals less with the primal porosity and the *passio*, and more with a creative *conatus* oriented to self-perfecting. I contrast his philosophical pluralism to a polytheism of creativity of the kind we find, say, in Nietzsche, and a monotheism of creation that we find in Aquinas. My own stress is on a metaxology of creativity where the potencies of original power emerge from the porosity, are received as the *passio*, and shaped as creative *conatus* or endeavor. And we must never forget the companioning power.

In *chapter 7*, I engage the remarkable ruminations, particularly on Romanticism, of Stanley Cavell. Cavell is a singular writer, emerging from analytic sources but expanding the practices of philosophy in thought-provoking ways, ways often at odds with more standard professorial practices. The voice of this singular thinker outlives the chorus of voices of the professors who do not always quite approve of the swerve into singularity. This reflection was originally intended to address Cavell's relation to German idealistic philosophy and Romanticism, but the exploration became a question for me of the recess of the religious in the dialogue of the philosopher and the poet. The matter concerns the migration, in Romanticism and its aftermath, of the sense of transcendence from its more original home in religion to the arts, and poetry especially. The recess of religion is not a true enough description of German philosophy or Romanticism, since the interplay of religion and art is very complex in both of these. The permeability of the religious and the artistic, even if under names that were more often heterodox than orthodox, surely served as an inspiring source of some of its great creative ventures. If we think in the terms of Hegel's philosophy of absolute spirit, with its triad of art, religion, philosophy, I explore how these three are differently in interplay in Cavell's practice of philosophy. I wonder if there is enough of the porosity, and the passion of being in Cavell's espousal of a moral perfectionism. I ask if the other can bear the weight of God that he now deems the other must. Mirroring the ruminative style of this philosopher, I touch on central themes like philosophical migration and inheritance; the death of nature, with some special reference to Coleridge; the equivocal displacement of religious redemption from religion to art with Romanticism; what the redemption of Romanticism betokens; and what this asks of the transcendence of thought and its sanity.

In *chapter 8*, I return again to the surface of things, but in the special human sense of the theatrical space of human drama. I offer a reflection on the theater of the *metaxu*, asking how in the porous space of the theater there is a staging of the between which participates in and brings before us the metaxological nature of our life. I am especially thinking of how human life takes form between different extremes: birth and death, nothing and infinity, abjectness and ecstasy, secret interiorities of intimacy and sublime exteriorities of vast indifference. Human being is a *between-being*, but these extremes are mostly recessed in the domestications of everyday life. My thought is that theater tries to stage something of this between-being and bring what it intimates out of its recess in everyday life. What I call a metaxological philosophy serves to illuminate this between-condition. "*Metaxu*" is the Greek word for "between," while "*logos*" can mean an accounting, or reasoning, or wording. A metaxological philosophy of the theatre would look on it as *staging the between*. I want to ask if we can consider the theatrical stage as a distinctive wording of the between. Can a metaxological philosophy throw light on what is staged on it, communicated in and through its intermedium? In light of this philosophy of the *metaxu*, I offer reflections on essential themes such as: the space of the stage, the intermediation of inter-action, the shaping of plot, the openness of endings, the tragic and the comic, the sacred and the profane. While the relations of philosophy and theater are not commonly treated topics, a reflection on the theater of the *metaxu* shows surprising intimacies of significance possible between the two. Worth remembering is that the origins of some of the most powerful forms of theater have something to do with a more religious or sacred occasion. In the theater of the *metaxu*, the companioning power may often be *incognito*, we may even try to force it to be gone, but it does not abandon the between.

In the *final chapter*, on redeeming laughter, I am again concerned with surfaces in this sense of the significantly superficial. I offer a variation on Nietzsche's theme of being superficial out of profundity, and perhaps the reverse too, being profound out of superficiality. I am asking if laughter has a metaxological wisdom, indeed idiot wisdom, to teach us. My question is: If we do affirm the low things, is this a low thing? Is there a noble laughter that in affirming the low things is indeed affirmative of the low things—without lowering of spiritual nobility, indeed rather with a surprising elevation? Is there the promise of agapeic affirmation? I do not shy off granting that there is much of absurdity in human life. Quite to the contrary, without such absurdity it is debatable whether human life would be human at all. I take it that to affirm the human is to affirm this absurdity. But *how* to affirm this absurdity, *what* is to be affirmed in this absurdity? Among the ways of affirming, I ask if one is to be found in what I call redeeming laughter. I mean redeeming laughter in a double sense: redeeming laughter from the imputation that it deals with the "merely" trivial or base because it trivially deals with the base; redeeming laughter as communicating laughter that is itself redemptive—an elemental power of festive affirmation of deep ontological significance. I am interested in laughter's radical intimacy with absurdity and its transformation from a malign absurdity into a benign surd. Does laughing at or with the absurdity do absurd things with the absurdity: turn it towards festive, ontological affirmation, without avoidance of the absurdity?

I want to connect such laughter with the passion of being and the body beside itself. To be embodied is to be the incarnation of worth before one more mindfully participates in diverse forms of worth, either derived from the already given world, or brought to form through one's own original contribution. This incarnation of worth, I think, is to be taken in an ontological sense; it has to do with the good of the "to be" in which we live, before we live it. I connect this sense of ontological worth with the passion of being that is prior to our endeavor to be. Our being embodied as *passio essendi* incarnates ontological worth, lives the good of the "to be," prior to our efforts to be this or that. The body is beside itself before it determines itself. There is a preceding, as well as outliving excess, beyond our determining and self-determining powers, concerning which elemental happenings like weeping and laughing are very revealing. They show the tension of the *passio essendi* (passion of being) and the *conatus essendi* (endeavor to be), though what is shown cannot be fitted into an exhaustive discursive conceptualization. We participate in what is shown, though what we participate in we do not, perhaps cannot, determinately know. We are made to be besides ourselves; and perhaps being beside ourselves is what we are made to be. Laughter is related to a discordance between the *passio essendi* and the *conatus essendi*. The release of laughter can return us to this *passio essendi*, overcoming and sometimes overturning every claim to self-sufficiency, including that of moral righteousness. That said, the sense of humor is not without its own ethical significance, since it expresses our character as attuned to the *passio essendi* and to the recurrent discordances between it and the overreaching claims of the *conatus essendi*. These discordances, laughably enjoyable, offer themselves for philosophical thought. There is metaphysical meaning in their being applauded.

The work concludes with a conversation with Steven Knepper entitled: "'Intimate Intertwining': An Interview with William Desmond on Art and Religion." Given the recurrent theme in this work of the threshold between the aesthetic and the religious, it seemed fitting to include this interview.

## III

To come to my second pass: how do we situate this work relative to some of my other works and the philosophical outlook that informs them? Art and the aesthetic figure in all my book in some way or other, as does the religious, or openness to it, even when not explicit. I mentioned *Art and the Absolute*, a set of studies bearing on Hegel's aesthetics, including the eclipse of beauty after him. One great significance of the gift of beauty is that we might refer to beauty as given or beauty as wrought, but we do not have to bifurcate them. Rather we are asked to ponder the fitting terms of an ontology of incarnation. There is an endowed dimension to all of gifted beauty. Our tendency to dualize nature and culture, and then to reconstruct them diversely, does not match the meaning of the aesthetic and artistic in their distinction and continuity. Without the festive celebration of flesh art sickens. Beauty as carnal is not governed by gnostic spirituality. Hegel is followed by many, as Danto saw, who allow the concept to assert pre-eminence over the aesthetic, but the passion of being as emergent in and from our flesh is enfeebled by this, with resulting enfeebling of aesthetic power. It is true that we might be thus an-aesthetic in theory, but this is not always matched in practice by the forms of being aesthetic that still prevail, for we remain carnal. And yet it can often be that Laputan artists are in the dominant, with their projects to concretize "interesting ideas," rather than let flesh word itself. Beauty is a rebuke to the conceptual abstractions of the Laputan projectors.

I want also to mention our being ethical, which certain forms of aestheticism tend to weaken relative to its more unconditional claims on us. I have written extensively on being ethical,[3] and Kierkegaard is not wrong is speaking of the aesthetic, ethical, and religious spheres of life. The question for me is, as with Hegel, how he understands them. How they overlap or pass into each other demands thought more subtle than laying them contiguously side-by-side in an existential self-becoming. Kierkegaard does not do this, of course, though I would say that the aesthetic and art, as much as our being religious and ethical, participate in a saturated equivocity in which significant ambiguity comes from the porosity of our being rather than from an endeavor to move from the aesthetic, to the ethical, to the religious, otherwise contiguously placed side by side. There is something about the permeability of these that continually resists their each being placed in their autonomous spheres. I am not accusing Kierkegaard of this, though the familial intimacy of the aesthetic, ethical, and religious is probably stronger in the philosophical view I develop.

About all three, in themselves and in relation, there are saturated equivocities that resist the univocal literalness of prosaic thought. These

3. Most fully in Desmond, *Ethics and the Between*, but also in Desmond, *Philosophy and Its Others: Ways of Being and Mind.*

equivocities find a place in thought somewhere between system and poetics. At the same time, these equivocities are not to be dialectically superseded by the higher univocity of a speculative system. Hegel's philosophy of absolute spirit has been recurrently a source of fascination and resistance in my own thought, which differently treats of this saturated equivocity. The equivocity is to be dwelt in metaxologically: as a sign of the surplus signifying of the overdeterminate ethos of the between; not as a medium allowing passage to conceptual thought, simply thinking itself at the end of all self-becoming. There is an aesthetic/artistic wording of the between,[4] just as there is a religious and a philosophical wording. Being ethical is the incarnation of that wording in a form of human life in fidelity to the call of being good. If there is a gift of beauty, aesthetic fidelity is also the fitting word to use to name the nature of its call on us.

Instead of the triadic sublation of art, religion, and philosophy in the unity of the concept at home with itself, there are metaxological intermediations that have a more fourfold character. The wording of the between is a crossing of the between. We can cross from in to out, from out to in, from below to above, from above to below. This seems simple enough at first glance, but there is nothing univocal about it. There is something about it hard to determine, something exceeding our self-determination, something not merely indeterminate but in excess as *over*determinate. In what sometimes seems almost nothing there is a too-muchness that shows finite being on a threshold, in a communicative, even revelatory sense. A metaxological dwelling with the saturated equivocity tries to think these crossings; tries to word plurivocal passages in the wording of the between.

Saturated equivocity means the importance of surface, of surfacing, as a passing from one space to another. Surfacing can be understood in terms of what comes to the surface and faces us, in terms of surfaces as facing us with what sometimes astonishes us, sometimes perplexes us, though we seek still to comprehend in the best terms possible. If we come to such thresholds, whether moving there up or down, in or out—if we stand there, precariously and poised—the threshold names a way of being permeable, of being porous. We can pass one threshold but it may be that we find thresholds on the other side that yet have to be traversed. Thus: We can go *in*, and discover within something more interior than our own intimacy with ourselves and its inner darkness. We may go *up*

4. See Desmond, "Wording the Between."

and find our own elevation to the superior position being exceeded by a superior excess that seems paradoxically to retreat as we come closer to it, that seems the more hyperbolically transcendent the more its astonishing immanence is insinuated. We may go *down*, and discover that there is space of significance to be covered in the infernal depths, unsuspected on one surface, but calling on us to surface differently again by exodus through darkest hell. We can go *out*, and awake to a land of waste, or find again the sparkle on given things that whispers of nature naturing, and beyond these whispers we are made to wonder about a secret voicing of the companioning power. Threshold leads to threshold, leading on and back, leading deep, as both above and below, leading out and leading in, as we are within and beyond, below and outside, all in all at the same time. This is perhaps what it means to be participant in the ecumenical *koinonia* of the intimate universal.

Worth recalling is how one of the central themes of *Art, Origins, Otherness* was the displacement of a sense of transcendence, traditionally understood in the space of religion, in the direction of art. At the same time, notice was taken of how after Kant art was accorded an unprecedented metaphysical significance. If there was such a displacement, it might also be taken as a sign that there was always sacred possibility and promise resourced in the aesthetic and in art, a promise not entirely betrayed in the claims of art to assert itself with an autonomy apparently hedged in by the hegemony of the religious. If religion and art are siblings in the same family, it should not be surprising that they share, so to say, certain ontological genes. If the one asserts its independence and otherness from the other, this will not do away with this familial relation. Rather it will either mask it, or turn it into a hostility perhaps, pursued just in the name of being other than the other. But the secret familial bond will not be set at nought, even when the one wants to negate the other.

The point is easier to grant if we are familiar with the long history of aesthetic and artistic manifestation. The secularization of art is the anomaly rather than the norm. Of course, this is open to different interpretations and evaluations. In the main it has been viewed and lauded as the justified emancipation of art from the supervising heteronomy of the religious. After some centuries, however, the ambiguities of claims to putative autonomy can no longer be hidden, and the unavoidability of freedom in relation to the other, that is to say, self-determination as relative to the other(s), rather than a univocal self-determination, brings to the fore the price of freedom so evacuating itself of a richer relativity to other(s). Ultimately it risks becoming just a hollow self-determination.

We do not have to assert our own freedom over against the other (*to heteron*), we do not have to think of the other as a tyrannical Big Other. A more hospitable intermediation between self-relating and other-relating is possible, and indeed actual in events of creative origination. In the concluding chapter of *Art, Origins, Otherness*, I spoke of "Art and the Impossible Burden of Transcendence" and explored how the sense of transcendence seemed for many more creatively invested in the artistic. But I also argued that this investment yielded issue only because there was a displaced-yet-secret religious charge to art, even in an age of the putative secularization of art. In all of this what was to be avoided was a *questionable equivocation* between the religious and the artistic. This asked not a reduction of one to the other, whether from one side or from the other, but a granting and exploration of permeability between the two, a permeability hidden by the dubious self-assertion of art as entirely justified through itself alone, for itself alone. I concluded that because we have not been entirely honest about this equivocation, art could not carry the burden of transcendence in the way it was asked. This has something to do with a deflation of the sense of transcendence as other, understood in terms of the sacred, and an over-inflation of self-transcending, understood as human creativity. Too much was asked of art in a manner that we now ask almost nothing of it. The present work is intended to explore this permeability in a variety of ways.

Though much more could be said about transcendence, whether in connection with art or religion, we have witnessed a certain prohibition on the transcendent since Kant. I connect this especially with an ethos of autonomy: our self-transcending is more concerned to keep and guard the circle of its own self-determination as absolute, as absolved as possible from submission to what is superior, as other. It would take what comes to it only on its own terms. Self-transcendence circles around itself and is diffident, if not hostile, to transcendence as other. Its own otherness is the height to which it often only allows itself to ascend, but this is a self-ascent, or indeed a self-descent. For often in circling around itself it discovers itself as an underground, as a cave, a darkness before it is rationally self-determining, and vertiginous descent into this darkness is sometimes more tempting and intoxicating than the arduous ascent to something above itself. This point has something to do with our tendency, at times, to show more fascination with the ugly, the excremental, the horrific, what strikes into our domesticated life with a brutality beyond the everyday, as opposed to the beautiful as breaking into our self-composure with the promise, perhaps, of a more benign intervening. In any case, in such an ethos of absolving autonomy we tend to have spiritual cramps relative to the granting of any excessive other that is superior always to our own self-determination, in a hyperbolic dimension of height, always asymmetrical to our every measure, even when it comes among us, and reveals its height through its agapeic lowliness.

When I speak of transcendence as other many quickly move into a mode of posing issues in terms of a *dualistic opposition* of immanence and transcendence. One response is the tendency to opt for the aesthetic/art as not asking the hard commitment to strong transcendence as other, while allowing a kind of creative self-transcendence in immanent terms. It will be said that strong transcendence sets us in opposition to rich immanence, and again in the terms of a dualistic opposition that leads to an "either/or" being enforced. This is not the way of thinking I advocate. I appreciate the power of dialectical thinking to deconstruct exclusive binary oppositions, and to offer in their stead a more immanent wholism, well suited to art and also the formed integral wholeness of the beautiful. I do not reject the latter, but I do modify it, and again in metaxological rather than dialectical terms. Here strong transcendence is not obviated or rejected or disguised under the camouflage of immanent self-transcendence. To the contrary, staying true to it directs us to a more radical sense of the immanence of the companioning power and in elusive intimacy with acts of creative origination. The way out and the way in cross, the way up and the way down cross, as do the radical transcendence and radical immanence of the endowing origin Those are issues I will not pursue further now, though they haunt other works I have written, as they do what I try to say in this work.

Worth mentioning is the eclipse of beauty in the wake of the sense of excessive subjectivity about which I spoke in *Art and the Absolute*. Beauty has an otherness irreducible to our subjectivity. If that subjectivity begins to exult in its own sense of immanent infinity, regardless of the equally granted sense of its own finitude, there can arise a feeling that nothing in otherness as such can bring to rest this excess of subjectivity, this excessive subjectivity. I will not speak the language of subjectivity here, and we have come to see some of the deeper equivocations of this subjectivity: at once a sign of something qualitatively more about our being, and also a source of a kind of existential wretchedness that cannot find itself at home in the world of finite things. We are excess, but what could answer this excess we, more often than not, cannot say. We are tempted to think there is nothing, and hence we become an anomalous overcoming of finite limitations in a freakish not-being-at-home—a not-being-at-home in principle—in the strangely mysterious world wherein we find ourselves: privileged freaks. But the anomaly swallows the privilege when the insight strikes home that there is nothing to answer our outreaching. We are ecstasies in the void, and in the end then ourselves merely void. This we see already at the beginning of Romanticism: a movement equivocal between the artistic and the religious, drawing some of its greatest inspiration from secretly sacred sources, sources not always explicitly acknowledged as such. The permeability is at work, endowing the sources of creativity, but only on occasion being acknowledged as such. Again among the themes of this book will be an exploration of this secret permeability.

What to do with this excess of "subjectivity" after Romanticism? Is it too much for beauty? Or is beauty rather too much for it? For the overreaching subject that comes to taste its own nothingness may be closer to the truth of beauty in that taste if it rediscovers itself as an original porosity of being, a *passio essendi* before it is a *conatus essendi*, a passion or patience of being before it is an endeavor to be; if it consents to its ultimate exposure to the endowing power, at the threshold of its own nothingness; if and when its self-transcending also turns into creative passing in the fertile void of the between. "I am nothing" finds some healing to its existential gall, and might offer itself as a purged availability to the endowment of the companion power.

Beauty offers a home for ecstatic desire, but if beauty is subject to the deconstruction of a hundred cuts or deformations, there is nothing there in which to find oneself at home. Of course, the presupposition here is that beauty is just a kind of finite wholeness in which a transcending, potentially infinite, cannot ultimately find itself at home. Perhaps it is not such a finite whole, but a kind of hyperbolic wholeness in finitude itself that gives signs of what itself cannot be finitized. This is something hyperbolic about the aesthetics of happening, about beauty, and not just about the sublime, as seems to be the preferred zone of concentration for centrifugal dissolution with some postmodern thinkers.[5] Centrifugal

5. On the aesthetics of happening as one of the hyperboles of being, see my *God and the Between*, chapter 6. I speak of aesthetic selving in *Being and the Between*, chapter 10.

dissolution itself is just a redefinition of the ontological not-being-at-home that is just the plight that is at issue. One can hollowly jubilate in what, *qua* solution, merely continues the question, a dissolution that presents itself as a solution when, of course, it cannot be. If that is all there is to say, we only *seem* to move beyond our predicament, for we must immediately end back in the empty nihilism from which we tried to depart. This is my question: Is there already a too-muchness in beauty, but of a strange sort, since it seems almost nothing—something that departs from the more usual contrast of the wholeness of beauty and the rupture of the sublime, something that already seeds radical unrest in the very rest that beauty does indeed offer to us. This will entail a different view of beauty.

To me, a telling point against the autonomy of art is this: art is grown in the aesthetic and both are double, metaxological. Aesthetic otherness is metaxological: it does not reflect back simply to "subjectivity"; the aesthetic happening of being percolates in our aesthetic body and the permeability of the two, the porosity of the two, is closer to the intimate truth of the matter. The nature naturing of the aesthetic happening comes to a second articulation in the aesthetic body and to a more express wording of itself in the art of the human, in song, for instance. As metaxological there is an aesthetic selving and an aesthetic othering, and the two cannot be so separated from each other as to be turned into a dualism. Aesthetic selving puts its unknowing roots into the aesthetic othering of nature naturing: we participate in that, and are not just a determinate form of nature natured. Likewise with art: artistic othering is not self-determining: it infuses a selving that is transported beyond fixed determinacy into a flow of energy and becoming. This energy can be shaped into a relative form of self-becoming, manifesting thus a qualified kind of aesthetic self-determination. But this last is only possible by its being befriended by this companioning flow-in, this infusion of creative energy that comes up from aesthetic othering in artistic selving itself.[6]

I am interested in the permeability of art, religion, and philosophy as reflecting an original porosity of being in which they all share. The issue is not the autonomy of any of them. This latter seems to me to lead to different dead ends: the end of art, the death of God, and the end of philosophy. We have seen these dead ends in art as communist propaganda or as capitalist commodity; in the wasting away of religious passion in

6. Many of these points are more fully explored in Desmond, *The Intimate Universal*, chapters 2 and 6.

the metaphysical cocoon of our self-warming humanistic world; in the evacuation of metaphysical seriousness in philosophy, whether by analytic technicians or hermeneutical rhetoricians. I seek a way of doing philosophy that allows the porosity of being to open up ontological promise in the permeability of all. If one says there is something postmodern about this, I will not object if I am granted that postmodernism has too often offered us an aestheticization of the religious in its rhetorical displacements of philosophy. Meditative patience is needed to dwell on the ambiguous threshold of aesthetic/art and the sacred/religious. On that threshold we meet the saturated equivocity that calls for metaxological intermediation and our philosophical meditation.

All this metaxological doubleness requires for us to think the porosity in both aesthetic happening, and in artistic articulation. The happening is the surface of what, in this porosity, is coming into song or into wording. The *passio* is before the *conatus*; receiving is before self-affirmation; being ready is before endeavoring. What is not at stake here is will to power. Nietzsche is often equivocal on this, but the note of self-affirmation is never allowed to be relativized sufficiently by the prior *passio* and porosity. Recall his description of artistic inspiration in *Twilight of the Idols*: Raphael as tyrant. This is almost the opposite of what I am saying here. Nowhere will I deny that there are tyrannical forms of eros. Nor will I deny that such forms shadow the creative venture of the artist. Despite themselves, these tyrannical forms too pay their complements to beauty. All this has relevance for the threshold between the aesthetic/artistic and the religious. Thought through more fully, we must not stay at the "level" of becoming and self-becoming. We must find our way to the space of coming to be. And further again we must pass into intimacy with the original porosity, into the "being given to be" that offers more primordially the "coming to be." There is a threshold between becoming and coming to be; there is a threshold between coming to be and being given to be; and these are thresholds where the religious and the aesthetic/artistic are permeable to each other, and in secret communication. If being religious is taken to signify our participation in the original communication of the porosity between the divine origin and what it brings to be, in the porosity there is the offering of the gift of singular becomings or our own self-becoming. It is on the threshold of communication with this that aesthetic glory shines forth, and that singular happenings of artistic creativity are seeded.

# 1

# The Gift of Beauty and the Passion of Being

## Disgust and the Gift of Beauty

Art shows its superiority, Kant tells us, in that it can beautifully represent things in nature we would find ugly, such as the "furies, diseases, devastations of war." However, one form of ugliness not to be presented is that which awakens *disgust* (*diejenige welche Ekel erweckt*).[1] One wonders if the representation of the disgusting is prohibited, or whether a disgusting representation is aesthetically anathema. The difference is significant. One might represent the horror of torture, say, and one might aesthetically participate in the horror of torture in the representation, but this is not quite the same as being an active participant in the torture. One might also represent the disgusting, and yet disgust is not the aesthetic response the representation evokes. Some of Francis Bacon's representations awaken a visceral horror before howling and deformed faces, and yet there is a haunting beauty, even glory in some of the paintings themselves. There is no prohibition on representing the ugly in Kant, so long as it is done with aesthetic taste. What would he make of the ironical "gesture," as one might take it to be, of Piero Manzoni's "Merda d'Artista"—cans of his own excrement, supposedly, bought by a number of major institutions of art for impressive prices. It has been said some cans

1. Kant, *Critique of Judgement*, §48. Hereinafter *CJ*.

have since exploded, perhaps because the technical finish of the canning was not up to long-term art conservation. I do not know of the state of scholarly opinion as to whether there was real excrement in the works, but if one were to open a can with excrement more than fifty years old (they were canned in 1963), surely some element of disgust would be aroused. And yet, apart from this distaste, who can resist chuckling at the "gesture."

However one interprets Kant's prohibition of disgust, the prohibition is transgressed with gusto by some contemporary art. Transgression often takes form as revolt against the form of beauty and the revolt can sometimes itself be revolting. Arthur Danto—analytic high priest of the Hegelian thesis of the end of art, reigning pontiff among philosophical aestheticians in advanced New York circles for decades—reflects on the revolt against beauty in contemporary art, as well as fascination with the revolting and the disgusting (Carus Lectures APA 2001). His example is telling: a work of the young Damien Hirst seems to present maggots breeding in the dead flesh of a mounted cow's head, and he tells of a friend's reaction who approached the work with anticipations of earlier canonical aesthetics about beauty. Initially puzzled, the light did dawn and the exclamation came: "How beautiful!" The person, expecting beauty according to traditional canons, finally did find beauty in the revolting. Of course, this was not the response sought by the Intractable Avant-garde, to use Danto's term.[2] The point was to play with our revulsion, not to find beauty in maggots or rotting meat. The person saw the disgusting as beautiful instead of the beautiful as disgusting.

An important point: the disgusting directly arouses a recoil in the *passio essendi*, the passion of being, and this is exploited in certain representations of the revolting. The disgusting intrudes viscerally, touching and arousing the *passio*. Since this passion is central to the appeal of beauty, it is right that we grant that the arousal of disgust belongs to the *same family of possibilities*, including beauty, that are the reserves of the passion of being. In these matters we must always be alert to saturated equivocities, equivocities replete with a twosomeness of appeal and revulsion, fullness and emptiness, promise and poverty, the beautiful and the monstrous. Such equivocities are not juxtapositions of opposites, not superimpositions of one on the other, not dialectical inclusions of one in the other. They are superpositions (to borrow a term from quantum physics) with a metaxological character, making it impossible to disentangle

2. Danto, *The Abuse of Beauty*, chapter 2. The exclamation of the beautiful is muted in the printed version of the lecture, but I heard it at the lecture itself.

absolutely one from the other. The importance of this metaxological sense of the saturated equivocity will come back to us again.

Apart from the disgusting, we find not infrequently a certain ambiguous attitude to beauty among some who pride themselves on their aesthetic cultivation. I take the following as a small sign: a recent book on *beauty* edited by Umberto Eco, though respectfully noted by its readers, was not a huge publishing success, while by contrast, its companion volume on *ugliness* was hugely lauded and brazenly outsold its more demure sister.[3] Is the idea of beauty bland to the putative avant-garde? Is it the consoling anodyne of the complacent bourgeoisie. Better by far something more disruptive and provocative. The ugly, the disgusting, the revolting arouse the thrill of transgression. They disturb in us something visceral and we recoil. They charge the beholder with a shot of energy; we cannot remain indifferent. We are to take disturbance as an index of the "really real." Beauty offers no promise of happiness, we are roundly reminded. Bland happiness is aesthetically blank; artistic peace is the death of "creativity."

How then be open at all to beauty as gift? I think we can keep in mind this taste for the ugly and yet inquire whether something is lacking if our tilt places primary emphasis on it. Can we look at beauty as suggesting peace: not the peace of death, but a peace, so to say, beyond war and peace? Remarkably, we often find ourselves at home with beauty, but we do not fall asleep before it. Beauty witnesses an elemental rapport between ourselves and what is other. There is nothing of a *vis dormativa* in this rapport. We are surprised by beauty and taken outside of ourselves. We behold something or someone as beautiful, and our breath is taken away, and it is as if the other beheld had taken the secret initiative in communicating to us. Our "beholding *of*" the beautiful is a "beholding *from*" the beautiful.[4] How else make sense of its surprise? We could not have expected it, and yet there it is, shining before us, arising out of the sea of the unexpected, before we are able to assert mastery of ourselves and take its measure. We are first receivers and only then perceivers and conceivers. The presence of the beautiful disarms our defenses, but the disarming

3. Eco, ed. *History of Beauty*; Eco, *On Ugliness*.

4. It is not lacking in importance that I first drew this way of speaking ("beholding from") from William Wordsworth's "Lines Composed a Few Miles above Tintern Abbey" (103–06): "Therefore am I still/A lover of the meadows and the woods,/And mountains; and all that we behold/From this green earth . . . ." Wordsworth, *Major Works*, 134.

is sweet and the surprise brings delight. If the surprise of beauty awakens delight, there is something *given*, something to which we are to be receptive. It is not first constructed by us; there is a deep patience to beholding what is beautiful. This patience is no lassitude but rather a paradoxical mixing of something given, something delighting, something energizing. We "behold *from*"—a consonance is communicated from what is other to our self-determination, and we come alive in a new and surprising way.

This is consonant with an element of exposure, availability, indeed vulnerability, in receiving the beautiful. This, in turn, is in tune with our being as marked most deeply by what I call a *primal porosity to being*. (*Consonantia*: one of the marks of beauty, according to Aquinas: "sounding with.") Beauty sensuously communicates in and through this awakened porosity. We human beings are first marked by a patience of being, a being received in being, before we gather our energies in our endeavor to be. I take this *passio essendi* to be on the boundary between receiving and responding—responding that may itself become creative in attempting to bring into being a work of art that directly or indirectly is in communication with the originating reception. More primally, nothing is originated without reference to the original porosity of being.

In modern aesthetics, as in modern culture generally, originating receptivity tends to be downplayed, if not repudiated, as supposedly a depreciation of our claims to creative power. The stress on human autonomy and self-determination has been predominant—and this to the recession of what is more receiving in our nature. We love only what we construct ourselves, not what we receive from often-enigmatic sources beyond our self-determination. The passion of being is driven out of the foreground by the *conatus essendi*, and this in consequence is sometimes tempted to a hubristic self-inflation. Anything given or received is a curb or threat or occasion of resistance to this *conatus*. From thence follows a guarded attitude to beauty, which communicates to us in the offer of a gift. We do not self-determine the originating occasion of beauty. We are more determin*ed* than determining, determined not in a deterministic way but in the mode of a free receptivity, a receptivity that is also releasing of freedom. As I put it above, we "behold from" in beholding something beautiful. This is why there is a surprise, a surprise of delight. One cannot self-determine surprise. One cannot construct surprise. One has to be opened, and lay oneself open to the occasion of its summoning, but not coercing, communication. There is something like a godsend in the truly beautiful.

This is not language that is currently fashionable, but I want to connect the gift of beauty with the erotics of being. The ancients obviously saw the intimate connection of beauty and eros—Plato most gloriously (see, for instance, *Phaedrus*, 250c7-e1). The erotics of being, as I understand the matter, testify to something self-surpassing, self-transcending, in us. Self-transcending is more usually connected with the *conatus essendi*, but I want to connect this erotics with the passion of being in the sense of *passio essendi*. This is the surprising patience to receiving the beautiful—in the sense of our being overtaken by it, overcome, taken out of ourselves, transported. Once again, this is not the language of self-determination, or the modern reconfiguration of the *conatus essendi* without fidelity to the *passio essendi*. Without such fidelity, the erotics of being undergo a mutation, something that also happens to our openness to the granting of beauty. Eros turns into a striving without any given or prior consonance with what is beautiful; its striving risks becoming a (sometimes secret) strife, and at a certain extremity a domineering form of will to power. The eros of our being becomes what the ancients called an *eros tyrranos* (tyrannical eros). Transgression becomes the mode of its quasi-activist transcending. There is a violence to its self-surpassing—violence that finds it hard to grant that the gift of beauty is granted from beyond itself.

What is here rejected, or closed off, is the *elemental pleasure* of being, our being pleased with being, that comes to us with beauty. This is pleasure as a "being pleased with," a *complacentia* as the medievals called it. When we close off, clog up, our porosity to beauty, there is nothing to be pleased with. The vehemence of our claims to be *self*-determining and *self*-surpassing exceeds all (other) claims on us, and produces in its excess a kind of eclipse of beauty. The delightful in being is not then for us a loving pause, a staying, or arresting of our will to power. Displeased with what is, we seek to transgress again, and again, all the way to the extremity of disgust and revolt at what is.

One asks: If we circle around the ugly as more thrilling than the beautiful, are we circling around our own lack, if the ugly alone is in the ascendant? Do we risk becoming ourselves the evil eye whose look on things sees nothing lovely? Whose look is itself the perishing of the beautiful, the worm that blights beauty while blaming beauty for not meeting an unloving demand the worm itself makes on it? I will not deny a kind of violence to beauty, but I ask: is there paradoxically a kind of *benign* violence? Think of *heart-stopping* moments or occasions or persons of beauty: the heart stops beating and one is as if dead, killed by the look of the beloved, and the knees seem to go from under one; but the heart starts beating again and one comes back to life in delight and quickened attendance. Does beauty kill us in that way and bring us back to life again?

## Incarnate Beauty and the Passion of Being

The view I want to offer is not that our *passio essendi* makes us merely passive. To the contrary, we are energized to creative work in receiving originating power. But there is an *endowed* character to our participation in creative power. We do not determine it through ourselves alone. We do not endow ourselves. We are endowed. If we are lacking reverence for the endowing power, and we couple this with the disposition to tyrannical will to power, the erotics of being is liable to degenerate into a pornography of the aesthetic, where reverence for the body and finesse for its intimacies gets overtaken by a bent to vile handling. The ravishing body is itself ravished.

Beauty is inseparable from our being as *incarnate* creatures. Vested in the body, beauty is the great incarnate refutation of (reductive) materialisms. It shows forth the worthiness of the body to be affirmed as a happening of delighting and delightful value. The aesthetics of happening are not to be confined to our senses as only subjective epistemic powers. Aesthetics bears on the sensuous showing of the happening of being, as itself saturated with a radiance or shine, more than any reductionist analysis into this univocal determinacy or that. The aesthetics of happening is *of happening*—not just of our sensory and intellectual faculties. The "is" of beauty reveals a transcendence to the thing itself. That given beauty there as other is not exhaustively determinable as just this or just that—there is an overdeterminacy at work in what shows itself as beautiful.

The ugly too is moving, because it can intrude on the *passio essendi* and move us before we move ourselves. The ugly can awaken a kind of visceral transcending in us. Does our tilt to this visceral transcendence paradoxically have something to do with the *loss* of exposure to the flesh of things in modernity? Why ask this? Because we tend to see things that are other as massively objectified and then reconstructed by us, while at the same time we understand ourselves as hugely subjectified. The otherness of things is held to an objectified standard, but there is nothing in their beauty that answers to this standard, hence beauty also must be handed over to the other side of the dualism, to subjectivity and its feel for things.[5] One wonders to what extent this objectifying mode of approach is still secretly embedded in our way of thinking—even when it is critiqued in the name of the aesthetic. We have not come to mindfulness of the ontological robustness of the aesthetics of happening. This cannot be fitted into an objectivizing or subjectivizing frame of things.

Consider how we mostly live in cities where the otherness of constructed materiality dominantly shows the stamp of our art. We have already worked on the otherness, and in it what comes back to us is only ourselves, betraying our loss of exposure to the flesh of things. Sometimes we make our peace with this, sometimes we suffer disquiet, sometimes we are tempted to revolt. Undernourished for nature as other, we are tempted to sentimentalize it—as if it too were just like us and a grizzly bear could be one's furry friend.[6] Perhaps we are better friends to it by letting it alone. But we leave nothing alone.

Does hatred of beauty in post-Enlightenment culture conceal a contorted anti-religious religiousness? Religiousness: this anti-religiousness is not devoid of its own hunger for an other transcendence beyond beauty. But if we are caught in contempt for anodyne beauty, what is beyond beauty? The sublime has had its devotees, and there is much to be said for the sublime, not least its power as contrary to the deadened machine-world of the Newtonian world-picture. In the deadened world, our transcending can take the shape of transgression as outrage. The adornment becomes an aesthetic mutilation, deforming rather than reforming the given form. Sometimes it is the outrage, provoking initially the sought howl of protest, pleasing to the provoker. The success of outrage breeds its own redundancy and we become bored with outrage. Instead of howling we yawn. If we are polite we say: how interesting! Meaning: how *un*interesting! The an-aesthetics of happening is reinforced instead of redeemed.

It is important to grant that the aesthetics of happening not only calls forth the passion of being but also allures our endeavor to be. This is something evident in our nature as *adorning* creatures. We adorn the world and ourselves. We augment given beauty, and this can be a giving on, a giving back, rather than just only our construction, or indeed a negation of what is originally given. All honor even to the kitsch of tatoos,

5. To the side of the so-called secondary qualities, as it was put by some of the early modern thinkers. Inherited elements of this are at work in the ethos of Kant's thinking, though in the *Third Critique* he is struggling to get beyond it—not with complete success.

6. I refer to the film *Grizzly Man* put together by Werner Herzog.

for there is sometimes a faded echo of, say, a sacred sign of initiation in the marked body. Think also of how some forms of adornment become changed through "cosmetic surgery"—indicative more often than not now of a refusal to accept ourselves as given. The passion of being raises questions about a deeper acceptance of being given. As adorning creatures we both accept and alter—if there is only violence to the given in the name of constructed beauty, we are on the road to sham beauty.

Perhaps this contrast of given and constructed beauty mirrors the long-standing contrast in aesthetics of *mimesis* (imitation) and "creativity" in art, the former the older conception, the latter the more recent, and now almost completely dominant. How do these conceptions affect the way we think of the gift of beauty? Does the former risk a passivity that is not quite true to the *passio essendi*? Does the latter risk a constructivism not true enough to finessed *conatus essendi*, that is, an endeavor to be supercharged into hyperactivity? The first, patience without creative activity; the second, activity without creative patience? We need more than this "either/or."

I would say we need a sense for the saturated equivocity of the aesthetics of happening. Such equivocity refers us to a metaxological doubleness in which we find a togetherness of self-relating and other-relating. This doubleness is not self and other just contiguous and side by side. Not a juxtaposition, it is not also a superimposition, either of other on self (*mimesis*) or self on other ("creativity"). Nor yet again is it an overarching position in which one and the other are mediating moments. As already suggested, it is more like a superposition of the two, an entanglement or interwinement, which I call metaxological. I call it that because its saturated equivocity points in the direction of a surplus of significance not reducible to univocal determinacy, dialectical self-determination, nor indeed only equivocal indeterminacy. The metaxological superposition draws on the aesthetic overdeterminacy of being, draws us to it as alluring, and on it we draw when we construct works that shine with its surplus.

This is also a reason why we need to revisit the elemental yet complex character of the eros of our being in connection with beauty. Among other things, one might draw on the *double* parentage of eros in the Platonic account of its origin, namely in *poros* and *penia*. There is metaxological superposition here of plenty and poverty. The *poros* as opening a way, as enabling a porosity, is not always recognized when we treat of desire as if it were only a lack. There is the memory of divine festivity in the birth of eros, and with this the endeavor towards beauty is already in receipt of the promise of more than lack, of a more fulfilled festivity. As I would put it, there is the promise of the agapeic in the erotic—the promise of a surplus generosity that comes to us in the delight of beauty. This festivity participates in an affirming "yes" to being. The gift of beauty offers this incarnate "yes" in a celebratory delight.[7]

Something not to be forgotten, however, more ominous than the disgusting: at the height of the erotic ascent we are opened out to the great sea of the beautiful (*Symposium*, 210d). I put a point Plato did not quite put. The sea of beauty puts us at sea; the wide sea opens to infinity, opens too the infinite porosity intimate to our own desire. Beautiful surprises may appear out of the sea of the unexpected; so also may sea monsters that arouse in desire both astonishment and terror. Remember: monsters too are sacred, and their haunt is the threshold between the aesthetic and the sacred. "*Monstrare*" means "to show": the monster is a show of the sacred, but there is a sacred show in the monstrance: golden carrier of the consecrated bread that is the body of Christ, once to be beheld, even on the streets of the city of man on the feast of Corpus Christi. *Ecce homo*: the sacrificial lamb on display. And the sea monster? The one who asked us to call him Ishmael speaks of how, whenever he found himself "growing grim about the mouth. Whenever it [was] a damp, drizzly November in [his] soul," he went down to the sea, noting the puzzle of all the people looking out to sea, looking out at nothing, then himself going to sea, to purge the burdened soul, to hunt the monster of the deep, Moby Dick, the blank Leviathan, whether innocent or malicious, who knows, mysterious beyond our moral measure of good and evil.[8] The saturated equivocity of beauty still tasks us metaxologically.

7. That the passion of being as in love with beauty is not a "mere passivity" but invigorating, only listen to "*Non piu andrai*" in *Le nozze di Figaro* of Mozart: it is a tonic to life, a vigor of exhilaration, a celebration of festive flesh, an intoxication. "Drive the Cold Winter Away," a piece of seventeenth-century English music collected by John Playford in *The English Dancing Master* (1651), comes to mind.

8. I am referring to the opening pages of Herman Melville's, *Moby Dick*. There is a beautiful Spanish film *Mar adentro* (*The Sea Inside*), 2004, but as it unfolds the seduction of its beauty risks being finally corrupted by its morality of death . . . in the guise of a higher morality of "choice," the choice of death. Such beauty can be made to serve lies, when it is overtaken by the urge to be preachy and ideological. All around lies the beauty of life and the love of people, but at the ideological core of the film is the right to choose as the right to death. An agenda film (like agenda philosophy) ends up exploitive of suffering.

## Beauty and Perplexing Transcendence

If beauty arouses a festive attunement in us, as we find ourselves in the company of something worthy of admiration and celebration, festive beauty is also capable of provoking thought. We do not normally couple beauty with perplexity and yet it does precipitate a perplexity when we try to think about what it is about beauty that arouses this festive state of being. There is something enigmatic here that calls for our pondering. We need a fidelity to perplexities that defeat the confidences of a more univocal rationalization. Beauty stretches our mindfulness, bound up paradoxically with a restlessness inseparable from a mysterious serenity. How do we think together the restlessness and the serenity? This is the restlessness not only of thought but of the human being as a self-transcending being. One is put in mind of the restlessness of the Augustinian heart, though with respect to beauty there is also something darkened about this restlessness if we couple it, qualify it, with a sometimes unrelenting perplexity, sourced to a degree, if I am not mistaken, in the darkened ethos of our time after the death of God.

Transcendence seems a word too sombre to invoke in relation to (seemingly superficial) beauty, and yet the word is fitting. Beauty seems to give pause to our restlessness and we rest in a contemplative appreciation of what now is before us. As thus resting, beauty appears to be contrary to transcending as always caught up in a movement beyond what now is. Do we have to divide the pausing from the surpassing, the resting from the restlessness? If desire and beauty are coupled, desire is inseparable from a finitely unsatisfied restlessness, certainly with respect to our self-surpassing eros. Philosophers like Schopenhauer have tried to decouple beauty and eros, in this respect: that art and beauty give us a moment of peace from this inquietude of the will, itself seemingly impossible to make tranquil. But if we were consistent with the decoupling would the festive delight not also vanish? Festive delight is not the death of desire but participation in an energetic fulfillment. A striking thing about Schopenhauer is that he speaks of a Sabbath of the will in describing those moments of release when the will is quietened. A Sabbath is less a matter of doing nothing and more one of being freed in time to enjoy the release of enjoyment in a sacred time. In Schopenhauer's death of the will there is an unnamed resurrection of willing as delight in a Sabbath. A true Sabbath of being is really impossible in the terms of reference of his metaphysics; yet he is true enough to acknowledge it or something like it, despite the explicit concepts of the philosophy. Does not the Sabbath of being that beauty witnesses ask for a different metaphysics? Such a non-Schopenhauerian thought is important here and I will return to Schopenhauer in a later chapter.

There is also the question of whether beauty relates to a sense of transcendence that is not reducible to human self-transcendence, even while enigmatically in intimate relation to it. The restlessness of human self-transcending can come in many forms, and a form that has been widespread is the self-transcending that in seeking beyond itself, *seeks its own beyond*, seeks again itself as beyond itself. This self-transcending seeks to come to itself as a higher level of self-realization, hence never radically breaches the circle of its own self-shaping, or finds itself breached by what exceeds its own self-shaping. The restlessness that most awakens un-rest is on the boundary of that breach. It is not just our self-transcending that is at issue but a more ultimate and radical sense of transcendence as other to our self-determining. Traditionally, of course, that transcendence has often been identified with the divine. If the corrosion of divine presence has worked its acid decomposition into the texture of the soul, it will be hard to grant that this is the sacred name that should still be invoked with reverence.

All of this seems quite heavyweight, and more redolent of the weight of finitude rather than the festive affirmation of creation. Wordsworth speaks of "the burden of the mystery," and this seems to signal something of the weight of finitude, but the festivity of beauty is not a burden, is not weighed down, but exactly the opposite. It releases something enigmatic in us. It lifts us up before we even know we have been moved beyond ourselves. It makes us ask if our restlessness makes any sense at all without our first being moved, insinuating the promise of some fulfilled resting. Once again: Must being at rest and being in restless surpassing be opposed? Is our exposure to something beautiful a place where the two are married? Does the disturbance that churns up the human soul in search of an ultimate—it knows not what it is or what its name is—come over us because a peace has been broken, and perhaps because a peace to come has been prefigured? Are we ever unburdened by transcendence? What does this resting in something worthy of a festive consent and celebration suggest about the relation of beauty to transcendence? Can a sacred restlessness easily become intoxicated with itself qua restlessness, giving itself over to a cult of hyper-activity, imperiously impatient with the enigma of being? Would not patience before that enigma then become useless? But without that patience is there any porosity to beauty? Does not Wordsworth also speak of a "wise passiveness"?

*Inquietum est cor nostrum*: thus Augustine in his *Confessions* about our unquiet heart. What is the heart, and what does this unquiet portend? Is being unquiet the same as disquiet? Is it the same as what Pessoa sometimes impressively, sometimes enigmatically, writes about in his book of disquiet?[9] Is it an unquiet opening onto a quiet that is less the death of desire's longing as recharging its intimation of belonging? The heart names what is most intimate to our being: stirring before the more self-possessed reason, stretching beyond the self-determining will: seat of emergent desire that often desire does not itself comprehend. Unquiet is our heart, but what stirs the heart, what perturbs it? The stirring is not only a perturbation, it is more intimately a passionate exceeding. The heart is the flesh of an opening of the more original porosity of being in us, and the emergence in that porosity of the passion of being. We are not offered a sedentary sanctuary but an impulse to movement and wandering. Such wandering moves perhaps along a pathway of wondering that, in being passed along, does not end in the death of wonder but in its augmentation in renewed, in new, delight. This passion of being flows into an endeavor to be, a *conatus essendi*, and this carries us beyond ourselves, both to what is other as well as to fuller forms of ourselves—our own selving in its othering towards both itself and the other(s) of itself. The heart is stirred up and perturbed at a depth that precedes the precipitation of our endeavor and that exceeds particular endeavors that give us this or that determinate satisfaction. There is a source of infinity in the porosity of the original heart. There is an unbounded promise of self-surpassing that strangely shows human desire as exceeding all deter-

9. Pessoa, *The Book of Disquiet* (2010). I owe warm thanks to Yuliya Shymko for bringing Pessoa to my attention. My intuition is that Pessoa's heteronymns come to be in the space of metaxological plurivocity and its potency for saturated equivocity. The Portugeuse title of his book is *Livro do Desassossego. Sossegar* is etymologically related to Latin, *sedere*: seat, settle, from which our word, sedentary. In *desassossego* there is unsettling, being unsettled. What I am communicating in the arrest, rest, and unrest of beauty is not exactly Pessoa's *dessassossego*: neighbor to perplexity, as I mean it, this seems more becalmed, less turbulent; something in the arrest/rest/unrest is more diaphanous, less blank; there is more of an energy of fluency, intermediary transience as porous to what is beyond; there seems more of a (secret) mourning in Pessoa that brings us to a kind of stop. Nevertheless, we are dealing with relatives that belong in the same family. A fuller account would need to call on what I say about astonishment and perplexity as ways of wondering in Desmond, *Perplexity and Ultimacy* and in Desmond, *The Intimate Strangeness of Being*. See also below on *uaigneas*.

mination in terms of univocal animal desire. There is a relation to what is more exceeding still, what exceeds our own self-exceeding, in the ever-renewed delight of wonder that exceeds all satisfactions with ourselves.

What brings quietness to the heart? Is it only death? Hamlet in his famous speech, to be or not to be, toys with the idea (III, 1):

> For who would bear the whips and scorns of time,
> Th' oppressor's wrong, the proud man's contumely,
> The pangs of despised love, the law's delay,
> The insolence of office, and the spurns
> That patient merit of th' unworthy takes,
> When he himself might his *quietus* make
> With a bare bodkin?

*Quietus.* The quiet of the grave: peace: *requiescat in pace* (RIP). "The end of art is peace": Coventry Patmore.[10] Is there an end of peace that is more than death? What then of the unrest of the soul—even infinite restlessness? Is it only quietened by its own mortal finitude that strikes fatally at it in its last hour? Self-transcending as *Sein zum Tode*, being to death? Eros as death-bound, twinned to Thanatos? Eros as a refusal of death, even in dying? Is there quiet that is not in bondage to death? For all the inquietude of the heart, there is in Augustine perhaps the most famous exclamation, the leaping prayer: *Sero te amavi! pulchritudo tam antiqua, et tam nova, sero te amavi!* Late have I loved thee. Beauty: so ancient and so new. The rest of the prayer is an extraordinary poetic outburst, with all the senses being invoked to praise what cannot quite be sensed: the hearing, the touch, the sense of smell, singing in such a way that exhales the fragrance of an aesthetic, almost erotic feast—the sensuous and the sacred married metaxologically.[11] If this is the quietness of the unquiet heart, intimate to it is an extraordinary festive mixing of ebullience and serenity. This mixture of buoyed restlessness and moving rest is of interest

10. In 1912, W. B. Yeats refers to "delight in art whose end is peace" in "To a Wealthy Man," *Responsibilities and Other Poems* (1916). Yeats, *The Poems*, 158–59. See also Seamus Heaney's beautiful poem "The Harvest Bow" in homage to his father.

11. *Confessions*, X, 27: this is a chapter that one should speak out loud, better sing, or at least chant: *Sero* te amavi, pulchritudo tam antiqua et tam nova, sero te amavi! et ecce intus eras et ego foris, et ibi te quaerebam, et in ista formosa, quae fecisti, deformis inruebam. mecum eras, et tecum non eram. ea me tenebant longe a te, quae si in te non essent, non essent. vocasti et clamasti et rupisti surditatem meam: coruscasti, splenduisti et fugasti caecitatem meam: fragrasti, et duxi spiritum, et anhelo tibi, gustavi et esurio et sitio, tetigisti me, et exarsi in pacem tuam.

to me. The word "interest" is itself relevant in its being on the threshold of a surplus doubleness—*inter-esse* is a "being between"—being between rest and unrest. Beauty is interestingly somewhere there between also.

## Sick Love and Beauty

One might talk of beauty and transcendence as other (not self-transcendence) in terms of being *overtaken* by something (or someone) beautiful. Being overtaken can sometimes mix with being taken over. Notable here is the permeability of free release and being in an enigmatic bond with something (or someone) other. But consider the opposed thought: beauty takes us over, but in a delusionary way. Schönberg suggested the need to be "cured of the delusion that the artist's aim is to create beauty."[12] Being cured: as if one were suffering from a disease, the delusion of beauty being that spiritual sickness. The cure crusades as a cultural revolt against beautiful music. Instead of a divine mania, love of the beauty might be likened to a kind of aesthetic hypochondria—a sickness that is no sickness because of longing for what is not. (We do sometimes say, of course, that "there is no cure for love.") Is it not ironical that the name "Schönberg" names a beautiful mountain, or perhaps mountain of beauty (*schön Berg*)?[13] But Schönberg descends from the beautiful mountain with missionary dissonance (in his "early" period he is considered an arch "late" Romantic). Adam in Milton's *Paradise Lost* (Bk 8, 530–34) confesses to the visiting angel Raphael that with Eve nearby "passion first I felt/commotion strange . . . [making him] only weak/against the charm of beauty's glance." Raphael warns that love is not in passion but in reason (8, 588–94). Delusion of beauty: think of Don Quixote's high regard for Donna Dulcinea del Toboso: a fantasy of the beloved beauty, the end of which is to be awakened and no longer to be enchanted. Beautiful music puts one under a spell, and once under the spell, the soul moves and is movable in modes that seem outrageous to the unmusical stiffness of the disenchanted consciousness. Let the music stop, let the spell be broken, and the sounds no longer enchant one, no longer resound in the capti-

12. Schoenberg, *Theory of Harmony*, 30. Concerning painting Barnett Newman says that, by contrast to the perfection attained by a Michelangelo, the impulse of modern art was the "desire to destroy beauty." See Newman, "The Sublime Is Now," 581.

13. It seems Schönberg came to use Schoenberg as the form of his name, having emigrated to the USA, and in "deference to American practice." See Foss, "Schoenberg, 1874–1951."

vated soul. En-chant: the spell-binding chant of the music puts the soul into a thrall, but it is siren song, a bewitching sea shanty.

Is this sickness really like falling in love? We do speak, of course, about being "sick with love," of "love-sickness." We can ask the question and echo a kind of Schopenhauerian suspicion of erotic love, but need we take it so? The cold one and the ardent one do not see the beloved other in the same way. The ardent one (ardor from *ardere*: to burn) is lit up, is alight. It is not that a light falls *on* the other, a light seems to fall *from* the other, and in it one is involuntarily enveloped. It is indeed like those spells in fairy tales of old: a kind of invisible mist descends on the one who is enchanted and while one is in that space one sees what the others do not see, one sees for miles and miles, one moves faster than light, one is there otherwise before one has othered oneself, there is involuntary communication in the field where a primal porosity seems to have opened up, and the barriers, the blocks outside the space of the porosity, do not exist.

It is all very mysterious when one is in it, and it is mysterious differently for those outside the space of this magic, for they can see "realistically," more univocally what is there, they hold. They see the person in love as a fool, as fooling themselves. This last cannot be quite true, of course, for one cannot fool oneself into a spell. One cannot deceive oneself into being spellbound—though one could be spellbound and also be deceived and self-deceived. But the spell qua happening that overcomes one, that overtakes one, that takes over, is not first an act of lucid choice or rational willing. It comes to one as a surprise, as a gift. One can be energized by this gift. It gives one a lift. It is not just like the second wind runners get, it is more like running and then there is a wind at one's back and almost unnoticed one moves differently. Wind and breathe: these are the elemental terms that from archaic times were the ways of wording the mystery of being in-spired. Being breathed into—a great magician breathes on one and one is different—no longer mud but human—a living being, itself breathing, and indeed as the breath begins to wake to itself also able to word its own self, its own mud. It can word itself, indeed sing itself, sing its own flesh. The archaic revelation tells us that God breathes into the *humus* and it becomes human. Breath of the divine: I would put it more intimately—God kisses the mud and it becomes a living soul. God's kiss is not just a blown kiss that dissolves in the air. It touches the *humus* and what it touches comes alive and breathes—breathes for itself, breathes as itself.

I come back to Schopenhauer: his deep-seated suspicion of the ruses of eros co-exists with a celebration of music as a direct image of the ultimate itself, the will his name for it. But his experience of the Sabbatical rest of beauty seems at odds with the way the will secretly grooms our desire, redeeming its promise with death rather than fulfilled love. Or love fulfilled as death: perhaps Wagner was right as a musical Schopenhauerian in *Tristan and Isolde*? Should not the spell of beauty also be a delusion against which we should revolt, *pace* Schoenberg? And yet Schopenhauer does not revolt and construct theoretically a systematic assault on tonal music. Mozart and Rossini were his favorites, and he was not enamoured of Wagner, despite Wagner's courtship. Schopenhauer in practice, though not in theory, is closer to seeing the spell as a granted accession to the space of the primal porosity. Into this space we cannot gain access through ourselves alone—since it allows access to all, for it is the presupposed openness that cannot be commanded on the basis of anything derived from it. In Schopenhauer, in fact, this is a kind of atheistic grace.[14] Only when a beloved other (this can be a song or a poem) appears is this porosity so reopened that we are, so to say, thrust back into it, now mysteriously unclogged. We are thrust back into ourselves almost as if by a sleeping magic that puts us out, and then wakes us up to a *second awakening* in our being already awake.

The delusion for Schopenhauer is in the spell of love as a ruse of nature to allow the *eros tyrannos* of the will to have *its way* with us to perpetuate *itself*. And yet why the strange anomalous peace of the will-lessness of beauty or art that brings a pause to the wheel of Ixion? Should we just think of that as an escape from the will, as Schopenhauer conceives it? Or should we see here something of the ontological spell of a more original origin coming to singing, coming to wording, coming to affirmation and a festive, indeed sabbatical, Yes? Again, the question about the doubleness here: *either* we bring the spirit of suspicion to bear on the gift of the beautiful and we become the worm decrying the deceit of the apple (though we ourselves have introduced the rottenness, we ourselves being the rottenness we decry in the apple) *or* we grant being overtaken by the spirit of a generosity that is not ours alone, though it is intimate to us, and comes out of and over us and rocks us back on the deeper porosity simply

14. See Schopenhauer, *The World as Will and Representation*, 1, §70, especially 404, where the sudden reversal into will-lessness is compared to the kingdom of grace (*das Reich der Gnade*).

to being present before us. This latter is more consonant with the idea of "beholding from," not just beholding.

There is a beautiful image in Plato (*Phaedrus*, 255): the eye, inlet of the soul, on being struck, is inundated with the divine stream of eros. Beauty is not quite in the eye of the beholder in the way we often mean this statement—it in the eye differently, not due to the beholder, but to this influx of a sea of light, filling, flooding the porosity of the soul. A glance exchanged, just one look: "beholding from" is not the same as "giving the eye," or "looking another over." "Eyeing someone": this is looking in the modality of serviceable disposability. To hold another's gaze is not an easy thing. To be held in another's gaze is to risk being lost. The eye is a glimmer of mystery, its light a delicate gloss on darkness. "Beholding from" is being beheld, and being beheld is being beholden.

When Nietzsche spoke of the Greeks as being superficial out of profundity, he was suggesting, among other things, how beauty is fertile with what I am calling the saturated equivocity. The doubleness in transcending is such that we can discover that up is down, down is up. I love the doubleness of the Latin word *altus*: it means both height and depth—above is below, below is above: *hyper* is *hypo* and the reverse. Beauty can be intoxicating, yet an enigmatic repose attends it. It appears a blank to one taken up into hyperactive self-transcending and there seems to be nothing there. Yet this blank seems to be the shine of a fullness, the too muchness of a festive vacation. Vacation: an abdication of our (heroic) self-transcending: nothing happening except perhaps the happening of nothing? Much more the first than the second, I want to say. Vacation: vacating, emptying out, doing nothing, being on holiday. But a true vacation is a festive kenosis, full of nothing, nothing but enjoyment of being. Has this something to do with the *incognito* of transcendence as other guarding the sanctuaries of a sacred peace?

## Useless Beauty and the Passion of Being

Why not just speak of "beauty and the passion of *transcendence*"? I prefer to speak of the passion of *being* for it allows us to foreground certain *ontological* perplexities in a general sense that cannot be separated from existential considerations in a human sense. "Transcendence" can be marked by certain post-Kantian equivocations between our self-transcending and a different sense of transcendence as other (pre-Kantians would have talked about the transcendent). I want to keep the more robustly ontological reference in the *passio essendi*, and our transcending seen as a participation in this. Our transcending participates in a "being given to be" which is not confined to our being alone. We surpass ourselves, but only because there is a being given to be—no *conatus essendi* without first *passio essendi*. There is a passion of being before we are as transcending beings. This *passio* is emergent out of a more primal porosity which cannot be described in the language of our self-transcendence. Rather it arouses perplexity about a transcendence as other that is enigmatically communicated in the opening of the more primal porosity. In the case of the aesthetic and beauty this is very much bound up with our being incarnate.

In the "passion of transcendence" we see something double: our passion towards transcendence in our own transcending; but also the passion of transcendence in the signs of its giving of itself beyond itself, and towards us. This latter would imply transcendence itself assuming the form of passion, assuming in the sense in which anything aesthetic or incarnate is itself a passion, a being given over to, a receiving of and into the flesh of life. In beauty the passion of transcendence is the being born as musical flesh of transcendence itself.

There is also the older sense of *beauty as transcendental*. This is much more than a moldy old Scholastic commonplace. This metaphysical-ontological sense of the transcendental is worth revisiting. Much discussion of beauty after Kant is transcendental in his sense, focussing on the "turn to the subject" and, since Romanticism, focussing on expressive subjectivity (as, say, Charles Taylor might attest). Hence, this "Kantian" sense is more amenable to discussion of art, if art involves our activity. But the offering of beauty is not simply a result of our activity—it comes to us, we do not come alone. Hence perhaps it is inevitable with the triumph of subjectivity that there should be a kind of eclipse of beauty.[15] The given as other is exposed to being overcome by a self-activating subjectivity. The transcendence of the beautiful as other is subordinated to our self-expressive power as immanent self-transcendence.

Yet transcendental, in the older sense, is also not simply "transcendent," in the sense of being beyond finite experience. "Transcendental" does refer us to something at issue in being itself—being true, being good, being one—something about being as true, as good, as one.

15. See my *Art and the Absolute*, chapter 6.

Perhaps beauty as a transcendental is contested or controversial because of the intimate tie with sensuous showing, so crucial, it seems, to beauty. Sensuous showing seems to bind us too much to the determinacies of the flesh. By contrast, the transcendental does refer us to a universality, though not of any ordinary kind. Transcendental signals a hyper universality, "hyper," above, more than, the "ordinary" universal, if by this latter we mean general kinds or categories, or empirical generalities. The transcendental is trans-categorial, just in its enigmatic reference to all of being—being as such as beautiful.

This sense of beauty cannot be referred to the primacy of self-expressive subjectivity—it is not our creation. Nor for that matter is the issue one of simple imitation of a fixed objectivity. It does not fully fit into our more general ways of thinking of beauty or art. There is something at play here that it is prior to our determination, and our determinate judgment of this or that as beautiful. We might refer to beauty as transcendental in terms of an enabling condition of particular beautiful things, and we might say this in echo of the modern sense of the transcendental. But even if this transcendental beauty were to refer us to an enabling, it is not just a condition of possibility but an ontological condition of being itself that is not something generalizable, something that also is not a particular thing or property or series or set of such properties. It is universal, but in the dimension of the "hyper": the overdeterminate. This "hyper" is not just "above" but also "in the midst"—and it includes as much the singular as the general. In a fuller discussion I would invoke the notion of the intimate universal in connection with this.[16]

In any case, some sense of the beautiful like this is really at issue relative to the passion of being, relative to the passion of transcendence. And it is quite useless, since "use" comes in another space of determination and self-determination. This uselessness is in the dimension of the overdeterminacy of being—beauty invites us to participate in the aesthetic festivity of being. The gift of beauty as the aesthetics of happening is a call to festivity that is self-delighting. The fire of this delight is not confined to self alone but self-communicative, and indeed it constitutes a community of festivity: not mine, not thine, but also thine and mine.

What does uselessness here betoken? The useful is, of course, very useful—without the useful life would be impossible. That granted, it is also the case that the useful is primarily defined in a relation to us: what

16. See Desmond, *The Intimate Universal*, 99–102.

is useful may concern something other than us, but that something as other is to be brought into a relation to our desire, which it then, perhaps modified, serves to satisfy. There are different kinds of desire and not all of them need be exploitative. I can desire what is good for itself, and desire for someone I love what is good for them, without an ulterior motivation of using the other, or merely using something to further an instrumental end. Nevertheless, there are desires that are exploitative: what we deem as the useful tends to be consumed in being so defined as such. The dominant senses of the useful bring the other in relation to oneself, and it is clear that it is oneself that is the primary term of the relation. Of course, in being in relation to that other as useful I must take its otherness seriously in some sense. In use, the other is for me, but its otherness, as unmodified initially and later as modified, is ingredient in the relation. There is already something given relative to what is put to use; this something given is for itself prior to being put to use thus. Gift precedes use, though use modifies gift, and sometimes use is an abuse of what is originally given.

In *Ethics and the Between* I offer the argument that even if gift precedes use, a totalizing of the useful produces the reign of serviceable disposability: here something serves our instrumental desire, and hence is serviceable, but when used, it is used up, and hence disposable. This point has some implications for the uselessness of beauty. There is something about beauty that is deeply and intimately beyond serviceable disposability. One aspect of its uselessness is precisely the way it opens up for us the dimension of the given qua given, prior to use, and beyond use. There is a transcendence of the beautiful to use. It is not there to be used up. Even in art, when it seems we transform the given, say, the material into something more beautiful than it was at the outset, the given has to be minded, even when altered. What is virtual in it as a promise has to be respected before it can be re-formed in the light of a beauty intimated as there but initially not overtly uttered.

I think here of the stone of Michelangelo—the figures in the stone call to him; he must listen to the calling from the rock, and be obedient to what it communicates to him—his intervention is a freeing of what is calling, into a more open, newly realized communicativeness. Think, by contrast, of Zarathustra:[17] in speaking of the dream of the superman, he uses the metaphor of bringing his hammer to the stone of human-

17. In the discourse "On the Blissful Islands" (*Auf den glückseligen Inseln*) in Nietzsche, *Thus Spoke Zarathustra*.

kind, now deemed the unformed material of the art of his creative willing. Zarathustra rages against the stone. What of the violence and pain? What does that matter to me, Zarathustra blithely rejoins. The stone is an otherness, initially recalcitrant, which must yield to the will of the creator. On it is to be imposed, superimposed, the creative will of the artist—super-imposed since it is this creator who thinks of himself as super—as "hyper," as above, as over the given, as over and above. This can be a tyranny and war. It is not a wooing of the saturated equivocity that gives a sign of the superposition of the above and the below. Where in this rage is there the creating obedience to the call of the promise in the rock? I find Zarathustra's creative rage hard to distinguish finally from a kind of higher instrumentalizing of the given. There is not enough finesse for what offers itself as gift, and hence not enough of the first passion of beauty which comes over us, and overtakes us. The first passion is not in what we take over, what we overtake. Michelangelo is more intimate with this first passion, more receptive to what is communicated in the original porosity.

It is worth recalling, of course, the approach to art and the useful strongly shaped by the capitalistic and exploitative culture in the nineteenth century and continuing into our time. Art serves to free us from a utilitarian bourgeois culture. This is understandable. "All art is quite useless"—thus Oscar Wilde, and he reflected a widespread attitude. Granted, this can generate an aestheticism that prescinds from given reality, and retreats into a self-absorbed and self-congratulating dandyism. While dandyism is not quite now so dandy, nevertheless the attitude to the beautiful as useless still reflects something of calculative bourgeois culture. One of the sources of the revolt against beauty is the perception that it panders to a philistine bourgeois culture. In being assaulted, such a culture (putatively) is provoked into betraying itself in philistine reactions, reactions allowing a second gesture of outrage to the dim aesthetic taste of the booboisie (H. L. Mencken).

I call to mind the great painting of William Turner, *Rain, Steam, and Speed—The Great Western Railway* (1844): the train a flash of unstoppable energy, crossing a bridge, devouring the countryside and its distance, and alongside these inexorable tracks, the blurred dot of a hare in alarmed flight. One of the fastest of the animals, the hare cannot outrun the hurtling of the machine. This painting has been extolled as Turner's tribute to the glories of the English Industrial Revolution, a witness to his own "being with" the times, a hymn to capitalistic invention and its unleashed mechanical speed.[18] But Turner is not painting the Industrial Revolution (nor colluding with the spirit of serviceable disposability it might harbor). Turner is painting the overdeterminacy, even in the Industrial Revolution. He is getting to the level of the "to be," on the threshold between the overdeterminate and the determinate. He is not painting the sublime Industrial Revolution, but the sublime *in* the Industrial Revolution, with respect to the overdeterminacy, prior to and beyond serviceable disposability. It is mute metaphysics, not propaganda for the progress of the Industrial Revolution. Seeing beyond serviceable disposability, his smear of paint that is the hare does not smear being. It is the too muchness of its "to be" as there. The smear glories in the overdeterminacy as giving the dynamic coming to be, including too the dynamic becoming of the onrushing train.

Admittedly, beauty is, in fact, often instrumentalized by capitalist culture to sell commodities. Why? Because it addresses us, commands our attention. It is the goddess made captive to serve the religion of shopping. A hidden honor is paid to beauty even when it is instrumentalized thus: its elemental power to move us, even before we realize we are moved so, or understand why.[19] The power of beauty to beautify is pervasive in human life, and even the most functional relations are lifted to another level by coming under the transforming power of beautification. Architecture offers a test case: a house must be useful if it is to be a habitation; but there can be functional buildings that in the beauty of their form uplift functionality to another level. The aesthetic in the general sense is here also at stake: what bears on sensuous and sensible existence (*ta aesthetika*).

Think, more generally, of the forming and transforming power of beauty in the humanization of the animal, even in the animal functions themselves. The mingling of the useful and the beautiful here indicate how use is made to transcend use, in use itself. Take the aesthetics of eating, for instance; or of washing; or of performing other biological functions. Duchamp's urinal is not a urinal, nor is Manzoni's "Merda d'Artista" mere merda. (Neither stinks.) It is impossible to sustain a dualism between the useful and the beautiful. The instance of architecture shows the power of beauty in the useful to transcend the useful. There is

18. See the BBC documentary, *The Genius of Turner: Painting the Industrial Revolution* (directed by Clare Bevan, 2013), see from fifty-three minutes onwards.

19. See chapter 3 below; for more on this, see Desmond, *The Intimate Universal*, 275–89.

a surpassing of mere use in the useful itself. Once again, what comes to offer itself cannot be just simply relativized to our self-enclosed desire as defining the given as useful. Something other is at work in our desires, qualified as so much of them are by considerations of the useful. We see this evidently in the erotics of the beautiful so far as this entails an energy that is aroused before use, and that passes in and through and beyond the useful—a more released opening within which, in the end, the useful finds itself taken up.

In a word, there are considerations about the beautiful that *precede* and *transcend* use. There is a more original sense of uselessness than the one rightly found problematic in the aesthetic critique of capitalist instrumentalism or bourgeois functionality. There is beauty beyond use, and beyond the critique of capitalist instrumentalism—such beauty is not to be instrumentalized by any anti-capitalist functionalization either. It is *trans-political*—more related to the sacred than the humanly measurable. It calls forth from us a kind of reverence for it. What is useful is always to some degree proportionate to us, proportionate especially to practical desire and the economy of means and ends. Reverence is beyond use. There is something intimated of the disproportionate in beauty—of uselessness in the dimension of the disproportionate. Yes, there are desires beyond the instrumental—there is an eros beyond use. Even the eros that concentrates on endeavoring to be itself in self-surpassing is still emergent out of something not itself the product of its own self-becoming. It emerges out of what enables, indeed endows, its self-becoming. I again invoke the *passio essendi*: a being *given* to be, before there is an *endeavor* to be; a coming to be before a becoming. This bring us back to a more original ontological porosity, where beauty most deeply strikes home.

## Being Struck and the Passion of Being

When in connection with eros the Greeks talked of Cupid's arrows, they were right about being struck. There is beauty beyond even the arrows of Cupid. The strike might be wounding, for after all an arrow is a weapon shot by a bow into tender flesh.[20] But more originally, it is a reopening of the porosity of our being; the wound reopens flesh closed in on itself. The strike may be felt more painfully as a wound if in the reopened porosity the beloved turns away or refuses the opening. Being stricken: a cut into

20. In one ancient understanding, Cupid was offspring of Venus and Mars (Aphrodite and Ares in Greek).

selving from beyond self. Struck into the reopening of the porosity, love can be precipitated in a fall exceeding self-determination, and in some instances astonishment, even awe before the beloved other can come to be. Awe and yet awful: and perhaps too the temptation to idolatry, so absolute the absorbing passion can be. The strike arouses the passion of being, but again this passion is no simple passivity, for in that passion we may feel the urge to construct new images of beauty. Nevertheless, it bears repeating that the *passio* of being is not just in what we construct in response to being struck. If use is subtended by gift in relation to the givenness of being, our using is subtended by a more original opening to what gives itself for use. What shows itself opens our more original porosity to what shines in the givenness. There is here something beyond both construction and deconstruction.

Being struck by what is beautiful—there is something of a violence to this. There can be something paradoxically peaceful about this violence. In a way, one is struck by nothing; for when we rub our eyes and look at what has thus struck us, we find it impossible to pin down anything in a fully determinate way. Yes, there is this determinate beautiful thing or person before us. It is as if something "more" streamed from it, striking us, impressing us, in the literal sense of pressing itself into us; but there is nothing that presses, like an unwelcome intruder; there is a passing into us of the beautiful that is, so to say, benignly violent. Certainly it violates our autonomy when this tries to hug itself *auto kath' auto*.

I illustrate with respect to music. This is a human art, of course, and as communicating a *wrought beauty* requires our activity in a way not quite the same as given beauty. But music is perhaps the most powerful art to return us to the porosity, while at the same time moving a *passio essendi*, prior to any rationalization of the movement of desire, and exceeding complete self-determination of it. We do not first move, we are moved. Think of Kant deeming music to have the lowest place among the fine arts (*CJ*, § 53, 199). He uses a very revealing image: he compares music to a person pulling a perfumed handkerchief from his pocket (*parfümiertes Schnupftuch aus der Tasche*); the smell of the perfume spreads everywhere indeterminately and one has no choice about being subjected to it (*CJ*, § 53, 196). "In poetry," he says (*CJ*, § 53, 197–8), "everything proceeds with honesty and sincerity . . . ; it does not seek to sneak up on the understanding and ensnare it by a sensible exhibition. It shows its hand." The words of poetry are subject to public scrutiny; they can be made more or less determinate; they need not violate self-determination.

There is something not quite above board about music. I find very touching what Kant says (in a delicious footnote) about the singing of spiritual songs (*geistlicher Lieder*): they inflict a great hardship upon the public by such *noisy* (and therefore in general pharisaical) devotions, for they force their neighbors either to sing with them or to abandon meditations (*CJ*, § 53, 200). It seems Kant lived close to a prison where the prisoners had to sing hymns, and one infers that Kant, forced to listen, seems to have been beside himself. I see this footnote as Kant *taking revenge* on having to endure such a situation. This is not the transcendental doctrine of beauty; it is the critical philosopher of pure reason as human-all-too-human. Or perhaps if the footnote speaks true, there is comedy in this—Kant forced to join in, to sing along with the spiritual songs of criminals! Irreverent imagination can sometimes get the better of one reading Kant.

Music comes upon us, as it were. It *moves us* without asking our reason or our will. We find ourselves caught up and moved. It is beyond rational will. Music communicates to and with the *passio essendi*, which, like Platonic *eros* and *mania*, is responsive prior to and exceeding the sway of determinate reason. Kant sees only an *intrusion* in this involuntary responsiveness of the *passio essendi*, and does not like it. He does not see the spontaneous surging up of a transcending that is powerfully moving, precisely as other to our rationalized and willed mediations. This power of music will be very important for thinkers like Schopenhauer and Nietzsche: it will be evidence of something other to human-all-too-human will. It will be the singing of aesthetic transcendence; it will be a metaphysical revelation of something other, named by them as will or will to power. Nietzsche revealingly confesses on occasion that his life would hardly have had a point were there no music: it is his *consolatio philosophica*.

Kant's negative judgment on music suggests a certain will to be in control. There is an indeterminacy about music; it offers only a *fleeting* or transitory impression (*transitorisch*), he says (*CJ*, § 53, 200); you cannot pin down, fix it univocally. You cannot fix why it so deeply moves us, and yet it does. We might look at that fleetingness in a different light. The fugitive transience of beauty is just its resonance with the porosity of being, its resounding with the *passio essendi*. There is an alighting of beauty, an alighting on beauty. Alighting suggests a prior flight that now comes to land, now comes to compose itself: something offers itself to us, no longer simply fugitive but paused or pausing in an interval that can enchant. Think of the way we ourselves are brought to pause when, as if in a kind of godsend, a beautiful butterfly alights before us, alights even on our hand. Our alighting on beauty, or its alighting on us, have to do with a certain resting or serenity with which beauty graces us. Beauty arrests us, and for a pause we are taken out of ourselves, sometimes lost in the enchantment of something marvellous before us. As Schopenhauer well knew experientially, the grasping, planning will is stilled and momentarily we enjoy a Sabbath, a release from what he also deems the penal servitude of the will.

It is this arresting, this resting, that interests me here in connection with transcendence and the passion of being. Arrest: something stops us. As with some arrests this stop can seem like an imprisonment. There is something involuntary about being arrested. But arrested, we rest: it is not a prison simply. The rest is an offering: an offering of a space of being taken outside of ourselves, even as we seem to do nothing but rest in ourselves. The rest shows a strange doubleness of a being-at-home and yet a not-being-at-home. The rest is not antithetical to the restlessness I mentioned earlier in connection with the energy of self-surpassing. To the contrary, this is rest that paradoxically also stirs something up—generates an unrest, but in another dimension to the functionality of a will that would manipulate and utilize what has come to alight before us. The offering of the beautiful mingles both ar-rest and un-rest: stops and releases; makes us still, and yet moves us deeply.

We can understand this doubleness in the arrest of the beautiful in terms of our doubleness as both *passio essendi* and *conatus essendi*. Even when the *conatus* takes over the *passio*, it still carries this doubleness, in so far as it is a *co-natus*, seen as a "being born with." There is always the relation to the other in selving's own endeavor to be, its striving to be itself. The arrest, while resting, stirs something up in the passion of being. There is a deep patience prior to functionality and beyond it. Being struck by the offering of beauty can incite the impulse to create something beautiful in the light of this offering. As there is the doubleness of ar-rest and un-rest, there is the doubleness of patience and endeavor, or aesthetically put, of inspiration and creation.

## Beauty and the Beyond of Wholeness

I would like to say something about the paradoxical conjunction of proportion and disproportion in beauty. This reflects also the saturated equivocity: the metaxological doubleness of selving and othering, the togetherness of receiving and endeavor, of "mimesis" and "creativity," suitably reconceived in light of the porosity of being.[21] As already suggested, this doubleness is not a conjunction of one and the other, not a superimposition of one on the other, not a sublation of the other in the one, but an aesthetic superposition of the two, a superposited togetherness.[22]

This entails we must resist the more usual juxtaposition of the beautiful and the sublime. One of the classical thoughts about beauty lies precisely in one term of this doubleness, namely, in the thought of a pleasing proportion between us and the beautiful. There is a consonance between us and the beautiful which is pleasing. Surely then the disproportionate is more suitable, either to the ugly as not beautiful, or to the sublime as discordant or disproportionate? One can agree: there is something of excess to the sublime. It is not pleasing simply but rather the occasion of pain. Paradoxically, it brings us down and lifts us up. It cannot be instrumentalized, for it is useless even to the point of threatening us with negation, though in fact we are not negated and some higher exhilaration is released in the face of the threatening disproportionality. I want to ask, however, if there is a disproportion in the proportion of the beautiful. If this is so, we need a revision of a strict contrast of the beautiful and the sublime. Uselessness as a kind of transcending of the proportionate opens up what is disproportionate to determination, disproportionate in terms of our own desire alone, disproportionate in terms of any determination or self-determination we might wish to impose on it. The passion of being, in the intimation of the disproportionate in the pleasing proportions of the beautiful, reveals the desire for transcendence coming forth in response to the call of the beautiful.

A fitting sense of harmonious proportion need not be rejected. Recall a related discussion of beauty with respect to pleasure, and my claim that we do not always do justice to the ontological reserves hidden in pleasure itself. If there is a call, there is also something pleasing; pleasure implies a pleasing, and pleasing harbors the notion of *appeal*. The appeal may take the form not only of asking but of thanking. It is interesting how sometimes we say "please" not simply to request something but in answer to something requested and given. As if the appeal in the "please" somehow could not be confined to one side of the pleasurable, namely

21. On this reconceiving, see Desmond, *The Intimate Universal*, chapter 2.

22. See Desmond, "Flux-gibberish: For and Against Heraclitus," on the saturated equivocity and superposited doubleness with respect to Heraclitus.

us being pleased into expressing a subjective gesture of gratitude. Pleasure of beauty: being pleased: *placet*. Again I think of *complacentia* in the medieval sense: "being pleased with." Being pleased with is not revealed in simple sensationalistic terms but in terms of a concord between the embodied person and the flesh of given being. We are not alien in the world, like gnostic spirits, pneumatics who are fallen into the vicious equivocity of the dissimilating world. Beauty is the living witness that this kind of gnostic transcendence is not true to how we are true to the earth in responding to beauty. There is a strangeness to being; there is also an intimacy. The pleasure of beauty is related to that intimate strangeness—strangeness in awakening us to the surprise of given beauty, intimacy in the pleasure that communicates in the secret concord. The "*cum*" of *complacentia*, of "being pleased with," might also signal a secret community of those pleased, pleased together. Something of the intimate universal is communicated in the pleasure of such *synousia*.[23]

One of the characteristics of beauty stressed in connection with harmony and proportion is the sense of *wholeness* marking the beautiful being. It is not that brokenness cannot bring beauty to mind, but some have suggested that in the fragment it is the intimation of a lost or coming or disfigured wholeness that draws us. Otherwise, the fragment is of nothing; and if it is of nothing, then it is just itself, and so a kind of whole for itself, and hence not just a fragment. Fragments are thus haunted by more than themselves. In any event, wholeness brings to mind a bounded totality—something that is for itself to be sure, hence not a mere means to an end—something justified in its own being. The arrest of beauty holds us in the embrace of some such wholeness. I do not want to say this is the last word, but it is relevant to the theme of transcendence and the passion of being. For do not wholeness and transcendence exist in tension with each other? A whole constitutes itself as such by being enclosed or enclosing itself in a bounding or self-bounding, self-binding limit. Like a circle, its beginning and end coincide and hence the whole seems to lift itself out of the succession of instrumental desires and grasps. There is something to this—say, the beautiful face as really striking manifests itself against the

23. Kant is getting at something like this concord of aesthetic pleasure, but in terms of the transcendental accord of faculties of imagination and understanding. I take a more robustly ontological sense from it all. On the *sensus communis* in Kant, see Desmond, *The Intimate Universal*, 94–97; on "being pleased with," 308–9. Augustine's distinction between *fruitio* and *usus* (in *De Doctina Christiana*) might come to our aid us here in naming a fitting way of "being pleased" with being.

greyer homogeneity of the ordinary looks of others, of the ordinary looks of things. By contrast to such a striking whole, transcendence seems to call all such boundings into question, at least to breach such wholeness. The framing of something associated with the aesthetic attitude is broken open. This frame is broken open. But in what way can an opening be framed? The broken frame seems on the side of the "trans" of transcending—and yet if the brokenness reaches a certain pitch of decomposition, there is no integral work there, and hence nothing of beauty. There have been many efforts to break the frame in recent times, but how far can you go and still have something that arrests one in the relevant sense? Is this breaking not a transcendence that exists in overt or concealed opposition to the poised integrity of the beautiful work or given beauty?

One thinks, for instance, of kinds of dissonant music to which our bodies have difficulty listening, or hearing, after a while. As a sensuous receptivity the body tends to shut down. There may be a theory behind the ordered disorder of the sounds, but the elemental body does not hear abstract theories. *Aísthēsis* is a certain *logos* too, Aristotle said (for instance, *De Anima*, 424a, 27–28), but hearing such a *logos* the embodied soul resounds; deprived of consonance, at a certain limit, the body shuts down. Relevant here is something more like Heraclitus's listening to the *logos* than having an abstract theory. The theory might make you continue listening longer, but are you listening or thinking of the theory? Or just hearing sound-effects corresponding to the theory?

Galileo uses the image of a rape of the senses in connection with modern mathematical science. And yet we *see* that the sun rises and is new every day. Heraclitus saw it too: "The sun . . . is new every day" (ὁ ἥλιος . . . [καθάπερ ὁ Ἡράκλειτός φησι,] νέος ἐφ' ἡμέρῃ ἐστίν: Fr. B 6). Looking: consider paintings that of themselves do not draw in the eye, and then one does not just look, one reads the card, only then to relax in relief—so that's what it is about! But is one then looking or beholding? Where is the sensuous arrest, the sensuous rest? Is the robust sensuousness of the beautiful supplanted by some idea that we are instructed to see as materialized? To what extent is this a *theoretical instrumentalization* of the sensuous?[24]

24. My point is not to argue against thought; the question is the relation of sensuousness and thought, or how the incarnate is truly an incarnation, such that one cannot separate the thought and the thing. How should we think of saturated immediacy as overdeterminate? Breaking the frame, dissonant music, and so on, were (once) intended to break the stranglehold of bourgeois beauty and free from the utility

The issue here: transcendence breaks open wholes, but is there something that is also communicated in the breach of beauty? *Is there a beyond to the whole that emerges within the whole?* Can we at all speak of the whole, or a whole, as if that could be taken out of the sustaining milieu that holds it up in its singularity? I suggest the notion of an "open whole" or "open wholeness" to do justice to what is at play: whole or wholeness to indicate the arrest, but open or opened to indicate the energy of transcending or unrest that is released in that arrest. There is a participatory side to all aesthetic receiving; it is not spectatorial in a detached way; it is engaged detachment, or interested disinterest. This participatory side means that, instead of the whole, we might speak of the open whole as a being in the midst in a singularly surplus way. We are in the midst, but we can be in the midst more intensively and with more unclogged porosity to what is showing itself, as a more engaged passion that cannot retract itself into a self-guarding being for itself. The open whole testified to a being in the *metaxu*, a being between. The beautiful as given, as well as the art work as a wrought beauty, offer a kind of between space for transcendence.

Of course, once we think more closely on the idea of an open whole it is not at all a mere contradiction between the closed and the unclosed. Even a fragment can serve, paradoxically, as an open whole: being itself an absence and a pointing beyond. Every being, as an endowed singular integrity, and as communicatively in relation to beings other than itself, is an open whole. This is especially so with the human being, a singular integrity who is just what it is in being beyond itself in relation to what is other. Openly whole and transcending: something beautiful pleasingly calls on us in the midst of things, calls us in its open wholeness into the passion of transcending that cannot be completely finitized. The true art work gives us an original image of this. There is always a double relativity of self-relation and other-relation, of creativity and mimesis. This is the basis for the surplus equivocity of the beautiful and of the art work.

---

of serviceable disposability. In time the transgression became established and subject to the same regime of serviceable disposability. The aesthetic elites, once sparse on the margins, now begun to gather crowds on the same margins, as the old center becomes vacated. The vacant center, no longer in the center, is now on these same margins. There we find cultural shadow-boxing with ghosts who should be long interred or exorcised. These ghosts, continually kept alive, are needful to keep up appearances—appearances of "resistance" to the bourgeois oppressor. "Keeping up appearances": how bourgeois!

Beauty ever gathers to itself and ever points away, points beyond itself. It communicates an open wholeness, or an opening of transcending in a surplus wholeness that cannot be enclosed in itself. Beauty is what it is in addressing what is other—the address to the other. Indeed, the address of the other is in the whole itself. The double relativity is there. The opening in the relativity recalls us to the more primal porosity of our being. In this porosity once again the passion of being is called forth. This is the basis of the disproportion that excites the proportionate—the hyperbolic in the immanent, the transcendence that yet is offered in what remains at home with itself—at home with itself in arousing a not-being-at-home.

If we were to speak here of the passion of transcendence, once again we see the doubleness of the "of." Is the "of" just of our self-transcending—which then comes back to itself and the whole binds itself to itself? Or is it of transcendence as other that arouses our transcending—not our opening to transcendence but our being opened by transcendence as other, and then self-transcending to follow? Everything about beauty, in view of the passion of being, turns us upside down, but this turns into downside up, and carries us as upended to what is above us. Coming home to the beautiful resurrects restless homelessness, being both ardent for the finite and awakened to what cannot be contained by finitude. Again: rest and restlessness, achieved home and homeless seeking beyond home, are not two things juxtaposed, previously lying side by side and now conjoined, but are superposed in a metaxological embrace that fleshes their *complacentia*.

## Begetting on the Beautiful

In one of the Platonic accounts of eros there is a perplexing stress on eros as leading to "begetting on the beautiful" (*Symposium*, 310b7: τόκος ἐν καλῷ). What might this mean? Has it anything to do with the suggestion of the open whole? For love of the beautiful is not simply love being responsive as passion, as *passio*; it is love responsive as endeavoring, as *conatus*, as willing new and more beauty to be. *Tókos* carries the sense of "birthing," mothering, a kind of nativity. Does "begetting on" suggest a wider sense of "begetting from"?[25] Wider than just begetting from one determinate finite source but fructifying from a source that cannot be so

25. The preposition *"en"* has a variety of meanings in Greek, including "in," "on," "upon," "amongst, "in accordance with."

finitized? Thus seen, "on" might signal perhaps something like an expanse of porosity, a between of erotic allure, a milieu of excitation towards the beyond of oneself. It is easy to think of self-surpassing as going beyond an already-achieved self, but what if the surpassing itself returns the "self," through its *passio*, to its own more original porosity, such that in a way there is no self, no fix(at)ed self. In the between the selving becomes an unselving and, womb-like, an excited opening to what is other or more than itself.

The open whole: we think of the whole as finitely determinate and bounded, and openness as initiating some aperture or unclosure of this bounded whole. But what if the openness of the whole already was participant in the porosity, not again simply as a quiescent passivity but as a restless *passio* that in inspired moments of increased excitation flows forth into energetic endeavor in relation to what is beyond itself, and indeed to its own beyond as already seeded or sleeping in itself. The doubleness of rest and restlessness, as a superposition of being-at-home and not-being-at-home, breaks out now more on the side of not-being-at-home and the quest for a new home never quite to be granted among finite things. The "on" then signals a *metaxu* of eros that is more than the plural participants drawn towards beauty and beyond themselves, participants often too in this drawing, being drawn, as if by a magic spell or enchantment. Schopenhauer, to mention him again, will see nature's ruse, see something of a lie to lure us on to further phenomenal life. Perhaps he is not entirely wrong, but he is not right enough either. For though there is a kind of sleepwalking character to being drawn thus, it is because something has awoken or become awake at more ultimate ontological depths: namely, the porosity as newly unclogged of determinacies that fix form on the indeterminacy, holding in check the creative overdetermination that in truth is too much for us.

On can think of the erotics of nature naturing (*natura naturans*: *tókos* again as birthing). Behold the manner in which animals generate, often going under as individuals for the perpetuation of the species. They are unknowing servants of the intimate universal of aesthetic nature. They immortalize in terms of the species, and hence pursue new life in a form of deathlessness in the mortal world. There is a ceaseless replacement of the old by the new—different but the same, the same but different. There is an erotic solidarity in generation—indeed a secret solidarity with the whole in the unwilled perpetuation of the species that comes from the unbidden excitation of the erotic *conatus*. In the endeavor to be sleeps, and now wakes, the desire for deathless being. The animals, the animated ones, thus are witnesses to their participation in the intimate universal. Eros is a living relating of dying creatures, with mortality a constant accompaniment, and the sway of the companioning power always accessory in the expanse of the relating.

Compare today the break between eros and generation when human beings turn back into narcissistic self-feeling, a contraction of the passion of being. The gift of the original porosity is still offering its promise, but the passion of being is overtaken by a *conatus* in which erotics circulates around itself as recreational sex rather than generational. This recreational sex is not re-creational, for it is not tied to creation, but is self-contracted, produced by a self-circling of the passion of being that allows no breach to a beyond of itself. We refuse the opening of the open whole, put the changeling of a whole closed on itself in its place: a counterfeit double of eros. One might say that true eros is recreational, creating again, generating beyond itself, cooperating in creation as participating in its begetting on the beautiful. "Recreational sex," in the meaning this term now has, enjoys no joy in new being, for it has nothing to do with re-creation as this begetting.

Even our *conatus* is not ours alone, if we play with the echo of the connatural in the *conatus*, and think of *co-natus* as a being born "with" (*natus-cum*). Our origination as selving is always bound to the terms of a "being with," a "co." A turn or return to the creative origin reveals itself as a connatural porosity to the intimate universal. Being self-related emerges as and out of a being in relation to other(s). This is relevant to an understanding of all forms of love. One of the Greek word for erotic union is *synousia*—literally "with-being." The intimate implication of "being with" another is signaled in the act of generation, in the doing of the act itself. (In the flesh: woman-man-the child as a familial concretion of this.) The same intimate implication is signaled from the side of conception coming to first fruition in birth in the "with" of *co-natus*. What is promised in the "with" will never leave us, or let us rest, in the course of our mortal life.

The erotics look like our self-surpassing, and thus our endeavoring, but a hint of the more primal porosity and patience might be detected in one of the myths about the origin of eros in Plato's *Symposium* (203a–204c)—namely, the tale told by Diotima/Socrates. Eros is conceived from the union of *Penia* and *Poros*: there is a poverty and lack (*penia*), yes, but there is more than that in *poros*. The tale tells of the feast of the gods, drunk on nectar, and *Poros* falls asleep, and somehow *Penia* manages to unite with *Poros* and conceive their child, *Eros*. There is a seed in eros exceeding finitude. The divine is seeded in infinite desire with a seed making us both extraordinary creatures and extremely foolish—from the animal point of view. The thought is that there is a kind of sleeping agapeics at the conception of eros, an agapeics in this sense of a divine festivity, the meal of joy as the gathering of the divine. In this agapeics, as in all such sacred festivity, there is a kind of seed of surplus generosity at the origin. This "too muchness" is there from the origin, and so eros, even while lacking, is always more than lack. It is the secret surplus of the divine agapeics that also companions its restless search for a fullness beyond itself.

The notion of the open whole might come across as unorthodox Platonism and rather as a mixing of Aristophanes and Socrates. In the story of Diotima/Socrates, the fuller unfolding of eros is not reducible to one whole. The emphasis is unlike that of the myth of origins so brilliantly told by Aristophanes (*Symposium*, 189c–193d): there the original whole—the being that is double what we now are—is split in two because its abundance was *hubristic*. The original humans challenge Zeus and are cut down to size, halved, cut in two. Such a surplus of hubris is not the agapeic surplus of divine "too muchness." In Aristophanes's story, archaic humans were one whole; now we are one of two halves, each of us in search of the lost whole, the other who is our own lost half and with whom we can reconstitute the one whole. In the account of Diotima/Socrates, by contrast, there is difference, but it is not the difference of a hubristic fullness. It is, rather, reflected in our doubleness as a mingling of *poros* and *penia*. *Poros* alone might perhaps tempt us to think ourselves as gods, were there not also the doubleness of our being neither empty nor full but partaking of emptiness and fullness. *Penia* alone might tempt us either to negate ourselves and become nothing or to negate our lack and try to be everything.

That this is not to happen follows from truthfulness to the doubleness, from fidelity to the fact that eros is the carrier of this different doubleness. Eros unfolds in both the anticipating openness of its poverty and in the porosity to divine agapeics inherited from the sleeping divinity of *poros* on the ground. Eros is not in our being cut in half as a punishment for the hyperbole of hubris. It is, rather, in search of a *hyper* above its own poverty, in search not just for itself, in search because the trace of the god is in the eros as a porosity to divine agapeics. There are also different ways of apprehending the *suffering* of the endeavor to be that is presented in these two accounts. In the one, there is the pain of being split in half and the pain of seeking oneself as other, the other as oneself. In the other, there is the strain of being twofold and the suffering is not just in one's lack alone but also in the seeking of the divine festivity, a seeking in terms of a seed of divine festivity in eros itself.

In sum, the passion of being emerges in a more primal porosity, and we find ourselves endowed as an energy of selving that is our own and yet not completely our own, an energy in and through which we define ourselves, though never out of relation to what is other to us. The passion of being, and the forms of love in which it finds incarnation, is not to be understood in any philosophy that tends towards the self-absolutizing of our activist character or our endeavor to be. In such a philosophy, in fact, we are taken in by the way the *conatus* tends to override the *passio*, resulting in what we might call a constructivist view of selving. In this view, we are not gifted with being what we are; we make our being, make ourselves as being for ourselves. We self-construct—even to the point of re-constructing, say, the bodies originally given to us. Witness today, in connection with eros and beauty, the cosmetic surgery industry: the language of *industry* shows the overtaking of elemental beauty by an economic project of reconstruction. We will not accept ourselves. Rather than love, we negate what is given and love only what we reconstruct. This means that the reconstructed self as loved is haunted by self-hatred.

Again and again there is an overriding of the patience of being by the endeavor. Being alive is to find oneself always tempted to this impatient overriding. In time we find that the fulfillment of life is impossible if this happens. We have not taken the proper time, and respected the rhythms of time, to attend to what is within us and before us, and hence to be truthful concerning our proper response to the promise of our being. One might say that the very perpetuation of life is conditional on a perpetual recurrence of the patience, and a perpetual receiving of the promise of life. Moreover, this recurrence is not only a matter of when the endeavor to be meets an external or hostile limit. It is always happening, and its gift of promise is always being offered, even though we do not notice or acknowledge it. It concerns the gift of life as received, granted to us in the first instance, but which, in the rush forward of the endeavor to be, is taken *for* granted rather than *as* granted.

In the sweep of a life, the external limits of encroaching others and the limit of mortal time—both internal and external—can serve as reminders of this more primal patience of being in which we may again consent to the goodness of the gift of life. In the light of recurrence and perpetuation, *eros* and *thanatos* cannot, of course, be absolutely sundered. But our intimacy with *thanatos* is not a death-drive. A death-*drive* overplays the energy of the endeavor to be as finally futile and underplays the wisdom of the deeper patience of being. Instead of granting that the gift of being at all is granted, we continue to turn against such givenness, just because it is given and not produced by us. We can so insist that everything be subject to our self-determination that we betray the joy of this gift, in the overriding of our own self-affirmation. Consent to death, in gratitude for the gift of life, may offer the final opportunity to make our peace with this patience. Eros, impassioned in being so patient, becomes porous to what exceeds the death-drive.

## Enhancement and the Counterfeit Doubles of Beauty

Given human multiplicity, there are different begettings on the beautiful. There are different kinds of immortalizing. I touch on the main ones in *The Intimate Universal*, generational perpetuation, immortalizing through works and heroic glory, the immortalizing of the great artist, the immortalizing of the sacred and of singular selving itself.[26] I would like to return briefly to one simple and elemental form: adorning. It helps us raise the question of the connection of enhancing beauty and counterfeit doubling. Cosmetics are an everyday form of begetting on the beautiful. The word "cosmos" refers us to a beautiful whole, and cosmetics to composing and recomposing the whole. Our faces are open wholes, and cosmetics opens the whole to the beyond of itself, promised in its givenness, more or less beautiful, though sometimes rather ugly. In adorning, aesthetic passion becomes artistic endeavor to be. In such a simple thing we have the lineaments of inspiration becomes creative. A true beautician is inspired: they see what is there in what is not there, or what is not there in what is there. In any case, they can be servants and artists of the superposition of beauty and ugliness. Sometimes they have to do hardly anything, the given beauty is so imposing. If there is given beauty, there is also beauty in enhancing. Beautification itself often involves enhancing the given.

What is enhancing? We do something, but it is not simple construction. There is a prior attentiveness to what is promising in what we hope to

26. Desmond, *The Intimate Universal*, 329–36.

enhance. There is no enhancement from nothing—enhancing is of something that already intimates itself as more than the dominantly current form of the given. There is an overdeterminacy to the given and it may take more than genius, it may take love, to see there what is more than the now-current dominant determinacy. The forming of the determinate points beyond itself to what is promised as overdeterminate, and the line to this redemption of promise passes through a creative indetermination which is not tyrannized by the determinacy. What it promises to be, it is as its own reserved to be. What it is to be is this, its often recessed promise. It is and it is to be. Enhancement as beautification exists between the promise and the process of its redemption.

A face is a face, but we sometimes think a face asks for a facial. How can a face put its best face forward, if the face is univocally simply what it is? A face is a possible surfacing of beauty, but the promise of the surfacing may be suppressed or retarded. The face might need a slight change of line there—the eyebrow a little plucking there—the cheeks need a little color here, less color there; and so on—and *voila*, the sow's ear is almost a silk purse. We talk of a "makeover," but a makeover is (made) over the "might be" of what now is. The face is what it is as what it is to be, and the "makeover" happens between what it is and what it is to be, two "poles" seemly different and yet not different at all. Finesse for aesthetic promise is part of the seeing appreciation of beauty. The intimate is as an intimating of what can be more in the given—what is the intimate(d) calls forth our cooperative creation. This cooperative creation brings in erotics as begetting on the beautiful.

There is the saturated equivocity of all this. Take breast enhancements as an example. Think of what extremes to which this can go—a woman is "made over" as a complex combination of chemicals and cleverly concealed surgical cuts. I am put in mind of Edmund Burke speaking interestingly of the smoothness of beauty, while dealing with gradual variations in beauty. He has a rhetorically impressive passage that shifts from the smoothness of round, soft doves to the dizzying effect of a woman's breasts:

> I have before me the idea of a dove; it agrees very well with most of the conditions of beauty. It is smooth and downy; its parts are (to use that expression) melted into one another; you are presented with no sudden protuberance through the whole, and yet the whole is continually changing. Observe that part of a beautiful woman where she is perhaps the most beautiful, about

> the neck and breasts; the smoothness; the softness; the easy and insensible swell; the variety of the surface, which is never for the smallest space the same; the deceitful maze, through which the unsteady eye slides giddily, without knowing where to fix or whither it is carried. Is not this a demonstration of that change of surface, continual, and yet hardly perceptible at any point, which forms one of the great constituents of beauty?[27]

You will find nothing like this passage in Kant's discussion of the beautiful and the sublime, indebted though he was to Burke. But even the Burkean swoon before the bosom would soon evaporate were self-consciousness of the silicone valley to intervene. The deceitful maze would no longer make him slide giddily. If self-consciousness intervenes, our response to such chemically enhanced beauty might well be to stop us dead in our tracks, for who could self-consciously love the stuff of silicone? These breasts are counterfeit doubles. A kind of innocence in the seeing seems needed. Perhaps we have as much to fool ourselves as allow ourselves to be fooled. Nevertheless, there is an erotic folly that is true. Indeed, if we take the beautiful thing or person apart too much, we are not enchanted. If this enchantment seems like a "lie" of beauty, it is sometimes more *we* who "murder to dissect." Seduction can be a kind of lying, though there is a wooing that is true. A beautiful woman can be seductive; but a beautiful woman is seductive because she is beautiful; she is not beautiful because she is seductive; she is not pretending to be beautiful. We fall in love with the flattering lies we are told; we fall in love with our own flattering lies. And yet, even in the equivocity, there comes a point where lucidity cannot be gainsaid—aesthetic beauty solicits the willing suspension of dissolving analysis. A *deus ex machina* is an erotic stopper. The god must remain hidden, to some degree, in what shows itself. I am thinking here of how self-reflective art can become a kind of self-cannibalizing of art, a violence of art on itself. Perhaps it is the loss of the innocence of enchantment that comes with age but age also brings senility.

There are occasions when bitter disillusion(ing) can express a revenge against beauty—revenge against the hour of consonance. Why?

27. *Burke, A Philosophical Inquiry into the Origin of our Ideas of the Beautiful and the Sublime*, 104–5. Burke remarks that smoothness has hardly been noticed as an essential constituent of beauty (104). In *Lysis* (216c-d) Socrates speaks of the beautiful as friendly and good, and so it "resembles something soft and smooth and sleek; that is why . . . it so easily slides and dives right into us, by virtues of these qualities."

Because it is fugitive. Important here are different relations of time to beauty. When young, we are easily infatuated, taken into its transport. The porosity is not perhaps so much on guard, and the *passio* of being surges with all the energy of an ardent endeavor. Older, one has the colder eye, and no longer falls for the wing and the sigh and the "come on." There is a way of saying "come on" that now means "get off," or "come off it."

Youth is in love with beauty—and it is right and wrong. It does not see when its eyes are everything—it is bewitched and unfree, and yet it is freed by some bewitching beauty—and hence there is more than itself at work in and through it. It is right, not knowing this, and when it knows it, it retracts into itself, and thinks it knows the score, but it does and does not. It has lost the vitality that woos life into continuation. Beauty cannot always live with too determinate knowledge—at least with an excessively univocalizing kind of knowledge. The vehemence of youth is in thrall to the *conatus essendi* in its seductive equivocity—there is often not enough of *passio essendi* in the mode of more mindful attendance.

Age is weary and it is right and wrong. The wrinkles come, the vitality withdraws, the paunch expands, the breasts sag, our séance with beauty proves too often to be too self-induced and the spirit of enchantment dissolves. Some can become bitter at this—for some this is one of the great "consolations" of age: to be able to denounce. But this is hatred, and we rightly deride bitter old age for being bitter. It is a cliché: we would rather graceful aging. It is a cliché because it is true.

And we are right. One might live in truth(fulness) and not know what is means univocally—but it is not easy, since we must cultivate patience for this grace and this is a *via dolorosa* to those who fancy themselves masters in control, sovereigns of eros. The ebb of the body tells us slowly that we are not masters, and that the exhilaration of erotic sovereignty is an evanescent ecstasy. We can will above the body, but only in a relative sense. Such willing wills a "makeover"—though it can strangely release sleeping energies that now no longer wake themselves. Where does this will come from, this willing to further life? We love beauty and we do not want it to die, do not want to die. The worm is already in the rose, but knowing this source of sickness does not always sicken the love of the rose. It can do, if we look on the rose with the evil eye, sometimes a worse worm than the worm in the rose itself.

We are a kind of clandestine ontological love. Like all human love, it is mingled with pain and envy and hatred—and with the dying of the dream when boredom palls our power to perceive the beautiful. The world is still full of its given glory and we see nothing except the withered husk of harvest and the shudder of coming winter. The wintry wind comes up when we call on the secret energies. The well is less dry as open to draughts that blow from eternity. Eternity is the vast desert that gusts now and then unpredictably through a vacation that always remains invisible, being more like nothing than something. The porosity must cede that it is porosity, not now to being but to no longer being. There is no wall we can build against the draught of eternity that takes our breath away, takes our breath back.

The passion of being can become compassion. Yeats in a bitter poem asks: Why should not old men be mad?[28] The old *can* be gifted with idiot wisdom. Childlike, the old one can strangely see the beauty—the useless beauty—no longer for purposes of serviceable disposability—but for itself. Time brings to Golgotha the self-circling desire of serviceable disposability. One is disposable but differently disposed. Perhaps with what Marcel calls *disponibilité*, one sees beyond the desire marking serviceable disposability. Desire beyond such desire springs up. Looking at the fresh energies of the young—innocent and mindless, not knowing that time will bundle them quickly to a place where the ugly face is the show of the beautiful soul, or the ugly soul—gifts one with compassion for transient beauty.

*Compassio essendi*: Compassion is a new quickening of passionate transcending that does not fit in. Everything is on the way out, and one is going out, exiting, perhaps with redeeming laughter as one leaves. Even the glory of creation is left behind, and perhaps only the glory of God is left. One sees glory again in the faces of the new ones. Old not before one's time but *in* one's time, one is young before eternity. There is a kind of sadness that shadows transient beauty. This is not any ordinary melancholy; it is a love of what is passing; the passion of being is love of the passing, and it is a compassion since the one who loves, like the one loved, is also passing. It reminds me of what the Irish call *uaigneas*, a word untranslatable.[29] *Uaigneas* is a kind of exile without an exile, a being intensely here and yet not here, a being neither here nor there, a kind of nostalgia and

28. Yeats, *The Poems*, 370.

29. See Ó Laoire, *On a Rock in the Middle of the Ocean*, 171–81, on *cumha* (on being lonesome, sorrowful) and *uaigneas*. I found this a marvelously engaging book, and illuminating also about laughter and tears (chapter 9) to which I will return in chapter 9 on redeeming laughter. *Uaigneas* is not quite the Portugeuse/Brazilian "*Saudade*," though there are family resemblances.

yet not sentimental but with a streak of the metaphysical, a homesickness that is yet at home, a wound and a release, a being struck and an ardor, a kind of loneliness, more of the soul than the memory, though if of the memory, sometimes more of eternity than time, or better of something in time that is of eternity, such that time and eternity do not stand opposed but cross, criss-cross in the porosity of the *metaxu*, and as they cross they have cut into one another with a longing that births a nameless transfinite reaching out, a be-longing as a longing to be, a longing to be otherwise and yet never more intimately so than one now is, a be-longing that longs along an arc of time prolonged into more than time, or already in longing for what more than time has begotten in time and still begets on the beautiful, a wound of longing that has no end and yet is healing.

## A Séance with Hell

Hell talked back to me and mocked:

> *Ah, beautiful, very beautiful! For you an old Platonist, a consolation and a consecration. But we are culturally sophisticated; we love the spirit; we hate the mortal flesh; its corruptible beauty is rotten. No, we answer differently the question of Plato's ghost, channelled through Yeats the medium: "What then?"*[30] *We echo and re-echo in answer: the ugly, the execrable, the disgusting, the thrill of transgression and the pleasures of inversion. We go down into the mud, and beyond. We do not kiss the mud and make it a living being. We pluck out the heart of mystery, and we pluck in the mud the flowers of evil. We are not priests of the glorious flesh but are the answer to Mr. Sammler's question: "Who had made shit a sacrament?"*[31] *We did. Our vocation is not a consecration to beauty but to desecration. Beauty is a gift but a gift is poison. It is a toxin which intoxicates but we purge ourselves of the delusion of beauty. Not even tragedy will console. Our pitiless eyes gaze blankly on a theater of horror. Dark transcendence yes, but down into Hades. What then, asks Plato's ghost, what then?*

A very good question. If I am an old Platonist, I am perhaps too heterodox a Platonist in celebrating the beauty of the flesh. Your voice recalls me to my opening with the disgusting. Would you have us now end in a

30. Yeats, *The Poems*, 349.

31. Bellow, *Mr. Sammler's Planet*, 36.

much worse place, that is, in hell? [32] After all, remember in Yeats's poem that good work has been done which has wrought a kind of completion. I cite the opening verse:

> His chosen comrades thought at school
> He must grow a famous man;
> He thought the same and lived by rule,
> All his twenties crammed with toil;
> *What then?' sang Plato's ghost. "What then?"*

In between: "Everything he wrote was read," "All his happier dreams came true . . . Poets and Wits about him drew." The refrain is repeated: *"What then?" sang Plato's ghost. "What then?"* Then the final verse:

> "The work is done," grown old he thought,
> "According to my boyish plan;
> Let the fools rage, I swerved in naught,
> Something to perfection brought";
> *But louder sang that ghost, "What then?"*

Notice: Plato's ghost haunts a *wholeness completed*. What then? The question queries something beyond the whole. And beauty? If it is an open whole, now the opening beyond the whole comes to be in the whole. And the question it raises is of life, or death, beyond life and death.

Yes, the passion of being is not univocal and its saturated equivocity can border an extremity of affirmation, as well tempt desire with a descending movement into darkness, touching on death, if not going into hell. Freud was not the only one to see the intimacy of *eros* and *thanatos*. It is there in Schopenhauer, for instance, and Wagner made enchanting music of the intimacy of the two in *Tristan and Isolde*. Begetting on the beautiful participates in the *agon* of *eros* and *thanatos*. Doomed love: intenser life. Death itself raises the ultimate question of the giftedness of beauty. It seems to rob us of this gift, destroying it, taking it back into nothing. It takes our breath away when first it is new; it takes our breath

32. Danto in *The Abuse of Beauty* opens his second lecture with: "Near the opening of *Une saison en enfer*—allegedly an allegorical account of his tumultuous relationship with the poet Verlaine—Rimbaud writes: "One evening, I sat Beauty on my knees; and I found her bitter, and I abused her." The "bitterness of beauty" became epidemic in the avant-garde art of the following century, but it was a rare thought in 1873, when Rimbaud published this poem." Now that the thought is not rare, the more constant lover of beauty may have to spend their season in hell.

away a second time, when our time is up, reclaiming the enlivening power, with death having the last word, it seems. But without death's companionship would beauty be at all what it is: a lure, an allure to affirming life?

The passion of being is intimately expressed in eros, and in our eros the endeavor to be can both glory in an exulting self-affirmation, as well as give itself over to what is other to itself, not least under the spell of this allure of the beautiful. The Greek feel for the lover as being struck with Cupid's arrow coexists with a finesse for the tyrannical possibilities of eros. The heart melts at the strike, but also smarts, especially when the strike stings as a humiliation. The strike of the eyes in "beholding from" becomes a "being beholden"—one has fallen under the spell of the beloved and one is no longer free. One thinks of the *geas* that Gráinne casts on Diarmuid, *geas* meaning spell, curse, though also gift. There is something sweetly tyrannical about the torture and ecstasy of young love: Romeo and Juliet. (One recalls, too, the story of Elvira Madigan.) And then? The tyrannical eros can mimic the heavenly, while the heavenly eros sometimes seems very like the tyrannical. And this last, not paradoxically when we are marked by sovereign self-mastery, but when eros shows itself as beyond rational self-control, or overtaken by desire beyond serviceable disposability. Because it is not always easy to separate the tyrannical and the heavenly, there can be a marriage of heaven and hell, as Blake instructs us. The poet too, like the lover, can suffer the tyranny of beauty, and yet word it memorably. I think of Yeats's passion for Maud Gonne McBride. She came to look Yeats over on the appearance of his first book of poetry, *The Wanderings of Oisín* (1889), an astonishing debut for a poet so young. Yeats's sisters, Lilly and Lolly, felt the radiation of her imperious gaze in not being seen, so utterly ignored by her were they. Yeats spoke of this first encounter with her as beginning "the troubling of his life." Out of that troubling, great passion and great poetry came to be.

*An intricate answer, if a tad long. Do not drift away from the "What then?" that death has whispered to you.*

There is no escaping: the whispers of the lovely are mingled with the many sighs of the hopeless. Yeats, in a famous phrase, speaks of "a terrible beauty," aestheticizing, mythologizing the Easter Uprising in Ireland, 1916. The terrible is not to be left out of the reckoning of beauty. Was not Rilke's great witness to beauty twinned with the terror of the angel? If the angel gives a name to the companioning power, these two poets are consecrated priests to the power of beauty to ravage and renew us, to bring us to death and brings us back to life. Shortly before he died, Yeats answered Plato's ghost and the mocking question of which he himself was the medium: "I am happy, and I think full of an energy, of an energy I had despaired of. It seems to me that I have found what I wanted. When I try to put all into a phrase I say, 'Man can embody truth but he cannot know it.' I must embody it in the completion of my life. The abstract is not life and everywhere draws out its contradictions. You can refute Hegel but not the Saint or the song of sixpence.'"[33]

I have found the ancient tale of the Bull of Phalaris as a fitting way to address the relation of beauty to hell, a tale as new now as once it was of old. Phalaris the tyrant is given the statue of a magnificent bronze bull by the architect Perilaus which Phalaris sends as a sacrifice to Apollo at the oracle a Delphi. Perilaus had constructed the bull as a kind of torture machine into which someone could be put, while a fire was lit beneath it. In time the heat would be hell for the imprisoned one, who would scream, but reed pipes in the nostrils of the bull—and this is fiendish—would transform the screams of the tortured into "the sweetest possible music by the auloi, piping dolefully and lowing piteously."[34] "A thing of beauty is not a joy forever, whose loveliness increases, and will never pass into nothingness," as Keats has it; it is a dissembled horror. The bull of Phalaris, marvellous in its aesthetic magnificence, is not exemplary of useless beauty. It serves political power, its artist is in the services of the tyrant. Why not, one asks, if eros is simply *eros tyrranos*?

*What then?*

Torture touches violently the *passio essendi*. It is a violation of the intimacy of being, intruding into our most vulnerable porosity. You ask: Does the artwork then reveal hell by means of concealing hell? Is its beauty a kind music wrung from hell, its howls of horror hidden by mellifluous harmonies of heaven? Yes, the art of hell counterfeits heaven as it camouflages horror. Is the gift of the beautiful then secreted from suffering poisoned in hell? A gift indeed.

*What then? Why not expose the secret of hell?*

33. Letter to Lady Elizabeth Pelham, January 4, 1939, cited in J. M. Hone *W. B. Yeats, 1865–1939*, 476.

34. *Lucian*, vol. 1, 17–19; the pipes, *auloi*, were reed instruments connected with the cult of Dionysus; hence used in music that communicated with the erotic, indeed the orgiastic.

Why not?

> *There is an element of that exposure in some self-reflexive art where the artist delights in breaking the illusion of art. We are taken backstage of beauty, as it were, where we behold the mechanisms of hell. We must take the cover off the counterfeit, show the flesh reduced to rotting meat, for instance.*

A striking scene: even Milton's Satan, on beholding Eve in the garden, is at first overcome and disarmed by her beauty—made "stupidly good" by it.[35] But is there not in all you say an old secret animus against beauty: beauty as seductress whose siren song must be resisted or silenced? Beware the troll within the beauty of the woman: *La belle dame sans merci*. Your disdain of beauty is not a love of the disgusting but an immunization against it—by way of excess? Beyond enhancement, you see the beautiful woman, but know that silently, secretly, her liver, earlier the organ of divination, is cancerous. The organs of the body are hidden, and perhaps not just for protection. If they are exposed, they are not beautiful in the way the outward body is beautiful. Exposed, they will die. The organs are profound—buried in the body. The beautiful body is superficial.

> *Ah you are too, too naïve! Are you not like Kant, about whom Nietzsche said in matters erotic he had the innocence of a country parson? Our self-reflexivity shows our superiority, we now being critically self-conscious, no longer duped by the aesthetic image. How could an old Platonist like you not rejoice? The poets have come over to your side, as agents of disillusion.*

Agents of disillusion are agents of dissolution at times (philosophers at times included). Idiot wisdom is not naïve and can secretly smile at the platitude of the parsons—and the slogans of the avant-garde. The self-reflexive mode seems profound and not superficial, but has it not lost the wisdom of the aesthetic, and indeed the lightness of being, which is

35. On first beholding the beauty of Eve, Satan is arrested, brought to pause: "Her graceful innocence . . . overawed/ His malice, and with rapine sweet bereaved/His fierceness of the fierce intent it brought./That space the Evil One abstracted stood/ From his own evil, and for the time remained/ Stupidly good, of evil disarmed/ Of guile, of hate, of envy, of revenge" (Bk IX, 459–66). "Stupidly good": not just stupid stupidity but being "overawed." A primal awe comes over Satan, and this is *idiotic*: more intimate than even the devotion of his will to malice. "[T]hen fierce hate he recollects" (470–71): Satan closes the porosity, the unrest of evil will returns and he resumes his project of desecration.

superficial out of profundity? I borrow again from Nietzsche, true son of many lines of country parsons. Suppose truth is a woman for Nietzsche, she is also Baubo. Only contrast: *An Cailleach Bhéara* is an old hag but as a goddess she is rejuvenated perennially as a beautiful young woman; and she is a *bean feasa*, a wise woman.[36]

Under the ground the dead lie. More lies in going under the ground than just the dead. In the equivocity of eros, the passion of our being can move up, or move down, or move up to move down, move down to move up. There are ways of going up that cast one down (say, the tragic hero's hubristic going up as thrown down by nemesis). There are ways of going down that lead up (say, the redemptive passage through hell of Dante, with Virgil as his guide). The porosity of being means we must affirm our own being as suffering: exposed to what is other, now uplifted with delight, now dejected and distressed. If beauty opens and reopens the porosity of our being, there is a vulnerability in being porous, and when the endeavor to be takes off, it can as much hate that vulnerability, and seek to triumph over it. The poison seed of hell is in that hate. The endeavor can also live out the vulnerability in love with finitude. Transcending upwards is shadowed by transcending downward. Beauty and hell are sometimes conjoined. There is nothing superficial about such superficiality. Blake again: The marriage of heaven and hell.

> *What if this marriage is made in hell not heaven? And does not the tyrannical eros rather dominate? Do not the shrieks of the tortured become lovely music to delight the tyrant? Does not the resonance of the surface music hide the suffering in the burning depths? Does not torture touch on what is most intimate, violating the* passio essendi *and the most vulnerable porosity? Beauty serves to conceal hell; we now serve to reveal it. We love the underworld, you the other world. What then?*

There is a half-truth to this, though as half of a marriage made in hell, it is more than half of an untruth. Hell is not far from the chaos out of which new beginnings can come. Hell makes what is good bad, and what is bad worse. It curses the darkness but reaffirms the curse of darkness. Re-affirms: a curse is a strange blessing of darkness. Hell is in love with heaven too, but it is a love that sours into hatred. Hell dissimulates itself to look like heaven, makes horror sound like sweet song, because it doubles for heaven. Hell is the counterfeit double of heaven.

36. See Ó Crualaoich, *The Book of the Cailleach.*

This is hatred mimicking love. Hatred loves love but hates itself for loving love, and so its loves hate love. Its form is envy, a malform of love. Hell's beauty is deforming death and not sweetening life. Counterfeit doubling is itself made possible by the saturated equivocity of the aesthetic. This means that despite hell, even in hell itself, beauty contains a trace of Eden. There is something of the pre-lapsarian secretly in it. There is a taste, a foretaste of a redeemed world in it. "If I ascend to the heavens, you are there; if I lie down in Sheol, you are there too" (Psalm 139). We are drawn by this trace, but find it difficult to say what it is towards which we are drawn. Like Ishmael we are drawn to the sea, the playground of monsters and the ocean of beauty. An artist might turn hell into song in a different redemptive sense. The artist might love this world as other, and the beauty of the other world shining in this world as other. One might be in the underworld, and the enchantment of song might serve to reopen the primal porosity of our being. The music of Orpheus brought tears in the underworld, and hearing it hard hearts softened. Music in hell sings of something more than hell. In the underworld it renews our passion for the upper world.

*What then?*

What then? On the surface, in between hell and heaven, there is something of the enchantment of the green world of the garden, though we are not green enough to forget the garden of Gethsemane and its agony. We can affirm the surface as the threshold where the depth comes to communicate itself. Beauty is such a surface and grants such a threshold. Heraclitus: "Dionysus is also Hades" (ὡυτὸς δὲ Ἀίδης καὶ Διόνυσος, Fr. B 15). Green growth strives towards the surface out of the darkness of the earth. Eurydice is led out of the underworld, with the promise of a posthumous life of love, but Orpheus looks back to Hades instead of ahead to the surface of the earth, and Eurydice is lost to him. Orpheus perhaps should have had patience, held in waiting the longing of his look, till both Eurydice and he had reached together the surface of the earth. Coming forth with the beloved from the realm of the dead needs new *passio essendi*. Orpheus's love was perhaps not patient enough. *Passio* is patience, *passio* is also on the threshold where *conatus* is aroused and excited. It leaps beyond itself and sometimes looks behind itself too soon, as if it had already emerged on the surface. Beauty that emerges from death shows the poise of patience and endeavor on the surface of the earth.

*What then?*

Heraclitus: "The sun . . . is new every day" (ὁ ἥλιος . . . [καθάπερ ὁ Ἡράκλειτός φησι,] νέος ἐφ' ἡμέρῃ ἐστίν: Fr. B 6). In its shine on things, depths can come to be on the surface. They then face us. But how do we face them? How do we live the interface of beauty? The surface shows what does not exhaustively surface. The face smiles, the face snarls; the same face smiles, but its smile is a snarl. Double face of renewing life and dying—the superposition of the saturated equivocity. The artist faces facing, and gives a sign. The sign, the de-sign shows itself in what faces us. We exist as facing what faces us. Fidelity to what faces us is asked in art, asked in philosophy.

Heraclitus once again: "The Lord whose oracle is at Delphi neither speaks out nor conceals but gives a sign" (ὁ ἄναξ οὗ τὸ μαντεῖόν ἐστι τὸ ἐν Δελφοῖς, οὔτε λέγει οὔτε κρύπτει ἀλλὰ σημαίνει. Fr. B 93) The artist as lover of surfaces is also a lover of what surfaces, what reveals itself and hides. But Heraclitus, one last time: "How can anyone hide from that which never sets?" (τὸ μὴ δῦνόν ποτε πῶς ἄν τις λάθοι; Fr. B 16). The philosopher, too, can be a lover and interpreter of beguiling surfaces—physiognomist in thought of the intimate depths of that from which we can never hide. Useless beauty and the compassion of being turn us, return us to the surface of things. Sometimes a sign is the thing itself and beauty the real presence.

# 2

## On the Surface of Things: Transient Life and Beauty in Passing

### Philosophy on the Surface

Different conceptions of life might be said to fall between two extremes. On one extreme, we find more objectifying, indeed reductive conceptions: here life itself seems to disappear in the very claim to account for it. On the other extreme, we find more subjectifying conceptions: here the sense of immanent self-relation and its dynamic enjoyment is held to make intimate contact with life as lived. A purely objective account seems difficult to endorse finally, if life *disappears* in its being accounted for. An entirely immanent orientation raises for us questions about the passing of life *beyond* self-relating enjoyment. By contrast to these two, one might suggest that life as *transient* (*trans-ire*: to go across) communicates more in the *passage* between these extremes. Our question then: How should we relate this transience, neither objective nor subjective, to the passing of life, to passing as passing?

In addressing this question, we need to recall that part of philosophy's vocation is to be true to the surface of things, in the transience of life on earth. Surfaces intermediate transient life. Beauty is crucially relevant as an intermediate happening, to be true to which, I will suggest, we have to be mindful of the *saturated surfaces* of things. In beauty the surface of life and the depth enigmatically communicate. Beauty is an intermediary of transient life that communicates what cannot be completely objectified and what exceeds every self-relation of the human subject. In beauty the surface and the depth communicate because *beauty is the depth communicating itself.* Life as transient is also an intermediate happening, and passes between being at all and not being. Beauty is intimately related to this transience of the interim of life, showing something of surplus significance on the surface of things. Beyond the excessively objectifying approach and the excessively subjectifying, it communicates an affirming sense of the excess of life itself, even in its fugitive passing. Fugitive beauty calls on our mindful attention.

But one might ask: Is it, in fact, part of philosophy's vocation to allow us to live on the surface of the earth? Have not philosophers repeatedly pointed beyond the surface and away from the earth? Do not Nietzscheans, reactionary to this pointing beyond, now point back and chant about remaining true to the earth? But surely we can only be true to the earth, behold what is on it, by attaining to the surface of things, a surface in no way exclusive of something above the earth? Not being able to be on the surface of the earth can be induced by various causes, some intellectual, some spiritual, some due to aesthetic and religious viewpoints that denigrate the surface, some due to lies in the soul that hinder us from seeing what is before us, some due to philosophical strategies that look only with suspicion on the surface.

Restoring what it means to stand on the earth and resurrect the surface of things puts one in mind, paradoxically, of the Platonic analogy of the cave. We live underground, and when freed we undertake a painful and blinding ascent to the surface of the earth, there to be able to behold a light only equivocally present under the surface. Platonic ascent is often now said to be treasonous to the surface of the earth, but we could read this ascent differently. Is it not the sun that enables the earth to be the dynamic, becoming, intelligible, indeed worthy and good reality it is? Without it not only the underground, but also the surface would be plunged into darkness. To live in the light of the sun we need to be on the surface and behold the shine on things. Indeed, is not *eidos* intimately connected with the "look" of things? The "look" of things cannot be separated from the surface that shows itself to our attentive mindfulness. The *eidos* shines on the surface of things to the looking that is mindful of the "look." Part of the ancient vocation of philosophy was said to be "saving the appearances." Such a saving knowing would be a matter of *doing justice* to what is shown on the surface. If on the surface there is surplus rather than defect, the justice of saving knowing might well have to draw on reserves of agapeic mindfulness.

Of course, the analogy of the cave recalls the ancient theme of Hades. One must ask: Is there not also a kind of hell with which we have to come to terms? In Hades beauty is under the shadow of darkness and the shades below seem to lack living beauty. But notice here how moving in the dark, whether coming to the surface, or sinking deeper into darkness, allows *different directionalities* for our underground motion. We can move up, we can stay where we are, we can also move down. Some movements in the dark in modernity have taken to heart the power of Hades, but rather than ascend to the surface, their motion is *descending*, into another darkness below the floor of the cave. We seem seized by the notion that our motion is not to come again to the surface of things but rather to descend below all surfaces where there is a truer darkness that the surface hides, even as the surface also shows some foreboding of it.

It is obvious that significant currents of contemporary thought have wanted to invert Plato, but what is the meaning of that inversion? Does it, in fact, allow us to live on the surface of the earth? I think the answer has to be qualified in the opposite direction. A true inversion of Platonism would less allow us to have peace on the surface as complete the disturbing descent, not only back into the cave, but below the ground of the cave into even more infernal darknesses.

This is what we have often found after Hegel. Hegel sublates the surface of things into self-mediating spirit in a philosophy of immanence where rational thought is consummated in absolute self-knowing. After him his ascent to absolute self-knowing is reversed, and the negative power of the dialectic produces what I would call a de-sublation. Instead of us being sublated to the highest standpoint of the identity of human and divine power, divine power is de-sublated to human power. Initially the fruits of that de-sublation are harvested in a claim that ingests the otherness of the divine into human power, sublates—that is, de-sublates—the transcendent otherness of the divine into human power. This is well known in Feuerbach, Marx, and others. But thereafter this follows a second de-sublation: human power is itself a surface, fronting for inhuman power or powers (however defined). It now appears that Hegelian reason is fated to front for some non-rational other, say, the machinations of will to power. The first de-sublation promises the ultimate power of the divine to us humans. The second de-sublation that follows now descends into what is below reason. The divinity of the human is a god that fails, and the subject becomes less object than abject.

Again there is the theme of depth here, but it reverses the Platonic analogy of the sun, which draws us beyond the cave towards the transcendence of the good. In the cave we are underground men, but now the analogy suggests a de-sublating directionality, pointing down and down into original darkness. We are digging below the cave to pits where the sun seems not to penetrate. Of course, on this view, even on the surface of the earth, the sun does not shine either, for there is no sun, and in the end all is dark. This turn away from higher transcendence and the penetration of our transcending into the lower underground is something we find with Schopenhauer, Dostoevsky, and Nietzsche, and many others right into our own time, for instance, Bataille. There is dissimilitude here, but it emerges from below. It is the abyss, the dark origin, it is the inhuman. The fate of reason is to be revealed to itself as not reasonable. The inhuman is the immanent other of the human. All of this has implications for our understanding of life, as we shall see.

Relevantly, in the Platonic directionality, beauty is the intermediate happening where the sensuous and supersensuous are in communication, and eros is not merely impelled beyond itself by its own negative self-determining energy but is drawn beyond by the loving lure of the beautiful or good.[1] Coming to the surface is an ecstasis that participates in that love of the beautiful. By contrast, in the scenario of inverted Platonism, below the underground, where could we find a comparable role to play for the beautiful? My suspicion is: nowhere. Rather, under the underground we are more likely to find more dirt, rather than tunnels of darkness that, were they to lead us back to the surface, would bring us to encounter again the glory of beauty. This would be a joyful occasion of renewing our love on the surface—rejoicing after the darkness that an abundance of beauty is there for us to behold on the surface. This return to the surface does not always happen. More likely, it is a certain fixation on the ugly that will engage our obsessions and anxieties. Here we find more the deformation than the form, more the repulsive than the attractive, more the disgusting than the serene. Even when the fluidity of life is

1 While Plato is generally said to stress the *eidos* as beyond, its transcendence to appearance, a certain understanding of the "look" of things suggests also a non-disjunctive sense where surface and beyond communicate, as is acknowledged to be the case with beauty in the *Phaedrus* (250d), for instance: "For the beautiful alone has this fate (*moira*), to be the most showing (*ekphanéstaton*) and most lovely (*erasmiótaton*)."

noticed, it is the disgusting fluids, or the fluids of life as disgusting, that contaminate us. We drown Christ in piss.

Has beauty restorative power? Returning to Schopenhauer, it is remarkable that for him beauty can save us, if only episodically, from the devouring darkness of the will. But how it can do so, is a good question. Despite the darkness under the underground, the beautiful frees us into a more serene comportment. Equally, Nietzsche preaches that it is art that saves us from the truth. The truth is the dark horror underneath, but art gives us the surfaces that protect us from that horror. The *"as if"* truths (that is, "lies") of art save us from *the* truth of horror. Nietzsche knew he was between a rock and a hard place. The Greeks were superficial out of profundity, he said—profoundly, in perhaps a tone of superficiality. I mention Schopenhauer and Nietzsche since with them there is some desire to recover, or at least come to terms with, the surface. To be truly on the surface of things need not be inimical to the gift of beauty and its restorative power. Whether their approaches are adequate to what restoration requires is another question and I doubt they are.

Some forms of post-Nietzschean thought practise what one might call *agenda philosophizing*, and of course the agenda here is to push through relentlessly the project of inverting Platonism. (Is it fair to say that Deleuze almost obsessively pursues this agenda?) If this is the agenda, why at all seek to come to the surface of things, to behold there things of astonishing beauty? If there is no sun, should not the "true" inversion take us below the cave into even more dismal darkness? But does not the desire to drive through this agenda of reversal show the logic of the reviled "Platonism"—now as inverted logocentrism, where everything is re-viewed according to the *idée fixe* of what is to be avoided? It would be better not to try to make any sense. And yet some "project" to make sense is still at work. The studied production of the senseless makes sense as the result of an agenda, but thus it finds itself contradicting itself, not quite senselessly, but in a manner that pays unacknowledged homage to what it would invert. Being dragged back down into hell as the true inversion of Platonic heaven is evident in the production of the ugly, according to the agenda of a certain aesthetic philosophy. Beauty comes to meet one, but one immediately crosses to the other side of the road; but to cross the road to escape means one has not escaped what one wants to avoid. Love of the ugly, hatred of the beautiful—are these Siamese twins? Are love of the beautiful, hatred of the ugly also twins? But suppose one truly were to love the ugly, would there not be something lovely about the ugly? To love the ugly—would this not be the love of a god? The god who looks on the lovely where we only recoil in disgust? If we were to follow this thought through ethically and religiously, would we ourselves not have to love those who are hateful? Would we have to affirm a God who loves even the evil, forgives it because there is more in the evil than evil?

## On the Surface and the Objectivizing Reduction

The sciences have diversely tried to define life,[2] but without decrying science, one could ask about certain *scientistic* temptations that recurrently emerge in reflections on its characteristic approaches. Important considerations include the following. What is given is rendered in terms of the theoretical neutrality of an objectified thereness. We are supposed to put out of play our own more subjective involvements, assume a more spectatorial rather than participatory orientation. This is all very well, in relation to close attention to what shows itself from itself, and not in terms of what we might impute to it in the likeness to ourselves. The injunction is that there is to be no anthropomorphism. We are not to project ourselves and our desires onto the otherwise neutral thereness, and all this in the light of knowing what is as it is. The greatness of this orientation can be an epistemic respect for the otherness of what shows itself as such, now truthfully granted its being for itself, outside the anthropomorphic projections we might otherwise impose on things. Similarly a scientific understanding of life is to be objective in that sense. We cannot project on it our own life, for then we would meet only ourselves again and not what is living as other to us.

Of course, putting ourselves entirely in suspension is impossible. For the objective orientation is itself one of our *valued* orientations, and while its directionality is said to regard the neutral thereness as other, it still is *our* orientation, and we cannot so escape ourselves that we are entirely removed from the picture. If we were entirely removed from the picture, there would be no picture, and hence no objective understanding of life in its non-anthropomorphic otherness. The project of objectification turns out to be a project of the subject—though its primal focus on the objective as other often disguises this from the subject so oriented.

It is also the case that reflection on the project of objectivity casts in doubt the merely spectatorial orientation I mean the orientation that

2. See Morange, *Life Explained.*

claims no involvement with what is beheld, no participation in the given reality under investigation. The more we wake up to what is at play in the scientific orientation, I would suggest, the more we see that it concerns the determination of *a certain kind of between*: between us and what is there, with concern to give an account of what is there, as precise, determinate, and univocal as possible. Determinability itself is inseparable from objectification, but determining is an engagement we undertake in a middle space between ourselves and what shows itself for this univocalizing consideration. Part of that determination is the effort to fix precisely the character of life, the precise enabling conditions that allow its emergence, conditions to which what happens on the surface can be reduced and rendered in exact mathematical formulations to the highest degree possible. In some quarters the point will be to determine the emergence of the living from the non-living. Thus is a certain extreme reached that mirrors the initial prohibition on anthropomorphisms. Remember that the prohibition barred the attribution of human characteristics to what is other than the human, in the interests of, at best, allowing the non-human to show itself *as other* to us. Here, with a more reductionist view of life, the point is not to project life into the enabling conditions that are necessary for the emergence of life. Rather, the non-living is that relative to which the living is to be understood. But to what extent then is this the claim to derive the living from the dead, a claim that surreptitiously projects a dead condition as the base ground, or the necessary enabler, of what emerges as not dead but living?

We are dealing here with *thresholds*. On one side of the threshold is the non-living, on the other side of the threshold is the living. How is the threshold crossed? We cannot but approach the non-living side of the threshold from some position *within* life. Hence, inevitably what we know of what is on the other side of the threshold is not entirely separable from our necessarily presupposed emplacement *within* life itself. How possible is it then entirely to neutralize a kind of projection of life on non-life? Do we not risk a kind of *inverted* anthropomorphism—that is, a projection guided by just the agenda *not* to find on the other side of the threshold anything that is redolent of the living side of the divide? Is not such a project of inverted anthropomorphism still a kind of anthropomorphic projection? A threshold is always a between space, and if the threshold is of crucial importance, can we ever, in fact, approach the happening of life without in some way presupposing our necessary emplacement in life itself? If we were to give an "absolute" account of life in terms of the non-living, would we have no account at all? Indeed, would the very project as such show its impossibility in its hypothetical realization?

Thresholds are very much related to surfaces. For a surface is also a between space—on one side, one reality, on the other side, another, and the between is the space of possible communication between those two sides. If there is radical heterogeneity between the two sides, would one have a surface at all? For on or in or through such a "surface" of heterogeneity, there would be no interface. Radical heterogeneity would allow no communication between the two sides, and hence no threshold could be crossed. For what is crossing but communication in and across a between? Must one not have rather a relation that mixes the like and the unlike? A threshold, like all betweens, requires an intermediation of sameness and difference, an interplay of likeness and unlikeness. A surface is the *metaxu* of this interplay. Hence, how we relate to surfaces is all important. There is no approach to what is hidden in the surface, or beyond it, or its depth, without genuine cognitive and ontological respect for the surface as such, that is, for the surface as a *metaxu*, and hence as an interface.

The issue then is whether there is any approach to life that does not necessarily presuppose life. If we seek to reduce the living to the non-living, or to show the conditions needful for the emergence of the living from the non-living, one still has to ask if this approach, indeed any approach, can entirely escape being already emplaced in the sphere of the living as such? Even if we try in the depths of life to discover the non-living as source of the living, can we do this without indebtedness to given life precisely as given—and given on the surface? The point I make is not to deny non-living conditions enabling life but to ask whether the univocal determination of these conditions can ever be entirely true to the happening of life as such. Life is presupposed as "more," even in the approach that would reduce it to the "less"-than-living. This self-confirming emplacement in the between of life, of course, is taken to be a limitation to be overcome by more reductionistic approaches to life. But the between of life is itself a presupposition of these reductionistic approaches themselves. There is something we cannot escape here, and we ought to ask if it has immense significance for the understanding of life.

A science of life that ends up with no life is in a fugue state relative to this inescapability. It has not remained true to the surface of things. In its plumbing of the depths it brings us death rather than life. One thinks of Wordsworth's famous words: "We murder to dissect." We take apart, we kill, we take the life from something to understand it. We do understand something, but life dies in this anatomy of life. If this is all there is to knowing life, knowledge is an invasion of, an assault on, what it seeks to know. Even then an assault is an act that *lives* from hostility. Would a knowing that does not kill have to be a loving of what it knows? One might ask if even the most extreme reductionism is in the debt of this love. Affirming something as true reveals a love of truth, and a love of the reality as so affirmed. But loving itself is always a living—a new living of the life known, and in a sense, a living augmented in coming to know in love.

Beauty, I would say, brings us closer to this loving knowing. It brings us closer to the erotics of knowing, perhaps even the agapeics, but I cannot dwell on this right now. In the main I now want to attend to the stress on univocal determinability that is worthy of note when the scientific orientation will express itself in determining certain structures as necessary for a living being to be alive at all. Suppose we consider the integrity of a living organism. The project of objectification might be satisfied with the determination of structures in so far as they can be expressed in the precisions of mathematical formulations. Well and good: without structure we seem left with a mere formless indeterminacy. But the issue of life is not a matter of structure as such but of what *passes* in the structuring. If we only stress structure, then structure and what is passing in the structure are disjoined from each other. We have to ask if rather here, with the living organism, structure indicates a *structuring* that itself cannot be simply determined in the language of structure—here now taken as an order that is fixed and determinate. One recalls Bergson's famous *élan vital.* I take this as a suggestion in the face of the tendency to a more fixed spatialization in the event of structure itself. Structure as such is not adequate to the temporalization, the becoming evident in life as life, in life as passing in the structuring and not just formulated in the fixed structure. The *élan vital* is rejected, of course, by scientists, because it resists precise univocalization. But perhaps the issue of life is not just one of scientific determinability and precise univocalization but rather a question of *passing qua passing.*

We do speak of life as passing. Structure is not a passing, though it may enable passage. Passing qua passing exceeds structure. There is no necessary life in structure qua structure. Is structure itself self-explicatory? You might say that it is immanently determining, indeed self-determining in the case of *organic structure.* There is obviously something to this: here is dynamic structure, since it unfolds in an active formation, proceeding from an immanent principle. If this is so, there is an *energy* of structure that reveals a (self-)structuring that, just as passing, cannot be just a structure. There is structure perhaps but the life that passes in the structure and as structure is not just a structure. Should we call these structures a matter of infrastructure—and then refer to what passes in and through the infrastructure? But if so, the point cannot be a dualism of infrastructure and what passes through it. This is a case where the great question of Yeats is apposite: How can we tell the dancer from the dance? Here we cannot tell—in an absolutely univocal way. In life, we cannot make an absolute division between infrastructure and what passes along it. This is especially so if we are dealing with an immanent becoming of life. This passing of life is a determining beyond determination. It is not beyond all determination but beyond *absolutely univocal* determination, which insists it is simply this and not that. For what is at issue is the transition *between* this and that—a transition that is not itself this or that. And so once again we are confronted with thresholds. These are not fixed boundaries, but moving thresholds, so to say. This is so, since the transitions here insinuate themselves into the determination of both this and that. And this means once again the "this" and the "that" cannot be univocally fixed in an absolute way. They too are what they are in becoming, in transition.

In sum, to identify any structure of life there must be presupposed something other than structure. The question is whether a purely objective account of any structure of life can be adequate to the passing of life qua passing.[3] It is not that determinate objectivities are to be slighted. The becoming of an organism, say, reveals a highly complex structure and a true investigation of its being tries to do justice to the amazingly intricate determinacy of its unfolding. Still to identify life in terms of structure presupposes life as living and lived in a non-structural sense. Structures

3. A rose flowers out of the earth. The rose is beautiful though the earth is dirty. Something shimmers in the appearance of the rose, though the earth from which it blooms is heavy and dull. The earth is a surface as well as a ground, and what shows itself on the surface is intimately related to what is in the ground, but it is more than its own enabling conditions. What passes from the earth and into the seed that shoots up onto the earth as the blooming rose? It is not just the earth; not just the seed; but the fertile life that must be buried in the earth to rise to the surface of the earth and above the earth. The laws of material nature are not themselves material. The law of gravity is not heavy, for instance—it does not fall, for it cannot be dropped or thrown, or leap. Flowers are beautiful but we do not (tend to) eat them.

as such, like mathematical formulations, even of life, do not themselves live. The recognition of life passes beyond structure.

Take the case of something beautiful, important for my chosen theme, for instance, that of the live song of a bird. Its music can be sometimes strikingly beautiful. It can also be measured, the determinacies of sounds studied, the connection with environment, and communication between mates explored, and so on. But none of this exhausts the living happening of the singing qua singing. What passes in and through the bird, what passes between this bird and other birds, what joy of being at all is sung out under the embracing sky, what is communicated in the song: to grant that all this is not so easy to objectively measure does not entail one derides objective measure. Suppose the music has something to do with the living subjectivity of the bird—the selving of its transient being? The singing is the living integrity of the being in communication with what is other to itself and with itself too as other. There is no derogation from determinacy, but rather the granting of an *overdeterminacy* in the happening as such. There is something more in communication in the happening of song. While determinate it is more than determinate, it is *over*determinate.

The making of music connects us with the long tradition stretching back to the Pythagoreans that connects mathematics with harmonies, a tradition well expressed by Leibniz who highlights the connection with determinability when, for example, he says: "Music is a hidden arithmetic exercise of the soul, which does not know that it is counting" (*Musica est exercitium arithmeticae occultum nescientis se numerare animi.* Letter to Christian Goldbach, April 17, 1712).[4] Music is unknowing mathematics. Singing does not know that secretly it is arithmetical determination. From the view I am suggesting, one wonders if it is the opposite that is more truly the case: not that music is secretly mathematics, but that *mathematics is a music the intellect does not know it is singing.* It is worth asking if song is more in communication with the overdeterminate, in which structure determinately participates but which it does not and can never exhaust. If we were to use the terms of another great mathematician and scientist, and connect music with the *esprit de finesse* and arithmetic with the *esprit de géométrie*, Leibniz's God comes across more as a God of

4. Schopenhauer cleverly reformulated this in the first book of *Die Welt als Wille und Vorstellung*: *Musica est exercitium metaphysicis occultum nescientis se philosophari animi.* Music is a hidden metaphysical exercise of the soul, which does not know that it is philosophizing. Arthur Schopenhauer, *The World as Will and Representation.* 2 vols.

geometry than a God of finesse.[5] The God of finesse is a God of music—a God of living beauty. One thinks once again of the justly famous jubilation of Augustine: *Sero te amavi! pulchritudo tam antiqua, et tam nova, sero te amavi! . . .* Living beauty, older than all age and younger than all youth. The God of finesse is one who sings the world into being and continues to sing it in being, in and through and with the cooing coaxing dovebird Spirit. This God is living not dead, this God is singing before calculating. For singing structuring is more than and before mathematical structure. The music of the spheres is not due to the geometry, the geometry of the heavens is due to the music.

## Interlude I

## On Objectivistic Non-Recognition of the Living

I offer two pictures of a revealing *disconnection* between the objectivistic reduction and the saturated surface of things. *First:* Descartes, it has been claimed, conducted vivisection experiments on animals. Animals are automata, they have no souls. The automaton reveals a mechanical autonomy in the sense of being entirely determined by the soul-less self-law (*auto-nomos*) inscribed in it. We stick a knife in the animal and it seems to scream in pain, but animals, who have no anima, feel no pain. They mimic our behavior, but they are soulless machines. So the pigs squeal when we cut into their living flesh. The squeal of the flesh is the surface of the thing. The reality is no pain. The pigs have no soul. Why then do we want to stop our ears to these screams? (Recall Galileo speaking of science and the "rape" of the senses.) The pigs have no pain, and if you say, listen they squeal, look they twist and kick, it is a mimicry, a counterfeit of a squeal or a shudder. The surface of things is not the thing.[6] We superior knowers scientistically do not hear the scream of non-human beings. The surface says life, the scientist says lifeless. The surface is nothing.

*Second:* the Dead Parrot sketch performed by Monty Python. There is a *comedy* of the surface and its denial. A customer buys a parrot, only to return to the shop to demand satisfaction, since the parrot is dead. The surface says "dead," but the seller says "alive." The surface screams "a dead

5. See Desmond, *God and the Between*, chapter 3 on the gods of geometry.

6. See Hans Jonas, *The Phenomenon of Life: Toward a Philosophical Biology*, foreword by L. Vogel (Evanston, Illinois: Northwestern University Press, 2001), 55.

parrot," but no, the seller says obdurately, it is only sleeping. The seller pokes the parrot and, of course, it moves, and the seller pounces, "There! It is alive! He's not dead, he was only 'stunned.' A Norwegian Blue, he's pinin' for the fjords." The cheated buyer explodes: "'E's not pinin'! 'E's passed on! This parrot is no more! He has ceased to be! 'E's expired and gone to meet 'is maker! 'E's a stiff! Bereft of life, 'e rests in peace! If you hadn't nailed 'im to the perch 'e'd be pushing up the daisies! 'Is metabolic processes are now 'istory! 'E's off the twig! 'E's kicked the bucket, 'e's shuffled off 'is mortal coil, run down the curtain and joined the bleedin' choir invisible!! THIS IS AN EX-PARROT!!" The seller finally relents. The truth of the surface triumphs.[7]

What does our laughter tell us? That there is a living recognition of a living being, the denial of which generates the nonsense of cutting off our noses to spite our faces. The laughter reveals the living recognition of the living, prior to all theories and more than our forced or false descriptions.

## On the Surface and the Subjectivizing Reduction

The above argument is that all approaches to life presuppose life as already able to relate to life, even if the preferred relation is one of reduction of the living to the non-living. This is more than a logical trick to critique the more objectivist orientation by invoking a necessary self-implication in the search for life itself, its intelligibility and truth. In fact, one of the major characteristics of the living being is some power of self-motion. It is already in passage, living itself is a passing, and in the passing the living being in some sense or other moves itself. Self-motion was one of the major characteristics that the ancients ascribed to *psyche* or *anima*, and hence to living beings. This moving is not just a matter of locomotion, the spatial displacement of an otherwise inert being from one location to another. There is the self-movement that is the becoming of the being—its self-becoming. There is an integrity at work but it is one in process. This integrity cannot be univocally fixed simply as this or that. In its becoming

7. One thinks here of the bird that brings forth the analytic anxiety of epistemological uncertainty: the goldfinch—real or stuffed or whatnot—at the end of the garden, in Stanley Cavell's discussion of J. L. Austin in *The Claim of Reason*, for instance, 50ff., 58, 73, 132–33, 160, 163, 194. For that matter, one is put in mind of Kant's fear of flying, when it comes to clipping the wings of genius, or bringing back to earth the dove of metaphysics that tries to soar into the high heavens, bringing the bird back to his miserable island of "truth," surrounded by the changing cloud-banks of illusion.

of itself, it is now this and now that but this and that cannot be frozen as too univocalized snapshots of instantaneity. It is both this and that, and moreover it is the transition between them. Its integrity in process is a nisus to be and become itself. It is an anticipation of a fuller realization of itself, and as more fully realized, it is as *a spanning of its own timing*—a spanning that is its being gathered into a new living and more or less poised integrity of being.

The integrity in self-becoming of the living being is the basis of its ability to move itself in relation to other such integrities and through between spaces, all diversely qualified. There is a certain rootedness and spread of ontological power in the living being. Here it is as this, and in a sense rooted in itself, but what it is entails a spread of itself to the space defining the parameters of its power to be. Some forms of life are more rooted—the plant. Some are more moving in this spread—witness the freer power of animals to range over their environment. All this is recognized by Aristotle in *De Anima*. But the living animated being resists reduction to more rudimentary matters in so far as the integrity in process answers to a unity that cannot be univocalized in a purely determinate way. Something of the power of its own self-determination is at work in its self-becoming, as well as its interplay with what is other than itself. This interplay is no less essential to defining the dynamic integrity that is itself in its process of becoming itself. The living being is transient in the double sense of being in self-becoming and in its passage between itself and other beings, living and non-living. Transience means a being's going from here to there, but its being there is itself again, so that while it moves from here, it does not just move from here, and thus comes to itself again there. Transience also means that it moves beyond itself in relation to what is other to itself. In some forms of transience, the point is not recuperation of itself—the living being is given over, or gives itself over to what is other. Transience means that the timing of the being in becoming is not only a growing and a maturing, it is also an ageing. Transience means that the interim of its time is temporary.

Here once again what shows itself on the surface is very important and it testifies there to the recognition of the living by the living. An objective science is not needed for this recognition. Rather there would be no science of life without this pre-scientific, extra-scientific recognition of life. A simple example: An animal sees an object lying there, seemingly inert. If it is willing to approach it, the important distinction for it concerns that between "living" or "dead." Is it alive or is it not? Is it friend or foe? It knows it is alive if it moves. To test it, the thing is gingerly poked or prodded. If there is no reaction, no movement, a certain equivocity is settled in the direction of the diminution of danger. Recognition of the motion of life is communicated in the signs of an inward vitality on the part of the thing seen as alive, and the thing seeing what is alive, for self-motion and the animation of life are bound up with each other. There is some univocity to the outcome of recognition. Not moving, the thing is not dangerous. If it is alive, it might be either an enemy or it might be food. It might be a form of life one might eat or one which might eat one. Surfaces and the interaction of the animal with them will help it tell the difference. The testing animal is alive and in the lack or not of movement in the other thing, the recognition of life by the animal is elemental. Animals love life—even in killing—the killing that comes with eating. Humans alone are able to hate life, killing in hate, even for no purpose—though the hatred is a mutation of the love of life.

Of course, it happens that some animals in danger play at being dead—they do not move, they play possum, and the lack of movement either makes it invisible to the perceptual powers of the attacker, or its "deadness" deceives with the impression that there is nothing of interest there. Only the living can play at being dead. The dead animal does not play at being dead. An animal also could play at being dead to induce a prey to come closer, only then to pounce at the unexpected moment. There is a certain asymmetry here in that life can in a living way relate to death and the surface of death—but the dead cannot do this. Does this mean there is a certain priority of the living? It does mean that the recognition of life is something primitive. This is not to underestimate the way the recognition is entangled in many possibilities of equivocity. The surface is not a matter of univocal clarity. It is an equivocal showing which hides as much as shows: in showing it also hides, even as in hiding it also shows.

From this I would stress a sense of the living that is prior to objectivizing reason. In objective life living is beyond the fully objectifiable. One might speak of the energy of the "to be" which, in certain formations, flowers into dynamic integrities of being which appear as self-affirming. Life is affirming itself, and one of the notable things about life, and lost in the more objectifying account, is this entirely *intimate self-relation*. I think one could speak of a certain intimacy of life that cannot be entirely exhausted with determinable accounts that approach it from the outside. This intimacy of life is also known intimately from within in the form of a certain self-affection. When Schopenhauer, for one, talked about the will as beyond sufficient reason, he could be seen to point to this character of life that exceeds the more objective fixation by determinate reason, determining reason. This more primordial life is lived from within, and in fact all of us know something of it in our own bodies. In our being embodied, there is no absolute dualistic disjunction between awareness and being alive in a bodily sense. I speak of a certain idiocy of being. Life has this idiocy in the sense of never being entirely reducible to the more determinable generalities or universals of neutrally available reason. Reason itself participates in this idiocy which is not something absurd but something irreducible in the relation of the being to itself—a self-relation presupposed by reason itself, if reason is to know what it knows as known by me. I know—knowing as a neutral happening does not know. This is not to decry the universal, but to say that there is an intimacy that cannot be rendered in the neutral language of abstract universals. There is a kind of *intimate universality to life* in that the living recognizes the living, the living knows itself as living and recognizes other living being as living with a kind of overdeterminate innerness that exceeds both the determinacy and self-determination of any particular being. (The power of beauty is very much bound up with this intimate universality.)

This self-relation has often been the basis for emphasizing something more "subjective" about life—and this is not wrong. But just as objectification does not always do justice to the overdeterminacy of given otherness, subjectification does not always do justice to the overdeterminacy of this intimate life. Subjectification fastens on the self-relation and rightly, but does not go rightly into this and rediscover the threshold spoken of above in relation to external otherness. There is also the threshold of an inward otherness that marks a between, across which the transitions are between the given life and its more ultimate giving source. I will come to this next when I talk about a more metaxological understanding of living.

It is important to grant that there is a plurivocity possible to selving. I would speak of selving(s) rather than subjectivity, since again the integrity in process is evident in this. In idiotic selving it is not a matter of autistic particularity but of a living and affectionate relation to oneself. We feel ourselves prior to thinking ourselves, or even thinking as ourselves—the intimacy, the idiocy reveals a pre-objective and pre-subjective self-relation—and this is the living relation of the living being to itself. Example: We sense something of it in the morning; we have this taste of self—before the day's determinations take over. We awake to ourselves and savor ourselves, brimming with new zest perhaps or dragging with weary disgust. This is not a determinate self-consciousness but a more floating indeterminate self-feeling—yet it communicates of how we are in relation to ourselves in the world we are shortly about to engage again more determinately. This is intimate life in its transience returning to the day of its self-relation and its relation to what is beyond it. It happens at a threshold, and hence most often it is not objectified, or not yet channelled into a more determinate or self-determining subjectification.

All forms of life might be said to be marked by a more or less relatively undeveloped senses of inwardness—of selving. All things selve in that respect. To selve is not the privilege of the human being alone. I think of Hopkins' great poem "As Kingfishers Catch Fire":[8] "Each mortal thing does one and the same:/ Deals out that being indoors each one dwells;/ Selves—goes itself; *myself* it speaks and spells,/ Crying *What I do is me: for that I came*." The surface of the thing as selving is the face of the thing. A face is the (micro)cosmos of facets that is the living surface of the selving being. Facets are surfaces and the higher integrities of being have faces that selve more and more intensively. In the sublunary world, the human being is the acme of this facing. We are a surface that faces the world, but we are our faces—the show of the intimate selving communicating itself. Is this why our faces are, in a sense, more intimate to us than even our intimate parts?

We can have many faces, and equivocity increases with surfaces like the human face. We have the ability to seem other than we are, to show

8. The kingfisher is not the dead parrot of Monty Python, not the stuffed/real goldfinch of Austin/Cavell, and has something of the spirit of the dovebird alive in it. So many birds to hear: the nightingale was the poet's bird in ancient Greece (Hesiod, Homer). Milton compares himself to a nightingale. The eagle was often the bird of poets, some Romantic (for instance, Lamartine and Pushkin). Shakespeare: the swan of Avon. Socrates, the poetic clodhopper, even tried to sing like a swan before his death. The *Schwanengesang* of Schubert: how hauntingly touching, and painful and sweet. Shelley likens the poet to a skylark. Wordsworth celebrates the lark too. There are other birds of life, for instance, the windhover of Hopkins. And nightingales pointing beyond this life now: Keats's Nightingale—"thou wast not born for death, immortal bird"; or beyond death, such as the golden birds of those great poems of Yeats's old age, "Byzantium" and "Sailing to Byzantium," birds that are "set upon a golden bough to sing/To lords and ladies of Byzantium/Of what is past, or passing, or to come." The bird may be beyond life and death, but beyond as living and not just imaged as the deathlessness of death. Only the golden sings. We do not want a base metallic metaphysics; we want a metaphysics of resurrected incarnation. The golden sings in Psalm 55:6, "Oh that I had wings like a dove, for then I would fly away and be at rest."

half-truly and to lie, to smile and hide hate in the smile. The power of equivocal surfacing is not confined to us. In *Being and the Between*, I pointed out the equivocity of the beautiful orchid, or the being other than what one is by being what one is, in the power of camouflage that surfaces in the selvings of animals, like the chameleon.[9] In this equivocity we find some of the reasons we often distrust surfaces. But the distrust of surfaces follows from what we learn from surfaces, not in isolation from what surfaces. The equivocity eludes complete univocal determinability, for showing is also always hiding; there are forms of showing that simultaneously are forms of keeping secret.

In any event, the self-relation of life to itself is very important and exceeds the terms of every objective determination of it. A living being is not subjective simply, it has its own objectivities, but as a living integrity of being it holds itself in a self-relation that comes to feel and know itself as such. I think of this as a very elemental opening or porosity to the intimate universal—not as entailing a rejection of the universal as such. It demands a rethinking of the universal, in fact, not its repudiation. All living beings participate in this intimate universal, and each is the singular surfacing of the energies of its "to be," but none exhausts it. One of the signs of this participation is its generation of the intimacy of life beyond its own self-relation, beyond its own possession of its own life. (The erotics of being is the passion of life.) The being knows it does not possess its own life—but knows that in its flesh, not in its head. This is why an erotics of life surfaces—the singular participation in the intimate universal is in passage beyond itself, passage sensing itself but not possessed in the flesh. This is something beyond determination, beyond self-determination, given that the living being is a nisus to generate beyond itself. This is more explicitly metaxological and again I will come to this. (The example of equivocity I cited above, the orchid, is intimately related to the erotics of naturing, and indeed without equivocity, the happening of human erotics would hardly be possible at all. In the erotics of life the surfaces of flesh are flushed, even engorged, with ambiguous significance.)

It is especially evident in humans that we have life coming to know itself as living. This self-knowing is not objective reason—it is living participation. The knowing of life is also the knowing of the transience of life. This is again not the knowing of a structure but of the passage qua passage. It is the knowing of life as in the passing of life itself as passing, and

9. Desmond, *Being and the Between*, 103–6.

knowing ourselves as participant in the passage as such. In connection with the equivocity of the erotics of life, I will here just briefly note how this self-relation can be taken in certain directions. The self-affirmation is evident in the Schopenhauerian will. What life reveals is the will to live—and this is a dark voracious energy in which we all participate and of which more often than not we find ourselves the victim. The matter at issue here is not only the nature of this "more" of life but the nature of love, and the love of this more primordial life. With Schopenhauer it has all the characteristics of a heedless *eros tyrannos*. The will is an erotic absolute, but without anything of the *eros ouranios* (heavenly eros) of Plato. In Schopenhauer it is voraciously self-insistent without end. It victimizes us when we think we can be agents of its or our own self-determination. Its greedy self-insistence makes it something vile rather than good for Schopenhauer. We cannot truly love a life whose aimless aim is to controvert every claim to autonomous self-determination we essay. Life is in an original guilt—it is not good to be—better not to be. We dip below the ground of the cave again.

We are still below the ground of the cave when Nietzsche tries to reverse the "yes" and "no" of Schopenhauer. The basic description of life persists. We live in foreboding of the Medusa below the surface—the horror that turns us to stone. Better to stay on the surface like the Greeks out of profundity. We are again dealing with the negotiation of thresholds, but here the threshold into the darkness goes down into an abyss of horror. Elemental life is this horror. It is reminiscent of the alien into which Žižek and others like to rub our faces. Of course, *the face has gone at this depth of darkness*. But the question of the surface does not dissolve. Is the surface the mask of horror or the face of something overdeterminate with an ontological good in which we participate and can never master? And perhaps not being its master has more to do with the giftedness of its good than the ruse by which the horrifying energy makes use of us for its own self-persistence and self-perpetuation?

In our time we find in Michel Henry a notable stress on life just as self-affection. He offers a remarkable development of the self-affection. Henry seems very insistent in setting the world (objectifications) over against Life. This is too dualistic perhaps, but I see in what he is doing a certain rightness in drawing attention to something crucial about the incontrovertibility of the life at issue. He transforms the transcendental subject in the direction of a remarkable transcendental Trinitarianism, so it strikes me, and which for me is closer to Hegel than Henry might like.[10] I note Henry had lots of respect for Schopenhauer and Nietzsche, and is right to remind us that they have seen something on the other side of objective representation, something in which we are and participate.[11] I think he does not see in both cases that the ontology of the "to be" is still defined by the modern evacuation of given being of all the traces of qualitative value. The "to be" is without the good of the "to be." Better not to be, in fact. This is nihilism, even when it protests against nihilism, as in the case of Nietzsche. In them the resort to this other path, of the "subject" beyond the "subject," is in an ethos of devalued thereness. In Schopenhauer it leads to the evil of being, in Nietzsche to the dream of a creative self-imposing of value on the valueless flux, and eventually to the dissolving of "self" in the same flux.

These strategies are not fully true to the self-affirming of life to which Henry perhaps is more true. But this self-affection, this self-affirmation, what is it? It is life loving itself—but what is this love? It is beyond reduction and objectification, but is it also more than every subjectification? Does it require more metaxological terms, in which there is always an opening beyond the self-affirmation of life? The affirmation of life is always between self and other—always in passing in the between, the passing in which we participate. It is very difficult to give an account of it, either in determinate terms or in terms of our self-determination. For all that, it is not a mere indetermination. There is something overdeterminate at work in its life. The interim of living passage is metaxological.[12] On the threshold, the between is worded; the between is sung.

## Surfacing on the Metaxological Threshold

By contrast with the objectivizing and subjectivizing reductions, these are now the considerations on which we must reflect. First, there is more to life than the neutral objectivities whose otherness entails no participatory involvement, since there is an ineluctable self-affirming of life even in its denial. Second, this self-affirmation, while undeniable, points to

10. See Henry, *I am the Truth.*

11 In the company of Schopenhauer, Nietzsche, and Henry, one might think of *Lebensphilosophie* more generally as seeing the irreducibility of life qua lived to the objectifications of science. One thinks again of Bergson, and also of William James's efforts to draw attention to "pure experience."

12. This metaxological view is systematically developed in my *Being and the Between, God and the Between,* as well as *Ethics and the Between.*

something more than a subjective self-involvement primarily circling around itself alone. As the otherness passes to self-affirmation, self-affirmation passes to the affirmation of otherness. Life is in the passage between these, and to do justice to the passage a different view of the self-affirming and the otherness is required. Living is a between process and a metaxological passage in the between.

Life is self-affirming, but there is more at play in this affirmation than just self. Self-affirmation is not the full affirmation. One way to indicate this is to look at the way in modernity the self-insistence of the living being has been called its *conatus essendi*, its endeavor to be. We find this in Hobbes and Spinoza, for instance, and also in Levinas, though criticized there. I would say there is more to the *conatus* than self-insistence. *Self*-affirming endeavor, so described, does not pay attention to the weight of either the *natus* or the *co* of *conatus*: a being born, a being born with. There is always a relation to coming to be, a being born, from an other "with" which the being is from the beginning. This opens a doubleness in the *conatus* itself. The living being endeavoring to be is received into being itself before it comes to affirm itself as for itself. The self-affirmation of the living being risks hiding from "self" the fact that this self-affirming is always "with" what is other. It hides the truth that to be self-affirming, it must be received from an affirming that is more than itself alone, and in which it always participates. In other words, the living being as self-affirming is not the bedrock reality, since the self-affirming comes to itself as "yes" to itself because already it is "yessed" in a "being born with." In the self-affirmation, life in a more full sense affirms itself. The overdeterminacy of life affirms itself in the self-affirmation, for self-affirmation is always more than self alone.

The *co-natus*, as a being born with, refers to what I call a *passio essendi* more primal than this endeavor to be. This passion of being is more primal because life opens us before we open to life. We are given to be as living before we give ourselves to be as determined, or self-determining, in accord with the particular form of life we are. The patience of life—in this sense of its being received from sources beyond self-affirmation—is often hidden from sight when the *conatus essendi* is wrongly claimed to be the essence of life itself. We are then prevented from looking deeper into the ontological sources at work in the incontrovertible self-affirmation. Put differently, there is a love (of life) more original than self-love, in which self-love itself participates, and which self-love distorts when it thinks itself to be the true form of love of life as such. In so loving our own life we do not love as we are given to live by the more original love and so do not love ourselves truly.

Thus, self-affirmation, in coming to itself out of being received, opens to an otherness of life that is not this or that determinate affirmation, not our own self-determination, but communicates of an enabling power in which all living beings participate. The *passio essendi* points back to the ultimate endowing source(s) of life. Suppose we start with the surface of things, start with our being in the midst of things. But we find ourselves open to things. We are open because we are already opened. Before we come to ourselves as more reflectively thoughtful, we already are in a porosity of being, and are ourselves as this porosity of being become mindful of itself. This is one reason I would speak of living in the between in terms of an *original porosity of being*, that is neither objective nor subjective, but that nevertheless is enabling of both, while being more than both, and indeed enabling passing between both. The porosity is a between space where there is no fixation of the difference of minding and things, where our mindfulness wakes to itself by being woken up by the communication of being in its emphatic otherness. Living as non-objectifiable and as exceeding subjectification reveals the transient flow of the "to be" in this porous between. More objective and self-reflective orientations come later. Already before we more reflectively come to ourselves, in the original porosity of being there is the more primal participation, and indeed we open mindfully to it in the mode of a certain astonishment.

To be is to be surprised by life—even if with later determinations and our claim to be self-determining we produce the dulling of the surprise of the overdeterminacy of being. In the living porosity, there is no fixed boundary between there and here, between outside and inside, between below and above. There is the coming to be of life; there is the becoming of determinate life in transient passage in the between; there is a relative self-determination with certain forms of self-becoming; but there is always the overdeterminacy, the "too muchness" of what gives itself to enable the coming to be and becoming of life. We find it again in our sometimes renewed astonishment at the surprise of life itself. There is a passage from what is into the awakening of mindfulness as, before its own self-determination, opened to what communicates to it from beyond itself. We do not open ourselves; being opened, we are as an opening. Living astonishment is not the neutral knowledge of objective structure, nor is it subjectivity simply in relation to itself. Rather it awakens the porosity of mindfulness to being, in the communication of being to mindfulness, before mind comes to itself in more determinate form(s). This living astonishment correlates with a more original "coming to be" prior to the formation of different processes of determinate becoming, and prior to the more settled arrival of relatively determinate beings and processes. Beauty is one of the happenings on the surface of things that can take our breath away and arouse wonder, that is to say, renew astonishment at the marvellous gift of life itself.[13]

The *passio essendi* and *conatus essendi* are always twinned; nevertheless a certain priority to the *passio* means always that life gives us to be before we come to ourselves as living. The passion of life is not originally of our willing, though the endeavor becomes our willing of life. Because of its source in the porosity of being the willing of life is always mingled with the possibility of nulling. My general sense is that the endeavor is always tempted to take over the passion of being. The active self-assertion of life overtakes the receiving of being, and to a degree tries even to null the receiving. Nevertheless, the receiving is more primordial. Truth to life entails more than endeavor on the surface of life but openness to this patience of being. To live in the *metaxu* is to be charged with remaining true to the original porosity. The *conatus* is to be given its full significance as a being "born with" (*co-natus*) against its contraction into just self-affirming of life. The endeavor to be is self-affirming, but self-affirming itself is witness to the double condition of twinned self-relation and relation to the other—in the *co-natus* itself. One is with oneself because one is "born with." Selving is not just self, but is a being endowed by virtue of a constitutive relativity to an other enabling source that is not oneself alone. When our selving loses any porosity to the more primal patience, its seeming self-affirmation mutates really into a kind of self-hatred. For this endeavor to be is in flight from itself, from what it is, from the patience of being that gives it to be at all in the first instance. The conditions that make possible its being at all are refused.

The *metaxu* as immanence is a given porosity of being, already in relation to what is beyond itself in being in relation to itself. If the

13 Important here are differences between wonder in the modalities of astonishment, perplexity and curiosity. Curiosity is more tied to objectifiable determinations of life; perplexity to an indeterminacy, especially bearing on the immanent life of selving; astonishment is ontological resurrection to the wonderful overdeterminacy of the *metaxu*, and beauty is its incarnational companion. On these three see Desmond, *The Intimate Strangeness of Being*, chapter 10, "Ways of Wondering: Beyond the Barbarism of Reflection."

between is porous it means that it is impossible to fixate univocally a "this side" and a "that side." What is most important is the happening of passage between—of passing. And this in an ontological sense—coming to be, passing into being, passing, passing out of being. All the pathos of life and death are contained in passing, passage in and through the between. Passing itself suggests a between since it cannot be fixed to any one moment or phase. Passing is as passing—just as a between is nothing without the enabling milieu of relatedness that sustains and goes beyond the beings upheld as existents in the relatively stabilized middle.

I suggest that this difference just indicated between *coming to be* and *becoming* has some relevance to the discussion of creation and evolution, though the relevance occurs on a level that is not customary in the reigning terms of the debate. Evolution is a becoming, but every becoming presupposes a coming to be. This coming to be is not an item in a process of becoming, it is not even the process of becoming as a whole. It is more in the givenness of becoming as such—in the "that it is at all." This is hiddenly presupposed in every becoming and in all of our approaches to becoming, the scientific theory of evolution included. To get some sense of the coming to be means being struck by the metaphysical astonishment that is amazed at the sheer being there of being. This metaphysical astonishment is not a matter of scientific curiosity and is closer to aesthetic marvelling and religious adoration.

Coming to be is a more original passage than becoming and the thought might be applied to life also. The question of the origin of life is often tied to the level of evolution as a becoming—and the effort is to articulate its scientifically warranted determination. But suppose there is an approach on the level of coming to be rather than becoming. Then there is no scientific explanation for the origin of life. It is always already presupposed by every explanation, and so in a certain sense the truer approach to life can never be the scientific one. Not only is this scientific approach a contraction of our participation in life but it can only see what is on the level of a determinate becoming. It does not metaphysically see surfaces as threshold of a coming to be—more truly a creation than a becoming. In that sense, creation is more primordial than becoming, but it is not another becoming. Hence, it is more primordial than evolution also, and is not this in terms of the big bang theory. We have to move in a different space of mindfulness. We have to see the surfaces of things differently. Rather than simply repudiate surfaces as superficial, the surfaces are the depths, if they are the thresholds of what is hyperbolic *in* immanent being, allowing and enabling passage of and to what is hyperbolic *to* immanent finite life.

This distinction of coming to be and becoming has applicability also to our tendency in modernity to put an emphasis on *self-becoming.* Recall that there is no self-affection of life without living in relation with others. The *co-natus* is itself between self-relation and other-relation, pointing back to a more original passion of living, itself emergent in a more primal porosity which enables passing between one being and another in the plurivocal relativity of the *metaxu.* The self-affirming of life is second—out of more original porosity. If I am not mistaken, the modern subjective view is witness to a certain contraction of the *conatus* to self-affirmation alone, though with this contraction there goes a kind of *expansion* of "selving," as the self-contracted self-affirmation of the *conatus* essays to overtake the *passio essendi* entirely. And then there is no patience of being, no receptivity of life from an enigmatic endowing source. Self-generating life is misunderstood as simply for itself alone. Its self-becoming circles around itself in an entirely immanent enclosure—life is all between it and itself—there is no opening of the porous between to an endowing source of life beyond all enclosed immanence. The circle of life closes on itself, even though its life is endowed, and even though without the source it would not be, or be for itself, at all.

Oddly enough, scientistic objectivism is implicated in a related overtaking of the *passio.* For the project of objectification, while seeming to free us from anthropomorphism, is another imposition on the givenness of life as such. There is no givenness, there is no received patience of being. The given conditions of life, on the surface of things, are to be reconfigured in terms of the secret *scientistic anthropomorphism.* Not surprisingly, this scientistic objectivism passes from the self-affirmation of life to a kind of mutation of love of life into hatred of the given conditions of life as other to us. A tyrannical autonomy (*autonomia tyrannos*) would impose on the neutralized conditions of life what it takes to be worthy of affirmation, and what is worthy of affirmation must serve it and it alone.[14] The de-humanization strangely serves a different project of the human. There is no patience for any givenness of life as such, except the waiting game that is needed to allow the day to come when we will be its masters and possessors. The anti-anthropomorphic project secretly serves us once again, and there is no true between. Between us and the

14. See Desmond *"Autonomia Turannos."* This is a recurrent theme in my *Ethics and the Between.*

otherness of life, the entire project is, in the final reckoning, a matter between us and ourselves. Even the inhuman, the non-human, is a mirror in which we see only ourselves. We see horror, but the horror is the mirror of our own hatred of life as given.

## Interlude II

### Life Granted on Metaxological Thresholds

I offer now four saturated surfaces that illuminate us about living on a metaxological threshold.

*First surface at the beginning of life*: The scream of the newly born infant on entry into life. Some will think of the scream in terms of horror at life. Lear: "When we are born, we cry that we are come to this great stage of fools." The scream is Munch's face before the horror of being. But is it quite so? For when the infant bawls there is relief and delight. The infant is alive and its scream communicates the self-affirmation of life. Were all quiet, we would worry something was wrong, something amiss. When there is no noise, we fear death. The infant affirms its own life, it communicates beyond its own life. This is being born as *co-natus*: from another, self-affirming, crying out, reaching out. We come to be from another, we are as reaching to another. What do we need to recognize the scream thus as the sign of life? Not science, certainly. And there is nothing neutrally objective about this recognition. Even in the self-affirming of the infant's life, there is also a communication beyond itself, though it knows it not, and thus there is more to the self-affirmation of life than self.

*Second surface from the middle of life*: I cite an interesting observation of Wittgenstein:

> Today I saw a poster saying: "'Dead' Undergraduate speaks."
>
> The inverted commas mean: "He isn't really 'dead.'" He isn't what people call dead. They call it "dead" not quite correctly. . . . It suddenly struck me: If someone said "He isn't dead, although by the ordinary criteria he is dead"—couldn't I say: "He is not only dead by the ordinary criteria; he is what we call 'dead.' If you now call him, 'alive,' you're using language in a queer way, because you are almost deliberately preparing misunderstandings. Why don't you use some other word, and let 'dead' have the meaning it already has?"[15]

15. Wittgenstein, *Lectures and Conversations on Aesthetics, Psychology and*

> In general, if you say: "He is dead" and I say "He is not dead" no one would say: "Do they mean the same by 'dead'?" In the case where a man has visions I wouldn't offhand say: "He means something different."[16]

I take these remarks to be striking reminders of the strange ways we sometimes use words. Yet Wittgenstein's remarks settle no issue, since what we mean by "dead" and "alive" still are shrouded in mystery. What are the meanings of "death" and "life" we already have? Even though we know, in one sense, what we are talking about, in another sense, we do not know. Ordinary usage will only get us so far. As far as the threshold of mystery: the surplus surface of too much, or almost nothing. Wittgenstein's dedication is to the "ordinary" meaning—but what is "ordinary"? It is on the surface of things, you might say, but what does it mean to take something at "face value"? It is not at all clear what "face value" is. And what if one were to think of resurrection? How ordinary can this be, or how extraordinary? How we use words will take us so far, but yet there will be something stunning about what surfaces—resurrects itself, from the grave of ordinariness, and faces us. Should we say that the Misfit in Flannery O'Connor's, "A Good Man Is Hard to Find," is closer to the mystery of surfacing when he growls: Jesus was the only one that ever raised the dead . . . and he shouldn't have done it? Or is the Misfit a kind of ordinary-language philosopher? He murders—though not to dissect.[17]

*Third surface from later in life*: The process of *ageing* as revealing, in the passing between of life, something neither objective nor subjective, but both. Ageing is important for the time of our life, for the time of living. In the timed body, aging makes finiteness evident on the surface. True, often now we try to refigure that surface—with cosmetic surgery, for instance. We struggle to keep time at bay by means of the youth of the surface. The struggle is always finally lost. In this respect also ageing is very much connected with beauty. Beauty blooms, but it is also fugitive and transient. It passes and it passes away. We more easily find beauty in youth than in age. We console ourselves by saying that the former is a surface physical thing, while in the latter we may find beauty of spirit or soul, which is not tied to the beauty of the surface. All this may be quite

*Religious Belief*, 65.

16 Ibid., 62.

17 See also Shakespeare's *The Winter's Tale*, with the statue of Hermione coming back to life at the end in the final scene. See Cavell, *Disowning Knowledge*.

true, and yet the importance of the surface of things is not to be denied. Ageing is a surfacing of time in our embodied being, and none can evade this surfacing, even if we can postpone it provisionally.

The between character of ageing is instructive. Ageing is not objective, is not subjective. It is both. It happens to us; but it is something sensed intimately. The time of the body is a living time, but it is transient and mortal. The loss of beauty on the surface goes with the time of our embodiment. Something is passing, neither subjective nor objective, and yet both. What is it that passes? It is life that passes, but as passing it still is life, and hence in another sense, it does not pass. It is what it is in passing, and yet still is life. And so the old do not always intimately know their own time as old. Lived from within, as lived, it still is young for itself, even if for others it shows the signs of decrepitude.

When we think of ageing we think of old age, but why should not analogous considerations apply to youth, being young. I mean the between condition of being neither objective nor subjective, of being a threshold of passing life. For surely the sense of the passing as passing applies as much to the process of growing as to that of declining, to becoming as to undoing, to passing to blooming as to passing the zenith and falling away from it. What is passing is held in a more pleasing poise on the surface of things with a younger beauty. The surface poise of old age yields to slackness in the tuning of the surface of things. What passes in the slackness is as enigmatic in its passing away as what passes more vigorously in the younger bloom. It is not a structure, not a form. It is a forming, an animating, an enlivening—but it is also a deforming, an anaesthetizing, a deadening. The sere, the yellow leaf, was once lush with green.

*Fourth surface close to the end*: I am thinking of a last illumination of life on the surface in *King Lear*, from almost beyond life and death, from life and its last breath. By comparison with the comic farce of Monty-Python, this last surface thresholds on a tragic extreme. The pig squeals, the dead parrot does not scream, the newborn infant bawls, but Lear howls at the death of Cordelia: "Howl, howl, howl, howl."[18] King Lear is

18. KING LEAR (5, 3):
Howl, howl, howl, howl! O, you are men of stones:
Had I your tongues and eyes, I'd use them so
That heaven's vault should crack. She's gone for ever!
I know when one is dead, and when one lives;
She's dead as earth. Lend me a looking-glass;
If that her breath will mist or stain the stone,

trying to ascertain if his beloved daughter is alive or dead. It is the surface that is attended to: Is there a breath in a mirror, does a feather stir with her breath? How delicate the images of life are: a breath that will mist a mirror—so fragile its being there is almost not there at all, even when life is thriving—an evanescent almost nothing that in death is indeed now nothing; a breath that will move a feather, but this is a mortal breath. It is an endowed breath that had its time. It is not quite the spirit of God that will be more than a feather floating, though it descend like a dove to brood on the earth, or ascend to the sky, also like a bird that for a while one can still follow and see, and then, almost instant-like, where before it was, it now no longer is, and it seems it has as if become nothing. A person has breathed her or his last. Why do we stand on the earth looking up? There is huge extremity in Lear's outcry when he realizes that the life is irrevocably gone:

> And my poor fool is hang'd! No, no, no life!
> Why should a dog, a horse, a rat, have life,
> And thou no breath at all? Thou'lt come no more,
> Never, never, never, never, never!
> Pray you, undo this button: thank you, sir.
> Do you see this? Look on her, look, her lips,
> Look there, look there!

Perhaps never has this word "never" been uttered with such agony. Of course, "never" is the negative counterpart to the word "once." The "once" of life—there in its mortal preciousness, its beloved beauty. Think how far we are from the neutralized thereness of the objectivizing reduction and how far too from the self-involvement of the subjectivizing reduction. The "once" is a gift of received beauty that gathers something ontologically good and unique to singular incarnation. The "never" is the return of the given to the enigma of the nothing from which it was given to be.

Cordelia is dead. Will there be more? Life beyond life . . . and death? If one were then to speak of saturated surfaces it would be so in a

---

Why, then she lives.
KENT: Is this the promised end?
EDGAR: Or image of that horror?
ALBANY: Fall, and cease!
KING LEAR: This feather stirs; she lives! if it be so,
It is a chance which does redeem all sorrows
That ever I have felt . . . .

paradoxical sense. The surface is as much a place of surplus as an opening into emptiness. It is the threshold between the plenitude of life and the emptying of its gift into death. It is at once both the surplus and the emptying. The surface is a little like eros: a double creation of a poverty and resource. Is the resource a *poros*, a porosity, beyond all mortal *penia*, within whose between-space opens a threshold between humans and divinity, mortals and immortals—a threshold that can only be crossed in death?

## Coming to the Saturated Surface: Hell and Transient Beauty

In these four saturated surfaces we have passed from birth into life, and through life to death, and perhaps beyond life and death to life. What then of philosophizing on the surface of things? In this last reflection I would like to return briefly to the connection between beauty and the porosity of being, with reference to transience on an extreme threshold, putting the accent on our being as suffering, as exposed to what is other to ourselves. Beauty opens and reopens the porosity of our being; but there is a vulnerability in being porous. Just as there can be a transcending upwards there can be transcending downward, and the latter can mean a descent into hell, though there are different ways of descending.

I return to the theme with which I opened, that is, a kind of "transcending" downward, below the ground of the underground—into hell. Recall again the story of the Bull of Phalaris: As a sacrifice to Apollo, Phalaris the tyrant sent to the oracle at Delphi the statue of a magnificent bronze bull, given to him by Perilaus, an architect/sculptor. Recall how the bull could serve as a kind of torture machine: a person imprisoned in it, a fire lit beneath it, and the screams of torture are turned in sweet music by reed pipes in the nostrils of the bull.[19] The shrieks of mortal despair serve as the source of aesthetic pleasure, but those who hear the music do not hear the shrieks. The artwork can serve, on the one hand, to reveal hell, on the other hand, to conceal hell. The perplexity this story poses for us: Is this then what beauty is: music wrung from hell, concealing hell as it is, and making it look like a heaven? The pipes bring forth lovely sounds, but what surfaces disguises the shrieks of the tormented. Is

19. See Harmon, trans., *Lucian*, vol. 1, 17–19. Some versions of the story downplay the cruel tyranny of Phalaris, others foreground it.

this beauty: not a face of the good, but a façade of dis-mal darkness? The surface of the beautiful hides the working of hell?

Remember, however, the equivocity of saturated surfaces as thresholds of transition. Think doubly of the night: night can be the time of nightmares, of blindness, of crying out from abysses of desolation and sorrow, of being overcome by monsters, of helpless struggle to escape, of dreadful quasi-movement, when one moves and one cannot move, lives but does not live. If one can be devastated by night, the night is also the time of rest and refreshment. It brings sleep that knits up the ravelled sleeve of care, the balm of the darkness, the tenderness of love, the softness of the shining moon and the healing nocturnal quiet when the longing for eternity wakes. In the dark divine dreams are given and messengers from beyond this life come to visit. Remember also that equivocity when, standing on the surface of the earth, an intrusive light so assaults us that we are victim of "light-pollution." Too much of the garish light of the metallic metaphysics, and we can no longer see. We lose the mystery of things. Life is night as well as day. We need the dreams of the night for the health of the day. These dreams might mingle horror and beauty, and yet without sleep and dreaming we go mad in the noonday glare. Beauty too is a seductive night of the soul that wakes its erotic porosity.

The equivocity surfaces here in relation to hell. For there might be a different sense in which the artist turns hell into song—there may be a redemptive sense. One is reminded of Orpheus, and his music in Hades. There are different ways of being in the underworld. His music could bring tears even in the underworld, and melt hard hearts. Enchanting song reopens even in hell the primal porosity. There is another way of being in hell, and communicating a power that is more than hell. Going below the surface can take us into chambers of horror, and we must spend our season in hell, but if this were the end of the matter, and there were no golden night of the agapeic heart, we would have no standing anew on the surface of the earth.

One of the most beautiful songs of the surface might be found in the final few lines of the *Inferno* of Dante. Virgil and Dante descend into the hell hole, but at a certain central point their descent turns into its opposite, namely, ascent out of hell, and upwards once again to the surface of the earth. They climb up over the fixed Lucifer and climb beyond hell. The frozen Lucifer is beyond all porosity, all permeability: fixed eternally in himself as himself—a parody of divine eternity. The center of hell is the closure of the porosity onto itself, and instead of the opening of the soul to what is beyond it, we find the frozen Lucifer who weeps eternally, as in his mouth he masticates the great traitors, Judas, Brutus, and Cassius. Virgil and Dante ascend beyond the frozen Lucifer and into an opening upwards. The journey through the Inferno has been long and replete in many scenes of horror and depravity. But this ascent now, once having passed through the heart of darkness, takes places quickly. The brevity of these last lines is notable, by comparison with the previous sojourn in hell and journey through it. But one feels there is a new invigoration of life palpable in the lines as they come to the surface and the two behold again the stars. These lines, ending on the threshold of a fresh beginning, are beautiful and worth recall:

> My guide and I entered that hidden road
> To make our way back up to the bright world.
> We never thought of resting while we climbed.
> We climbed, he first and I behind, until,
> Through a small round opening ahead of us
> I saw the lovely things the heavens hold,
> And we came out once more to see the stars.[20]

It is night over the world when the poets come to the surface. But there is a light that shines on things, and in the night it is the borrowed light of the stars. Still more, there is a source of light above the sublunary world, beyond the stars. In the beauty of the night we do not directly see the sun, but we are not entirely cut off from its light. To come thus to the surface of things, after hell, we begin again to open to the marvel of things. We even begin to wonder if the saturated surface of things is the place of consecration where God gives himself for praise.

20. Dante, *The Divine Comedy: Vol. I Inferno*, Canto XXXIV, 133–39. Lo duca e io per quel cammino ascoso/ intrammo a retornar nel chiaro mondo;/e sanza cura aver d'alcun riposo, /salimmo sù, el primo e io secondo,/ tanto ch'i' vidi de le cose belle/che porta 'l ciel, per un pertugio tondo./E quindi uscimmo a riveder le stelle.

# 3

# The Shine on Things: Given Beauty and the Order of Creation

## Opening

Recurrently throughout modernity, certain scientific orientations to nature have tended toward the reductive. Of course, one might immediately object that it is a *scientistic* rather than scientific orientation that exhibits this tendency. And, it is true, we must make a distinction between the scientific and the scientistic. I take the *scientistic* to be a philosophical interpretation of science that claims that the scientific approach can solve, at least in principle, all the essential questions or problems. The *scientific* approach, by contrast, can well be more chaste in its claims to be the measure, if only in principle, of all essential questions. Open to the real as it is, true science is willing to confess its fallibility. Yielding in the acknowledgement of the limits of its knowing, it may also grant that there are certain perplexities not in essence scientific. The curiosity of science participates in a more primal and open wonder at the astonishingly intricate intelligibilities that come to show themselves in the order of creation. Surely that order, and the intelligent astonishment that is opened to it, is not betrayed by the determinate curiosity of scientific inquiry.[1]

1. It is crucial to keep in mind important differences between wonder in the modalities of astonishment, perplexity, and curiosity. Curiosity is more related to objectifiable determinations of given being, perplexity to indeterminacies we cannot quite

Granting such an epistemic-ontological openness of science, one might still ask if the opening is itself twinned with a tendency toward the reductive. Scientism, in one form or another, seems to be a recurring default position haunting science, a besetting temptation when the larger significance of science itself is philosophically, and indeed theologically, in question. We find something like the following from the beginning of modern science: The surface of things, with all the qualitative textures things exhibit, tends to be relativized in the direction of a more neutral, valueless objectification. Accompanying this, our pre-scientific orientation to what is given is often subjectivized, and in the language of earlier modern science, the surface of things yields merely secondary qualities rather than primary.[2] True, in due course science comes to find astonishing orders at work in nature. The primal epistemic-ontological opening to the being of nature as it is cannot be gainsaid. Nevertheless, the given beauty of creation tends to be subjectivized, if not ontologically weakened. One might say: the shine is taken off things. What stands before us is a valueless, neutral thereness. And what the beauty of creation communicates, if it communicates at all, tends to be deprived of metaphysical and theological significance.

Generally, postmodern attitudes to order might seem quite different to more scientistic orientations. One might put it thus: where the scientistic tends toward the reductive, the postmodern tends towards the deconstructive. Yet there is a kind of overlap in their different stresses, namely, that finally there seems to be no *given* order of beauty. The surface of things is invested with an equivocity that, whether reductively or deconstructively, we can only approach with epistemic-ontological suspicion. That is, given orders are said to be invested with a kind of false sacredness, or "naturalized," such that their origins in human construction or will to power are disguised. The point now is said to be an unmasking of given order, and a revelation of the secrets of power. If there is an order of creation, this postmodern orientation does not seem very hopeful in approaching it. More often than not, such an order of creation is denied outright.

---

make univocally determinate, astonishment to ontological porosity to given being in its wonderful overdeterminacy. Beauty is to be correlated with this third modality as its incarnational companion. On these three modalities, see Desmond, *The Intimate Strangeness of Being*, chapter 10.

2. Whitehead's account of this in *Science and the Modern World* is still marvelously fresh.

Of course, there is a side to postmodernism where art and the aesthetic play a huge role, and one might well ask whether that role could be played at all without some sense of order, or aesthetic form. I think not. While celebrating the aesthetic, postmodern thought tends to be equivocal about the religious. And yet one can ask if there is a secret familial bond between the aesthetic and the religious that points to something beyond deconstruction or complete reduction: the given order of creation, as itself presupposed by all human claims to creativity. One could well ask if given creation and the endowed creativity of the human being communicate something of the giving source, or the ultimate endowing power.

In the following reflections I want to focus on the connection of given beauty and the order of creation in light of these issues. Beauty itself is inseparable from some sense of formed wholeness. One must grant, of course, that such aesthetic wholeness does not preclude the possibility of disorder; and yet there is consonance in the dissonance, harmony in the struggle of opposition. The question is whether there is a givenness to beauty in nature which belies the (postmodern) claim that order is just an imposition of (our) power on flux. I would say that the notion of creation is inseparable from the origination of order, but the order *comes to be*, arises from originating sources that allow forms of beauty to be that are more than our determination or self-determination. Creation is more than an imposition on flux, for something original, something marvelously original, comes to be, comes to shine. Things come to shine, there is a shine on things. But what shines on things when we come to appreciate their given beauty? Is it just *our* shine on things, as if we were the sole source of light? Is it the shine *of* things, as if the things were luminescent in their own being there? Is it a shine *on* things, such that the source of the light was not just ours, nor confined to the thing of beauty?

Postmodern thought has inclined to look on beauty as something merely domesticating, and has tended to stress the *sublime* and its excess to every formed whole.[3] The beautiful tranquilizes, the sublime disturbs. Perhaps this attitude is taken to counteract the valueless thereness of the objectivizing reduction, above mentioned. The sublime liberates from aesthetic staleness. This is not untrue, but beauty, I will argue, does

3. A sample of works in this regard: Lyotard, *The Inhuman*; Lyotard, *Lessons on the Analytic of the Sublime*; Battersby, *The Sublime, Terror and Human Difference*; Courtine, ed. *Of the Sublime*; Silverman and Aylesworth, eds., *The Textual Sublime*. Not quite postmodern, but illuminating and engaging, is Crowther, *The Kantian Sublime*.

not domesticate being in terms of a closed whole, but witnesses to the promise of what I have called an "open whole." Beauty reveals no merely tranquilized totality, nor need there be any exclusive "either/or" between beauty and the sublime. Finite wholes, in the aesthetic happening of things, open beyond themselves to what gives them to be. Revealed as creations, a light shines on things from beyond every closed whole. The shine on things has metaphysical and theological significance, beyond reduction and deconstruction. We behold the lilies of the field, but does the shine on things tell of a light that endows our power of enlightening? Does this light, neither of us or things, give things of beauty whose lustre wakes in the soul a song of praise?

## Creation and Postmodern Order(s)

In connection with the theme of creation, order, and postmodernism, normally we think of postmodernism as assaulting order, in the sense of deconstructing orders that, supposedly, have been "naturalized," even "fetishized," while their origins in human construction or will to power are disguised. The unmasking of such orders, the deconstruction of the secrets of power they disguise, more often than not are said to reveal some covered-over otherness, more inhuman than human. As I already put it, order is an imposition on flux, and when we see through the imposition as our imposition, no order can give orders. Something of its credibility is weakened. We cannot surrender to it without suspicion. At most, order is a provisional and transient stabilization of flux. If there is a *given* order of creation, this cannot be the last word. We must ask: Who or what gives the order? Are we giving the orders, or are we given order, perhaps even under order? The gift of beauty can offer some illumination here. More, it can offer opportunities for reflection that need not be "merely" aesthetic. The gift of beauty relative to the order of creation has some bearing on crucial metaphysical, and indeed theological, matters.[4] The foregrounding of the aesthetic in postmodern thinking often co-exists with the recessing of the religious, indeed metaphysical and theological,

4. See notably Balthasar, *The Glory of the Lord I: Seeing the Form*. Of course, some postmodern currents do try to recover some sense of the sacredness of nature and the given order of creation, in particular those philosophies and theologies that have an ecological and holistic orientation. In Desmond, *God and the Between*, I have discussed the holistic God(s) of pantheism and panentheism (chapter 11), as well as what I call the theistic God of creation, beyond the whole (chapter 12).

dimensions of the issue, but it is a question if, finally, these can be avoided in a (renewed) postmodern thinking of the order of creation.

Given the prominent role art and the aesthetic play in postmodernism, we cannot avoid asking from the outset whether this role is possible without *some* sense of order, or aesthetic form. We do note a recurrent trend that seems more intent to deform the form, to break the frame, to desanctify the fetishized given, and in one way or other, reduce to the status of a false exaltation everything claiming to elevate and ennoble. Aesthetic order seems again and again to be put in the doghouse. I recall again a relevant instance I cited in my opening reflection, namely, how Umberto Eco's book *On Beauty* was a moderate success as a publishing venture, while a sequel *On Ugliness* was a signal success.[5] We seem to find an elective affinity for the ugly, the monstrous, the execrable, just to the extent that order seems defeated by disorder, form by formlessness, purity by blemish, serenity by horror. I think of how in the paintings of Lucien Freud human flesh is on the verge of mud—humus with the divine breath withdrawn, or withdrawing; while in those of Francis Bacon flesh is meat, screaming meat.[6]

The traditional argument is that it is hard to make proper sense of the ugly without its secretly being parasitical on some sense of the beautiful. How make sense of disorder without some hidden sense of order?

5. See chapter 1, note 3.

6. It would be interesting to reflect on Lear's howl and Bacon's screaming popes. That Bacon had regular recourse to a medical book on facial deformities is not an incidental biographical detail. His paintings on figures at the base of the crucifixion speak less to a hatred of bland bourgeois beauty as to the menace of an indeterminate monstrousness at a threshold just below determinate form. The torment of the communicating face in a shriek of horror reminds us of Beckett's "Not-I." But beauty is in how the thing looks as well as in how we look. We are to behold the lovely as the to-be-loved: loved because lovely, though lovely too because looked at with love. If we look with indifference or hate, the lovely is not seen as lovely. Looking with love or hate, how we look, is like a wave breaking on the shore, but the source of the wave is way out there, comes from afar, far in remote deeps. Bacon's look at bodies does not see flesh but assaults it in a kind of discomposition—a composed decomposition.

The look of Lucien Freud at the flesh of the sitter does not bring to mind a look of love—a disenchanted look of sorts—and what it sees reveals as much of the looking as of the sitter beheld—if beheld is the right word. One is keeping disgust at bay. There is a kind of curl in seeing that with a little more curling would curdle into disgust. The distance in which the flesh of the other is seen makes it verge on not being flesh or flesh in transience towards meaningless thereness. There is no dream, no enchantment. One thinks of troll-like people, the flesh of these trolls reminding one of something analogous in Bosch: peasant creatures just up out of the earth.

How make intelligible the (non)sense of deformation without some operative form, albeit *incognito*? Some sense of aesthetic order must be at work, even if we are to enjoy the thrill of transgressing aesthetic order. The case is analogous to evil and the good. It is undoubtedly true that in recent centuries humanity has "supped full of horrors," to borrow a phrase from *Macbeth*. We are like Macbeth who says: "Direness, familiar to my slaughterous thoughts/Cannot once start me" (V, 5, 14–15). But have we too much hugged the horror? Have we become too yielding to slaughterhouse thoughts? Have we grown direly suspicious of any consent beyond horror?[7] There is a trend where we reveal ourselves to be engaged obsessively and (oddly) easily with radical evil,[8] while all the while we remain silent about the astounding question of *radical good*. Who poses *that* question? Silence about this question should not exist at all, if we are honest about the evil itself which, it is reasonable to argue, cannot be made sense of without as honest an exploration of the promise of the good. This issue of evil is also connected with creation, and indeed the good of creation as given. If we have a diminished feel for the beauty of given creation, it is not surprising that we have an enfeebled sense of the goodness of creation as given.

Relevant here is the concern of postmodern currents with *the sublime* rather than the beautiful. After all, the sublime ruptures form and brings a breach to our more domesticated forms. Its breach provides an opening to something of excessive otherness. This is true and very important, but of course much hangs on the sense of the excessive otherness that might be glimpsed in the breach of finite order. Someone like Lyotard draws attention to this, and draws on Kant, a point well known.[9] The unrepresentable is somehow presented. The unrepresentable is

7. I want to thank Renée van Riessen for her engaging and thoughtful remarks in response to an earlier version of my reflections, and am at one with her in granting we cannot avoid the horror. Admittedly, my search here concerns more the consent than the horror. I have treated of evil in a number of places: Desmond, *Beyond Hegel and Dialectic*, chapter 5; Desmond, "Dialectic and Evil"; Desmond, *Ethics and the Between*; Desmond, "Sticky Evil"; Desmond, *God and the Between*; Desmond, "Ethics and the Evil of Being"; Desmond, "Creation and the Evil of Being."

8. A sample of recent works diversely dealing with evil: Copjec, ed. *Radical Evil*; Lara, ed. *Rethinking Evil*; Neiman, *Evil in Modern Thought*; Bernstein, *Radical Evil*; Matuštík, *Radical Evil and the Scarcity of Hope*.

9. See Lyotard, *Lessons on the Analytic of the Sublime*; also Desmond, *Art, Origins, Otherness*, chapter 2 "The Terror of Genius and the Otherness of the Sublime: On Kant and the Transcendental Origin."

reminiscent of the God of monotheism of whom no graven image is to be made, but there are multiple ambiguities here. If we connect the transcendent with the religious, in the rupture of the sublime we are also breaching the circle of aesthetic autonomy, and rightly so. But this runs against the grain of both modernist, and to a degree postmodernist, aesthetics. The modernist wants an art freed of the religious, though, in fact, the modernist invests the aesthetic with something of the displaced ultimacy of religious transcendence, and in my view the religious passes into art in an often unnamed way. There is resistance to bringing that name of religion out of anonymity. You might say the postmodern breaches the autonomous order of modernism's aesthetic form, and yet there is a sense of uneasiness in being forthright about the religious as such. It is as if our dissatisfaction with modernist autonomy is still in thrall to the same (aesthetic) autonomy, though this is now lacerated. We cannot come quite clean on naming the religious dimension of the issue as such.

Remember also that the postmodern sublime is more often than not a *wrought* sublimity. One thinks of some works of artists like Mark Rothko and Lyotard's engagement with Barnett Newman.[10] The given order of nature as creation is not the originating occasion of the postmodern sublime but the image of the imageless wrought by artistic construction, or deconstruction, or perhaps abstraction or subtraction. The rupture of the unrepresentable seems to owe more to the constructing/deconstructing "activity" of the artist, albeit shrouded in the enigma of its own night, than to the sublimity of nature as other and given. It is a sublimity that strangely remains too tied to the human, even as it seems to free the human into the inhuman or the transhuman.

I think it prompts a query concerning the extent to which postmodern thought or art is the thought or art of *the city* rather than that of the country. If this is so, such thought or art is always distanced from creation as given, and hence from a sense of order that, while not human simply, invests (the) human order with its distinctive potencies. Such a thought or art would be more concerned with human constructions rather than given orders in which human construction participates, orders in which the human shares rather than overarches.[11] In the city in its familiar

10. See Newman, "The Sublime Is Now"; also Lyotard "The Sublime and the Avant-Garde"; also Lyotard, "Newman: The Instant."

11. On technological sites, skyscrapers, the Golden Gate Bridge and suchlike, as places of spectacle and tourism, see Nye, *American Technological Sublime*. On technology and the sublime in contemporary American writing, see Tabbi, *Postmodern*

strangeness the human being is reflected *back to itself*, in the wrought order. This seems so even when the face reflected back is a strange face—the alienated face is still our own. Where there is an inhumanity to the city, this inhumanity is still humanity's own inhumanity. By contrast, the face of nature (as creation) is not simply our own. Even when we do our utmost to humanize it, there is an otherness to it beyond human determination and self-determination. The order of country creation, if I might so call it, is not the mirror in which the human is so easily confirmed, or as now seems more beloved on the terms of postmodernism, disconfirmed.

Remember Kant's moralization of the sublime: the sublime may seem to make small the human being as a creature of nature but it really leads to the elevation of the human being as a moral being.[12] The otherness of the sublime is moralized, even morally tamed. In postmodernism we do not find the moralization of the sublime, but more the demoralization. Witness Nietzsche: he would de-moralize all of being, and return us to the so-called innocence of becoming (*die Unschuld des Werdens*); but return to *homo natura* is also return to the inhuman, if moralized humanity is our measure. The equivocity of the sublime otherness so granted by some currents of postmodern thought seems to remain too equivocal to be given an honestly religious name. The breach of autonomy yields a lacerated autonomy rather than a different freedom that releases us to the fullness of creation as other.

It is worth remembering that the (re)emergence of concern for the sublime in the eighteenth century itself had strongly religious overtones. Mixed in with it was a reaction, religious as well as aesthetic, to the anorexic abstraction of the deistic transcendence and the dead thereness of a mechanistic nature. In question was something of the glory of creation as other to us. Sublimity, thus approached, is something on the boundary between the aesthetic and religious. That boundary is important for rethinking the aesthetics of creation and the kind of order that is at stake here.

It is interesting to recall that Hegel had a sense of the sublime that touches on this issue. It is especially bound up for him with the majestic transcendence of the Jewish God, a God who for him is also connected with the doctrine of creation. While he calls Greek religion, the "religion

---

*Sublime*.

12. Kant, *Critique of the Power of Judgment*, § 27.

of beauty," he calls Judaism the "religion of sublimity."[13] But it is the transcendent otherness of the sublime that is for Hegel both its greatness and deficiency. For Hegel, Jewish transcendence is superseded by Christian immanence, and hence the sublime God must give way to a divinity more self-determining in immanence, an immanent God also more modernly compatible with humanity's own immanent self-determination. The old order of creation and its sublimity are surpassed in spirit's cultural self-determination. Creation is the self-creation of God, and there ensues the relegation in spiritual ultimacy of the sublime. The spiritual domestication of its aesthetic happening qua happening is not pursued by Hegel in the direction of postmodern disorder, and yet he submits to the secular evacuation of the aesthetic happening of the sublime of its religious significance. Hegel's dialectical-speculative evacuation of divine transcendence yields, I would argue, a counterfeit double of God, and this applies from a Christian point of view, as well as a Jewish.[14]

Whichever way we turn, and to underline the present point: the postmodern does not seem so hospitable to the idea of order as such, since the spirit of suspicion lingers that all claims to given order are false faces of hidden powers. Their surface beauty conceals brutal realities. Apply this thought to creation in so far as there is beauty in its given order, and we must suspect that this seducing face of beauty hides a darker Medusa-like visage, into whose eyes we look with peril. For what we then see in truth is *horror* and our chilled souls are instantly turned to stone. I have just named something that lies very close to the heart of Nietzsche's vision of the dark Dionysian origin against whose more exposed truth we need art to save us, the same Nietzsche who alternatively is the patron saint of postmodernism or its mischievous Peter Pan.

In short then, in relation to the ontological status of order, we find a certain doubleness. The postmodern is both a breach with and continuation of the modern: order as the determination of "geometry" in one, becomes order as the surface of chaos in the other; autonomy as first lauded in one, then becomes autonomy lacerated in the other, at the end becoming autonomy that is not so much self-legislating as self-lacerating, self-cannibalizing. The break and continuity of the modern and postmodern has something to do with a loss of the sense of the order of creation as

13. Hegel, *Lectures on the Philosophy of Religion*, 328–74.

14. Desmond, *Hegel's God*, *passim*.

given. It has something to do with the need for a finessed beholding that would follow from a different sense of the aesthetics of happening.

## Creation, Modernity, and Beauty's Eclipse

Of course, one might argue more generally that what has happened as modernity has unfolded is a certain *eclipse* of beauty. As I put it elsewhere,[15] in Romantic and post-Romantic aesthetic culture a subjectivity in excess of all finite objectivity comes to dominance and it can find no balancing consonance between itself and the beauty before it. I will return to this point. It is true that in popular culture and entertainment physical beauty is a thing massively sought after, but in cultural circles of a more avant-garde character beauty is treated with diffidence, if not disdain. It revels in the dubious consolation that serves to tranquilize the false consciousness of the bourgeoisie—so it might go. One of the sources of the revolt against beauty in some aesthetic quarters is the perception that it panders to a philistine bourgeois culture. In being assaulted, such a culture (putatively) is provoked into betraying itself in philistine reactions, reactions allowing a second gesture of outrage to the dim aesthetic taste of the "boobs" (H. L. Mencken's term for a member of the "Booboisie"). Admittedly, the case is more complicated in that beauty is, in fact, often instrumentalized by capitalist culture to sell commodities. Beauty addresses us, and gets our attention, and hence is an easy servant to shanghai or press gang the consumer into collusion with the capitalist need to sell. Beauty is groomed as the consort goddess who serves the last god of the religion of shopping.

All this is quite true. While some aspects of this are to be decried, there is another sense in which the whole thing pays *a secret tribute to the power of beauty*, even as it uses it for purposes that are not always very beautiful. Beauty moves us. There is something elemental and deep and not understood about our being so moved. It is this moving or being moved that is deflected in the direction of the shopping mall and the cash register. Bait and switch, I think it might be called in the jargon of the salesman—a very distasteful experience, even for a shopper (speaking as a shopper). You want to buy one thing, but the seller, having one fish in the bag already, wants to sell you something else also. Beauty is made to

15. Desmond, *Art and the Absolute*, chapter 6.

serve the lying and dissimulating—all in the name of the highest moral imperative, to sell to the customer, who is always right, another lie.

It is quite understandable why lovers of true beauty would hate this. What they love is being prostituted. But, of course, it is part of the power of beauty to beautify—and this is essential to human existence. It is important to remember how pervasive beauty is in human life. Recall how one half of the human population spends a lot of time looking at the other half with more than half an eye to beauty. I am thinking of the way man looks at woman and woman looks at man. Without beauty would we look at each other at all? Less intensely, but not insignificantly, even the most functional of relations (the useful) are lifted to another level by coming under the transforming power of beautification. If the useful were merely the useful and the beautiful only the beautiful and the twain should never meet, then use would degenerate into an ugly functionality within which humans could not make a home or find themselves at home. This would be a degradation of the useful into the merely instrumental. Meanwhile, the beautiful as useless would pine away in its preciousness, protecting us from intrusion by anything other, but now destined to vanish into the consumptive impotence of the beautiful soul.

I think we need to take a view broader than the instrumental exploitation of beauty. I would connect what looks like the slow eclipse of beauty in philosophical reflection with a certain *denaturing* of the human being in modernity. The human being does not find peace in the otherness of given creation, overreaches, overtakes, and reconfigures its givenness. Our *technē* becomes more ultimate than any given beauty of creation. This is usually presented as a great advance in some quarters. Finally, it is said, we are freed from natural necessity and can assert our power over the conditions of our life. We can forge ahead for the only prize purportedly worth fighting for—our own autonomy. It is notable how in modernity freedom has become perhaps the only uncontested value, while freedom in turn is very frequently identified univocally with autonomy. It remains contested as to exactly what true freedom is.

This denaturing has sometimes been attributed to or blamed on the notion of creation—God has made us lords of nature and by divine endowment we assert our overlordship. What is given serves us. We are not the steward who serves but the lord who dictates. Perhaps often we find ourselves caught in an equivocity here between an attitude of superiority sovereignty and one of generous, respectful service. Nevertheless, the accusation against the notion of divine creation is too equivocally formulated. The service of the steward is not the determination of the dictator. There is a just dominion that is not tyrannical domination.

As is agreed by many, the premoderns dwelled in the world with some sense of it as a cosmos. This is explicitly inseparable from the aesthetics of being, as the word "cosmos" (cosmetics) indicated—a well-wrought, harmoniously ordered whole—a thing of beauty. Recall the demiurgic art of Plato's god—he works the world as a work of art. One might say this is a matter of *technē*, but it is not a neutral imposition of form on matter. The fitness of the whole is in view. The demiurge as the best (*aristos*) makes the most beautiful (*kallistos*) cosmos possible (*Timaeus*, 29a). The demiurge looks to geometrical paradigms, but geometry seems subsumed into aesthetic and religious finesse for the beauty and goodness of the wrought cosmos. The cosmos is likened to "an *aesthetic god* that is an icon of the noetic."[16] "It is everyway necessary that the cosmos be an icon of something."[17] Geometry and finesse are twinned in the divine art. We might say that human beings are called to a certain finesse for immanence that attends to the beyond of finitude—finitude signed as divine art.

The order of nature in modernity seems tilted more and more towards a God in whom predominates the *esprit de géométrie* rather than the *esprit de finesse* (in Pascal's terms). One recalls the mechanism to which we are accustomed in earlier modernity. This is no cosmos, no beauty, and its aesthetics reveal merely secondary qualities. The aesthetic is not invested with ontological weight, or indeed with any sense of the sacred that we find in the sacramental universe of the medievals. We also find a kind of breach between being and the good. Our objectification of being purports to offer a neutralized thereness, while subjectivity as autonomous purports to be a source of value and indeed to invest things with what worth they possess. But beauty is the sister of the good, and the sister is even more subjectified than the good in this now-stripped-down cosmos. As Yeats put it: "Descartes, Locke, and Newton took away the world and gave us its excrement instead. Berkeley restored the world."[18] Leaving aside the interpretation of Berkeley, loss of the world/restoration of the world is somehow at stake in the eclipse of beauty, and the return of the light that shines on things.

16. *Timaeus*, 92c: *eikon tou noētou theos aisthētos.*

17. *Timaeus*, 29b: *pasa ananke tonde ton kosmon eikona tines einai.*

18. Yeats, *Explorations*, 325.

In this context, the reaction of Romanticism to Enlightenment is understandable. This was a reaction to the loss of the world by, so to say, a rampant *esprit de géométrie*. Enlightenment rationalism often went hand in hand with a deism that superficially granted a God beyond the immanent mechanism of nature, though at the price of making the immanent mechanism threadbare of divine intimacy. I would defend a form of superior transcendence, but there are forms of oppositional transcendence that want to safeguard divine transcendence and yet end up generating the opposite—the vanishing of God as transcendent. The king (now suitably modernized as a clock-maker) is secure in his high castle on the high hill, but a wall of brambles grows around the height, and nothing seems to be communicated any more to the sublunary world, and at a certain point of non-communication the silence turns us away from transcendence on high to immanence all around us. In this light one might see pantheism as an understandable reassertion of the signs of divinity in immanence itself—an effort to restore the world, to see something of the divine shine in and on it, or from it.

There are theological issues here into which I cannot go more fully, not least in connection with the sacramental sense of the world, assaulted alike by the religious iconoclasts and the scientistic secularizers. The religious iconoclast can share with the scientistic secularizer the domineering urge to reduce the equivocity of the religious image to imageless univocity.[19] Suspicion of the aesthetic can look on the image as the temptation of an idol, and the aesthetics of being can be devalued in consequence. While the iconoclast has an important justification in connection with the God beyond all aesthetic images, it is still the case that the emptied space produced by extreme iconoclasm can just as easily become the *focus of nothing*, as the focus of the God beyond all images. Protecting God from the aesthetic image can generate its own atheism. There is the fact too that, in the emptiness, other images can come to be generated, and these are not necessarily friendly to the God beyond all images. They blank out transcendence, but the hunger of the soul does not rest, and it reaches out into the emptiness, and alas the hungry soul tends to people it with images of *itself*, or even with monsters that spring forth from its own darkness. Out of itself can come not pure piety but also

19. If the imageless univocity of the scientistic is believed to come with the rational perfection of science, the imageless univocity of the iconoclast is held to come, say, in an assault on Catholic veneration of sacred images or supposedly "Papist worship" of images of the saints.

deconsecration, then alas desanctification, and then even the desecration of all that is glorious in the aesthetics of the given happening of creation. In desecrated creation the shine on things that might aesthetically tell of the divine is not only dulled but execrated.

The loss of the creation, coupled with the subjectification of the human being and the objectification of the given otherness of nature, readies the space for the release of a certain project of human autonomy. The work of autonomy, not the gift of unmasterable grace, is thought to become the engine and master of history. I see the shadow of this even in the moralization of the sublime with Kant, short-circuiting the religious possibilities of the sublime. After Kant and Hegel, a related secularization proceeds much more radically. There is a deep paradox here. The more art has proclaimed its autonomy from religion, the more it has tended to smuggle in earnest concern with an *incognito* sacrality, in order to sustain its own claims to ultimate seriousness. As I have detailed it elsewhere,[20] there is a displacement and migration of ultimacy from traditional religious form into the aesthetic. In all this the name of the religious becomes harder to utter, since in the regime of immanent autonomy, religion is thought to be too tainted with the bad repute of repressive heteronomy and old transcendence.[21]

Could one venture that there is a loss of exposure, so to say, to the flesh of things in modernity? As I implied before, our stress on human construction reflects how so many of us live in cities, where given creation and the otherness of its materiality always shows the stamp of our

20. Desmond, *Art, Origins, Otherness*, especially chapter 8, "Art and the Impossible Burden of Transcendence."

21. In the German infatuation with the Greeks from the latter part of the eighteenth century onwards, we find a hunger for rich (spiritualized) sensuousness in immanence. Is it because one was barred from going back to medieval Catholicism that pagan Greece became the shining beauty on the hill? This shine is as much a projection of the German lover of Greece as anything else. Yet it is testament to the impossibility of separating the religious and the artistic, though the name of religion might not always be uttered in this connection. After all, the Greeks were not atheists. As pagans they were religious, perhaps even too religious. *Kunstreligion*, religion in the form of art, is what Hegel called their form of religion. He also called it the "religion of beauty." We find something not entirely dissimilar in Wagner and Nietzsche and others. Nietzsche's hope for the renewal of tragic culture had a sacral side; it was not just merely aesthetic. A different liturgy was sought—an aesthetic pagan liturgy, so to say. One thinks of the *ersatz* liturgy of the Wagnerian opera—a sacrament without a consecrating god—with the opera as *Gesamtkunstwerk* creating itself as its own redeeming divinity, a kind of *causa sui - als ob* (*mar dhea*, as we say in Irish).

*techné*. We have already worked on it, and in it what comes back to us is only ourselves. There is a loss of the exposure to the otherness of creation, and undernourished for nature as other we tend to sentimentalize it—as if it too were like us and a grizzly bear could become a teddy-bear and be one's friend.[22] Of course, one is often a truer friend to it by letting it alone. We leave nothing alone.

Things as other are massively objectified, while we are just as hugely subjectified. This too is reflected in the way the otherness of things is held to an objectified standard, and then there is nothing in their beauty that answers to this standard, and hence beauty also must be handed over to the other side of the dualism, to subjectivity and its feel for things—to the side of so-called secondary qualities, as it was earlier put. One has to wonder if this objectifying mode of approach is still secretly embedded in our way of thinking—even when it is critiqued in the name of the aesthetic. We have not come back to the ontological robustness of the aesthetics of the happening of given creation, which cannot be completely fitted into an objectivizing or subjectivizing frame of things.

Is the eclipse of beauty, then, to be called a lunar eclipse? *We* become a hindering moon that comes between the sun and the light it shines on things? Remember how in Romantic and post-Romantic culture an excessive subjectivity, claiming (quasi-)religiously a kind of infinite inwardness, ceases to find itself aesthetically at home in given beauty as other to it. Its inwardness, as (quasi-)religiously infinite, exceeds all finite being, and no object, even one that is a beautiful formed whole, can stay its infinite restlessness and striving (*Streben nach dem Unendlichkeit*). But does the light this subjectivity claims to cast not, in fact, blind it to the finite beauty of given being? It seems to shine *on* things, but there is no shine *of* things. And so like a hindering moon, paradoxically, it takes the shine off things, and they sink into shadowy secondness. The infinitely restless subjectivity can find no rest in things, and indeed no rest in itself either. Any given beauty is not enough for it, just because it is given. And any beauty it constructs itself is only prelude to its own deconstruction.

22. See Werner Herzog's film, *Grizzly Man* (2006). Herzog seems to want to communicate the violence of amoral nature. Nature is not good, not evil, though often it is more like evil than good from *our* perspective. We are tempted to see something blind and merciless. But there is a kind of ecology of fittingness in the interchange of life and death, and one wonders if the amoral way of approaching things remains also too anthropocentric, all appearances notwithstanding.

I come back to something about the postmodern sublime: ostensibly a breach of humanistic self-satisfaction, and hence a rupture to excessive objectivism and subjectivism. But if postmodernism is more hyper-modernism or later modernism, one wonders sometimes if it is an accentuation of just the twin pillars of modernity, objectification to an extreme, subjectification to a matching extreme. Thus, we find together these two sides: on one hand, a tendency to reductionism in which the human presence seems to be absent (the death of the author, the death of man); on the other hand, a difficulty in seeing the aesthetic sources of origination in anything other than human making. Human constructions maybe testify to something other, something even inhuman. But given that we cannot name this other without circling back to ourselves, in practise the high priest remains the human being—even if a strange priest. As I put it above, the work remains the work of the city—but it is the work of the city of man rather than the city of God. The sun and the earth *both* grow shadowy in the eclipse. The hyper-reflection of the human to itself in the artificial city results in the loss of the human to itself in the infinitely multiplied reflections of itself, for in these infinitely multiplied reflections there seems no longer to be any original true self. Self-infinitization produces a false double of the divine in which, at the end, the divinity of the human itself goes under in its own self-proliferation. Can such proliferation and undergoing really be called creativity? Or do they too risk being the counterfeit doubles of creation?

## Beauty Given Again

Relevant to the matter under consideration is the question of the significance of a certain *givenness* to beauty. Givenness as such is a notion often rejected in modernity. Epistemologists speak of the "myth of the given," cultural theorists claim to resist the temptation to "naturalize" as "given" forms of life that are historical constructs, and so on. If there is any given, it does not count as significant till we reconfigure or reconstruct it in accord with our determination of significance or worth. Nothing is to be accepted as such unless we give it to ourselves. We call the shots. Just as the given order of creation is made problematic by attitudes to nature that would reconfigure the conditions of life in accord with our desire, so beauty as given is less well attended to in an ethos where we stress the constructive activity of the human being. And yet the givenness is notable in that there is something *striking* about beauty. A beautiful face, say, stops us, arrests us, and opens a porosity and receptivity on our part that is less a languid passivity as a being-taken-out-of-ourselves in relation to the face itself as beautiful. It calls us out of ourselves (*to kalon*, it has been suggested, is related to the call). In beholding something beautiful there is a kind of "beholding *from*": something is communicated to us. There is also in such beholding a resting in something worthy to be affirmed, indeed something worthy of a kind of festive consent and celebration. The offering of beauty is not simply a result of our activity—it comes to us. And hence perhaps it is inevitable with the triumph of subjectification, mentioned above, that there should be a kind of eclipse of beauty. But the power of beauty is to return that triumphant subject to a more primal receptivity

I would connect this receptivity with the *passio essendi*: patience of being, a *being given* to be, before there is an *endeavor* to be. Vis-à-vis creation, there is a coming to be before a becoming. A being, or beings, or processes of becoming, must *already* be, be already *given* to be, as coming to be before they participate or shape their own (self-)becoming. Creation does not effect its own coming to be, though beings created can contribute to the shaping of their own becoming, contribute to it by way of the power to become of the *conatus essendi*. Coming to be relates us back to a more original ontological porosity, where beauty most deeply strikes home. Recall how in connection with eros and beauty the Greeks talked of the arrows of Cupid, and a point I already noted in a previous reflection: they were right about *being struck*. But there is beauty beyond even the arrows of Cupid. The strike arouses the passion of being, and in that passion we may construct new images of beauty. But the *passio* of being is not just in what we construct in response to being struck. All our use of things is subtended by a more original gift of being to us, subtended by a more original opening to what gives itself for use. As we are made porous to what shines in the givenness, there is something beyond reduction, something indeed beyond both construction and deconstruction.

Being struck by what is beautiful—being struck has something of both a violence and a peace to it. We rub our eyes and seem to have been struck by nothing, for we cannot exactly fix what has struck us. At the same time, the replete singularity of the beautiful one before us fills us with delight. There is a shine from the other, as if something more flows from the other towards us, though again there is nothing there. And yet something passes into us, and we pass outside ourselves in a kind of stupor of ecstasy.

I have illustrated this more original porosity in connection with music, and though this is a wrought beauty, yet there is a giving in it that aroused the passion of being. Beauty, be it given or wrought, reopens the porosity of our being. The simple distinction between the given and the made does not help us much. One might ask, of course, if there is a given music of creation that has already sounded or called in our souls, before our souls even wake up to themselves. Music, one might say, is perhaps the most powerful art to return us to the porosity, while at the same time moving a *passio essendi*, prior to any rationalization of the movement of desire, and exceeding complete self-determination of it. We do not first move, we are moved.

I think again of Kant's revealing comparison of music to the perfumed handkerchief, how the perfume spreads everywhere indeterminately and one has no choice about being subjected to it.[23] The words of poetry, open to more public, determinate scrutiny, can be made more or less determinate; they seem relatively controllable. He does not quite like the way music moves us before we move ourselves. It sweetly violates our autonomous self-determination. Music comes upon us, steals upon us, as it were. It moves us without asking prior approval of our reason or our will. We find ourselves caught up and moved. It is beyond rational will. Music communicates with some intimate in our being that is responsive prior to and exceeding the sway of determinate reason or will. Kant responds to this as only an intrusion we have not sought, and though we find it hard to resist it, he seems unhappy with its impertinence to autonomy.

Notice that there is nothing here that one can absolutely fix with univocal determinacy. There is indeed determinacy, often very intricate, but it is communicated in the passage of a dynamic forming that has a kind of wholeness to it but it is not a closed whole. Beauty communicates an open wholeness, or opening of transcending in a surplus wholeness that cannot be enclosed in itself. It is what it is in addressing what is other—the address to the other, and perhaps more elementally the address of the other that is communicated in the aesthetic whole itself. There is a kind of double relativity in this dynamic forming. The opening in the relativity recalls us to the more primal porosity of our being. In

23. Kant, *Critique of the Power of Judgment*, § 53.

this porosity once again the passion of being is called forth. This is the basis of the disproportion that excites the proportionate towards something beyond the order of merely finite form. Perhaps here we might find a *permeable threshold* between the beautiful and the sublime? Perhaps here also one might say that beauty is an offering of something *hyperbolic* in the immanent, a transcendence that yet is offered in what remains at home with itself—at home with itself in arousing a not-being-at-home, and a movement beyond self.

To reiterate a point I made in chapter 1: if we were to speak here of the passion of transcendence, we would have to note a certain doubleness of the "of." Is it just of our transcending—which then comes back to itself and the whole binds itself to itself? Or is it of a transcendence that arouses our transcending—not our opening to transcendence but our *being opened by* transcendence as other to us? I think we are enjoined in this second direction. Everything about beauty, in view of the erotics of our being, turns us inside out, upside down. But upside down is downside up, for it carries us as upended to what is above us.

The open wholeness of beauty, in the language I use, testifies to a being in the *metaxu*, a being between. The beautiful as given, as well as the art work as a wrought beauty, offer a kind of between-space for transcendence. Of course, once we think more closely on the idea of an open whole it is not at all a mere contradiction between the closed and the unclosed. Every being, though it exists as an endowed singular integrity, has its being communicatively in relation to beings other than itself. It is in this sense an open whole. Something of this comes especially to manifestation with the human being. We are marked by a singular integrity that exists as just what it is only in being beyond itself in relation to what is other—it is openly whole and transcending. Something beautiful pleasingly calls us in its open wholeness into the passion of transcending that cannot be completely finitized. This we find in the given beauty of the aesthetics of happening. The beautiful artwork also gives us some image of this, such that neither simple imitation nor sheer self-creativity does justice to the double relativity of other-relation and self-relation. The surplus equivocity of the beautiful and of the art work communicate aesthetically this double relativity.

If we return to the order of creation we would have to speak of the aesthetics of happening, but "aesthetics" would not just have a bearing on our senses as subjective epistemic powers. Aesthetics would bear on the sensuous showing of the happening of being, as itself saturated with a radiance or shine, more than any reductionist analysis into this univocal determinacy or that, and more than any expression of our own powers of self-determination. The aesthetics of happening is *of happening*—not just of our sensory and intellectual faculties, nor indeed of our power at all. We are moved to affirm that this "is" beautiful but this "is" of beauty reveals a transcendence to the thing itself. But again what is given there as other is not determinable as a mere fixable this or that. There is an *overdeterminacy* at work in what shows itself as beautiful—this is not simply an indeterminacy, but a "too muchness" that, while determinate and not hostile to our efforts at self-determination, exceeds all univocal determinability and our claims as self-determining beings to be its ultimate measure.

The point with the shine of beauty, then, is not a matter of the univocal certainty of a scientistic and geometric sort. It is more a matter of finesse for the overdeterminate which communicates to us in the sensuous ambiguity of aesthetic happening. This finesse is a matter of the reading of signs, of designs as signs that are not a matter of the fixation of rigid univocal orders. There is an aesthetics of order as well as a geometrics. It is not the case that geometric order necessarily excludes aesthetic order. I think of William Blake's great poem that speaks of the tiger, "burning bright, in the forest of the night," and of the hazardous question it poses for us: "What immortal hand or eye dare frame thy fearful symmetry?"[24] "Fearful symmetry": this brings us to pause on a hazardous threshold. There is order, yes, symmetry, but it brings fear, perhaps even awe. And yet too fear of the Lord is the beginning of wisdom. Atheists of a neutralized nature deconsecrate the symmetry and do not feel the fearfulness. Pascal did—and was terrified. Creation is bound up with glory and terror. Even if we cry out, like Rilke, to the angel, we know that beauty too is the beginning of terror. Job is silent before the Voice who does not answer questions but multiplies unfathomable perplexities. Questions are answered by unanswerable questions. Where were you when I laid down the foundations of the heavens? Have you descended to the springs of the sea or walked in the unfathomable deep? Have the gates of death been revealed to you? Could you lead the Leviathan by the nose? Or keep it on a string like a song-bird for your maidens? These are questions

24. The opening stanza is: "Tyger, Tyger burning bright/In the forests of the Night/ What immortal hand or eye/Could frame thy fearful symmetry?" The last stanza repeats this opening stanza, except the last line now is: "What immortal hand or eye/ *Dare* frame thy fearful symmetry?" (emphasis added).

from the hyperbolic dimension of the overdeterminate. They are from the hyperbolic and about the hyperbolic, and themselves so hyperbolic, no determinate science with an order made to human measure could answer them truly. It could answer, but it would still find itself in the "too muchness" that could never at all be diminished. This is something disproportionate.

And hence one must query the search for an order that is only proportionate to us. Creation tells against this. This is not to deny, as beauty so powerfully witnesses, that there is an affinity between us and orders in things. Leibniz was not entirely wrong. But the harmony is exceeded by something more than our measure. There is a permeable threshold between beauty and the sublime.

Beauty witnesses to the beyond of wholeness. And there can be both glory and horror in the intimate things, in the small things. Or religiously put: creation itself testifies to an open wholeness that tells of something beyond all finite wholes: the God beyond the immanent whole.[25] Paradoxically that sense of the beyond can be communicated in a tiny particular. I recall a confession from Whittaker Chambers: atheist that he was, on seeing the ear of his new-born child he was struck with the conviction: God is.[26]

## The Shine on Things

I would like to conclude with a meditative reflection on beauty and the shine on things. Rather than a univocal argument or a linear exposition,

25. See Desmond, *God and the Between*, chapter 12, "God beyond the Whole: On the Theistic God of Creation."

26. Being struck: this is an example I recall from Whittaker Chambers's autobiography *Witness*, xlv. He was a card-carrying communist, with the programmatic atheism that went with that. He saw the ear of his new-born infant and was immediately struck by the thought: God exists. The birth of his first child was "the most miraculous thing that had ever happened in my life." I would say there is a kind of revelatory power to the beauty of such surplus immediacy: a too-muchness in almost nothing; something more. It was not the functional design of the ear that struck him—this is not an inference, an argument from design, though it may be the intimate source of this argument which itself becomes orphaned in the development of the argument. There is a strike of beauty, a being struck, and a being called out—and nothing is the same afterwards. The same is the same and yet not at all the same. One not only looks differently, not only do things look different, but as the same world looks different, one lives in the world differently.

I would like to call on the aesthetic suggestiveness of this metaphorical way of speaking.

I note the word "on." We think of one thing on another, and it is a plurivocal notion. We say: a mood of despair lay *on* the gathering; the wall collapsed *on* him; he was *on* top of her; peace was *on* the sea. The shine on things is more like the last. On: but in a mode of pervading presence—a presencing, nevertheless, impossible to fix or pin down.

The shine on things is not just a matter of the shine *of* things. For then "of" would mean a confinement to the things, as if they possessed the shine and it was theirs and theirs alone. It is not that there is not a shine of things, but the shine on things is more than that.

There is a certain radiance that at first might seem to come from things, but that more truly comes to things—it comes from things because it has first come to them. They have first been endowed with what comes to shine before that endowment itself comes to shine from them.

This sense of radiance is connected with beauty. For beauty has much to do, as we suggested, with a certain radiant wholeness. Wholeness reminds us of a harmony that is formed, but something of the energy of forming, or coming to form is in the radiant whole itself. And so there is nothing merely static about it, even though there is a kind of repose about the beautiful thing. If there is such a repose, it is the poise of an energy rather than the going to sleep of a dynamism. Radiant beauty is this double thing: in repose and entirely energetic, a reverent stillness and an appealing motion.

What shines on things? One might perhaps give three main answers. First, *things themselves* shine; second, *we* shine on things; third, (if I may be permitted to speak religiously) *God* shines on things. I know this is too bald for some philosophers, but sometimes we should not beat around the bush. Sometimes beating around the bush with much philosophical fuss serves only to hide the fact that, for all the beating, there is nothing in the bush.

The first answer—things themselves shine—is important: there is a radiance to the things themselves—a thereness that is not valueless or neutral—a givenness that is alive with qualitative worth—a singular concretion of the good of the "to be." But there is nothing self-enclosed or self-contained about this shine of things. Quite to the contrary, the more we dwell with the shine *of* things, the more we come to wonder about the shine *on* things. The things themselves are there, but they are not self-derived. They become from other things, but all the things carry the mark of not being self-derived. They tell of *coming to be*—beyond all the complications of their becoming themselves, from this or that antecedent source. Coming to be: the shine of the idiocy of being, the marvel "that they are at all."[27] If this idiocy does shine, it is not a merely absurd idiocy—there is something of a more benign idiocy. The shine on things, all idiotic, comes on things from what is beyond all things.

That said, it is still a very important vocation today to recuperate the shine of things—given the objectification, the reification, the reduction to valueless thereness so pervasive in western modernity. We are called perhaps not just to recuperate but to glorify. Think on the witness of pure praise in the poetry of Czesław Milosz: "I stare and stare. It seems I was called for this: To glorify things just because they are."[28] Pure praise is graced consent beyond horror. Though we cannot do it, come to it alone, we can try to be in readiness for it.

The second answer—we shine on things—is one that has been quite pervasive in modernity. We shine on things because we are the source of the light. Then things are as just above described—valueless therenesses, but we invest them with value, we project into them what otherwise is not to be found at all in the things themselves. The world of things remains in its dull thereness till we enliven it with our energies, our projections. Of course, taken in one direction, this means that there is no shine of things and indeed no shine on things, if we withdraw our light. The things are darkness, we are the light shining in the dark.

This might sound marvellous, but it means there is no community between us and things, or between us and creation. There is no creation, we are said to be creative. The view is widespread, but lurking in it is a kind of nihilism—without our shining, there would be no radiance of intelligibility or truth or good or beauty in things. One thinks of the constructivist claims made for cognition—we know what we make—until

27. More fully on the specific sense of what I mean by the idiocy of being see, for instance, chapter 3 of Desmond, *Perplexity and Ultimacy*; also Desmond, *The Intimate Universal*, chapter 5.

28. Miłosz, *Conversations*, 144, from "Blacksmith Shop" in *New and Collected Poems 1931–2001*, 503. Interesting that the bellows of the blacksmith blows the air that feeds the fire that makes malleable the iron that allows the smith to shape the matter into working tool or shoe. It is not quite God kissing the mud and making a living spirit, but the directed force of the air vitalizes the fire that enables our making. Behold and glorifying: not robbing the fire like the thieving Titan, Prometheus; in the poem a boy (unstated, one surmises) unshod (stated) "At the entrance, my bare feet on the dirt floor,/Here, gusts of heat . . . ."

we shine, until we project and make, there is no light there in the things. One might even try to erect it into a revolutionary principle. Think of the Copernican revolution in the Kantian style: this has to do with the shine on things, but there is no shine of things, and we, the active constructive knowers, are the sun that shines on what otherwise lacks light.

If *we* become the sun, this is very un-Copernican, I would say. The Copernican view is heliocentric, not anthropocentric. Plato is heliocentric—is Copernican in that sense. The sun is the *analogon* of the good, Plato says (*Republic*, 508c). But the sun shines on things. It is not simply we who shine. In the Kantian way, we are "suns"—but we are strangely sterile suns, since we do not know the shine of things (only mere appearances), and we do not know the shine on things, except it be our own. Where is the sun in Kant that shines on all things, ourselves included? If one answered that Kant has his moral God, this is an "as if" God. How does an "as if" sun shine on all things?

But we are moons not suns: we shine with a reflected light—and when the other sun sets, the moon has no light of its own to cast. In modernity generally and after Kant especially, we are moons who pretend to be suns. We do not grant the borrowed nature of our light. We claim for ourselves the privilege of being the sole source. We are moons who purport to be "as if" suns. Coming between the earth and the sun, we occlude the sun above us, and create a lunar eclipse, and the earth grows dark.

This is reflected also in the understanding of beauty and its eclipse. It is neither the shine of things nor the shine on things—it is our shine on things, which as other to us, hardly count as things—they finally count as mirrors in which we come to know ourselves more lucidly. There are no beautiful things, there are no sublime things; there are occasions in which we cater for the harmony of our faculties of imagination and understanding, occasions where the seeming excess of the scene other to us, by a detour of seemingly humiliating the human being, serves rather to elevate the human being even more, beyond all measure relative to the things of nature themselves.[29] We are, so to say, subrepting *als ob* "suns," which darken further our own lunar finitude. Afloat in spaces of

29. I am thinking again of the way Kant describes the sublime as entailing a *subreption*—a subreption, as he says, attributes to the object what is properly *of us*. Hence, it can be recuperated *for us*, from its alienation in another (to speak Hegelese). The otherness qua otherness does not ultimately count but serves as the occasion of a mediating circuit of self back to self.

emptiness, spellbound by ourselves, we rotate in the nocturnal orbit of ourselves. This is to make a sham of the shine on things.

The third answer looks to a source of shining more than things and more than ourselves. Plato calls it the good, the monotheistic religions call it God. It is transhuman and more than a natural thing or the complete totality of things. Who or what is it? In order to approach it, I think we have to grant two things at least: that things do shine and that there is a light on them; that the human being is not the creator of this light, though we may participate in the gift of this light—be "creative" in a relative sense, while not being the creator. "Shining" may not always describe radically enough what is at issue here: perhaps "creating" is a better word—and all that "creation" entails in a metaphysical and theological sense, especially in regard to the *given* beauty of creation and the *endowed* creativity of the human being.

This third response also means that one has to grant the worry about *idolatry*. The worry about idolatry is not the same as the enjoinment of iconoclasm. The idol is not the same as the icon, as Marion challengingly argues.[30] We must attend on the icon, as well as the idol, with the appropriate religious *finesse*. Creation may be God-given, but it is not God. As evidencing a kind of fertile equivocity, shining can be potentially duplicitous.[31] What glitters is not always gold.[32] There is fool's gold even though it gleams and bewitches.[33] The iconoclast displays a suspicion concerning the aesthetics of happening generally, and this is in part understandable since there is a kind of equivocity constitutive of the aesthetic. This is one reason why we require something like a religious poetics of nature

30. *Inter alia* see Marion, *The Idol and Distance*; Marion, *In Excess.*

31. One thinks of how in German *Schein* carries something of the meaning of dissembling appearance, *Erscheinung* a more positive sense of appearance, a doubleness of which, for instance, Hegel makes some dialectical use.

32. See Ross, *Gifts Glittering and Poisoned.* The title of the book is a phrase of mine, and I responded to the book in "On Festival, Ecstasy, and Masquerade."

33. On a plea for a retrieval of the Greek gods without God, see Dreyfus and Kelly, *All Things Shining.* Is this plea for a renewed polytheism credible? Do its authors religiously believe in the Greek gods, or is the matter only *aestheticized religion without religion*—in Hegel's terms, *Kunstreligion* without true conviction of *religious* reverence? (One sometimes wonders if postmodern "polytheism," like Lyotard's, for instance, is paganism without the blood, an "as if" polytheism" that nobody believes in a truly religious sense.) If the title of this book of Dreyfus and Kelly (*All Things Shining*) recalls the closing lines of Terrence Malick's 1998 film, *The Thin Red Line*, for a theological-metaxological interpretation of all things shining, see Simpson, "All Things Shining: Desmond's Metaxological Metaphysics and *The Thin Red Line*."

as much as a geometry, an aesthetic hermeneutics as much as a dianoetic science. This would be in the services of finesse for the metaphysical and theological dimensions of creation that strike us outside the frame of geometric univocity. But neither a poetics nor hermeneutics as reading signs can deliver the precise univocity so demanded by the scientific ideal. Forms of scientism fetishize this univocity and, oddly, they can be guilty of their own idolatry in demanding from the image what the image cannot give. There can be idolatries of theory as well as of paint and sound. An idol can be made of concepts as well as wood. Scientistic theory can falsely invest the finite with the ultimacy of the infinite. Is this not something we have to reckon with in every claim of the divine to reveal itself? Revelation is not the evaporation of the mystery, but its shining in a non-reductive way. The hyperbolic is a showing of the mystery that carries mystery in showing itself. There is no dissolution of the mystery, though it is named and indeed more truly praised in wonder and rejoicing.

It seems to me that an incarnational religion must rejoice in the glory of creation as aesthetic happening—notwithstanding the risk of aesthetic idolatry. There is also scientistic, philosophical, and indeed religious idolatry—is not all idolatry finally religious?—and hence even aesthetic idolatry pays its tribute to what it mimics. This is part of the hazard of participating in the cooperation of creation in its becoming. The given beauty of creation and the endowed creativity of the human being together point to this. We sing in the sublunary world, but the source of the song comes to us from above the moon.

# 4

## Soul Music and Soul-less Selving

### Why Soul Music and Not Self Music?

WHILE THERE IS SUCH a thing as "soul music," there is no such thing as "self music." Why is this? What is the difference between the two? And is not the language of "self" all pervasive in our cultures, while the language of soul seems to have gone into eclipse, especially among the more modernly educated persons? Why is this? What might be at issue in the music of the soul in soul music, and the music-less self without soul. "Oh self, self, self. At every turn nothing but self"—so expostulates Charles Dickens's Martin Chuzzlewit.[1] And yet for all this all-pervasiveness, why no self music and why soul music, music of the soul? It is true that Walt Whitman's celebrated poem is called "Song of Myself."[2] But the song of

1. Dickens, *The Life and Adventures of Martin Chuzzlewit*, 95: Chuzzlewit has just burned a new will in exasperation after an exchange with Picksniff—everyone wants his money. Is Chuzzlewit immune from self, self, self? For he goes on to say: "Heaven help us, we have much to answer for! Oh self, self, self! Every man for himself and no one for me!" Then the narrator offers the thought: "Universal self. Was there nothing of it in these reflections, and in the history of Martin Chuzzlewit, on his own showing?" Of course, Dickens had a genius for names, for the signature of souls, so to say, even when to all appearances, there is nothing but self, self, self. In his feel for the music of demotic English, he also had great "negative capability." He referred to himself as the "great imitator," and would mimic his characters in a mirror, rush back to his desk and put them then down in words; as if he had no self, and yet was the fertile place where selves with soul come to expression—even his soul-less selves have souls.

2. Opening lines: "I celebrate myself, and sing myself,/And what I assume you

myself, when it is truly singing is soul music—it is not just self, self, self. We speak of having a soul-mate, and there is something beautiful about this. But having a *self-mate* (if one were to speak that way), is there not something out of tune about this? And so the question again: Why soul music and no self music? Why, even when there is a song of self without the music of the soul, might there be no singing selving at all?

A first remark: soul music is associated with certain styles of black singing. Ray Charles has said: "Some people tell me I'd invented the sounds they called soul—but I can't take any credit. Soul is just the way black folk sing when they leave themselves alone."[3] Leave themselves alone: get out of the way and let soul pass through . . . .

One huge thing worth noting is the history of suffering of such a people—a suffering endured, yet turned into song, and indeed transformed by singing. One need only think of Gospel music, and how out of Gospel music so many other forms of passionate, pathos-filled, and vigorous singing emerge to branch off into the wide world.[4] Blues: the color of a *soul;* not the experience of a *self.*[5]

Speaking of color, I cannot help but draw attention to the category of "blue-eyed soul." The eyes are the windows of the soul, it is said, but what is blue-eyed soul? A soul that is blue, a soul colored blue? One might suggest that the term "blue-eyed soul" refers us to an *entirely non-dualistic* way of speaking, since crucial features of the body, the focal features of the face, the eyes, are in the soul, *are* the soul as embodying itself, singing out itself to us. Blue-eyed soul is the name for black music not sung by a black but by a white singer who sings black. The voice of the singer rings forth as black though the singer is white. Rings forth from a world that in one way is inimitable but that in another way can be shared and, more, can be intimately lived together, from within out. The source of the voice is more than the white surface of the skin. It is *soul.* I admit many now might cringe in political correctness at this use of words like "white" and "black," charged are they can be with social and political agendas.[6] But

---

shall assume,/For every atom belonging to me as good belongs to you."

3. See Cousineau, *Soul*, 1.

4. Of course, the ways of the world are also exploitative and Martha Bayles in *Hole in Our Soul* shows us how soul can be for sale, indeed the many ways soul-music was often sold out. Her fine book is a celebration of the soul of the music and a lamentation for its abuse.

5. See James Baldwin's celebrated story, *Sonny's Blues.*

6. Think of the blue-eyed rhetoric of the white music of the Aryan nation. Think

blue-eyed soul is not an agenda but a singing from a space of being, *prior to* and *beyond* such agendas.

My favorite blue-eyed soul singer from a youth not entirely misspent: Dusty Springfield. With such a singer how could one lose one's soul or squander its longing? Growing up in England of Irish Catholic stock, her real name was Mary Isobel Catherine Bernadette O'Brien.[7] What a singer! When one looks at some of her performances on YouTube a thrill along the spine still comes with some of her singing . . . there is an entirely singular signature, and in that sense she is self, herself and nothing but herself—but it is not the self of the singer that communicates the spread of the thrill—it is *soul* . . . blue-eyed soul. There is loss, loneliness, lament, appeal, longing, amazement. The voice raises the banal to the exalted, making more of the less, transforming, ensouling all things simple and deep, intimate, heart-broken, and sultry. "I close my eyes and count to ten, and when I open them you're still here; I close my eyes and count again, I can't believe that you're still here . . . ." This is a song of the primal astonishment of being in love, astonishment before the being of the beloved. The ordinary perception of seeing and not seeing is disturbed and disarrayed—and yet the seeing is more fully completed in being again and again surprised by the loved one, simply as there before one. The song sings the incredible miracle of love surprised.

Enough singing the praises of Dusty, and back again to the question: Why then is there soul music and not self music? Or are we entirely to give free range to self language in a tuneless modality—hearing nothing of beauty, singing nothing of soul? Can we relate soul and self in a manner that also restores to selving something of its soul, something too of its music? Is there a music of soul that spreads itself abroad even more universally and soulfully than soul music and in which soul music participates?

## Soul-lessness

Soul, under many names, has echoes of a primal word in many cultures: *atman*, *psuche*, *anima*, *Geist*, *nephesh*, *prana*, *duk*, breath, the principle of life. It is difficult to define, and yet resists reduction. Even in an age of

---

of such black-face minstrels as Al Jolson, now not to be respectably heard.

7. See Bartlett, *Dusty*.

science and technology, these ways of speaking persist. People will not forfeit their souls easily.

Nevertheless, if the soul has lost its meaning for many (Cavell speaks of "soul-blindness"), there are diverse factors involved in this.[8] I think that certainly attention must be paid to the ambition to *univocally determine all being* that has expanded in modernity into a project claiming to be on a par with the whole. I want to suggest that there is more to soul than can be made the object of such univocal determination. Being more, it is also not indeterminate; there is something overdeterminate to it, in excess of determination and self-determination. There is a mystery to it, in the end. Moreover, the project of determination passes seamlessly with a project of self-determination, and hence the huge presence of the language of self coexists with a view where there is nothing so absent as self. Soul suffers in the projects of determination and self-determination. We need other ways to think of selving to allow soul to communicate out of its overdeterminate mysteriousness.[9]

Relative to the project of determination and determinability: I am thinking of the objectification of being, wherein all that is is determined to be an object of scientific investigation and possible technological exploitation. The qualitative textures of things do not count in this project of universal quantification, this *mathesis universalis*. Of course, if things are massively objectified, this goes with the huge subjectification of the human being, the "self," as it will come to be known. Which comes first: the subjectification or the objectification? Since objectification is a project of the subject, there is a sense in which the subjectification is prior, even though this may not appear so at the outset. We make things objective, but changes in ourselves then set in motion other changes, not only to things other to us but also in how we relate to ourselves, how we understand ourselves. One of these changes has to do with the de-souling of nature as other to us (following the objectification), and with this the creeping soul-lessness of the ensuing self (following the subjectification).

8. See Barrett, *Death of the Soul*.

9. What I say here has some relevance to the recently debated question: What comes after subjectivity? I have spoken of this in Desmond, "Agapeic Selving and the Passion of Being." There I also reflect on the language of throwing, *jacere* as in pro-ject, ob-ject, sub-ject, intersub-ject: this is not the language of soul but a version of the *conatus essendi* that covers over the porosity of being as the matrix of souling—and truer selving.

We find this twinning of objectification and subjectification in the Cartesian language of the *res extensa* and the *res cogitans*. The extended thing is determined by the thinking thing, and then the thinking thing is subjectified. As subjectified the thinking thing does not tap into its root in nature: it is over against nature, it is above nature, determining it. It is feathering its own nest of self-determination, and perhaps not feathering it but fouling it. And then we find self, self, self: self circulating around self. We might say that the univocalizing on the two sides, the subject and object, hides a flight from the equivocity of soul music, and indeed any possibility of an ensouled world (*anima mundi*). In addition, there is the taking over of what the ancients took as the key mark of soul, namely as principle of motion, as self-moving. This now is driven in the direction of autonomy (self-motion) and self-determination. I would venture that the reason why an entire configuration of human being as autonomous did not earlier emerge had nothing to do with the absence of freedom but with the fact that it was not evident that to be free was to be autonomous, and autonomous in connection with determinability and univocalization. *In actu* there was too much of porosity to othernesses that did not enter the self-circling of autonomy. Modern autonomy is a construction of freedom erected on the basis of soul-less selving and the soul without music.

The soul is sent underground in this, or sent beyond "nature," beyond the body. It is not there as participating in the body of being—on the surface of things. For on the surface there is an aesthetic communication of depth and surface. The body is a singing word—it is there where the first languages find utterance. Here we find a certain separation of body and soul that makes the body into a neutral thereness, and the soul into the ghost in the machine. There is then no soul music of the body; no musical bodying of the soul; no wording the body. We become deaf to what Vico heard: song as the first language.

I want to stress at the outset that the loss of the soul in the vocabularies of science and philosophy does not obviate the persistence of expressions of the soul in our existential lives. What other kind of life is there finally, if not existential? We do not live in theories. We should take this persistence (of the expressions of soul) very seriously as thinkers. The theorist is not himself or herself a theory. I have argued earlier (chapter 2) in connection with life that the surface is a threshold of communication with the deepest; the threshold is a saturated surface, for there sur-faces what communicates itself. This is like the face of another: absolutely there, and yet there as a mystery beyond subjectification and objectification. One can be intimately in communication with this person, this before-one-present mystery in the sur-face that faces one. There is no need of a dualism of surface and depth, outer and inner—the outer is the uttering of the inner, the inner is the intimacy of the outer communicated. The sur-face is the threshold of communication where the mystery of singularly embodied being is offered. I will not repeat the arguments I offered in chapter 2 in favor of a way that is neither objectivizing nor subjectivizing with respect to life, but *mutatis mutandi* these considerations also have relevance to the enigmatic persistence of soul.

There is no need to have a negative view of scientific findings, but philosophically one cannot take these as the acme of truth. They are truths formulated in a well-determined framework, which itself is configured according to inclusions and exclusions, that is to say, in abstraction from the full overdeterminacy of given being as such.[10] The framework is set forth with as much univocal precision as possible, but, as the word "precision" suggests, there is a *cut* (*scisio:* scissors) in the fullness of the given, a cut that, as abstraction, is manipulable and determinable in a way that the full overdeterminacy is not—for all determinations ultimately derive from it as the original matrix of being and intelligibility. Manipulation is itself a cut—cut out from, perhaps cut off from, the fullness of the overdeterminacy. (The phenomenologist makes the point sometimes in terms of the *Lebenswelt.*) What I have called the saturated surface of things hints at a less abstracted figuring forth of the fullness of the overdeterminacy. The view is that what flowers forth in human existence, apart from any prior permission from a scientific scheme, can be immensely revealing about the truth of the matter. So even if scientific discourse has dispensed with

10. I begin to suffer from glaucoma, and sometimes what I see is a blob, more or less distinct, but more indistinct than earlier. I might take these blobs for what is there, but I know there is more sharp determinacy there, since I have seen it. Yet the other conclusion is not warranted: namely, that what I see is an indeterminacy which I make determinate. To the contrary, the sharp determinacy is saturated—it is surplus to what I could ever determine; it is overdeterminate not indeterminate—and if I were to see by a more powerful light, and if my eyes were up to it, I might see more of the overdeterminacy, but I would not see *all* that is there. (St. Augustine is the patron saint of sore eyes, as well as of theologians, printers, and brewers, but can he help me here?) The blob seems indeterminate, but I have seen more, and know it is not such a blob at all. Think of the refreshing of a landscape after a heavy rain, and the same determinacies shine with a new freshness, as if a new light fell on them. One might be graced by sight, by access of the light and see the same things but see them in this other light; but what is there is no less an overdeterminacy for us, not an indeterminacy in itself.

the soul, the issuing forth in life of such a happening as soul music can be of great importance in communicating something true(r) about soul.

There are different pathways to different truths, and the pathway of science may not at all be the right one when it comes to soul. (The same point applies to rational psychology, as I will indicate below.) The pathways through music, art, religion, the ordinary ways of talking, may be the truer ways. In that regard, what perhaps we need to do is not offer a scientific theory; it is to search out traces, signs, reminders of something, once named soul, exceeding determination and self-determination. No scientific certainty can be offered in such a probing exploration. More often than not, metaphorical, imagistic ways of speaking have to be invoked, not because of an evasion of thought, but because the appropriate thought of soul must necessarily clothe itself in metaphorical and analogical likenesses. The saturated surfaces of things are signs communicating of living realities like soul. Hence, the notably metaphorical character of quite a bit of, say, the *Phaedo*.[11]

## Souling: From Animation to Reification

I will return to selving below, but I want to illustrate the loss of the soul in modernity by looking briefly at Aristotle's vision, contrasting it with the reification of soul that occurs after Descartes. It might seem more appropriate to contrast Plato and Descartes as offering two forms of dualism. There is a tendency in this direction in Plato, though there is more at play in Plato, and if there is dualism it is not of the same sort as in Descartes. But that is a tale for another time, though I will return below to the musical Socrates on the vigil of death.

With Aristotle, as with many of the ancients, it is the living being and its unity, as well as its power of moving itself, that is centrally at stake. The soul is not some dematerialized stuff haunting the grosser stuff of the body. Soul is in the deepest intimacy of the living being and on the outermost surface of its bodily communication. It is hard to describe the intimacy of this unity without risking, in modern-wise, some kind of reduction to unfinessed materialism. Much of our modern materialism takes form according to the heritage of the objectifying-subjectifying

11. Though there is our need for dialectical argumentation, there is also our need for myth; see *Phaedo* 114d. Also *Phaedrus* 246a: to speak of the Idea of soul would be an entirely divine and blessed discourse, nevertheless it is within human power to describe the soul in a figure (or likeness/icon: *eikōn*).

dualism already suggested, but Aristotle's unity of soul and *soma* is in a different metaphysical space, reflecting a different ontological ethos and dwelling in the world than the more typical modern one. The ensouled being is a living integrity, even though it can be marked by a plurality of powers. Soul shows itself in the pluripotent integrity of the living being that is and becomes itself. The powers are revealed in how it is, how it does itself, how it goes and utters itself. The soul is the original of the powers, and in some beings the original pluralization of powers is richer than in others. Hence, Aristotle's fruitful scheme of the vegetative, animal, and rational souls. In all cases, our attention is drawn to a dynamic integrity of being, which displays a pluralization of powers, up to the instance of beings manifesting themselves in rational powers.

The soul is the living self-pluralizing integrity. Soul is in the body and enfolds body in its manifest materiality, and so too the body is in the soul: there is a rich immanence that cannot be either dualized absolutely or materialistically reduced. The ensouled integrity is also ecstatic as well as self-relating—it is out beyond itself in communication with what is other; and yet in being out beyond, it is a holding of itself together in that dynamic integrity of being that it is.[12] See the plant out beyond itself in the flower turning to the sun, later folding into itself at dark; and yet in turning out and turning in relative to what is other, it is always itself. Consider the animal's mobility: witness to an increased range of power, marking the spread of its self-transcendence, as not rooted in one place, like the plant; and yet in this spread, the animal *is itself* in its sensitive and sensible self-transcendence. And most of all with the rational being, the being of logos, we find the being out beyond itself and yet entirely intimate to its own integrity of being. There are the famous enigmatic sayings in Aristotle's *De Anima*: somehow the soul is everything (431b, 21–22); *nous* is the power to be and become all things (430a14–17). I find these famous sayings (echoed by Aquinas: intellect as *potens omnia facere et fieri*) to be very important for our music of the soul. For music, in its fluid resonance, is like the water of Thales. In one way, water is everything in being able to take on all forms, and yet in another way it is nothing in that it is never there if we try to fix it as one frozen form. I would not say it is a nothing and an everything (in *posse*) just as an indeterminacy awaiting determination, and self-determining. I would

12. Joe Sachs gets at something of this in his translation of *entelecheia* as "being-at-work-staying itself," in *Aristotle's On the Soul and On Memory and Recollection*, 189–90.

say it is an overdeterminacy—more than everything determinate and self-determining, and nothing as enabling the determinate and the self-determining.[13] A potency that is a plenipotency is not a mere potential but already a kind of fullness (*plenum*) and hence not just an indeterminacy. Because it is a plenipotency, it can be a pluripotency. I will connect this below with the porosity of being.

Aristotle's is a marvelous thinking of the soul. I notice that he situates his reflections on the soul as part of *physics*. Of course, the sense of the physical (*ta physika*) here is not the mechanical order of earlier modernity when the soul comes to be put in question. *Physis* as *natura* is as much *natura naturans* as *natura naturata*, nature in its overdeterminate power of becoming, nature as determinately natured (which need not mean mechanically determined). The soul in relation to *physis* cannot be thought of as a dematerialized spook. What nature means here is not the objectified concatenation of centers of effective power that we find in the modern version. It is emergent, it is growing, it is blossoming, so well described by the twentieth-century Aristotelian, Heidegger.[14] It is the matrix of the self-becoming of beings, beings that are more than ontological centers of *becoming*, since to be at all they have to have *come to be*—given to be before they can begin to become themselves, or give themselves to themselves. Determination and self-determination always derive from sources more primordial and not to be described as just determinate or self-determining.

But let us now look, again briefly, at what becomes of the soul in modernity, and Descartes is the familiar and obvious paradigm. The movement is from *animation to reification*, and the reification marks

13. See Emily Dickinson's poem, "The Brain—is wider than the Sky—." Should we perhaps not say, with a bow to Aristotle: "The Soul—is wider than the Sky—?"

14. See William James's "Concerning Fechner." On Fechner himself, see Fechner, *Religion of a Scientist*. There is music of the soul in Fechner—see the lovely description of plant life that James cites—it is reminiscent of a lyrical Aristotelianism. James is enthusiastic and diffident at once. Enthusiastic: in being enchanted by the vision of Fechner—a thick version of idealism/panpsychism, not the thin version of American transcendentalism, as he suspected that to be. Diffident: in that his own skeptical side, coming from science, keeps him from going overboard in terms of voicing the vision as *his own conviction*; he delights in playing the music of another, and it is as beautiful as James can sing, but it is of another, and so he cannot be accused of being the singer simply—he would sing, one feels, but he could not quite, so song becomes reporting another, even a little singing of another (a "cover" as the musicians say), but it is not quite the pouring forth of the song from one's own being, as one's own being. In that sense, it is not quite soul music.

both the objectification and subjectification of being. In Descartes there is the now-familiar dualism of the *res extensa* and *res cogitans*. This might seem to fall within a Platonic paradigm, but what we find is the project of mathematical and technological objectification, for the certainty of which philosophical reflection is to provide the epistemological warrant or certification. The famous *cogito* argument is not to be eschewed, though it has been relentlessly assaulted in more recent times. It is a peculiar argument—there is indeed something incontrovertible in the denial of self (if this is the right word). What is being denied is doing the denying and hence is affirmed even in the denial itself. The issue now, granting a certain incontrovertibility, is what is it that is doing the denial and affirming itself in the denial.[15] Here the answer: the *ego cogitans*—and this *res cogitans* is then identified with *spiritual substance*, set off by an ontological gulf from the *res extensa*, the neutral wax-like stuff of the world around us. The term "*res*" carries the objectification: "thing," but with the implication of a determinability that fixes itself and nothing but itself. I mean this not only as an objectification and determination but also as a certain univocalization. It is as a consequence of univocal determinability that we find ourselves fixed in dualism; for to be the one thing it is, the *res* must incontrovertibly be *not* the other things, and between the one and the other there opens a gulf of difference, in the end not intermediated or open to intermediation.

The *res extensa* seems to open up the vista of objectified neutralized thereness; and it seems also to define by necessary complement the *res cogitans*, the subjectivity for whom or for which this neutralized other is there at all. But this subjectivity itself undergoes a reification in being determined as thinking *thing*. It is in this determination, identified with the soul, that the soul begins to be lost. For the soul is *not a thing*. This is not at all intended as a depreciation or making inferior of things. I would defend things as ontologically thick,[16] in fact, and see no point in an absolute dualizing of things and persons, say. But qua *res*, the univocal fixity of the soul begins to live a life that is continuous with the modern project

15. It is only too well known that something of this incontrovertibility is affirmed by Augustine before Descartes, but Augustine has no "project" to found a new science of nature. The incontrovertibility counters the soul's evasions of its own truthful porosity to truth—truth as intimate and other to the soul's claim to be the truth. The soul music of Augustine is prayerful and not geometrical, and sung from a space of sacred intimacy more hyperbolically interior even to the soul's own intimacy with itself.

16. See my *Being and the Between*, chapter 8, "Things."

of determinate objectification, even though carried out through a process of subjectification. My point is this: soul music ceases, because it is the determinability, the fixability that is now at stake. Music witnesses to *flowing form*; but flowing form requires more than univocal stasis for its determination—for it is more determin*ing* than determined—and hence exceeds complete determination. Fluid form is a *forming in passage*; and if we see a unity in the flow of passage, it is a strange unity that is itself by exceeding itself, and that yet is in intimate self-relation in this being beyond itself, in this being of itself in the moving of itself.[17]

Of course, music is not mathematics, though both are intimately connected, as the Pythagoreans long ago realized. Mathematics tends to form, while music tends to forming. The music begins to fade with the project of the modern mathematicization of nature. Think of the difference of Kepler and Galileo. Nature for both may be the book written in the language of mathematics, but the former still heard the music in the mathematics, while in the latter the mathematics had taken over in a form that recessed the music.[18] My question: does not the same happen

17. Aristotle connects soul and *nous* with form (the form of forms: *ho nous eidos eidōn*, *De Anima*, 432a3). I would say that there is more to form than form—there is form*ing*, and its dynamic power has to be taken into account. Form as articulated points beyond itself to forming as articulating. There is life that is passing in the form, and hence the form is not *just* form. This is why the fluid form of music is so appropriate to the soul as souling, and indeed perhaps also to the self as selving. The source of the fluid form is not just another form and hence there is an element of beyond determinability and self-determination about its power(s). This also is consistent with the overlap of mathematics and music, in respect of form, but if the form is forming then in a sense the music is more primal than the mathematic, for it is attuned to, it is the attuning of, the source powering the forming qua forming, and not just crystallized in (determinate) form. A more general point might be made relative to all beauty in so far as we think of this in terms of *splendor formae*: form has no splendor if it is only form considered as a determinate structure; for form shines, but shining with splendor is more than fixed form; thus we say a picture shimmers, that is to say, radiates, and exceeds fixation in determinate form, even though it is in the determinate form itself that the radiation of the splendor is singularized. The same point holds for the communication of music, and hence Kant's metaphor below of the perfumed handkerchief is not at all inapposite: it is the diffusion that is at stake, the diffusion beyond the determinate and determinable boundary of fixed form; the diffusion of the music is carried by the moving form, the fluid forming as it is in passing. One might note also the musical reference of soul in respect of the image of the lyre in the *Phaedo* (86c), an image that occasions criticism of soul considered as a harmony; though the source of the music as forming beyond form is not the same as the musical instrument on which the music is played. See *De Anima*, 407b30–408a10 for criticism of soul as a harmony.

18. See Desmond, *Being and the Between*, 95–97.

to music when the self comes to the fore, when the self is intent on being the source of determination and on being itself the realization of self-determination? We find it hard to hear soul music; we find it perplexing even to know what it means to listen for it. That is why *all the arts*, and music not least, are *guardian angels of this easily lost listening*. An ear for music is asked of all the powers of the senses. We have to listen when we look, listen when we touch and shape, listen when the body dances, listen when the tongue tastes and words.[19]

What of the long-standing argument that connects soul with *simplicity*? Is not this consonant with the desire for univocal determinability? Is not this too the meaning of simplicity? But this is too simple by far. Simplicity is the most unsimple of things. God's simplicity—what is this? Surely this simplicity is infinitely rich, just in its being uncompounded. On first appearance, it would seem we have to think an origin that in its uncompounded character seems to leave no juts of complexity by which we might hang our determinations by the skin of articulated differences. Otherwise, this would be "the night in which all cows are black," in Hegel's sarcastic jibe at Schelling's absolute as the *Indifferenzpunkt*.[20] And yet this divine simplicity is the absolutely *full*, the absolutely *over*full. Here we begin to border on paradox, indeed touch on mystery: the infinitely overfull is so absolutely simple that when we try to determinate it, it comes before us as nothing—nothing in particular. This paradoxical doubleness is deeply important for the soul: the soul as surplus seems beyond finite determinability and yet seems like a nothing, but it is a nothing that is the power to be or become everything (again with a bow to Aristotle).[21]

The language of self begins to take over with the *res cogitans*, with this self of reification in a double sense—reification of what is other to itself as objective, reification of itself as spiritual subject. Thus one can make sense of the paradoxical development in this modern univocalization:

19. Augustine (*De Trinitate*, XV, X, 18) refers to the words of the heart (*locutiones cordis*) and how in the soul the outer distinction of seeing and hearing is abrogated: seeing is hearing, hearing is seeing (*non est aliud atque aliud videre et audire*). On this see Chrétien, *The Call and the Response*, 49.

20. Hegel, *Phänomenologie des Geistes*, 19; *Phenomenology of Spirit*, §16.

21. One reason soul as simple is not determinable simply or simply determinate is because it is the determining source of singular determinations and in excess of complete determination; and it is also not "self" as formation of self-determination. Not that there is not self-determining going on but the soul as source of determining is more before determination and more beyond. "Selving" comes to be on the surface of this mysterious source, is the sur-facing of soul. More on this below.

it can go in the direction of a more brutal reification and reduction, or likewise veer in the direction of an unleashing of subjectivity unmoored from any anchor in being. So we find: the materialisms of modernity on the one hand, the idealisms on the other, and their de-sublations.

True, the Cartesian view of the soul seems a fit made for the question of *immortality*, and this with respect to its simplicity.[22] But with the reification, there is the recessed being at work of the soul and this too unanchored from nature; and as a non-natural thing, it is a question as to how we are then to determine it, how then to pin it down. This is not at all easy, and can come to appear scandalous when the project of univocal determinability has matured to the point of demanding an analogous univocalization of the soul. But there is no mathematicization of the soul, no technology of its music. We are tempted with a material science, whether phrenology in earlier centuries, or neurophysiology in our own time. The de-naturing of soul contributes to a desire for soul's determinate objectification, which in turn leads to the disappearance of soul and its replacement with a variety of other seemingly plausible forms of determinability. But there is no such soul.

In the quest of the substantial soul, the issue deteriorates also on the side of the empiricists. I think of Locke's description of substance as an "I know not what" that yet has to be invoked to sustain the properties of the thing taken in as impressions by the acts of sensation. How sustain the claims made about an "I know not what"? Of course, if determinability is required big time we are in a pickle. One thinks of the arguments about Lockean substance by the divine Stillingfleet to the effect that it cannot be an "I know not what" if we can say about it that it is an "I know not what." And then there is the relentless assault by Berkeley following on this as to the redundancy of this concept of substance, certainly material substances as such. There remain only spirits, as Berkeley calls them, all

22. Descartes talks about the soul as being the most easily known of all. I think this has to do with intimacy. In one sense, what he says is true; there is this (elusive) intimacy of being; but what is the nature of the knowing of it? If it is an intimate knowing, how determinate or determinable is it? Most close to itself, most far from itself; most known to itself and most unknown to itself? Since the knower is the knowing and the known, there is no "distance" of objectification (by and through which the subject can determinately grasp itself). For we are not only participants; one *is* it—and yet there is more to it than one can univocally determine. It is a mystery rather than a problem, in Gabriel Marcel's sense. Even at that, it is not easy to say *what it is*, since the saying of what it is intimately participates in it. Compare Descartes on the soul as the most easily known with Heraclitus (fragment 45) on the impossibility of finding the limits of the soul, "so unfathomable is its *logos*."

perhaps rather too cliptly. Of course, the overdeterminacy of the issue of soul tends not to be honestly enough acknowledged in all of this, and the kind of sanity of the Aristotelian fidelity to nature is not given its proper due. Berkeley claims to demolish material substance, Hume tries to demolish spiritual substance, and the self, considered as a fixed substance, is held to dissolve in a flux of impressions. Of course, Hume had to be himself to look for his self, and had to continue to be himself when he himself (who is he?) found there was no self to be found. The aesthetic determinability of soul proves a failure with the empiricists, as the dianoetic determinability does with the rationalists.

## Soul, Self(-Activity), and Kantian Equivocation

I take Kant here as a witness to the mess. I refer to his discussion of rational psychology, a scholastic discipline dealing with the soul, but soul considered as this simple substance. We find this in his treatment of the paralogisms of pure reason in the *Critique of Pure Reason* (Second Division, Book II, chapter I). What seems to be at work here is Kant's strategy of showing a contradiction, indeed an illusion reason cannot avoid, a deep-seated equivocity in reason itself concerning the notion of the soul as simple substance, and as treated in a speculative theory. Rational psychology equivocates between the dianoetics and aesthetics of the matter, between claims made by reason and claims that seem to offer an empirical affirmation. That is, in treating of the soul as simple substance, we claim to make assertions about the soul purely on the basis of reason, and its consideration of the "I think"; in the process we move from rational considerations but end up with seemingly empirical claims. For Kant, however, nothing of cognitive worth is to be ascribed to these claims. One might say, apropos of the twinning of subjectification and objectification, that we move from the side of rational subjectivity but only it seems to end up on the side of an empirical reality. This move cannot be justified. Rational psychology is vitiated by contradiction and equivocation.

At face value, there seems to be here a certain working out of the doublet of the *res cogitans* and *res extensa*, considered as amenable to univocal determination.[23] This discussion of the paralogisms was seen by many as dealing a death blow to rational psychology. Or is it the death of the soul? A death warrant perhaps, but not direct death. It is the death warrant of a certain way of conceiving the soul, but this cannot be taken to exhaust the issue, or to deliver us over to a truer approach. In fact, Kant does bring the soul back, *via* his practical philosophy, where the autonomy of the moral self is sovereign, and *via* the postulate of immortality. Practical reason can still address the great themes of special metaphysics, God, freedom, the soul. But where is the *music* in Kant's moral philosophy? Is there any soul music in this postulate of its immortality? I cannot hear it. I hear nothing.

It bears remarking that this turn to practical philosophy is configured by Kant in terms of *moral self-determination*, which does what univocal rational determination cannot do in a theoretical sense. There is nothing of the living overdeterminacy of souling in all of this. And, of course, the recessed presuppositions of the dualistic contraposition of the *res cogitans* and *res extensa* are still very much at play. If we find these presuppositions problematic in terms of understanding soul—as we must—then another approach is required. Perhaps the problem is the recessing of the intimacy of soul in the dualistic language—the self either as a determinable thing or as source of self-activity. We have difficulty seeing the determinate and self-determining self as the outcome of a process of selving, itself reaching more deeply into intimate sources of souling and being ensouled. These intimate sources are idiotic from the standpoint of surfaced determinations and projects of self-determinations of the selving. As intimate they return us more into the *passio essendi* and deeper still into the porosity of being, which is neither active nor passive.[24]

Another important upshot here with Kant is the turn away from soul *towards self-activity*, and so towards the being of selving as *conatus essendi*, and following this the emphasis on practical willing as most essential to the being of selving. Soul is pathological, as intimate with the

23. One could say that Kant's critique of the paralogisms is continuous with his critique of the *ontological argument*. There is no justified transition or inference from rational concept (possibility) to reality or existence. There is a gulf between the two that cannot be bridged by rational thought alone.

24. Nor is it *prōtē hulē* either, though there is a likeness to the Platonic *khōra* (this interests me more than what deconstruction has made of the *khōra*). The matrix of ongoingness is neither simple being nor becoming. How speak of that mother? Paul Weiss speaks of the dynamis and I return to this in the next chapter, "Creativity and the Dynamis."

*passio essendi*; and there is also the matter of the primordial givenness to itself.[25] This is a complication taken over by the great idealists, where the quest to give an articulation of pure activity is to be found (consult the whole problem of spontaneity and receptivity here). Moreover, the matter is there developed in a manner that again wants to embed self in nature. Hegel and Schelling do this somewhat differently. I will say something below about this in relation to Hegel who, while recuperating something of the ontological embeddedness (evident in his great respect for Aristotle and his *De Anima*), has a view of spirit and nature that, in the end, comes to remind one more of the modern conception rather than Greek *physis*.

One might wonder here how in Kant the farewell to rational psychology, and the promotion of moral postulates, leave us with regard to music and the soul. Undoubtedly music does not fare very well. Kant has a very diffident attitude, perhaps even an easily irritated attitude. So I infer from the things he says in the *Critique of Judgement* where—as I mentioned in a previous chapter—he compares music to the dandy and his perfumed handkerchief. The perfume works on everyone involuntarily. It does not ask of us our permission, but with no by-your-leave it works on us before we can insulate ourselves in the circle of self-determination. It is as if we would be better off, if only we could be *Stoics without noses.* Music, like perfume, touches us, "gets up our nose," caresses us or hits us, in any event, it moves us at a level of being below or beyond the defenses of our autonomy, self-circulated in its rational security. It moves us before we know we have been moved. Perhaps just as bad, it seems, is the unsavory aspect of its relative indeterminability. Music is not above board, we recall Kant avers. In this it is unlike poetry, which shows its hand, as he puts it. Like perfume, music can be everywhere and nowhere, passing through the pores of our bodies, indeed our souls, proving so moving that the body (self-moving like a soul) might move itself to its beat and tap its feet, clap its hands, and more outrageously, even make it desire to dance. Music ensouls, animates the body. Indeed the moving power of music passes beyond fixed determination and self-determination, gets through to the porosity, reopening it, and resonating with the soul.

We can see here how selving configured as autonomous self-determination is diffident about the intimate communication of music which

25. I have articulated the meaning terms like the *passio essendi* elsewhere, for instance, *The Intimate Strangeness of Being*; also in *The Intimate Universal*. Something of their meaning will become more evident as we proceed.

touches us at depths of soul before rational self-consciousness. This is all pathological for Kant. There is no soul music here. I find that the interesting thing about music is that it would give the lie to the notion of soul substance as a spiritual thing. In that sense, it would confirm perhaps one side of Kant's discussion in the paralogism, but what this would open up for consideration does not find its place in Kant's way of negatively critical thinking.

A last remark on soul in Kant, concerning his move to the level of pure practical reason where the antinomy of moral autonomy opens beyond itself towards the immortality of the soul.[26] The argument is that we must postulate the immortality of the soul as part of the resolution (*Aufhebung*) of the antinomy of pure practical reason. This is the antinomy between virtue and happiness, resolved in the *summum bonum* that, through God, ensures that merited happiness is enjoyed by the virtuous in exact proportion to their moral worthiness to be happy. What is this deathless soul that is implicated in overcoming the antinomy of pure practical reason and completing the moral doctrine in the *summum bonum*? Where is the music of the soul in the other world? Just as Kant seemed somewhat irritated with the singing of spiritual hymns here in this life, one suspects that Kant did not anticipate much singing there in the next world either. What an eternal irritation it would be to him, given that it was such a terrestrial agitation that he had to take his revenge in a footnote.[27]

Be that as it may, it seems the moral toil goes on, as each soul tries to earn its right to be happy—its rightful worthiness to merit happiness. There is no free music for this soul. Singing will never earn the soul a moral supper. Kant's doctrine of freedom means there is no free supper—whether sung for or not. Kant seems to moralize the glory of eternal life, now somewhat faded in true glory, since he does not allow the soul to enjoy itself there until it has paid its moral dues. Otherwise heaven would be like *spiritual South Sea Islands* whose natives seem to him disgustingly happy in eating, lounging around, and, *mon Dieu*,

26. Death, of course, means *facing the music* and we must not forget the ethical and religious dimensions of this question of deathlessness, evident in Plato's *Phaedo*, and in the Christian thinkers like Augustine and Aquinas. These ethical and religious concerns are bound up with *eschatological justice*. The rational psychology of modern thought is not richly attuned to the issue of eschatological justice—though there is a pale echo of it in Kant's postulates of immortality and God.

27. Kant, *Critique of the Power of Judgment*, § 53; see my *Art, Origins, Otherness*, 78.

breeding (*Fortpflanzung*).[28] For Kant there seems no great banquet in the divine eschatology, with wine, woman, and song (if you like, resurrected in the dimension of hyperbolic transfiguration). God forbid, again. God is not the mysterious donor of overabundant gifts to whom we sing but the paymaster general of moral merit. There is no hymn of soul music in eternity. The pagan Nietzsche is far closer to soul music when his Zarathustra sings: all joy wills eternity, wills deep, deep eternity!

## Substance, Soul, Subject: Hegel's (Self-determining) Spirit

I want to pay some attention to Hegel since he is amphibolous in a revealing way: he tries to recuperate something of the Aristotelian way in a post-Kantian space, but in the end he tilts towards a superposition of a logic of self-determination on the living overdeterminacy of soul. The result resounds in his philosophy of music, whose notes are quite close to the music of the soul, but not concordant. There is something out of tune.

Hegel speaks about soul in connection with his philosophy of subjective spirit. Technically the discussion appears first under the heading of anthropology, which he connects with the soul in nature, passing thence through phenomenology, where we encounter the soul coming to appearance out of nature, coming finally to psychology proper, wherein Hegel's philosophy surpasses soul as such in the direction of a more adequate expression of spirit.[29] Overall, Hegel is dealing with the emergence of spirit from nature, and its development out of this toward its own liberation from nature as such. This liberation from nature is into spirit's being for itself and into its more and more consummate self-determination. While the details of his account are often richly suggestive, and while he praises Aristotle's *De Anima* as in a class of its own (*Encyclopedia*, §378), the unfolding of his account as a whole is oriented to the emergence and consummation of subjective spirit, and its *Aufhebung* and supersession by objective spirit. The whole process is governed by the teleology of spirit as journeying towards the (self-)constitution of its own proper self-determination, finally consummated at the level of absolute spirit.

28. Kant, *Groundwork of the Metaphysics of Morals*, 74–75.

29. Hegel treats extensively of the soul throughout the section on subjective *Geist* in Hegel, *Enzyklopädie der Philosophischen Wissenschaften im Grundrisse*; Hegel, *Hegel's Philosophy of Mind*; Hegel, *Lectures on the Philosophy of Spirit*.

The soul is explicated as the first appearance of spirit out of nature and its externality. The true root for Hegel is not nature but freedom. I would say Hegel takes over the critique of soul as simple substance and he needs to do so if he is to move to the self-activity of spirit. Noticeable in his discussion is his reaction to any dualism of matter and spirit, body and soul; such dualism leads to his critique not only of materialism but also to his critique of questions so dualistically posed about the relation of body and spirit as two substances. Hegel makes references to Descartes, Malebranche, and Leibniz as seeking through God differently to bring the two substances into unity or community. He criticizes this way of thinking. In a sense, materialism is to be dematerialized, while spirit is to be concretized in its determinate appearance.

Hegel is one of the idealists who developed the notion of pure activity (an idea in Fichte). One can map something of this in terms of a certain reaction to the spiritual substance of rational psychology and Kant's critique of it. This critique is accepted at one level, and at another level, there is an extraordinary expansion coming from the critique that might be summarized in Hegel's words: From substance to subject.[30] This is a central catchword for the *Phenomenology of Spirit*, and it adds significantly to the theme. Substance is selfless, lacking in true subjectivity, as Hegel suggests in connection with Spinoza's substance. Moving from substance to subject is the phenomenology of spirit, *Geist*, the *logos* of appearing spirit. What of soul in this? We must give up simple substance to make the move and transformation of substance to subject, but soul can find some place in this process. It provides something of the needed threshold and transition between nature and spirit.

I note that Hegel is Aristotelian, but not entirely so. Where he discusses the soul in his anthropology, it is just on this threshold between nature and spirit, where the transition from the former to the latter is effected. The embeddedness in nature is Aristotelian, and the emergence from nature mimics Aristotle in one sense, in that with the rational powers we come upon the fullest form of soul. But Hegel's account is not Aristotelian in another sense, in that the threshold, once crossed, tends to the subordination of nature in the very act of spiritually sublating it. Hegel's is an intrinsically interesting discussion, but it is very modern with regard to nature and spirit. Nature is something that spirit will *overcome*—nature is spirit in its self-externality, not spirit in its full and hence

30. Hegel, *Phänomenologie des Geistes*, 19; *Phenomenology of Spirit*, §17.

proper self-relation. There the idea is outside of itself and in a sense it is scattered abroad. The soul initiates the bringing of the scattering back to self-relation. It does so as in the body and as emergent in the body. For obviously the body and our being embodied are important for Hegel. More, as the expression of spirit, the human form is the only true vehicle of spirit in nature, as he puts it in his *Aesthetics*.[31] Yet in the end *Geist* is self-surpassing, not only of nature, but of itself also, and is not to be reduced to bodily form only. I might put it: the selving of *Geist* is more than the aesthetics of souling. The soul as witnessing to spirit emergent in nature has about it an immediacy, but immediacy is connected with a beginning and thus with a sense of indeterminate possibility. Hence if there is an opening of soul here the immediacy must be mediated. Finally, with mediation we traverse a movement from the indeterminacy of the immediate, through various forms of determination, towards the end of more and more fulfilled self-determination.

Note that while we might find here hints of the porosity of being and the *passio essendi*, they tend to fall under the governance of a teleology of endeavor (the *Trieb* of the Idea?) where the *conatus essendi* is in search of fuller and fuller rational self-determination. The soul does seem to be intimately idiotic in one sense, but it is more idiotic in a deficient rather than a saturated sense, an indeterminate rather than overdeterminate sense. And once having crossed the threshold, nature does not show itself to have quite the blooming surplus character it might be said to have in the Greek notion of *physis*. Where then is the soul music in Hegel? It is not denied, but there is a spiritual selving more ultimate than soul, and to invest in soul too much is to hinder the self-completing process of this selving.

Pure activity determines itself in a plurality of forms—but practically speaking it is oriented to "the free will which wills the free will," as Hegel puts it in the *Philosophy of Right*.[32] There is more, of course, than a bare free will that wills the free will. Hegel is a complex modern thinker in offering a teleology of selving oriented to *social self-determination*, not an archeology that finds soul called up from surplus naturing, and that finds uttering from the idiotic sources of the intimate affirmation of the "to be," with its porosity and *passio*, with its suffering and endeavor. In the move from substance to subject *via* soul, there is more stress on

31. Hegel, *Hegel's Aesthetics*, vol. 1, 78; (abbreviated, *HA*); *Vorlesungen über die Ästhetik*, in Hegel, *Werke in zwanzig Banden*, Bande 13–15, I, 110 (abbreviated *VA*).

32. Hegel, *Outline of the Philosophy of Right*, §27.

the end through human endeavor and activity than on the sacredness of suffering and receiving. Suffering and receiving may be beginnings but they are not the end, and the end is what determines the point of the whole. This concern with the end, the *telos*, is very Aristotelian, of course, but once again Hegel is not fully an Aristotelian, even when he crowns his *Encyclopedia* (§577) with a speculative hymn covering Aristotle's thought thinking thought (*noēsis noēsis noeseōs*). One suspects Plato was the greater at offering an archeology of the good and not only a teleology; moreover, archeology that points back to the intimate soul in its own cavernous darknesses, its prenatal intimacies with true being, its outreach to the good above itself, above us all, the good that gives us to be here and now, that allows us to stand on the surface of the earth and in the light that gives us being and intelligibility and growing. Hegel talks about the impotence of nature. It does not seem to be the mother, matrix of all fertile possibility. *Geist* is the true progenitor. Hegel is not a dualist, to be sure, but he is more concerned to complete the modern turn towards self-determination than return to or retrieve forgotten archaic resources.[33]

And what of the music of soul? Interestingly, Hegel importantly sees the connection between music and the soul. In line with his teleological tilt to self-determination, and his location of soul at the beginning, which is only indeterminate, we find him identifying *music* with the romantic art *par excellence* (*HA*, vol. 1, 88, 528; vol. 2, 889; *VA*, I, 122; II, 141; III, 133). Romantic art is the art of interiority. Hear Hegel:

> For expression in music is the object-free inner life, abstract subjectivity as such. This is our entirely empty self, the self without any further content. Consequently the chief task of music consists in making resound, not the objective world itself, but, to the contrary, the manner in which the inmost self is moved to the depths of its personality and conscious soul (*Seele*). The same is true of the effect of music. What it claims as its own is the depths of a person's inner life as such; it is the art of the soul and is directly addressed to the soul (*Gemüt*). (*HA*, vol. 2, 891; *VA*, III, 135)

33. In his later *Lectures on the History of Philosophy*, Hegel gives more evidence of a sympathetic appreciation of the ancients—though again perhaps as too much prefiguring his own ultra-modern, totally up-to-date system.

There is much that is suggestive about this and that bears thought,[34] but something about the indeterminate immediacy of soul does not bear enough thought for Hegel. Thus we find him remarking on the thoughtless virtuosity we sometimes find in music:

> . . . musical production may easily become something utterly devoid of thought and feeling, something needing for its apprehension no previous profound cultivation of mind or heart. On account of this lack of material not only do we see the gift for composition developed at the most tender age but very talented composers frequently remain throughout their life the most ignorant and empty-headed of men. (*HA*, vol. 2, 954; *VA*, III, 217)

We hear, once again, that it is the indeterminacy of beginnings that is stressed by Hegel, and with this also a certain deficiency of determinacy, not to say immaturity of rational self-determination. It is not the too-muchness of the musical soul that he hears but the not-enoughness of the indefinite, of the immaturity of the too indeterminate, of a dearth and poverty of thought and spiritual culture. The overdeterminacy of fullness that pours forth in soul music is not heard, overdeterminacy of fullness even in the emptiness of indeterminacy, as like the voice in the wilderness. Hegel thus:

> Music, for example, which is concerned only with the completely indeterminate movement of the inner spirit and with sounds as if they were feeling without thought, needs to have little or no spiritual material present in consciousness. Therefore, musical talent announces itself in most cases very early in youth,

34. One thinks of Hegel's understanding of the human voice "as the freest, and in its sound the most perfect instrument. . . . [T]he human voice can apprehend itself as the sounding of the soul itself, as the sound the inner life has in its own nature for the expression of itself, an expression which it regulates directly . . . in song the soul rings out from its own body. . . . So, for example, the Italians are a people of song, *ein Volk des Gesanges*"(*HA*, vol. 2, 922; *VA*, III, 175). "[The] free sounding of the soul in the field of music—this is alone melody" (*HA*, vol. 2, 930; *VA*, III, 185). Hegel makes a positive reference to Pythagoras (*HA*, vol. 2, 924; *VA*, III, 177–78). Music is connected to tone and tonality: "music takes the soul of tone, working itself free from spatial matter, in the qualitative differences of sound and in the movement of the ever-rolling stream of time" (*HA*, vol. 2, 894; *VA*, III, 139). Here he mentions mathematics, and also compares music and architecture. In an inward sensuousness heard in the inner ear, the development and unfolding of tones is by way of interplays of repetition and variability, sameness and dissonance; and while the unfolding is fluid in its variability there is a return to itself. Something of this is connected to the feeling soul. Still this is the "I" in its barest of immediate indeterminacy; the soul or "I" here is all but nothing.

> when the head is empty and the heart little moved, and it may sometimes attain a very considerable height before the spirit and life have experience of themselves. Often enough, after all, we have seen very great virtuosity in musical composition and performance accompanied by a remarkable barrenness of spirit and character.
>
> In poetry, on the other hand, it is quite different. (*HA*, vol. 1, 28; *VA*, I, 47)

You might interpret some of these statements of Hegel as touching on the porous idiocy of the soul, but their significance as idiotic for Hegel is precisely to be superseded in the direction of a more rational self-determination. On the threshold of this idiocy, Hegel can only drive forward to more and more rational self-determination. The "object-free inwardness" (*HA*, vol. 2, 892; *VA*, III, 136) that music expresses is too indeterminate for him. There is a logic of self-determination always at work. The soul is an immediacy in the sense of indeterminacy, not in the sense of a secret overdeterminacy of living. There follows the drive from soul to selving and then selving is in essence a matter of self-determination. The self-determination takes over the souling, and wins over its porosity—wins it over not by the wooing of the music but in terms of the will that wills itself. The *Trieb* of the *conatus* defines the move from the indeterminate to the determinate to the self-determining. The selving then proves not porous enough, risks losing its intimacy with the *passio*. In its music the soul does not sing itself as received into being. The soul does not know itself as wooed and wooing. In its music it does not receive the given note from the secret source; it works on its own notes.

I find a redeeming feature to Hegel's way of thinking in his appreciation of dialectic as enabling a dealing with *transitions* and *thresholds*.[35] This shows something of the capacity for "two thinks at a time," as James Joyce put it. A threshold opens up on more than one side, and hence we can move back and forth, we can move up and down, we can move out and in. The fluidity of moving on the threshold is important, and this is very relevant to the fluid forming that we can be said to experience in music. Interestingly, the Muses in the Greek world, from whom we get music, were connected to springs, running water, streams, fluidity. The question of how we move on the threshold is all-important, and whether we are so driven to the end that the antecedents are either left behind,

35. See Stone-Davis's essay "Music and Liminal Ethics," which also touches on the subject of music and thresholds with regard to the notion of liminal ethics.

or perhaps used as stepping stones to attaining the end. In Hegel's case, the antecedents are not simply left behind and also are not simply stepping stones. The antecedents are taken up into the unfolding process and hence contribute to the living substance of that unfolding, now taking new and sometimes surprising forms in the unfolding itself. Nor are the stages of unfolding stepping stones simply, since stages might take on the fuller form of an entirely developed world that is fully for itself, if not the absolute fullness itself. It is not a means to an end merely, even if in the end, it does serve the becoming of a fuller end beyond itself.

These complexities in Hegel's understanding are not to be underestimated or undervalued, but the tilt of the unfolding in the process is still in the direction of the end, with the beginning understood as an indetermination to be further determined, in view of the self-determination to be attained rather than attuned in achieved teleology. The threshold serves this teleological process of self-determination, as does the indetermination of the beginnings, as well as the plural forms of determination we find along the way and its stages. But music as threshold, as soul music, intimates a different sense of origin, and hence also a different sense of determinacy and self-determination. This I have called the overdeterminacy, though again without hiding the need of paradoxical language of fullness and emptying. The surplus character is intimate even in the minimalism of the least unfolding; you might say, the affirmative is in the negative, but in a way that does not fit Hegelian negativity.[36]

As with Kant, it is not surprising that in Hegel there is a final preference for poetry as preeminent, and one can see in this a predilection for determination and determinability. In a way too it is also a preference for the promise of the diurnal life of the spirit, a preference for the nocturnal intimacy of the musical. The spiritual is understood as more essentially diurnal than nocturnal.[37] Is there a dark night of the soul in Hegel's way of thinking? I cannot conceive Hegel as writing a hymn to the night (as Novalis did). I cannot see him like Zarathustra singing a *Nachtlied*; nor for that matter that most tender song that came to Nietzsche on hearing

36. See Hegel, *Science of Logic*, 56 where he talks about "the inner negativity of the determinations as their self-moving soul, the principle of all natural and spiritual life."

37. It is worth asking: Would there ever be soul music without the black churches in America and their Gospel music? And would there be that black music without Africa? Go figure, Hegel! Riddle me Africa. But Africa for Hegel does not figure in his scheme of world history. It is an indeterminacy whose night does not get the honor of offering even a small fillip of progress in dialectical determination. Ironically, black Africa is blank.

at evening the voice of the unseen gondolier from the bridge in Venice. It is hard to think of Hegel as a musically Orphic thinker, and for all his talk of staring the negative in the face and converting it into the positive, as one with the power of music to descend into hell and even move the powers of Acheron. In fact, Hegel sardonically suggests that the notes of Orpheus "sufficed for wild beasts which lay around him tame, but not for men who demanded the contents of a higher doctrine" (*HA*, vol. 2, 908; *VA*, III, 157).[38] One wonders, of course, who could be such a singing thinker. Perhaps only a god or God could be the singer of such soul music that all horror is forgiven, all broken promises of the good reinstated, indeed festively fulfilled. Were one allowed to mix Greek and Jew, such an Orphic singer would be Christ.

## Selving with Soul

The Hegelian "self" determines itself "upwards," so to say, through the rational self-sublation of its own soul. But hell knows no peace. And what if the dialectical negativity that moves up thus might also move down, and now not preserving but negating the rational self? Might it not lead to a de-sublation of *self without soul*? In truth, after Hegel, one does see signs of this de-sublation and it does not bring us back to the soul, rather more to the ab-ject "subject" rather than the rational subject. The thrown-down self, the ab-ject, goes back into the dark, but it is not the dark night of the soul. Indeed, in this going down, the "self" is a kind of dark night where every dawning is a false dawn, masking, surfacing over, what lies down deep beneath. This going down is to be found in Schopenhauer and Nietzsche and others later.[39] But where is the soul in entry to its own

38. See Marchenkov, *The Orpheus Myth and the Powers of Music*.

39. One sometimes thinks the world here is like the Bull of Phalaris for Schopenhauer and Nietzsche. It is the dark cave in which the philosopher is roasted in fire. It is the belly of the Beast (say of the Ophites), the Leviathan Art saves us from the truth of the horror of being. Nietzsche suggests in Zarathustra that once he believed in a tortured, suffering god at the origin of all, but that he overcame this view—but did he? The world is a work of art giving birth to itself, but in the hidden womb where the birth is first generated the secret at its core is the scream of pain. Is this still the suffering of the tormented god? Dionysus is also Hades, as Heraclitus said. Nietzsche sought heaven on the surface of the earth. Schopenhauer saw the hell, not the heaven. The jars are not half full, but always half empty. What's more, they are leaky jars, always emptying, even while they are being filled. We might think of the Danaids, Tantalus, and even Sisyphus: the futility of going up, coming down, going up again . . . to no

night? And does it not also seem as if what makes the living being to be living at all (formerly, soul) lies "behind" or "below" it as the "thing"—obscene and a horror and not good: not the soul but the evil "thing." If so, self-sublating subjectivity is de-sublated and subjected to the "thing." We might call this *the horror version of reification*—the subject not merely objectified but subtended by the "thing." When the "subject" knows it as thus subtended, it sees itself as the abject subjected by the "thing."

This is a motive to come back directly to the theme of soul music and soul-less selving. Even if there is a stress on self, self, self, that is not good for the soul, the point cannot be to do away entirely with self.[40] Not at all. I spoke above of soul and *selving* when considering objectification and subjectification. I adopt "selving" as a term from G. M. Hopkins and adapt it now in tune with the present theme. I quote Hopkins:

> As kingfishers catch fire, dragonflies dráw fláme;
> As tumbled over rim in roundy wells
> Stones ring; like each tucked string tells, each hung bell's
> Bow swung finds tongue to fling out broad its name;
> Each mortal thing does one thing and the same:
> Deals out that being indoors each one dwells;
> Selves—goes itself; myself it speaks and spells,
> Crying Whát I do is me: for that I came.

In this marvelous poem, we are arrested by the eye-catching flare of fire, but also by the resonance of music in the splash of water that has entered deep in the well, or in the tolling bell that tongues perhaps

end, endlessly.

40. Think of Charles Taylor's suggestion of the "buffered self" in *A Secular Age*, 27. This for him is a modern construction. But where he sees the premodern self as "porous," I see the porosity of being as elementally constitutive in an ontological sense, not just an historical-cultural mark of "earlier" peoples. To be is to be porous. Buffered selves lose their souls. See Desmond, "The Porosity of Being: Towards an Agapeic Catholicity. In Response to Charles Taylor," 283–305.

The porosity of being is related to what Keats speaks of as "negative capability," earlier mentioned in connection with Dickens. Keats also spoke, of course, of the "vale of soul making . . . ." In one sense, the soul is not made, it is created, and endowed with powers, and with these powers it participates in making a self: the world is a vale of self-making in that sense. But prior to making is what is not made but what enables making; and what enables making is in itself not self-enabled. It is enabled not as self-made but as endowed, that is, as received into being from a source other than itself: God (speaking theologically).

its angelus, the message broadcast being that mortal things word themselves. Their wording is their selving.

How now relate selving and soul? A suggestion: the uttering of the soul is its outering, and this uttering is where selving takes form. Selving is the outering of souling; this also entails the wording of being ensouled. Souling is not to be reified in the ensouling of things. This is why it, the wording, is more like a singing. The souling comes to the embodiment of a selving, coming to be from a secret origin, given to be as itself, an intimate and finite origin(al). For it is received into being as creature—as singing creature, both created and creative. Being created and being finitely creative are mirrored in the doubleness of the *passio essendi* and the *conatus essendi*. Soul, then, is witness to an intimacy of being more original than selving, but in the intimacy of souling, there is something more than soul, that gives it, that endows its being. Soul comes to itself as enabling selving from a source beyond both selving and souling.[41]

How relate this to what has gone before? To recall the narrative I offered: as soul has been objectified and self subjectified, being a self has tended to become enmeshed with determinability and self-determination. Self is a relatively surface event, if that is the right way to put it. We are often tempted to speak of layers or depths of self and this is not wrong, but the implication is this: we standardly take for self what has been firmed in terms of a more available determination. This is the selving that has come to be the more constant character, and our fix on this is not always with patient attention to the more recessed selving out of which the self is expressed. We do not attend enough to the saturated surplus of the surface, and hence we miss the soul. To attend to soul asks of us to be attuned to the recessed reserves of being. But again, this is not entirely accurate, if we think only of a vanishing depth, since the soul is as much out as in; it outwards itself and is the inner in the outer, which is never just outer, just as the inner is never just inner. My suggestion is that the soul-less selving of modernity comes to be in the collusion of objectification and subjectification, and does so not only in terms of more fixed determinability but in terms of what is stirring secretly in the soul—the urge to be free, the urge to be released. But here this urge now takes the form of a quest for self-determination. This is a quest for an autonomy that risks forgetting as much the inward otherness of itself,

41. Emerson is wonderfully suggestive in relation to the Over-soul: "Man is a stream whose source is hidden. Our being is descending into us from we know not where" (Essay IX, "The Over-soul," in *Collected Works, Volume II*, 159).

as of the outward otherness with which it is always in communication, always co-implicated.

There is a variety of ways of being free, ways that are not necessarily just autonomous, for instance, not just self-circling self-determination, but our being released; or our being sung into being from beyond ourselves; or our singing selving of ourselves beyond our self. In being self, in being itself, this soul-less selving sets itself over against otherness outside, also made soul-less, and sets itself over its own inward otherness—both of which then are thought to be heteronomies to be subordinated to autonomy. The *conatus essendi* takes shape as the will to self-determination, but in doing so forgets its own more original *passio essendi*, which is itself as more intimately and vulnerably porous. It forgets the porosity of soul that makes it participant in an open space of communication, indeed communion. It covers over the porosity of soul as an empty abyss, a threatening nothing within innerness, as well as reconfiguring outer otherness as a soul-less heterogeneity separate from itself. The selving on the surface of self-determination thus tries to snip the umbilical cord that ties it to its own soul—and no nourishment from the womb of the porosity comes up to it, even though in this, all its endeavor is still an affair of being "birthed with" (*con-natus*). It thinks it gives birth to itself, and forgets its being received into being, its being initiated—always through an other or others—an other or others who are with it, before it is with itself. Soul music opens access to the *passio essendi* and the porosity, and when the opening is allowed, we ourselves are allowed, free(d), released differently—into the song of life that is never our own, even when it is most intimately our own.

Thus, I would use the language of selving, and in a manner that carries the resonance of souling. I cannot go into the fuller dimensionalities of selving, beyond recalling that out of the idiot self comes the aesthetic selving, bound up more articulately with our full aesthetic being in rapport with the aesthetic happening of being as intimately other to us; recalling then the erotics of selving where the thrust of self-transcending in search of another comes to itself in being with the other; recalling further the agapeics of selving, which witnesses to a surplus generosity of being at work in the selving that is not simply for selving itself and alone but for giving beyond self. This last is selving in service of goodness, that is willing to be there and to give of itself fully there for the good of the other as other. For it does not find just itself in the other but finds the other as other, and finds that just finding itself is not what finding or being found is all about.[42]

Soul(ing) reminds us that there a radical intimacy to the living being, which empowers communication but which is more than this or that communication. This is why its powers are not more ordinary determinate powers, since these powers invoke the *porosity* and the *passio essendi*, relative to which we have to grant the priority of being given to be to giving beyond ourselves, as well as give up insisting on self-giving that gives only self or gives only for itself. Souling reminds us of the secret endowment of which we are in primal receipt before any acting or endeavoring on our part.

Soul is particularly connected with the intimacy of the idiotic self as naming the threshold of night and day, the night of our being and the day; the threshold of dawning and awakening; the threshold allowing intimacy with the nocturnal powers slumbering in our being; the threshold releasing passage into the diurnal powers we more normally associate with the self, with the processes of selving. The soul is night, the selving is day. In the passages from the idiotic through agapeic selving, there is a dawning of day, even as there is also return to night. This means there is no selving without suffering, though this is double, since return to night with us can mean both the horror of the nightmare and the healing of the prophetic dream.

When I say the soul is something idiotic, idiocy here has the meaning of the intimate, to be sure. It also has the meaning of the idiosyncratic, in the sense of the singular. This is connected with the sense of simplicity associated with the soul. But this intimate singularity is not autistic in the sense of being turned back into self as a closed or enclosed monadism. Rather, it is a singular opening of an intimate field of communication. Here is the connection with the porosity of our being. This is itself not initiated by us, but rather it is a between-space where we begin to wake to ourselves and other things, where things dawn on us, where we dawn on ourselves, where the others dawn on us. This prior field of communicability is indicated by the word "idiot" as when we speak of an idiom—a singularly inflected way of communication. There is no need here to set self-relation and other-relation in opposition. Our participating singularity in the open porosity of communication births us in the promising

42. On selving, see again Desmond, *Being and the Between*, chapter 9.

field of the intimate universal. This intimate field of communication is related, one might suggest, to our nature as *beings in prayer*. Is this field of communication perhaps why the thought of a kind of panpsychism or *anima mundi* cannot be quite suppressed, when our participation in the field of communication, in the porosity of being, indicates no final or absolute impermeability between ourselves and what is other to us? It is not that the "more" is like us, or that we are like it, but that we are together in a metaxological community that cannot be defined by *partes extra partes*. It is a kind of metaxological "all in all." Sometimes it seems even like a kind of mystical promiscuity in which, nevertheless, a mysterious and absolute chastity marks the being together of all things, when they are themselves in their most intimate truth. Interestingly, there are forms of music in which we have that double experience of pure chastity and nuptial *sun-ousia*. We are being penetrated and penetrating; receiving joy and offering back rejoicing.

There is here a connection with my above remarks on Kant and Hegel on music, a connection that brings to mind the renegade Kantian and Hegel-hater: Schopenhauer. If I am not mistaken, Schopenhauer has a feeling for something prior to the determinate and self-determining self. He speaks of this in terms of what he calls *the will*, but he should have talked about the *passio essendi* and the *porosity*. There is too much of the *conatus essendi*, the striving of the will (*Streben nach dem Unendlichen*) in his description of the ultimate metaphysical origin. He realizes the problem with the Kantian dualism. Kant does not pursue the way "self" puts its ontological roots intimately into a certain darkness of being (even though he does refer to an unknowable X). This is why Schopenhauer is close to the heart of the matter when he talks about music as the direct copy of the will—except it is not a copy of the will. Music comes out of the intimacy, the porosity, rather than the will. It comes out of the soul, in the sense I am here trying to suggest, not the modern spiritual substance.

Recall again Kant's attitude to music and the porosity of being, his irritation that his autonomy might be overcome, as it were, with perfumes. Think of his phobic reaction to the threat of a sweat coming on: he would stop his afternoon walk, rest under the shade of a tree, until the danger of the sweats passed and the porosity sweating brings; safe again, the pores of his being closed up, he would resume his walk. Might one see this as a protection against the infernal condition of which G. M. Hopkins, seer of spirit, spoke with witness?

> Selfyeast of spirit a dull dough sours. I see
> The lost are like this, and their scourge to be
> As I am mine, their sweating selves, but worse.[43]

Now consider Schopenhauer. He thinks there is a release from the relentless striving of the *conatus essendi*, a release that we find in the artistic genius and more radically the saint. The artist as genius, as excessive contemplative intellect, somehow escapes the fate of being in the bondage of the will. The artistic genius is free(d), if only for some few privileged moments, while the ascetic saint is graced with or sustains this freedom more fully. Lifted above the incessant becoming of will, its ever-renewed lack and restlessness, the artist attains the Platonic Idea in a contemplative composure replete with metaphysical significance about the most ultimate nature of being, which is named by Schopenhauer as will. The individual arts offer will-less knowledge of Ideas, an indirect knowing of will itself, but music alone is not knowledge of Idea but directly of will itself. This is its privileged position.

> Unlike the other arts, then, music is in no way the image of ideas; but rather the *image of the Will itself (Abbild des Willens selbst)*, whose objective form the ideas are also: it is for this very reason that the effect of music is so much more powerful and penetrating than that of the other arts: since the latter only speak of the shadow (*Schatten)*, while music speaks of the substance (*Wesen*).[44]

There is more in the primal root of the soul, retreating into darkness.[45] Schopenhauer shows himself attuned to the power of music to open up the porosity of being. Music speaks to what is profoundly *intimate* to the human being. Melody: the "secret history of the intellectually

43. This is from Hopkins's dark sonnet: "I wake and feel the fell of dark, not day."

44. Schopenhauer, *The World as Will and Representation*, vol. 1, 257.

45. Platonic erotics does not deny that darkness, nevertheless the soul's eros is brought to its consummation in relation to beauty, and one might say that there is a *musical logos of philosophical reason* that gives harmonious voice to that eros. The soul's eros is not lost in the night. Schopenhauer's recommendation of music and its metaphysical consolation comes out of a desire for escape from the tyrannical eros, the dark origin named will. Schopenhauer less redoubles Platonic themes as *doubles* them in a way that is not Platonic, given his view of the ultimate origin as a tyrannical erotic will. See Schopenhauer, *Art, Origins, Otherness*, 152–53; also 240n32 on Heidegger and song.

enlightened will"[46]—not quite the right way to put it, but moving in the space of a right attunement. My question: Whence comes that festive joy we often have in music? Whence the peace even in and through dissonance, if the will as origin is as Schopenhauer describes it? Surely it cannot be an *eros tyrannos*; there must be more of the agapeic in it?[47] More often than not, Schopenhauer's sense of the will corresponds dominantly to the *conatus essendi* rather than the *passio essendi*. Sometimes perhaps he mingles these two together, but I would say it is to the *passio essendi* that music first addresses itself. The language of the will is not the most apt way of talking here. There is something *before* the will that wills itself. The *passio essendi* has to do with our *being given to be*, prior to our giving ourselves to be, determining ourselves this way or that. Thus, there is something on the *other side* of will, something *not voluntary*, about the intimate appeal of music. The appeal has to do with gift. It has to do with what is secret to the idiotic selving. The power of music to open up again the porosity of being is remarkable. It communicates its intimate appeal beyond the fixation of this or that determinate formation of our selving. If music has this significance for the intimacy of being, and its porosity, its ultimate origin cannot be as Schopenhauer describes the will. Schopenhauer's self-insistent will cannot account for the opening up of the porosity of being in which the powers of communicability and communication come to form, and within which the expressions of music, and all art, show themselves intimate with the *passio essendi* prior to our *conatus essendi*. The original giving of the porosity is agapeic.[48]

46. Schopenhauer, *The World as Will and Representation*, vol. 1, 259.

47. One should not forget that the original will, the *Wesen*, is itself even darker than all the shadows. An ultimate darkness that casts shadows (of itself)—how is this possible at all? Any shadow needs light, but an original darkness is devoid of light, so how then can it cast a shadow of itself? With light, or a light other than the darkness? But what could that light then be, given the ultimate (pre-)supposition that everything is the outcome of will, the dark origin? This is a theme I will take up in the following chapter.

48. What words to call on to express what is prior to determination and beyond self-determination? My suggestion overall is that our stress on "self" has been so foregrounded that we become less attuned to what is recessed, just in that foregrounding. Will, will to power: these are not good ways of describing the recessed. They offer languages more at home in the foreground rather than the recessed intimacy of being. The ethos of self-determining will becomes more self-affirming, but the patience in the selving does not get the right acknowledgment or mindfulness. But it is out of what is thus recessed that music springs. This indicates something about the nature of the recessed that is not entirely one with describing the expressed in the language of will

It is difficult to avoid paradoxical language in regard to this prior porosity: neither passive nor active, but *both* passive *and* active; neither beyond nor immanent, but *both* beyond *and* immanent; neither strange nor intimate, yet *both* intimate *and* strange; not mine, not thine, but *both* mine *and* not mine at all, and *both* thine *and* not thine too; not unknown nor known, but *both* unknown *and yet* as if known already; neither one nor many, but *both* one *and* many; not simply given nor giving, but *both* given to itself *and* self-giving. This paradoxical language is beyond the dialectical language of the coincidence of opposites. It is more resonant of the metaxological poise between opposites, in the fluent passage between them.[49]

## Soul Music and More: More Than Self Alone with Itself

To round off these reflections, though not quite in any finale, I want to broaden the question and ask: More than soul music as a genre of music, should we perhaps understand soul music in something like the broader Greek sense concerning *ta musika*, the musical things? The musical things have everything to do with what a later age will deem humanistic studies, or indeed liberal arts (*artes liberales*). A self without soul music is devoid of these liberal and humanizing arts. These call for finesse and not

(to power). Thus, Schopenhauer is a participant in soul music, as it were, but he cannot quite make sense of the meaning of this participation, how it touches the intimacy of being, as it does. We are released from will into a Sabbath of peace, but his language of will does not quite jell with the festive celebration that is part of the meaning of Sabbatical festivity. The mutation of autonomy into tyrannical eros does not help soul music, for this music breaks forth to console even the tortured self in its subjection to the inexorability of will. The abject self lurks already there in this inexorability—even though later, whether defiant or abject, it will be even less willing to confess its confused, even corrupt condition.

49. The soul is self-moving in both Plato (*Phaedrus*, 245c–246a) and Aristotle (*De Anima*, III, 9). Soul names an originality of moving, an initiation of moving, of life, of being. But if the soul is self-moving, is one "side" of it mover and the other "side" of it moved? Hence one side passive, one side active? How are we to make sense of this? Or is there a middle, neither passive nor active? There is an intriguing connection here between soul and the middle voice (see Davis, *The Soul of the Greeks*, chapter 12, "The Grammar of Soul," 207). One might connect the active with the endeavoring *conatus* the passive with the *passio*, and the middle with the prior porosity. The modern selving tilts in the direction of the endeavor as self-determining; selving as *conatus* overtakes the *passio* and the porosity, and hence loses the middle and its meaning.

just geometrical technique. There is a Platonic sense of soul music in this regard, and its care is for the pedagogy of the *psyche*. Without that care soul-less selving produces results in which the music of life, the poetry of being, evaporates—and we have *technē* without art, art in the more deeply wooed sense called for by music.

Selving springs out from, and must always remain in contact with, soul in this musical sense, and hence must be marked by ontological fidelity to what is *before* its own determinacy and self-determination, and what also is *more*, in pointing beyond self to what is above it. One should remember that music refers us to the muses, and these recall the gift of receiving from sources of inspiration we can call on but cannot command. We can call on and can recall, and we must listen to those sources, if our own being is to be animated by soul-music—if our existence is to become a singing life.[50] The muses are the daughters of Mnemosyne—and memory in the deep metaphysical sense is connected to music. The more deeply wooed sense of art comes only with true courtesy for these daughters.

I mention three indicators here. A first indicator has to do with *origin*. I find myself thinking of Nietzsche and his first-born book: *The Birth of Tragedy from the Spirit of Music*.[51] One must stress this last part: origin in the spirit of music. One can see here a kind of regress to, if not recuperation of, sources of animation prior to the determinations of reason, out of which human outering and uttering come richly. We have to drop back down into the darkness of this prior animation for creativity to come. But again it cannot be commanded. The Greeks were right: it has to be wooed and we have to accept our recipient status. We are beneficiaries of its gift, honored by it, not masters of its energy. To a huge degree this source is identified with the Dionysian by Nietzsche and there are questions to be asked about this. As far as I can see the matter in Nietzsche, there is no true trace of the agapeic promise of the gift. The gift-giving virtue (*die schenkende Tugend*), as Zarathustra calls it, is not agapeic, though it mimics it (a matter I have discussed elsewhere[52]). There is too much of *eros tyrranos* and its equivocity, not least inherited from Schopenhauer and turned in a different direction, putatively "yes-saying." In truth, there is a sign of the porosity here, though it is

50. There would be then a song of self not the same as the song of myself of Walt Whitman—though in truth his song is more than of himself, it sings of that more.

51. Nietzsche, *The Birth of Tragedy* in *Basic Writings of Nietzsche*.

52. Desmond, *Is There a Sabbath for Thought?* 221–28.

then taken over by a *conatus essendi* as defined by will to power affirming itself, sometimes ferociously. Nietzsche never worked out the equivocities of receiving and self-affirming. Nevertheless, the redeeming power of music comes. If there is a kind of "aesthetic theodicy," as Nietzsche does suggest, what does this say about the saving power? If there is a Sabbath of the will, as Schopenhauer says, what does this say about the redemptive power of the releasing source? The source does not have to be taken in their willful sense, their godless sense. One might see them both as trying to restore the soul music to the self but with the sometimes forced strains of the soul-less self.

A second indicator has to do with *end*: I am thinking of Socrates at his end. Nietzsche touches on the point of the "musical Socrates" and this is very germane to the matter. The matter now is the eve of death and the perplexity about the deathlessness of the soul, broached by Socrates and his companions in the prison. The setting of their conversation is the anticipated end of a singular life, the beginning of perhaps another life. Eschatological perplexity hovers over the dialogue—perhaps the most dualistic in one sense, but one has to consider the occasion: this is not the beginning of a Dionysian orgy but a farewell into death, the greatest mortal mystery perhaps, not less than the mystery of life itself. The setting in prison is dictated by the religious duty to avoid polluting Athens by putting someone to death during the sacred time of the yearly festival during which a state ship is sent to Delos to thank the god Apollo for delivery of the youth from the sacrificial death exacted by the Minotaur. It recalls Theseus in the labyrinth, finally gaining release from the appeasing sacrifice of fourteen youths to the Minotaur. In the case of Socrates, there has been a long interim between judgment and execution, the interim prolonged by the delay in the ship's return. The ship is now close by. This stay of execution creates a time in between life and death, which is entirely enfolded in sacred festival. In that between time, neither immersed in life nor yet passing over into death, the worry of Socrates is about the dream that has come to him in the past, and that now again has visited him, namely, with the admonition about making music: "make music and work at it" (*Phaedo*, 60e). He does try his hand at music, and since he is not a maker of myths, he takes some of the fables of Aesop as the substance of his songs, though a hymn to Apollo is also mentioned (*Phaedo*, 60d).[53] He comes to wonder rather if he should continue what

53. Some have mocked this, Nietzsche included, but there is something elemental about Aesop—there is nothing aesthetic in the foppish, "cultured" sense about such

he has always been doing since he thought that perhaps philosophy was the true music and that his dream was like the cheers that encourage runners of a race. Nevertheless, Socrates thought homage must be paid to music, and the musical soul, and there is something sacred about it. That is clear.

Clear also is that there is a musical moment even when the arguments for the deathlessness of the soul do not always completely convince, in the sense of putting all perplexity to rest. Yet even if the *logoi* give no apodictic certainty, there is to be no misology. At certain limits argument becomes appeal and exhortation. Further, Socrates is quite honest that in face even of the crestfallen deflation of argumentative certainty, we still might resort to charms and songs (*Phaedo*, 77e) to keep the soul primed and not lacking in confidence or hope. There is edifying music on the boundary between life and the beyond of this life.

All this is by way of qualification also of the stark dualistic picture most frequently associated with Plato and the *Phaedo*. Further, the immortality of the soul is not just a matter of offering a univocal theoretical argument about a simple substance. It is not that we must eschew metaphysical arguments but metaphysics here must acknowledge the issue of eschatological vision. An eschatological vision is not the same as a teleology of self-determination (*pace* Hegel and Kant above). There is something beyond the logics of determination and self-determination. The question is tied to the matter of the last things (*ta eschata*), of ultimate justice and ethical judgment on the singular soul. This is metaphysical in a metaxological sense as dealing with a threshold where a perplexity about ultimate justice cannot be entirely resolved within immanence itself but in immanent time points to the beyond of immanence. The eschatology of the *metaxu* crossed the boundary between metaphysics/ethics and religion. Thus, the issue is also trans-ethical (if we think of ethics in the Kantian sense). It is beyond immanent autonomy, since the divine measure that will judge cannot be also folded back into any morality of autonomy and (social) self-determination. The soul music resounds from beginning to end . . . even unto eschatological judgment where there may be glorious song, but perhaps also not music but weeping and

fables; they come from below up, from the often-inarticulate ground of the demos and its folk-memory. Folk wisdom comes from nowhere, and yet it has a ground and hold in the elemental constancies of the human condition that, again and again, keep getting resurrected.

gnashing of teeth.[54] The question of eschatological vision is bound up with what I speak of in terms of *posthumous mindfulness:* mindfulness beyond the normal division of life and death, and on the lookout for the worthy to be affirmed in life, and in death . . . the good of the "to be."[55]

There is a sense in which Nietzsche is not so un-Platonic after all, not so different to Socrates at the end. One thinks of his own anticipation of arriving in Hades into the company of great figures and of him having converse with four pairs of thinkers: Epicurus and Montaigne, Goethe and Spinoza, Plato and Rousseau, Pascal and Schopenhauer. Over against their greatness, he would be tested, he will be perhaps purged, he will judge and be judged.[56] This is uncannily like Socrates' anticipation of meeting the heroes on arrival in the next world, and putting them to the kinds of questions that have consumed his soul in this life (*Apology*, 40e–

54. On the need for myth, see *Phaedo* 114 d. See Pieper, *The Platonic Myths*. The *Republic* is centrally concerned with justice, but in the myth of Er Socrates is concerned with justice in an *eschatological perspective*, as he is with the vision of the other world in the *Phaedo*. One notes also how all these visions seem to have an essentially underground dimension, and their concern is emerging from under ground to the surface of a beautiful world. One thinks of the images in Plato comparing us to the fish that lift their heads above the water, and get a glimpse of another world (*Phaedo*, 109b–10b); or of the chariot rising and falling in the empyrean (*Phaedrus*), a vision of our earth, if not seen from above, touched by what is above, and touching it; and then there is the prophesy of the other world to come, where we will not have *images* of the gods, but *the gods themselves* actually will dwell in the sacred groves and temples (*Phaedo*, 111b–c).

55. When one witnesses the astonishing singularity of an infant once born, one is perplexed in tune with Plato's perplexity about the prenatal intimacy of the soul with being; and one wonders about pre-existence, beyond determinate life and death, and our being delivered into life, being delivered over to life and death.

56. One notes at the close of the *Birth of Tragedy*, the reference to sacrifice: the voice of an "old Athenian . . . with the eyes of Aeschylus," and the invitation to "follow me to a tragedy, and sacrifice with me in the temple of both deities" (*Basic Writings*, 144). In "Mixed Opinions and Maxims," §408 (*Human all too Human*): "*The Journey to Hades*: I too have been in the underworld, like Odysseus, and I shall yet return there often; and not only sheep have I sacrificed to be able to talk with a few of the dead, but I have not spared my own blood. Four pairs did not deny themselves to me as I sacrificed: Epicurus and Montaigne, Goethe and Spinoza, Plato and Rousseau, Pascal and Schopenhauer. With these I must come to terms when I have long wandered by myself; they shall tell me whether I am right or wrong; to them I want to listen when, in the process, they tell each other whether they are right of wrong . . ." (*The Portable Nietzsche*, 67). The allusion is to Odysseus in Hades (*Odyssey*, Book 11) in response to Circe's instructions (Book 10). Odysseus encounters many in Hades: his erstwhile companion Elpenor, his mother Antikleia, Ariadne, Tiresias, Agamemnon, Achilles, Ajax, to name some.

41c). Again we have to cease to think in simplistic dualisms—of which I would not accuse Plato. In the *Pheadrus*, it is said that to give an account of the idea of the soul would be divine and that a likeness is more fitting for us humans. We are not totally bereft of articulations. Hence again our need for the image and the myth (the chariot, the horses and charioteer, the singing cicadas—their sound can be heard as ugly, as noise, yet these singing insects are communicators of the sacred[57]). The sacred story is more resonant of the music of the soul than is the bare concept. The image and myth tend to be concretizing and sometimes even singularizing in ways that the concept does not and cannot be.

Soul may have lost its meaning for many, but if we follow the path I have indicated we are brought to the threshold of mystery, where soul is not a bad name for something that has evaporated in the self-determination of selving in our time. It is a matter of acknowledgement of an overdeterminacy rather than knowledge of a determinate matter that we can pin down with univocal fixity. There may be no positive knowledge of the soul in the sense of an absolutely determinate concept, but this does not mean we do not know the soul. Beyond absolutely determinate and univocal knowledge, there can be a kind of *metaxological nescience on the threshold*, especially on the boundary of the ultimate between—between life and death, between death and the life that is beyond death. Heraclitus (fragment 45): "You could not search out the furthest limits of the soul, even if you traversed all of the ways; so unfathomable is its logos."[58] All the ways Heraclitus mentions are the songlines along which the aboriginal ancestors went on walkabout. Without soul, the selving goes on pointless walkabout, for it cannot hear the songlines. It sees only wasteland around it, not secret sources of support.

My third indicator comes back to the *middle*: I must be content to conclude by returning to the poem of G. M. Hopkins that helped me hear the music of the word "selve." I have already cited the first part of the poem, and it brings out the sense of everything as selving, and indeed of the musical sounding of selving. But there is more than selving, even in selving, and to see this one needs to recite the second part. Body and

57. On the singing cicadas by contrast with the bull of Phalaris, see Desmond, *The Intimate Universal*, 311–15.

58. Deserving of more attention is W. B. Yeats's poem "A Dialogue of Self and Soul" where soul "fix(es) every wandering thought upon/ That quarter where all thought is done:/Who can distinguish darkness from the soul? Yeats, *The Poems*, 284–86. I have said something about that poem in connection with forgiveness in Desmond, "It is Nothing: Wording the Release of Forgiveness," especially 13–15.

soul are together in a vision of the incarnate God. The incarnate God is more than the Nietzschean body, more than the Platonic soul. The music of the soul is called to hear the song of the divine, in the saturated surface of all things, in the elemental self-affirmation of all being, and then in the selving that the soul makes for itself in being pleasing in the sight of God. Here is the second part:

> *Í say móre: the just man justices;*
> Kéeps gráce: thát keeps all his goings graces;
> Acts in God's eye what in God's eye he is—
> Chríst—for Christ plays in ten thousand places,
> Lovely in limbs, and lovely in eyes not his
> To the Father through the features of men's faces.

I perform a variation on a theme of Hopkins. I say more—but is it more of the same? More of the self? Yes, and no. We have come to the selving of all things, and there was music in things before this express affirmation. But there is more: The just man justices. If justicing keeps grace, there is more to the just self than its own moral justice. *Keeps*—but what keeps and what is keeping? I venture this keeping is not a matter of possession, but of safeguarding, safekeeping, a sacred duty of holding in trust, as we do when we are confided a gift or an endowment. (An older usage: one has a job to do and one gets one's keep—the shelter and essential nourishments that sustain one's life.) To keep grace is to guard grace, to husband it, to shepherd it. To be the shepherd of this gracing is to be a graced self. In graced selving, the sacred source of soul brims up from the bottomless well and, so to say, christens the selving. With such soul music, we taste ourselves, but the taste is not bitter, not sour. (I am hearing the echoing air of the darker sonnet of Hopkins, cited above.) We are not gall to ourselves, we are not heartburn. Selfyeast of soul no longer a dull dough sours. Our lot is not to be as are the lost, our own sweating selving. If we sweat, it is the porosity coming to be unclogged again, being purged, the selving no longer clotting on itself. The soul is leavened and as song rises in it, it rises into song. This might even be a song of myself, but if so, this is the music of no longer soul-less selving.

# 5

## Beauty under the Underground: Art, Religion, and Schopenhauer's Dark Origin

### Dark Beauty

Schopenhauer's philosophy raises a crucial issue for any affirmation of beauty and its gift: how to reconcile this affirmation with the evil of being. I say evil of being not to endorse this position but to attend to a recurrent tendency human beings display, a tendency that recurs in human history in a variety of forms, religious and anti-religious. Gnosticism most notably might be a paradigm of the religious form, but there are atheisms—and I think of modern revolutionary atheisms—for which being as now given is an evil to be overturned and destroyed, and a new reality constructed by us out of the overcoming of past and present being. Schopenhauer has no time for such revolutionary dreams and does display an aesthetic finesse for beauty, and yet the metaphysical bass tone of his thought resonates with the evil of being. There is his invoking of Dante's hell, not to endorse it straightforwardly, but to exceed it: *this world itself is a hell* surpassing Dante's vision, and every man is a devil to every other.[1] Though an atheist, Schopenhauer does not turn his back on

1. Schopenhauer, *The World as Will and Representation*, 2:578 [hereafter *WWR*]. In *Parerga and Paralipomena*, 2:§229, Schopenhauer has very disparaging things to say about Dante and the idea of a divine comedy.

Luther's bleak picture of fallen creation and the prince of the world, its evil lord. Evil and beautification: "The prince of darkness is a gentleman" (*King Lear*, III, 4, 1935).

The evil of being is felt by Schopenhauer in the flesh itself: instead of the glory of the human body, we know ourselves to be hapless victims of the sexual urge. Erotics offers no enchanting intercourse with the beautiful, the beloved; instead when the will affirms itself in generation there follows shame, repugnance, disgust, and a "peculiar sadness and remorse."[2] Eros: humiliation to rational autonomy. The intoxication of eros is toxic. Schopenhauer's philosophy: sweating out of his system the poison of eros. And while "unconsciousness is the original and natural condition of all things,"[3] yet all beings strive to be. Though there is a will to existence—call this a certain *conatus essendi* universalized—still the truth of this is that all life is a constant suffering.[4] The passion of being is pain only, suffering and suffering alone. How could there be any soul-music, much less richly generous selving, if the basic forms of willing are shared "in common with the polyp," while the "fundamental error of all philosophers" is of making "thinking the essential and primary element of the 'so-called soul'"?[5] In one of his better-known adages, "life is a business whose returns are far from covering the cost."[6] In many ways, Schopenhauer throws up his hands in exasperation at "the whole catastrophe" (as Zorba the Greek called marriage and family): "no one has the remotest idea why the tragic-comedy exists." Life "by no means presents itself as a gift to be enjoyed, but as a task, a drudgery, to be worked through."[7]

There is an asymmetry between evil and good, but here the tilt of the balance falls on the side of evil. Evil "can never be wiped off, and consequently can never by balanced by the good that exists along with or after it."[8] And a paradoxical point to which we will come: the true end of life "is the *euthanasia of the will*."[9] One might say: euthanasia of the endeavor to be; and this, not to reopen the porosity of being and be patient to the gift of the "to be" (*passio essendi*), but to nihilate the will to be and

2. *WWR*, 2:569.
3. *WWR*, 2:142.
4. *WWR*, 1:267 for instance; 2:635.
5. *WWR*, 2:204, 206.
6. *WWR*, 2:353
7. *WWR*, 2:357.
8. *WWR*, 2:576.
9. *WWR*, 2:637, italics mine.

the *esse* of our endeavor, all endeavor. The will exists as self-discordant in the struggle of different beings for life and against each other; and yet too the will can turn against itself.[10] But how will can turn against itself and become will-less is hard to understand. Here the significance of art and the religious appear as helping effect this turn away of the will from the will. And yet is there not a kind of odd pride in Schopenhauer that he is such an apostle of the good news of the evil world? "Only with me are the evils of the world honestly admitted in all their magnitude."[11] The excellence of the better religions was just their nihilistic attunement to the evil of being, and the original evil of the human being. Kierkegaard, as is evident from some late journal entries, was delighted when Schopenhauer began late in his life to enjoy a certain renown. At last, a dark man who was intimate with the darkness of man—a darkness that no social or political ameliorization could dispel. One does get the impression, however, that Schopenhauer's darkness was as child's play compared to the darkness the true Christian, and by extension Kierkegaard himself, had to suffer. Schopenhauer too much prides himself on giving asceticism "a place in his system," even turning pessimism into the "interesting"—an aestheticization Kierkegaard rejects.[12] Still, in any event, the shadows of suffering and enduring evil continue to *disturb* the bright high noon of idealistic enlightenment—just as also there continue to be thinkers who *relish* the darkness.

How then is it possible to talk at all about the gift of beauty on these terms? That this gift is offered is undoubtedly true, and it is undoubtedly

10. *WWR*, 1:146–47, 412, 391; 2:635; see also Schopenhauer, *Parerga and Paralipomena*, 2:418–20.

11. *WWR*, 2:643.

12. Kierkegaard, *The Last Years*, 77–79, 170–72, 218–19. The entry 170–72 is more abbreviated than the same entry from 1854 as more fully translated in *The Journals of Kierkegaard, 1834–1854*, 234–40; there it comes across that Kierkegaard is struck also by a certain inversion between himself and Schopenhauer, manifested in their names A.S. (**A**rthur **S**chopenhauer) and S.A. (**S***øren* **A**abye Kierkegaard). I mentioned above the humiliation felt by rational autonomy relative to eros, but see *The Last Years*, 68–70 where Kierkegaard's views of woman come across as no less misogynistic than Schopenhauer's: "First and foremost men are humiliated by women. One may generally assume that every married man is in his inner heart crestfallen, for he feels that he has been made a fool of, when all that high-flown stuff of the days of falling in love, all that about Juliana being the very incarnation of beauty and grace, and the possession of her being the summit of blessedness, end in a false alarm. This is the first blow the man receives." Compare to Schopenhauer "On Women" in *Parerga and Paralipomena*, 2: chapter XXVII.

true that Schopenhauer was appreciative of it, even granting his evil eye for given being. And yet the appreciation that would grant beauty given as gift is coupled with a metaphysics that evacuates every kind of gift of the generosity of being that it most touchingly communicates. In his early notebooks (between 1812 and 1814), under the influence of Plato, Kant, and the Upanishads, he talks about a "better consciousness" that seems to give us access to something higher than ordinary consciousness; but there is controversy about the meaning of this, as well as its coherence with Schopenhauer's metaphysics as a whole.[13] I myself ask if perhaps this issue is connected with the absence of terms in this metaphysics that would allow us to make some acknowledgement, if not a kind of philosophical sense, of the porosity of being and the *passio essendi*, and indeed the *conatus essendi*, no longer now seen as the voracious will that wills itself and nothing but itself. For the will that wills itself and nothing but itself can give nothing in the generous sense at issue; and givenness as such becomes the opposite of the generous gift of being—it becomes no more than an absurd happening from which we must escape. Of course, we too are absurd happenings and so every project of escaping absurdity is itself absurd, short of the hara kiri of the will, itself also on the terms offered to us, the absolute in absurdity, since what cannot but will itself cannot will itself not to be. This is a strange Lucifer at the center of hell, in one sense like Dante's, frozen and weeping, but here not gnawing on the great traitors Judas, Brutus, and Cassius, but *gnawing eternally on itself.* Instead of the will as a primal love of itself we have will as a primal hatred of itself.

There seems no escape. If will is more primordial than the principle of sufficient reason (a point to which I will return), it is without any reason. It is an ultimate without a why. Mystic Angelus Silesius: the rose is without a why. Schopenhauer, gloomy deliverer of kakodicy: the will is without a why. Will: before reason, exceeding reason, and if we were to call it a god, it would be an evil god, not neutral, but more like the

13. See Neill and Janaway, eds. *Better Consciousness*, 10n.2, where Christopher Janaway helpfully lists the persistent references to the "better consciousness" from Schopenhauer, *Manuscript Remains*, vol. 1. In *Parerga and Paralipomena*, 2:274–5, Schopenhauer speaks of being beyond the separation of subject and object, knower and known in death, as we were once before birth: "we are shifted only into the original state which is *without knowledge*, but is not for that reason absolutely *without consciousness*; on the contrary, it will be a state that is raised above and beyond that form where the contrast between subject and object vanishes." Could we say of pre-natal and posthumous being: being once and being again in the pure porosity?

evil genius of Descartes. The effect of the latter supposition, we recall, is to reverse all the signs, positive and negative, good and evil, and in the process make us the dupe of a kind of universal dissimulation. Images of the original seem like light, but this original is a dark origin and so the images are images of nothing but this darkness. We too are made in the image and likeness of the darkness of this dark origin.[14] The *conatus essendi* is most like an *eros tyrannos,* a point Schopenhauer is not at all inhibited in putting. It is a ravening want that, as wanting, seems to be a lack, but as voraciously wanting, it is an energetic insistence on what it wants, and which it seems to get circuitously when it does not get it directly. Perhaps mimicking God, the ways of the will are truly mysterious to man. The human being is its unwitting host. Chasing after beguiling beauty, all the while, unbeknownst to us, we are being groomed for death.

This is hell, and again Schopenhauer does not desist from offering us many images of hell. But at the core of his right remembrance of hatred and hell, we have to wonder if there is metaphysical incoherence, and indeed perhaps a blindness to the power of agapeic generosity. And this despite his ethics of compassion, which is not agapeic generosity, appearances notwithstanding, but a kind of self-pitying counterfeit double of it. It is not for the other *qua other* that compassion goes forth but for *oneself* and the identity of one's suffering in the suffering of the other. Does such compassion brings us home to ourselves in the whole, hence not truly release us to the beyond of ourselves? *Tat tvam asi*—thou art that—but is this the agape of compassion? To state again the question above implied: How can the will at all mutate into compassion if there is not in its deepest sources the seeds of agapeic generosity, seeded in the original porosity of our being and our *passio essendi*? And if there were these seeds, and this promise of love, would the will be at all the will as Schopenhauer describes it?

14. Is this why, at times, one notes in Schopenhauer a striking mixture of acuteness and crudeness? For instance, he strikingly sees that there are two places on the human body where are significantly hairy—the head and the *pudenda.* He takes the head to be the seat of the brain, and hence to correspond to the Idea, while the genitals are the seat of sex, and hence the focal point (his word *Brennpunkt*: literally—burn(ing) point) of the will.

## On the Dangerous Threshold of the Sacred

Schopenhauer's philosophy of the dark origin might be said to navigate an ambiguous and sometimes dangerous threshold between the aesthetic and the religious. We do not normally think of him as a religious thinker, and yet there is a sense in which he is one of the first of the *religious atheists*: self-proclaimed atheists who yet take back into their philosophical thinking orientations to the world that have had their first home in the space of religion and that now, suitably reconfigured, are given a new place within what seems to be a post-theistic ethos of being. Whether the ascription "religious" can finally be upheld is a question, yet there are forms of atheism that are sometimes close to religious thresholds and indeed some of these thresholds are inhabited, indeed traversed, by aesthetic sisters or artistic brothers that soften the gulf between atheism and religion. Schopenhauer can be looked on as such a kind of atheist. He confesses that though his philosophy ends on a negation, in terms of what one must give up, "it is precisely here that the mystic proceeds positively, and therefore, from this point, nothing is left but mysticism." This supplement can be found elsewhere, and Plotinus, Scotus Eriugena, Meister Eckhart, and Jacob Böhme are among instances mentioned.[15] True, his religious atheism is particularly hostile to faith in the goodness of God, and from this hostility complications ensue: ensue not only relative to any sense of final release or redemption, understood religiously or atheistically; but ensue also relative to Schopenhauer's own love of the beautiful, sister of the good, in the older metaphysical tradition. For how can one love the sister of the good if the good itself is in thrall to the secret evil of being? These issues are at stake in the thoughts to come.

We also often pay more attention to Schopenhauer's reflection on art than on religion, given that art and the aesthetic since Kant seem to offer just such a reconfigured space where traces of the sacred persist, though never explicitly named as such. We can play with the possibilities of art without the danger of more explicit religious commitments and yet in all of this not lose some of the flickerings of mystery that come with the lingering ghosts of the religious. I have already suggested that the sense of transcendence migrates or is displaced from its original home in religion to a seemingly more accommodating aesthetic space in post-Kant aesthetics, and this we see to a degree with Schopenhauer also. Schopenhauer does invest art with a remarkable metaphysical significance,

15. *WWR*, 2:612.

and yet he is not reluctant to cite the figure of the saint as perhaps of even more ultimate metaphysical significance than the artistic genius in his or her way of looking at things. What art does episodically, religion does more completely and conclusively, particularly in its radical ascetic forms. But how could there be such things as atheistic saints? How at all could ascetic atheists be brothers or sisters to the saints?

Crucially significant here, I think, is what amounts to a philosophical apostasy to univocal rationalism in metaphysics, and the claim for a more ultimate origin that is on the other side of the principle of sufficient reason. This ultimate, as already stated, Schopenhauer calls will, but ultimate will is not only beyond this principle, in a certain sense it is mysterious. For it cannot be completely determined in rational terms—to the contrary it secretly determines the terms on the basis of which reason itself ultimately erects its constructions. The will or dark origin is thus a name for mystery, not entirely unapproachable, and yet not reducible to what the principle of sufficient reason determines as intelligible, precisely because it is the more ultimate, the ultimate determiner of that principle itself.

It is this broad sense of mystery that places Schopenhauer's thinking on a threshold where it can swivel productively, now in the direction of the aesthetic, now in the direction of the religious. Hence, notably again, though he is a self-proclaimed atheist, he does take pains to grant that the images and myths of the "higher" religions prefigure in representational or symbolic form what is more rationally expressed in the metaphysical concepts of his own philosophical system. (What can "higher" mean at all in this way of thinking?) In this he is not at all unlike Hegel, except that what he means by representation and concept is different to Hegel, a difference going all the way to the ultimate root of what they consider to be the basis and character of all being. His atheism has a religious tinge to it, just as also his appropriation of art is not lacking in the need to resort to the mythic language of the sacred to communicate its most essential insights. I want to consider how this way of looking at things has a bearing on a familial relation between this sense of the dark origin and religious mystery and aesthetic contemplation. I want to look at what seem to me to be equivocities in this sense of things, where aesthetic contemplation and sacred mystery can be as much ontological delights as metaphysical escapes. They tend to be the latter for Schopenhauer, whereas I would put a different stress on the former.

When I speak of him as a religious atheist my primary point is more than just to acknowledge rightly the important influence that Eastern religions had on him, both confirming his metaphysical views (as he grants himself), as well as influencing them.[16] This is an important consideration: that a professed atheist might exhibit no simple agenda-driven hostility to some of the great religions, no callow rationalism that is deficient in imagination as to what might be communicated in sacred signs.[17] Whether he approaches these religions in the best way is a question, and I would question the nihilistic interpretation of ascetic religions, Christianity especially not excluded. I am interested in the metaphysical role played by the will, by the sense of the ultimate will as on the other side of the principle of sufficient reason, and whether, and to what degree, this overlaps or diverges from an appreciation of mystery with respect to the ultimate or divine, so crucial in religious traditions. I will have occasion to note his thin take on the agapeic, but I will have something to say about the erotics also, and indeed the other hyperboles of being as I call them.

There is, in Schopenhauer, a peculiar mixture of porosity, *passio* and *conatus*: I am very unsure he has a sense of the truer equipoise between these. Will for him is an ontologically generalized *conatus essendi*, with results also for the *passio essendi*: this tends to mirror Schopenhauer's sense of will thus conceived, not the sense of patience, and reception of the gift of being. And yet, paradoxically intruding into this absolutized *conatus*, the power of art is affirmed as enabling, in my terms, a reopening of the porosity of being, with *passio* now communicated as released from the relentless will into a new will-lessness. The mixing of porosity, *passio*, and *conatus* is important for metaphysics, but also for how we understand religion and art. For metaphysics: bearing on the ontological

16. See *WWR*, 2:169 where he concedes Buddhism's "pre-eminence over the others" in relation to his own philosophy, and expresses his pleasure in finding this philosophy confirmed there.

17. A significant doubleness in relation to religion, mixing outright hostility and qualified sympathy, is evidenced, for example, in his essay "On Religion" in *Parerga and Paralipomena*, 2: chapter XV. This is so in the dialogue between Demopheles and Philalethes (§174), but revealingly in his anti-Judaism (he speaks repeatedly of the *foetor Judaicus*) and his hatred of the opening of Genesis with God's "It is very good" (370ff., 381). What is good about Christianity comes from the East, probably through Egypt, and Jesus was an avatar (383). The Fall is the central doctrine, Augustine perfected the doctrine of original sin (363–6), contra the superficial optimism of the Pelagians, and (in his time) the rationalists who are well-meaning but shallow (386–89). A fascinating diatribe, I would recommend it as indispensable preparation for understanding Nietzsche!

structure of being and the human being. For religion: bearing on the original porosity as opening the primordial communication of the human and the more than human, the divine in religious traditions. For art: bearing on the secret sources of human originality and creativity and receptive beholding, as beyond univocal determination and dialectical self-determination. The *passio* communicates something prior to the *conatus*, as a receiving of the energy of being before the self-activation of the endeavor. Selving itself is to be seen as gifted before seen as constructed—with tremendous repercussions for both religion and aesthetics, and indeed also for metaphysics and the practise of philosophy. The ascetic religions are themselves mixings of the porosity, *passio*, and *conatus*. While Schopenhauer intuitively touches on these in diverse ways, it is questionable whether he does justice to the true intermediations between them. This has repercussions for being on the threshold of the sacred, repercussions that can issue in counterfeit doubles of the holy.

## From under the Underground

I have referred before in previous reflections to a tendency in recent centuries in philosophical thought that departs from Plato's ascent *above* the cave and rather descends *below* the cave into deeper darknesses where the sun's light seems entirely extinguished. Schopenhauer's philosophy is illuminating on the matter (if one can speak properly of illumination at all at such a depth of darkness). Here is a first pass at being under the underground. Of interest here is that we often think of Schopenhauer as a *post-Hegelian thinker*, given his hostility to Hegel. We also couple him with his successor Nietzsche, so much so that we overlook the fact that Schopenhauer's *World as Will and Representation* (vol. I, 1818) was written at a time very close to Hegel's *Science of Logic* (1812–16). Perhaps we fail to take much notice of this because Schopenhauer only exerted influence well after Hegel's death. More than a mere historical contingency, I find this overlap of philosophical significance. In Hegel a certain rational idealism reaches its culmination and yet the Hegelian hymn to *ascendant reason* is contemporaneous with the Schopenhauerian *descent into a more ultimate darkness prior to reason*. Hegel speculatively ascends to thought thinking itself, Schopenhauer philosophically descends to what is other to thought thinking itself, the will willing itself. Can the ascent of one be divorced from the descent of the other? Do we still think and live out of the consequences of that ascent and descent?

Due to that descent under the underground, Schopenhauer's philosophy of the dark origin still speaks to us today. Why so? Partly it is due to a skepticism about reason, in some ways initiated in the critique of pure reason by Kant, critique wending its way along more irregular, even nihilistic ways after Kant. Partly it has to do with the over-inflation of confidence in reason by the Enlightenment generally and Hegelian idealism particularly, each of which produced its reaction of a long deflation in confidence in reason. Perhaps more importantly, it resides in the sense moderns have of the ethos of being—that is, of a thereness that has no inherent value, the worth of which we have to "create" by "projecting" our value(s) on its otherness, if it is to have any value at all. This devaluation of the ethos of being has its origins in the scientific objectification that extrudes any purpose or final causality from its sanctioned scheme of intelligibility. Instead of the given ethos of being communicating of traces of inherent value, it stands over against us as valueless, all but as an alien other. One might even suspect something like a gnostic suggestion in this valueless ethos of being, a suggestion of something not merely indifferent but hostile to the human being. Rational confidence in the inherent intelligibility of being passes over into suspicion of the bright face of intelligibility. We worry that intelligibility is the mask of something darker and lacking intelligibility in itself. We detect aspects of such a metaphysical attunement, or dissonance, not only in Schopenhauer but in Nietzsche, as well as many other thinkers, too numerous to mention.

Many of these considerations are mingled together in any reflection on a dark origin, but I will mention this last one, namely, the stress on the will as such, in Kant and after. Reason is and must be the slave of the passions, Hume said, and Kant's philosophy of the good will, the rational will, sought to testify against this enslavement. Nevertheless, the suspicion of something darker in will than reason seems more persuasive when the eros of endless striving seems more fitting for human beings refusing limits to their own autonomy. Indeed, in that endless striving, the human being might seem no longer passively to mirror the devalued thereness of nature as a mere mechanism, but actively to participate in living in an organic nature alive with a darker, sublimer energies.

Philosophers have always been concerned with the search for origins, or the origin: be it the sources or resources of knowing, the sources and grounds of intelligibility, or most extremely, the origin of the "to be" without which nothing determinate would be at all. Some might say that we live in post-metaphysical times, and that such questions belong to a surpassed past, but while particular approaches to such question might be no longer entirely viable, the questions themselves are elemental and perplexing, and we will never get beyond them finally, even when we essay our best answer. They call forth what for Kant was the ineradicable metaphysical impulse, addressed by perplexities it can neither answer in an entirely definitive way nor put aside as now no longer of consequence. To be blessed—or cursed—with such perplexing questions is to be a philosopher and, no question about it, Schopenhauer was a philosopher.

That he was such a philosopher needs to be reiterated, since attention to his work in the last century has been much dimmed, to the degree that his star was eclipsed by Nietzsche, his spiritual son. Nietzsche has some responsibility for also eclipsing the above-intractable perplexities, especially metaphysical perplexity: his mockery of the metaphysicians (coupled with that of the heavy Germanic guns of Heidegger, and the perhaps lighter artillery of his French followers) had its desired effect of making thinkers ashamed of the question of origin—ashamed of being philosophers. Of course, if Nietzsche himself had not encountered the bracing inspiration of Schopenhauer it is an interesting (if hypothetical) question as to how he himself might have developed as a philosopher or anti-philosopher. We are often forced to read Schopenhauer in Nietzsche's shadow and we forget the immense influence Schopenhauer had on major artists and leading cultural figures in the nineteenth and well into the twentieth century.

Perhaps some may share my experience: I had read Nietzsche extensively before I had studied Schopenhauer intensively. I had been indoctrinated by Nietzsche's self-promotion, repeated endlessly by many of his admirers: when I was a child I put on Schopenhauerian ways, but now that I am a man, I am Nietzsche, the antipodes of Schopenhauer—he is pessimist of the great "No," I the herald of the great "Yes!" Yet when I studied Schopenhauer more intensively, I was astonished to discover how he had read Nietzsche so closely! Schopenhauer, the gruff bear, had fallen under the spell of the dancing *Maestro*! I had to rub my eyes to be released from this magic spell. Of course, enchanted by Nietzsche, I was seeing things back to front. In truth, so much of Schopenhauer lies at the back of Nietzsche. Schopenhauerian blood always circulated in the body of Nietzsche, even while a different body grew; strong or sick, Nietzsche remained Schopenhauer's blood brother to the end. Christopher Janaway is right in the main when he says: "Schopenhauer . . . is the system behind Nietzsche's anti-system"[18] The rhetorical brilliance of Nietzsche masks some of these more systematic considerations, and perhaps it is Schopenhauer who rather offers us a needed lucidity on hard issues. Perhaps also Schopenhauer is the more radical and honest about the nihilism that comes with a vision of the whole that proclaims its overall purposelessness.

Such purposelessness returns us to Schopenhauer's sense of the dark origin. Will, he holds is primordial, but the primordial will has no purpose—it is a blind, insatiable striving. It is a dark self-expressing energy, but there is no point to its striving beyond itself, and this is no point to it all, for there is no point where it comes to an end. It is endless striving that emerges out of its own darkness, passes through what looks like spaces regulated by more rational norms, only to show that the latter are themselves derivatives, and in the end that is no end, the derivatives are overtaken once more by the purposeless striving or futile will.

This is a bleak vision no doubt, but let us step back from its darkness to throw light on some important factors inspiring it.

## Platonic Half-Light

Two significant philosophical influences are acknowledged by Schopenhauer, namely Plato and Kant. Schopenhauer offers a peculiar melding of Kantian and Platonic factors: on one side, there is the legacy of a "subjective idealism," on the other side, that of a form of "objective idealism"—since here the Platonic Idea is not just the objectification of the individual will but of the will itself, considered as an ontological origin. Both Plato and Kant are philosophers in which the powers of *logos* or reason seem to reign supreme. Further, what is original is also seen in the light of *logos* or reason. With Plato we make intelligible sense of being by reference to the Ideas, with Kant with reference to reason, whether theoretical reason in the complex synthesis constituting our scientific knowledge of phenomena, or practical reason in its autonomous determination of the moral law, or reason in its regulative projection of Ideas with respect to anticipated totality.

Looking first at the matter with Platonic eyes, Schopenhauer's view effects a revision, indeed reversal of the principle of sufficient reason. Reason is derivative from something more primordial, the will; something

18. Janaway, ed., *Willing and Nothingness*, 2.

excessive about will seems recalcitrant to complete rational comprehension. Schopenhauer wrote in the time of the high noon of idealism, but he was attuned to perplexities in that noon concerning what is *other* to reason entirely at home with itself. He philosophizes in the equivocal half-light, half-darkness of phenomena in Plato's cave, but there he begins to tunnel below the floor of the cave rather than simply climbing up above and out of it. The Platonic cave is constituted by a mixed interplay of light and darkness, but it is not only that we are in the cave; rather *we ourselves are a cave, a second underground.* More radically still, there is something *subterranean even in that underground*, whether of the first cave, or of the cave we ourselves are. Will is a more primordial origin than the half-and-half world of phenomena, the cave in the first sense, or of ourselves, double creatures of will and representation, the second cave.

In a crucial passage, when talking about access to the thing in itself of Kant, Schopenhauer says "we ourselves are the thing-in-itself"; a "way from within (*ein Weg von innen*) stands open to us. . . . It is, so to speak, a subterranean passage (*ein unterirdischer Gang*), a secret alliance, which, as if by treachery (*Verrath*), places us all at once in the fortress that could not be taken by attack from without."[19] It would be an interesting question to reflect further on this passage and the language of secure self-enclosure of the thing in itself and our betrayal, but we must stick with the underground that we ourselves are.[20] In truth, speaking Platonically now, in whichever cave we are, first or second, Schopenhauer's vision is so dark that we are perplexed as to what we can *see at all.* He sees the subterranean passage as a way to truth. But if the thing itself is a dark origin more primordial than the half-light/half-darkness of the cave, or of our own half-light/half-darkness, what at all can we see by the light of its darkness? In that dark vision, or vision of darkness, what can it mean to say there is an underground to the underground cave? And what would the consequences be of burrowing below its ground?

Think of it this way. Schopenhauer's major work is entitled *The World as Will and Representation.* Will is the thing itself,[21] the original, while representation is its image. If we were to liken the world as representation to Plato's cave, could we liken Schopenhauer's "will" to Plato's

19. *WWR* 2:195.

20. For instance, Schopenhauer's *Verrath* brings to my mind Heidegger's claim in *Being and Time* §29 that wresting the truth of *alētheia* from its hiddenness (*Unverborgenheit*) is like a robbery (*ein Raub*). Suspicion of a crime hangs over the thing.

21. *WWR* 1:110.

"good"? Surely we would have to consider the reverse possibility? For will is no sun, is no good, but as a dark origin it is darker even than the shadow land of representation. If we were to call it a first principle, it is a more like an other under-ground, *beneath* the first underground as its origin, not above it as the good. It is an under-ground beneath us humans also. But can we then meaningfully speak any more of what is *above*, above either the "normal" cave of everyday life, or ourselves as denizens of that cave? We have to wonder if, long before Nietzsche, Plato is already being reversed here—reversed more radically.

I will come back to the fact that Schopenhauer holds on to the Platonic Idea, and hence seeks to mitigate some of the more extreme consequences that would follow from this line of thinking. That said, the extremity of what follows from Schopenhauer's view is worth reiterating. For if the representations are shadow images of the will, then they are not shadows of light; they are not even shadows of shadows; they are shadows of this original darkness. What kind of strange shadow is such a shadow of original darkness? What kind of strange original is this, if its darkness casts shadows only apparently more lightsome than the original itself? To know this thing itself would be to know an original that, in a way, is no original, for it casts less images than vanishing shadows of "itself." Do not these shadows then *compound* the darkness, rather than dispel it? What could philosophy—or art or religion—possibly do to dispel the shadows of this impenetrably dark ground under Plato's first underground?

## Strange Shine of Light

What of the shine on things, the strange light, despite all of this? We might turn now to how Schopenhauer is shadowed by Kant's idealism: his acknowledged debt predominantly centres on Kant's coupling of transcendental ideality and empirical reality. Recall reflection in a previous chapter (chapter 3) on the sourcing of the shine on things in the transcendental subject. This is relevant here. Schopenhauer is (at least initially) a subjective idealist for whom there is no object without a subject. "The world is my representation": Schopenhauer opens his *magnus opus* with this imperious announcement. Showing immense confidence, he claims that everyone will recognize this proposition as true: it is comparable to one of the axioms of Euclid. No object without a subject, for in order for there to be an object there has to be a subject for whom the object is or appears. The defect of realism is its assertion of an absolutely identical object, totally irrespective of a subject to which it is appearing. The principle seems hard to reject, though much turns on the *meaning of the subject* for whom the object is or appears, and the nature of the *relation between* the subject and it. If initially there seems a confident naïveté about his idealism, his exploration undermines any naïve notion of the subject, for there is an immanent otherness at work in the subject, related to the dark origin, and which erupts as much immanently in the self as externally in the world of nature.

Why here with Schopenhauer do we *not* get a triumphant subjectivism in which a self-knowing transcendental subjectivity trumpets its epistemological or ontological ultimacy, or something like the self-transparency of Hegelian absolute knowledge? One reason is the Platonic exigence that philosophy "must go back to what is first and original." This "going back" will bring us to more than "subjectivity," back to something like Platonic Ideas, but more importantly to *will as absolutely original*, will that is a family relation of eros, not an overt Kantian concern, but certainly crucial for Plato. With this we come back, and in the intimacy of "subjectivity," to an otherness that shatters the pretensions to the immediate self-certainty of subjectivity, and that certainly blocks the way to anything like the triumph of Hegel's absolute subjectivity. In a way that reminds us a little of Schelling, Schopenhauer explodes idealism from *within*, though he might not put it thus himself. Triumphant subjectivity defeats itself in its triumph over itself; but its triumph is its discovery intimate to itself of something over which it cannot triumph in an entirely rational way. It discovers that what drives it to master itself is marked by an immanent otherness over which it is not, and cannot be, sovereign master.

Wittgenstein remarked that solipsism coincided with realism (*Tractatus Logico-Philosophicus*, 5.64), and perhaps something analogous happens here. Starting with subjective idealism, Schopenhauer's exploration leads to will as thing in itself, but this leads to an ontological claim: the nature of original being as will is read off from the self. If we find here an ontology of subjectivity, we also find an ontology of the inward otherness of selving itself, which directs us further to the ontological power of original being. What follows is an explosion, rather implosion, of subjective idealism from *within*: the unruly otherness is within the putatively sovereign idealistic subject. Even more, there is a sense in which the subject is no longer within itself; it too is the effect of the original ground/origin as other to it: given to be, before it gives itself to be, or relates to being other than itself. Schopenhauer does not quite put it like that, but I see here the form of a subject that is *beside itself*. Again I am reminded of the importance of eros (indeed mania) in Plato, and will return to this.

Contra Kant, Schopenhauer says we can know the *thing in itself*. Interestingly, he here agrees with Hegel, who says even more loudly that the thing in itself is the most easily known. But the difference between them is crucial. In knowing the thing in itself, for Schopenhauer, we know the will, which we cannot absolutely know, in the sense of entirely encapsulating it in a system of concepts. "My body and my will are one."[22] "Everyone finds himself to be this Will, in which the inner nature of the world consists."[23] The knowing is first in the intimacy of our own sense of embodied will; then the intimacy of embodied will is known as the energy of a source of being that, as more original than the intellect, can never be mastered by the latter. Something remains beyond, even while acknowledged as immanently embodied. The rational concept, while needed, betrays something about the intimate knowing of the embodied will itself. If we intimately know the will as embodied, we are not far off from thoughts about the energy of eros, itself emergent from secret sources in the obscurity of our embodiment, even as it sets us in motion in an unfolding of self-transcending. I might say more here about the relation to the emergence of the *conatus essendi*, in continuity with the *passio essendi*, out of the more original porosity of being, but I will just note that most original for Schopenhauer is *will* and not this porosity. This has consequences for his foregrounding a form of the *conatus essendi*, and without a finessed enough appreciation of the *passio essendi* and its significance. By contrast with Schopenhauer, when Hegel says we know the thing in itself, he asserts the superiority of rational thought over any resistant otherness. Rational thought is just that power that overreaches both itself and its other; rational thought can overreach the other because the other is itself nothing but thought, the two are the same. This is just what is denied by Schopenhauer in his doctrine of will. The will as the other of thought *is* the other of thought. Instead of the Hegelian overreaching of the other of thought, it is the other way round. It is the dark origin that overreaches thought, for thought is a derivative of this origin, an emergence from a ground beyond thought.

22. *WWR*, 1:102.

23. See, *WWR*, 1:125; also *WWR*, 2: chapter XVIII.

If will is said to be the primordial metaphysical principle, all being manifests will. Will is the original source of being to which we have the most direct access through ourselves as embodied will. As aware of our being embodied, we are intimate with ourselves *both* as subject and as object, as both will and representation. When we realize this philosophically, the world is opened up for us, opened as both will and representation. See in this Schopenhauer's acceptance, with significant revisions, of the so-called Copernican revolution of the transcendental turn. Very strikingly, he reverses the claim that man is a microcosmos and the world a macrocosmos. Rather, we should say that the world itself is an *macranthropos*: the world is, so to speak, the human being writ large, not the human being the world writ small.[24] But in turning to the intimacy of the human will, Schopenhauer is catapulted towards the will as transhuman, and hence, in a kind of immanent summersault, this macranthropomorphism seems reversed. If we ourselves are an underground, we do not find that we are univocally identical with any *inward sun*. Certainly, the more ultimate will is not at all like Kant's rational good will. One could argue that will as origin must be dark relative to more determinate forms of cognition; beyond the normal split of subject and object, it is the primordial source out of which plurality and differentiation are subsequently derived. Will is not a determinate rational structure, though it may take form as structured. That Schopenhauer's describes it in terms a blind, goal-less striving says something about the darkness of this primordial origin.[25] This "thing in itself" does not "see." "Seeing" emerges derivatively from a more primordial blindness.

Put somewhat differently: rational thought is a moment within an original otherness, not as Hegel would have it, the speculative whole

24. *WWR*, 2:642; German: *Sämtliche Werke*, 2:824–25 (herafter *SW*): "*Ich habe den Satz umgekert und die Welt als Makranthropos nachgewiesen; sofern Wille under Vorstellung ihr wie sein Wesen erschöpft. Offenbar aber ist es richtiger, die Welt aus dem Menschen verstehn zu lehren als den Menschen aus der Welt . . . .*"

25. There are many passages to this effect in Schopenhauer. See, for instance, *SW*, 2:771ff., which disputes the optimism associated with giving priority to knowing rather than to blind will. Rationally speaking, the existence of the world is groundless: *Daher wenn einer wagt, die Frage aufzuwerfen, warum nicht lieber gar nichts sei als diese Welt; so lasst die Welt sich nicht aus sich selbst rechfertigen, kein Grund, kein Endursache ihres Daseins in ihr selbst finden, nichts nachweisen, dass sie ihrer selbst wegen, d.h. zu ihrem eigenen Vorteil dasei. – Dies ist meiner Lehre zufolge freilich daraus erklärlich, dass das Prinzip ihres Daseins ausdrucklich ein grundloses ist, nämlich blinder Will zum Leben, welcher als Ding an sich dem Satz vom Grunde, der bloss die Form der Erscheinungen ist und durch den allein jedes Warum berechigt ist, nicht unterworfen sein kann*" (*SW*, 2:741–42); see *WWR*, 2:579ff.

within which original otherness becomes a mere moment. Thought thinking itself in Hegelian fashion claims the whole contains the darkness within itself. Thought thinking its other in Schopenhauerian fashion suggests that it is the darkness of the whole that embraces the frail light of thought within itself. And no matter how expansively this light extends, it will never overreach the darkness, for it is the latter that will always be the more fundamental ground of the former. Of course, we can still ask whether the darkness might be *mysterious without being absurd*, whether the light might be more enigmatic than our reason can comprehend. Recall my remarks at the outset as to whether Schopenhauer, despite being an atheistic philosopher, is on the threshold of a sense of mystery, itself perhaps more at home in the family of the sacred.

Will as dark origin must externalize itself to come to some self-realization of what is hidden in the initially intimate idiocy of its will to be. There is something idiotic about the origin in Hegel, as in Schopenhauer, since in the beginning it does not know itself; its self-becoming is its self-articulation and its pathway to self-knowing, beyond idiocy. Schopenhauer objected to what he took as the excessive anthropomorphizing of cosmic *Geist* by the Hegelians, as if the whole of nature and history simply served the narrow ends of European man at the beginning of the nineteenth century. The darker consequences of his macroanthropmorphism tell against the rational optimism of the idealistic anthropomorphism. Kant spoke of subreption as projecting on the other what properly belonged to oneself, claiming this happens with the sublime. We meet in Schopenhauer another afterlife of Kantian subreption, though one that points towards distinctly non-Kantian ends. For what belongs to ourselves also turns out to have its own immanent otherness and we cannot master ourselves in full self-transparency. If there is an immanent sublimity, there is also, as always with the exhilaration of the sublime, the horror. We too are the horror. In itself, in its intimacy in our own inward otherness, the origin remains dark, remains idiotic.

## On the Idiocy of Will and Its Aesthetic Reversal

One might ask if willing transcends itself in terms of what I would call its idiotic, aesthetic, erotic, and agapeic manifestations.[26] By idiotic I refer

26. See Desmond, *Being and the Between*, chapter 10 on idiotic, aesthetic, erotic, and agapeic selving; also Desmond, *God and the Between* on the hyperboles of being.

(as above) to a certain intimacy of being that is not fully amenable to expression in public generalities. By aesthetic I refer to everything dealing with the sensible and the sensing. By erotic I refer to the self-surpassing movement we meet especially in desire overcoming its own lack. By agapeic, I refer to a self-surpassing towards what is other that is from surplus generosity rather than from a desire that lacks and seeks to fill itself. I have just referred to the idiotic, but clearly there is an aesthetic and erotic manifestation to will. I will return to the erotic and agapeic, but let me put some flesh on the above considerations by looking at some of Schopenhauer's aesthetic reflections.

These reflections serve to mitigate some of the bleaker aspects of Schopenhauer's views. There is something more than the horror. Again here Schopenhauer appeals to the Platonic Idea in connection with art. Some commentators have suspected incoherence in this appeal, but it is consistent with a desire for some release beyond will. Will in itself is not a static substance but a dynamic power that objectifies itself at different grades that, he tells us, correspond to different Platonic Ideas. The artwork serves to lift the mind to the contemplation of the Platonic Ideas. Indeed, an aesthetic metaphorics suggests itself when we try to understand the objectification of the will at all. If in itself the will is idiotic, as I put it, to come to itself, perhaps to know itself, it must express itself, objectify itself. One is tempted to compare this to the artist's need to externalize himself to come to some self-knowing of what is hidden in the initially impulse to create. Prior to creation nothing is known, only a groaning striving. Schopenhauer is not alone in this. Schelling was one of the first to entertain the aesthetic possibilities of Kant's transcendental self-activity. We find some such aesthetic metaphorics in Hegel's understanding of *Geist*. We find it obviously in the younger Nietzsche, but also in the later, when he refers to the world as a work of art giving birth to itself.[27] In all cases, a turn to the originality and immanent otherness of aesthetic selving is crucial for an interpretation of the process of being as a whole.

Schopenhauer views genius as an instance of exemplary, perhaps original, selfhood, and yet something other to original selfhood emerges

27. On this theme in Schopenhauer and others, see my *Art, Origins, Otherness*. I draw here on some of ideas in chapter 4: "Art's Release and the Sabbath of the Will: Schopenhauer and the *Eros Turannos* of Origin." The reference to Nietzsche's world as work of art giving birth to itself is *The Will to Power*, 419 (§796); *Der Wille zur Macht*, 533.

in immanent consideration of what makes its creativity possible. Like many of the Romantic period, he was also fascinated by the significant proximity of genius and madness.[28] This is a theme reminding us of Plato's *Ion*, and the question of the difference of *theia mania* and just mad madness. We meet a startling reversal: beginning with will as dark origin, art emerges as an end in the process, an end of the striving, for through it the will's restless striving is stilled. One might say that to understand madness, not to mention genius, one must not be mad, though one might well need a touch of divine madness. On the whole, Schopenhauer's tastes strike one as more soberly classical than Nietzsche's, closer to Hegel's. Schopenhauer retained a sobriety, mostly. True: the mere thought of Hegel did put him in a rage, did make him "lose it," as we say colloquially, lose this astringent sobriety—though again, since there is something operatic about his furious rage against Hegel, one wonders if there was an element of hamming going on.

Kant spoke of genius as that favored one through whom nature supplies the rule to art. Genius is the figure exemplary with respect to aesthetical ideas, those representations of imagination that occasion much thought without, however, any definite thought being entirely adequate to such representations. Genius stands at the edge of rational articulation in its more rule-bound forms, but the powers of articulation of the genius dip into the dark inarticulate ground of nature. It is nature, after all, *pace* Kant, that gives the rule to art, through the genius. The genius is intermediary. Kant is as cautious here as Socrates is about Ion's claim to inspiration: the dark origin may not always shine with reasonable light and like nature in disturbance may erupt into the unruly. Kant has a double attitude: genius is necessary for art, but it is also necessary to subject genius to rules of decorum and civilized taste.[29] Schopenhauer casts off Kant's caution, and is ready to celebrate genius, especially in his or her *excessive* nature.[30] Genius erupts against a dark background of the chaotic and irrational: this excessive upsurgence testifies to the energy of the dark origin, the will itself, prior to its splitting into subject-object. Genius, it seems, is more *intimate* with the thing itself, will, unlike the ordinary mortal, the mere empirical subject manipulating phenomenal objects in accord with the principle of sufficient reason.

28. See *SW*, 1:272ff.; *WWR*, 1:§36; *SW*, 2:514ff.; *WWR*, 2:399ff.

29. On this see chapter 2 of Desmond, *Art, Origins, Otherness*. In chapter 1, I address the issue of *thea mania* in Plato.

30. See *SW*, 2:484ff.; *WWR*, 2:376ff.

There is a turnabout here that occasions some astonishment. Will-less knowing emerges, but how can it, since it seems to have to *turn against* the very conditions of its own emergence, namely, will itself? My perplexity comes back: How can an upsurge of darkness bring light, how can blind energy bring sight? Schopenhauer suggests that the excess of genius shows a *surplus* of intellect and of disinterested contemplativeness.[31] Through this surplus, the genius *sees* the will in the form of its *universality*, prior to the subject-object split and the dispersion of will into the multiplicity of phenomena. The genius rises above this, or digs below it, to a freer, more composed, more universal comportment. The genius, in this way, is the aesthetic prefigurement of the universal sympathy of the saint. In its excessive manifestation, excessive with respect to ordinary science and everyday pragmatic concerns, will paradoxically begins to be *liberated from itself*. It begins to wake up to itself, to its own pervasive universality, and indeed to its own final futility. As become self-conscious in the genius, will, the dark origin, no longer is simply dark to itself. Will drives forward, darkly, blindly; but in the excessive intellect of the genius it produces an enigmatic reversal of itself into will-less knowing. Pushed further again, this knowing might produce in us the will to self-annihilation, that is, a will to do away with will. The will that wills itself wills now against itself, wills to be or become will-less.

Again there seems an interesting overlap of Hegel and Schopenhauer in so far as each claims that, despite the darkness of ontological origins, the original "self" *needs to know*. Nietzsche throws a question mark on this need when he wonders if the need for truth is a necessary illusion. Despite the fact that Schopenhauer has been seen as one of the first post-Kantian "irrationalists," there is something quite traditional in his proposing the Platonic Idea as the objective of the desire to know. Less traditionalist, Nietzsche's will to power will swallow this eros, and there will be no Platonic Idea: nocturnal desire will engulf diurnal reason. If reason is only instrumental, and in the services of the more primordial will, which is not rational, how can we avoid a final *antithesis* between will and intellect? On this way of thinking, intellect is and must always be subordinated to will. Do we just escape the tyranny of a totalism of abstract reason to fall foul of the tyranny of a totalism of blind will?

The relation of will and Idea is intimately bound up with the contrast between the genius and the "ordinary" person. The latter is defined

31. See, for instance, *WWR*, 2:370, 379–82.

by the everyday phenomenal attitude wherein we are both the products and victims of the will. Products: as embodied beings, we are driven by an insatiable desire that can only be temporarily allayed, only then to sweep onward ever in further dissatisfaction. Victims: because desire erupts in us unbidden, crystallizing us into an ever-renewed dissatisfaction. We are metaphysically doomed to lack and unhappiness. In Schopenhauer's graphic image, we are the beggars who are thrown crumbs for today, only for tomorrow to be hungry again. Desire is without end and becomes a vanishing infinity because eventually it is an objectless restlessness. Nothing can satisfy it, no finite thing will ever satisfy it, hence its initial hyperactivity, its intermediate anguish and its terminal apathy.

We are victims in this further sense: in the phenomenal world desire is driven deterministically, and (the voice of Spinoza breaks through) free will is illusory. By contrast, the artist as genius, as excessive contemplative intellect, somehow escapes this fate: he is free, if only for some few privileged moments (the saint sustains this freedom more fully). He is lifted above the incessant becoming of will, its ever-renewed lack and restlessness. His intuition of the Idea attains a contemplative composure that yields metaphysical insight into the deepest nature of being, namely the will itself.

Ideas for Schopenhauer, as was said before, are objectifications of will itself; hence, art as will-less knowledge of Ideas is only indirectly knowledge of will itself. Music alone among the individual arts is not knowledge of Idea, but more directly of will itself. Hence its privileged position in Schopenhauer's aesthetic. To cite again a crucial claim:

> Unlike the other arts, then, music is in no way the image of ideas; but rather the *image of the will itself (Abbild des Willens selbst)*, whose objective form the ideas are also: it is for this very reason that the effect of music is so much more powerful and penetrating than that of the other arts: since the latter only speak of the shadow (*Schatten)*, while music speaks of the substance (*Wesen*).[32]

We tend to feel consolation at remarks like these. But this shows that we have forgotten that the original, the *Wesen* itself, is more radically dark than all the shadows!

We come to this striking tension in Schopenhauer. The artwork gives us metaphysical knowing, and some kind of salvation from will; yet

32. *SW*, 1:359; *WWR*, 1:257.

this knowing ambiguously strains against the very metaphysical conditions of its own possibility, namely will itself, and indeed precipitates a metaphysical *turning against* this will. It reveals a metaphysical truth that seems to be *at war with itself in the very peace it claims to offer*. It reveals a metaphysical truth that, from the opposite angle of the same perspective, seems hard entirely to separate from metaphysical absurdity. From this last perspective the final truth is, once again, the futility of being. The basis of intelligibility is itself unintelligible. Is the metaphysical knowing Schopenhauer claims for art both the most intelligible and the least intelligible? Passing over the threshold of mystery, we do not escape absurdity, but compound its futility.

## Dark Eros and Will

Appreciating why Plato and Kant are the only philosophical predecessors to whom Schopenhauer confesses a deep debt, I would now like to elaborate another significant overlap with Plato, one not explicitly exploited by Schopenhauer himself. While Schopenhauer's will is not Kant's good will, there is a connection with Platonic *eros*. The genitals, as he famously said, or shamelessly, are the metaphysical organs and focal point of the will. Indeed, I think we should understand Schopenhauer's dark origin to be a kind of erotic absolute.

Platonic eros, as Diotima tells in the *Symposium*, has one its sources in lack (*penia*), the other in resource (*poros*). Deficiency is the driving source of desire and will in Schopenhauer. Lack dynamizes the human self into restless search for some satisfying fulfillment or peace. In Plato it is beauty itself (*auto to kalon*) that confers peace and completion on *eros*. Likewise, direction to the Ideas can stabilize desire's otherwise wavering motion and guide it to fitting ends. Schopenhauer tends to stress lack, and if there is *poros* (resource) to desire, it becomes instrumental to negotiating with the infinite hydra of lack. We do not find the archaic trace of divine festivity that slumbers in the (re)sources of Platonic *eros*. Schopenhauer's understanding of will reminds us of the horror of being at all. It is better not to be, as Schopenhauer, echoing the tragic wisdom of the Silenus, reiterates. Art is a compensation in the face of this horror.

If Schopenhauer's will tends towards being an *eros tyrannos*, there is, to my knowledge, no direct significance invested in something like *eros uranios* (heavenly eros), though one might see his strategies of escaping *eros tyrannos* as trying to address the misery generated by tyrannical eros. Given this, one can understand how an unrelieved stress on *eros tyrannos* might well spell the death of the Platonic vision of the higher *eros*. Of course, will for Schopenhauer has greater overtones of Romantic, post-Christian inwardness than Plato's *eros*, but Plato was deeply concerned with limitless desire, revealed for him in the figure of the tyrant. Plato's depiction of the ultimate misery of the tyrant finds significant echoes in Schopenhauer's description of the will as finally the source of man's ineradicable wretchedness. For Plato, the tyrant and his will to power were a deformation of desire,[33] not an incarnation of the dark origin, taken as primordial. Thus too, beauty for Plato is not the extirpation of desire, but crowns the full unfolding of desire. Here there seem in Schopenhauer to be continuing, unresolved tensions between will and Idea. With respect to the release of art, will as dark origin seems counterposed to a peace "beyond" will conferred by contemplation of the Idea. But what can this "beyond" be? There seems no "beyond." Beyond the temporary alleviation of the misery will engenders, there seems no ontological basis for peace, if will is ultimately a kind of *eros tyrannos*.

If I am not mistaken, one can detect here a silhouette of Nietzsche coming to form out of this tangle of desire. "Nietzschean" desire is multiform, even hydra-like, yet even when it claims to affirm, a bleak dark sap comes up from hidden roots in the secret chaos of the origin. The horror of being at all is deeply hidden down there, in the idiotic recess of our intimate being. Nietzsche too repeated the tragic wisdom of the Silenus: It is better not to be. Unlike Schopenhauerian desire, Nietzschean desire claims to be a defiant, not melancholy, rejoinder to the darkness. It wills to say "yes." It says it says "yes," but finally how affirmative is this "yes" if its celebration is inseparable from defiance of darkness? Is it fair to call its metaphysical music a kind of whistling in the dark? Whistles in the dark are no less dark than the darkness they only *seem* to alleviate. If Nietzsche reverses Schopenhauer's "yes" and "no," does he return to where Schopenhauer began, indeed where Nietzsche himself also began? And one has to wonder if Schopenhauer already brought us to the point without the detour of Nietzsche, and that Nietzsche arrives back there, but dissimulates the darkness that lies under it all: art as redemption now simply means our need for the *necessary lie*.

33. See my "Tyranny and the Recess of Friendship."

Of course, different songs can be whistled in the dark, and perhaps not all darks are voids of horror. Perhaps also the idiotics of some forms of intimate being are not revolting, but rather marked by love. We have to ask here about Schopenhauer's moral doctrine of compassion? Is this marked by an agapeic surplus of generosity for the plight of the other, beyond lack? But it seems that, for Schopenhauer, in identifying with the suffering of the other, it is my own suffering I see in the plight of the other, and hence the bent of compassion circles back to myself. One thinks that perhaps, yes, Schopenhauer's heart is in the right place, but his understanding of compassion only mimics, while lacking any friendship with, or agapeic love of, the other as other. How could this be possible for any will that is the will willing itself?

That said, something about Schopenhauer's bleak vision does have its attractions. There is his phenomenological appreciation of the labyrinth of desire, its insatiable hunger, the bitterness of repeated disappointment. There is his openness, even as an atheist, to some of the originating sources of religions, East and West.[34] We desire salvation, but the way of our desire itself blocks salvation. I see a likeness between his will and Hegel's "bad infinite," but without Hegel's presumptive consolation of completeness attained. When we think we "ought" to be happy, our very craving for happiness guarantees our inevitable unhappiness.

Also attractive is Schopenhauer's preference for music as the metaphysical art *par excellence*. Music sings to the intimate idiocy of the soul. Kant and Hegel opt for poetry as "higher" than music, and thus reflect a different response to the *passio essendi* of human existence, and the nocturnal passion of creative origination. The darkness of the origin resounds in, so to say, the logical silence of music. Music can be more powerful on this score than Kant's "aesthetic ideas"—namely, as occasioning much thought without any definite thought being adequate to it. Nietzsche will concur in privileging the "musical," to the chagrin of the "logocentric" Platonists. Music lets us sing the will, hear it, heed it, beyond logic. One might ask if the Kantian and Hegelian option for poetry does justice to *poetry as music*: not the prose of origination, subject to conceptual determinability, but its singing speaking, beyond determination and our self-determination?

Once again, the relation, indeed balance, of Idea and will is important here. Ideas refer us to determinability, but *eros* and will refer us to

34. See *WWR*, 1:385 where he speaks of "atheistic religion" as well as "theistic."

what exceeds determinability, since they express passages of determining power. The Schopenhauerian genius "sees" the Ideas, they are not subjectivistic constructions; we do not determine them, but their form gives form to our otherwise-formless striving. There is, I believe, a precarious balance between the creative power of the Schopenhauerian artist and the ontological weight accorded the Idea. Tilting the balance more towards the creative power of the artist, his successors will identify "Ideas" more with *projections* of genius, indeed, eruptions ("subreptions"?) out the dark origin itself. Nietzsche again comes forcefully to mind. The strong "self" *makes* the "Idea," he does not find it. There is nothing "eternal," "metaphysical," about "Ideas"; they are secret idealizations of will (to power), and can as equally be deconstructed as constructed. Of course, the strong "self" as secret source is itself also an upsurge or project or "subreption" of will to power. It is not released, finally, from the dark origin, now of will to power, out of which all comes to be and into which all things pass, as into an ultimately inarticulate night. Not surprisingly, one of the most haunting passages of poetry in *Also Sprach Zarathustra* is Zarathustra's Night Song.

With respect to the Idea, Schopenhauer evidences a return to Plato (something non-Nietzschean), but he also opens a way, no doubt unintentionally, for the more thoroughgoing Nietzschean dissolution of Platonism. As an heir of Kant, he is also an influential middle ground between Kant and Nietzsche. For Kant, the Idea is a regulative principle of reason that we project to anticipate totality (Kantian reason: the *eros* of philosophy pretending *eros* does not matter). For Plato, the Idea allows *eros* to be made whole. For Schopenhauer, the Idea is our savior or escape from *eros*. For Nietzsche, the Idea is *eros* falsified and so must be metaphysically unmasked. Nietzsche radicalizes the activist subject to eviscerate the Platonic Idea, though further again this evisceration also eviscerates the activist subject, and the Platonic Idea cedes primacy to Dionysian ecstasy. Schopenhauer would not have endorsed the more extreme consequences of the Nietzschean subversion of Platonism. Remaining something of a Platonist, perhaps he is not entirely antithetical to the Hegel he hated, though instead of Hegel's rational version of the erotic absolute he offers us a wilful version.

With respect to some of his significant inheritors, Schopenhauer is perhaps more prescient in at least implicitly drawing attention to the need to balance the originating "self" (here, genius) with the ontological context of origination (here, will and Idea). Cut loose from ontological moorings, human originality risks mad madness, not divine madness. Of course, one might still charge that the Idea here, finally, cannot be anything other than a consoling gloss on the darkness of the origin. Generally Schopenhauer is admirable in refusing to fake failure as success. But given the ineradicably dark origin, can one affirm *any* possibility of success, aesthetic or otherwise. Nietzsche might revolt against this, dispense entirely with the Platonic Idea, lift "logocentric" restraints on the origin, in an intoxicated outpouring of its Dionysian darkness, but is this not the same darkness again? Does not his revolt again surrender to that against which he revolts? Does not he hide the horror in drawing attention to it? Does not the origin under the ground of the cave drag all things back into original chaos?

## Art and the Sabbath of Willing

When speaking of art's deliverance from the will, the *eros tyrannos* of the dark origin, Schopenhauer's language is revealing in mixing the aesthetic and the religious: art, he says, offers us a *Sabbath* from the penal servitude of the will.[35] My question: can there be *any* Sabbath here? The original Sabbath religiously recalls the seventh day on which the Creator rested from creation and saw that "it was good, very good." Schopenhauer invokes the Sabbath, but how can we take him at his word? The question arises not from his atheism as such, or indeed significant touches of anti-Jewishness in his thought, but with relation to the dark origin. Is it possible *at all* to say "It is good"?[36] Schopenhauer's will willing itself seems to hold us in the vice of its *eros tyrannos*. What release can there be? Can there be here any *Sabbath* of the will, without an other sense of *eros*, an other sense of origin, perhaps an agapeic sense?

35. *SW*, 1:280; *WWR*, 1:§35. Other images he uses to describe the endless, futile willing from which art offers release—such as the wheel of Ixion, or drawing water in the sieve of the Danaids, or Tantalus as eternally thirsting—are borrowed and adapted from Greek mythology, again a sacred source. He explicitly likens the peace of art to "the painless state, prized by Epicurus as the highest good and the state of the gods." 1:196.

36. See *Parerga and Paralipomena*, 2:§174, where his anti-Judaism, expressed in the language of the *foetor Judaicus*, is connected with his contempt for the opening refrain concerning creation in the book of Genesis: God saw that "It is very good" (370ff., 381; see also 310 in connection with suicide). *Sed contra:* such joy in beholding beauty and good surely is *just being sabbatical.*

There is here a family of philosophical possibilities with respect to will as ultimate. One thinks of Kant investing the good will with *unconditional* worth. One thinks of Hegel speaking (in *Philosophy of Right*, §27) of the "free will that wills the free will." Each thinks that this will is *rational*, but Schelling will claim that will is absolute being, but without the rationalistic consolation of Kant or Hegel. With Schopenhauer's will there is even less comfort. Nietzsche, surprisingly, comes along here trying to be a comforter: will to power finds *joy*, its ultimate "yes," in its "yes" to itself, but beyond reason, and morality.

Here and there Hegel refers to the notion of God as "love disporting with itself," and one is made to wonder if Schopenhauer's dark origin as an *eros tyrannos* is also a "love disporting with itself." Insatiably insistent, it seems to be contracted on its own self-seeking, and finally it seems alone with itself and nothing but itself. Hegel's God disports with itself by playing with the whole world, nature and history; seeking to be at one with itself, reconciled with itself. One suspects there is more honesty in Schopenhauer about this "God" that disports with itself. Honesty, because the good God has flipped into its opposite and shows a face more like the *evil genius* disporting with itself. One thinks of Schopenhauer's response to Spinoza's *Deus sive natura*. God may be an honorific name to offer to nature, but there is something dishonorable in the Spinozistic formulation. Big fish eat little fish, Spinoza and Schopenhauer would agree, but to throw flies to spiders and to laugh with glee, as his first biographer Colerus told us that Spinoza did for fun, this Schopenhauer could not stomach.[37] St. Augustine tells us of his own watching of a lizard or spider catch flies (*Confessions*, 10, 35), but his response is quite different to Spinoza's glee: praise of God displaces the concupiscence of curiosity and of the eye.

One is reminded of the blinded, comfortless Gloucester in Shakespeare's *King Lear* (IV, 1, 36–37) who cries out: "As flies to wanton boys are we to the gods, they kill us for their sport." Gloucester *sees* in his blindness. If Schopenhauer's will as dark origin has some family resemblance to the evil genius, is it too like a wanton god whose disporting with himself is staged in the horrors of nature and history. Hegel talks piously of nature and history as God's two temples, but if these two were "objectifications" of the dark origin they would not be temples but torture chambers and charnal houses. The logic of an *eros tyrannos* with no immanent good in

37. See *Parerga and Paralipomena*, 1:73.

it is more forthrightly shoved in our faces by Schopenhauer. Again one is forced to ask: can Schopenhauer's will willing itself ever be released to any Sabbatical "It is good"?[38]

Aristotle spoke of tragedy evoking terror and pity, or horror and compassion (*phobos* and *eleos, Poetics*, VI, 2–3). Schopenhauer and Nietzsche are strong on horror, but equivocal on compassion. Schopenhauer's saving release in face of the horror of will might be called an "aesthetic compassion," even though the origin cannot source an "It is good." Nietzsche is more tempted by pity, not only for us, but for the dark god of tragedy. That god too cannot say "It is good," but Nietzsche in his pity will say "It is good," for him. Nietzsche shows us horror, and warns against pity, yet he shows "pity" (or its surrogate) in the comfort of his "yes." Schopenhauer shows us horror, and enjoins pity, yet he is often pitiless.

Does art too begin to look like the sport of the wanton god? Our willing blithely builds its crystal palaces. Then it finds itself miserable in them. Then again it proceeds to destroy them. Then once more it proceeds to repeat its futile building. Thus, will comes to itself in its creations as finally *nothing*. The active lack that drives it to being, that drives its "to be," is everything and nothing. There is no plenitude of glorious being in itself; no glory of existence communicated to the other in the release of the creation. The drive from will to something other is only a *quasi-move*. It is a drive from lack to nothing. What is in-between is the vanishing medium of its own self-deluding willing of itself. Schopenhauer's will as an erotic origin is the dark mirror—or image in reverse—of the self-certain, self-mediating reason of Hegel's absolute. But if "full" self-knowledge of this will were to hit us, we would be hit with absolute "emptiness" and we would struggle to stifle the cry of horror.

Is there something more honest than Hegel when Schopenhauer reverses Leibniz, and now this world seems the "worst possible"? If the evil genius holds sway, rather than the good God, no wonder it is "better not to be." Can art and the holy release us to an "It is good"? The honest answer on these terms of Schopenhauer must be "No." The only release is an escape from the "It is"—the "It is" as evil. There is no Sabbath. The release of art and the holy cannot bring us to life or towards life as worthy. They can only turn us away from it as unworthy. But if they too are participants in life, what source makes them worthy in their turn?

38. See my *Is there a Sabbath for Thought?* chapter 10.

One can see Schopenhauer's dark origin as turning, returning us to the otherness of existence, with a gusto sometimes coarse, sometimes remarkably perspicacious. There is a kind of existential gusto in Schopenhauer's dark philosophizing. I see this as reactive to idealistic thought thinking itself. This thinking can produce a kind of ontological malnourishment, and there comes a point of recoil at the sense of emptiness it seems to produce existentially. (One senses something similar in Kierkegaard.) One might then return to the overdeterminacy of being, its too muchness. But how does one return if the hunger of one's desire cannot be slaked at all? There can be a hunger gone so far in ontological lack that the "too muchness" of being in its splendor always exceeds it. It is tempted to seek out darker fruits, but what nourishment is there in them? Having endured a long ontological and metaphysical fast, one's transcending desire can glut itself on everything and anything, so long as it is not just the *thought* of food. This too, however, will come to nothing without renewal of the love of being. Disgust with being can erupt that mirrors, in an "irrational" register, the idealistic turn into "reason," away from the splendor of being. One wonders if Schopenhauer was saved from this in his living by the irrepressible affirmation of life itself, and not by his philosophy of negation. Schopenhauer called Hegel an "intellectual Caliban," but one asks if there was something of the gusto of a different Caliban in his own joy, his own festive hatred of being.

The matter is not merely of historical interest, for we have as much difficulty now, as then, in saying "It is good." In fact, we seem more comprehensively deprived of a Sabbath than ever, in a world defined by the dominion of serviceable disposability.[39] There everything is a means, and nothing an end, and art seems to place itself in servitude to that dominion, servitude less penal now as too well paid. We do live culturally and philosophically with something like Schopenhauer's legacy, its continuing influence, especially as transmitted through Nietzsche in regard to art and the "beyond" of reason. Schopenhauer's suspicious anti-Hegelianism also makes him our contemporary, but can we, must we, chose between the Schopenhauerian and Nietzschean reversals of optimistic idealism? The first tends towards resignation, awaiting a change of being reminiscent of a gift of grace; the second commands an intensification, not abnegation, of self-affirming will, of the will willing itself. The darkness of the original will remains ultimately *dark for both*, regardless of

39. See Desmond, *Ethics and the Between*, chapter 14.

whether the transfiguration is renunciation of *eros* or intensification. In the light, or darkness, of this origin, it is the *similarity* of renunciation and intensification that strikes one. Whether one says "yes," or "no," this dark origin remains thus dark.

Shadows of something like Schopenhauer's dark origin have had afterlives into more recent times. I think of André Breton's *Second Manifesto of Surrealism* in which he recommends the "vertiginous inner descent" and the "ceaseless promenade in full forbidden zone."[40] I think of absurdist existentialism and the literature of the absurd. Quite Schopenhauerian also are some of the presuppositions of psycho-analytic thought, reminding us of the sly ineluctability of the id, the horrifying despotism of the Thing (*das Ding*), the ceaseless desiring and dissatisfaction of the libido, the tyranny of the original eros. Unlike Schopenhauer, however, Freud says psychoanalysis "has scarcely anything to say about beauty. . . . All that seems certain is its derivation from the field of sexual feeling. The love of beauty seems a perfect example of an impulse inhibited in its aim."[41] Postmodernist thought, in its Nietzschean variety, suggest a skeptical, *ironical* version of Schopenhauerian pessimism, secretly, or not so secretly, conscious of its own final futility. Oddly enough, the ethical Levinas comes to mind in thinking of Schopenhauer's dark origin. Levinas reiterates, not only the horror of the *il y a* ("there is"), but the *evil of being* (*la mal de l'être*, as he puts it in *Existence and Existents*)[42] in the relentless self-insistence of the *conatus essendi*. Interestingly too, Plato's good beyond being helps Levinas escape *la mal de l'être*.

How can there be a Sabbath of life where the evil of being holds sway? Are we not rather led to expect that under the underground there are *metaphysical sewers*? And after the first thrill of excremental transgression, desolation comes and descends on us and with it the (self-)hatred of purposeless life. This is not purposiveness without purpose (in Kant's terms) but life purposeless in purposing, and when self-consciousness hits, purposing to be purposeless. The will willing itself to be reverses into the willing willing itself not to be. The self-enjoying self morphs into the self-hating self: an abject self-lacerating self-contradiction—marked by a torture self-inflicted that mutilates its own being. The *conatus essendi* brings on itself the *accidie* of endeavor, sometimes disguised in a

40. Breton, *Oeuvres complètes*, 1:791.

41. Freud, *Civilization and its Discontents*, 30.

42. Levinas, *De l'existence à l'existant*, 19; *Existence and Existents*, 19.

hyperactivity in flight from itself, and sometimes as a passivity that counterfeits the *passio essendi* in its non-responsiveness to the splendor of all beautiful things. Earlier times might have spoken of *spiritual death*—though here this death reminds one as much of an abortion of our spirit as of its despair. We also find the execration of the beautiful as the hated harmony of being at home with oneself, with the others, with the world, and with the divine: to be dismantled, scourged, spat upon, mocked, and crucified. This is no redemption of the horror but the reiteration that all there is is horror. This is a kind of love of the execrable. And indeed one might *endorse* a love of the execrable. But this here is the counterfeit double of an *agapeic love of the execrable*, for this latter love still sees in fallen beauty the mustard seed of the good.

Whether our faith is modernist or postmodernist, we stand in the shadow of the too-forgotten Schopenhauer, and often recess our secret entanglement in many of his metaphysical assumptions, which, finally, no amount of talk about being "post-metaphysical" can completely hide. We are frequently less candid than Schopenhauer in confessing the ruses by which we protect ourselves from the darkness of the origin. Schopenhauer carried through a line of thought that many successors continued, even while they thought they were beginning a new line with the "yes" and "no," the plus and negative signs exchanged. If the dark origin is the principle of the whole, then any reversal between "yes" and "no," plus and negative, while seeming to free us from that origin's tyranny, takes place *within its embrace*, and will inevitably be swallowed again by its darkness. One must ask if not a few of Schopenhauer's successor have only arrived back at this starting point, where their end is Schopenhauer's beginning. We must not fool ourselves that we have made a move from darkness to light when we have only made a quasi-move, and have only come full circle from darkness to darkness.

# 6

## Creativity and the Dynamis

### Opening: Paul Weiss and Creative Ventures

PAUL WEISS THINKS THAT philosophy is not essentially marked by creativity. This is thought-provoking from an honored thinker creatively in pursuit of philosophical understanding. Weiss wants to understand the truth, he will insist, and the truth is not the *product* of a creative venture. The truth is something we quest and *find*. Philosophy is knowing, not making. Yet Weiss's quest and finding have resulted in the making of an outstanding portfolio of philosophical works. These works span an extraordinary range of themes, showing not only singular ambition, but high daring and risk in the venture of thinking. Not least of these books is his work *Creative Ventures*.[1] If there is a philosopher who might lay claim to tireless thinking, thinking venturing and issuing in an ensemble of created works of philosophy, it is Paul Weiss.

The theme I have chosen for consideration—creativity and the *dynamis*[2]—is a persistent concern of Weiss, as well as providing focus for a fundamental philosophical issue. I had chosen this theme and title before *Creative Ventures* had appeared, sensing an important connec-

1. Weiss, *Creative Ventures*. Hereafter cited in the text as *CV*.

2. I have transliterated this Greek word as *dynamis*, following the SBL style, but note that Weiss transliterates it as *dunamis*. I have chosen to maintain the consistency of my own transliteration throughout the book but to avoid italics when using the word to speak of the philosophical notions Weiss seeks to articulate.

tion between creativity and the dynamis. On the appearance of *Creative Ventures* I was gratified to see that Weiss's article on the dynamis was reprinted in the book as an appendix.[3] Is there any significance to the fact that Weiss singles the dynamis out for special mention among what he sees as the ultimate conditions? At least I was on the right track, I thought.

Weiss has always been concerned with the nature of creativity, most especially as applied to the arts. This is evident in books like *The World of Art* (1961), *Nine Basic Arts* (1966), *Cinematics* (1975), *Religion and Art* (1963), and again most recently *Creative Ventures*. But this concern with creativity is not confined to its artistic specialization. This is very clear in *Creative Ventures*. The title of the work already signals a recognition of the plural manifestation of creativity in a variety of different ventures.

We might stress the term "venture" as well as the term "creative." The adventuring spirit of the human being, the being of the human as a venture, is at stake, at stake in its intertwining with our creative potential. To venture is to make an attempt, to take a risk and strike out into the unknown and the possibly new. An adventure is undertaken with the hope of coming to something, coming upon something that is not initially known as determinate from the outset. The preposition "ad" signifies a certain going towards something, a movement from an origin toward something that, at the outset, may not be known with clear determinacy. There is risk in this going towards at the outset, as one does not explicitly know where one will end. One has to throw oneself forward into the hazard of the initially unknown.

Of course, the process of going towards becomes more determinate as the adventurer proceeds. The venture seeks an initially indeterminate goal towards which it aims its creative power; in the process of actualizing this power we may become more and more determinate as to what it is that draws the creative venture forward. The goal is a determinate work that is the incarnation of an ideal, dimly sensed at the outset of the process, capable of being lost or betrayed or deformed at each stage in the process of making the idea concretely determinate. Nor does this exhaust the venturing self in its transcending dynamism. The created work offers an actualization of this dynamism, but not an exhaustion, and the creative venture renews itself in its transcendence of its individual stabilizations.

3. "Dunamis." *Review of Metaphysics* 40.4 (1987) 657–74.

What I have just said is very close to what Weiss says. We find ourselves participating in and involved with a certain energy of creative transcendence. Here the theme of "creativity" comes to appearance, not as particularized in the arts, not as pluralized in a host of human ventures, as in art, mathematics, science, leadership, and so on, but as an ontological principle ingredient in the constitution of all concrete realities. The creativity evident in human venturing is not a human creation simply but invokes "creativity" itself as something to which we must appeal to understand the nature of all being. This is especially clear if we wish to do justice to the dynamic and original, to dimensions of reality as in process of becoming. The creative becoming of the human being cannot be abstracted from the becoming of creativity in all being. There is no understanding of human transcendence apart from an understanding of the energy of transcendence at work in all being, and singularized in unique and often astonishing ways in the human being. This will be central in my thoughts here: the ontology of creativity as suggesting something other to the human being, yet other in a way that the human being participates intimately in it. There is something other and intimate about creativity. And while, in Weiss's case, we cannot call either creativity or the dynamis by names derived from the sacred, yet it remains a question whether humanistic names are true to the matter also. Is human creativity companioned by a power other than the human? Is Weiss's dynamis a name for this other-power? If so, how so? If not, why not, and how can we think otherwise of this other-power?

I mention in passing that the stress on venturing seems to tilt towards the endeavor to be, the *conatus essendi*, rather than the *passio essendi*, the being given to be, that has a certain priority to the endeavor. Weiss's ventures are determinations of something initially indeterminate, but the significance of this initial indeterminacy does not seem to be the same as what I call the porosity of being. I would say that creative venturing emerges out of the passion of being, itself emergent from the more primordial porosity, and while it issues in an endeavor that seeks to originate something new, this new origination is at best only half described if we do not do justice to the *passio* and the porosity. Again to stress these latter is not just to emphasize something more passive by contrast with something more venturing, something more active. The more usual contrast of passive and active does not adequately describe the *passio essendi* and the *conatus essendi* in my understanding of them. The danger with a too strong teleology of the *conatus* is that it shortchanges an archeology of the *passio*, an archeology that if pursued would transform the normal couple of the active and the passive. One could also bear in mind this point when below I discuss Weiss's dynamis, which is not the porosity, and yet might be seen as not entirely irrelevant to a description of the porosity as naming a more original enabling condition of possible creativity. It is a point too large to enter here, but I think we need to distinguish "coming to be" from "becoming" to do justice not only to an archeology of origination but also to a teleology of creating. Creative becoming points us back to a more original coming to be. Relative to creative becoming one is inclined to deploy the venturing endeavor of the *conatus essendi*, but for coming to be we need the more originating sources named by the porosity and the *passio*.

My reference above to creative becoming will call to mind process philosophy, and though Weiss is not a process philosopher, he was shaped by his friendship, philosophical and human, with the father of process philosophy, Whitehead. Whitehead has his principle of "creativity," not just to explain human creativity, but to acknowledge what is universally at work in all becoming. Weiss's view of creativity is not Whitehead's, though there are affinities to which I will return. Still, both share the recognition that the creativity of the particular occasion or actuality cannot be fully understood apart from a more englobing sense of the work of creativity, not confined to the human being.

Hence any adequate study of creativity, even when it seems to focus exclusively on the human being, must invoke a metaphysical reflection on the nature of creativity, indeed creation, in the most embracing sense. Weiss's concept of the dynamis is important for this requirement. I will come to a more extended discussion of the dynamis, but we can say immediately that, among other things, it is invoked to explain the character of universal ongoingness that marks all processes of becoming. The energy of transcendence, as I see it, is not necessarily exhausted by this universal ongoingness, yet the latter is one manifestation of the basic dynamism at work everywhere in being. Weiss baptizes this simply, elementally with the name: the dynamis. Though the name is simple, elemental, what it names is enigmatic and perplexing. It points, perhaps to something that is even more perplexing, as I shall try to indicate.

For the moment I paint in broad strokes some of Weiss's procedures and claims in *Creative Ventures*. Weiss gets to work immediately *in medias res*. The lame reader will sometimes find himself limping behind. Initially one is puzzled, for his strategy is progressively to build up complexity and concrete richness through a multifaceted unfolding. This strategy seems to mirror philosophically his own description of a creative venture as a movement from an initially indeterminate ideal through a complex process of concrete determinate realization. Weiss claims that his method is reconstructive. It traces what is available in daily events back to their sources and ultimate conditions. It then claims to show how such sources and conditions enter together into the process of a creative venture. The creative venture is not confined to artists. In addition to artists, there are creative mathematicians and scientists, persons who create great characters for themselves, creative leaders, and creators of states.

In all creative ventures five ultimates or conditions are said to be variously at work. These Weiss singles out as *the voluminous*, which is most pertinent to the arts; *the rational*, which is most important for creative mathematicians; *the stratifier*, which is an ordering, assessing power, most relevant to the creation of a good character; *the affiliator*, which allows the supportive inter-involvement such as we find in creative leaders; finally, the *coordinator*, which is prominent in the creation of states. All these conditions are at work in every occurrence, but they receive distinctive expressions in the different creative ventures.

In addition to these ultimates or conditions, any creative venture involves the primary pulsating ground call the dynamis. There is also the privacy of the creator and obdurate material. The creative venture also requires an ideal which is initially indeterminate, but which the progressive unfolding of the creative venture makes more and more determinate, and this through the joining together into a harmonious inter-involvement of the conditions, the dynamis, the privacy, and the material. The outcome of creative ventures is the production of the work of excellence, which as a rich whole concretizes a new complex togetherness of all these factors.

## Creativity and Singularity

### With Bows to Nietzsche and Aquinas

I will now try to put two questions to Paul Weiss, the first reflecting the particularization and pluralization of creativity in human ventures, the second concerning the ultimacy of "creativity" itself relative to the ontological happening of being in its actuality. The first question bears on the use of the term "creativity" in contemporary culture and what restrictions, if any, ought to be placed on its use. The second question, not unrelated to the first, has to do not only with the radical nature of genuine creativity, but its participation in the ultimate origin of creation which cannot be called human creativity.

Relative to the first question, I begin with the contrast of imitation and creation.[4] Here I have the most to say about art, even though Weiss is also interested in mathematics, science, the good life, leadership, and the state, each as a distinctive creative venture. In reflection on the aesthetic, we find a dominance of the first idea of imitation in ancient and medieval thought, and a certain ascendancy of creativity in modernity. Of course, in the premodern world, mimesis entailed much more than some facile naturalistic copying. Among other things, it implied participation in the original power of being, understood in its otherness to human subjectivity. It also implied the recognition of a certain metaphysical dangerousness in the human being ascribing to itself the exclusive possession of creative power. This latter ascription always carries the risk of hubris, indeed of a kind of blasphemy: one appropriates the creative power for one's own possession, and this was thought to be fundamentally misplaced and disordered.

Modern selfhood is often too blithe in respect of the dangerousness of sacral power and the ambiguities of our relation to it. It is a well-recognized theme in aesthetics that beginning with the Renaissance the ascription of some kind of "creativity" to the human being becomes increasingly common and also increasingly unmoored from its previous theological and metaphysical anchorings. In line with an overall desacralization of being, we find that a desacralization of the powers of creativity. The first question to be put is: now at the end of modernity has not our use of the term "creativity" become too indiscriminate?

I am not accusing Weiss of this lack of discrimination. Quite the opposite: his work is finely attuned to differences. Yet there seems little doubt that it is the *pervasiveness* of the creative impulse that interests him in creative ventures. This emphasis on its pervasiveness risks certain ambiguities. What I mean especially is a kind of democratization of "creativity" such that its impact ceases to be felt. I think here of Shaftesbury's pithy and prescient statement relative to human beings: "We have undoubtedly the honor of being originals." Shaftesbury was still bound to a version of Platonism (he calls the artist "a just Prometheus under

4. I have treated of this contrast of imitation and creation in different places including, Desmond, *Art and the Absolute*, chapter 1; Desmond, *Philosophy and its Others*, 87ff.; *Desmond, Art, Origins, Otherness*, chapter 1.

Jove"—even the Titanic artist stands under the justice of a higher god). But what has happened in the last two centuries is that this honor has been seized by all. Now no one wants to be a "mere imitator"—this is almost an ontological insult to our very being. Emerson's words are famous because they hit the bull's-eye: "Imitation is suicide."

We all now can claim the privilege of being putative originals. Creativity and originality have been democratized. The question is whether this democratization has also led to a flattening of the idea. Now all one has to do is tie one's shoelaces, or cock one's cap, or brew coffee, and one can claim to be creative. Best of all: attend on the weekend a "creativity workshop." One hears of creative lifestyles, creative budgeting, creative blah blah.... Culturally speaking, has creativity known become a catchall for conceit?

My point is not to deny genuine creativity. Nor does Weiss offer us a vision of creativity so all pervasive that it loses its outstanding marks. Let me cite two thinkers to further the question: Nietzsche and Aquinas. First, Nietzsche hated the flattening effect of modern democracy, and his entire philosophical demeanor was a kind of call for aristocratic creativity. Yet, Nietzsche produces the hyperbole of creativity, and his emphasis has been taken up not by the few but by the many. Quasi-Nietzschean rhetoric lies in the current indiscriminate use of the term creativity. Nietzsche himself implied that you could not have a full conceptual analysis of creativity: like Archibald MacLeish's poem, the creator was to be, not to mean. Acting is superior to thinking, being creative is superior to the analysis of the intelligibility of creations.

For all his hyperbole about his own uniqueness, Nietzsche remains himself heir to a tradition that emphasizes the figure of the hero, aesthetically incarnated as the genius. In this respect, our contemporary use of the term creativity conceptually bobs in the confused backwash of the great originals of high Romanticism; but the spiritual robustness of these great originals has been vulgarized. Again my question is: does not genius imply the uniqueness of certain singularly creative selves? If this very uniqueness has been democratized, the consequent egalitarian flattening is at odds with the original stress on singularity: *everyone* now is to be creative, absolutely original, unique—that is to say, everyone is absolutely the same, indifferently the same. Does not genuine creativity vanish in this situation?

It seems to me that the thrust of Weiss's account in *Creative Ventures* is diffident about any view tinged with Nietzschean aristocratism. There is the strong confidence that the nature of a creative venture can be analyzed in terms that are publicly available to all. On the whole, Weiss tends to see any reference to the enigmatic nature of creation as an abdication of the philosopher's duty to make articulate sense of things. As I indicated above, he offers us an account in terms of the ultimate conditions, the dynamis, the privacy, the material. The creative venture makes a prospective ideal, which is initially indeterminate, progressively more and more determinate, by joining together in a work of excellence the harmonious inter-involvement of the conditions, the dynamis, the privacy, and the material. Nevertheless, he says that a creator "does nothing that is not in principle possible for anyone to do" (*CV*, 30).

One may sympathize with the democratic principle, but how helpful is this in enabling us to understand the difference between, say, a Salieri and a Mozart? The aesthetics of democratic commonality is indifferently applicable to the mediocrities and to the greats. Yet it is the Mozarts, the Shakespeares, the Rembrandts who continue to attract us and baffle us, and the more so the more we determinately know about them. In fact, there are no Mozarts; there is the entrancing and yet mysteriousness of a *singularity*. There was one Mozart and *only one*.

For all his diffidence about Nietzschean singularity, Weiss shows an uncompromising recognition of the *non-duplicable* nature of human privacy. This is something Weiss has always stressed from his earliest writings. While the privacy can be and is given public manifestation, it is never completely manifested. In a language that Weiss himself does not use, there is a certain inward otherness to the human being that is inexhaustible. This does not mean incommunicable. But it does mean that there remains a reserve of inwardness that is not completely communicated. (I also speak of the idiocy of intimate selving.) The creator moves more intensively into this privacy, the better to more richly express it and anchor it in the determinate work. There is a singularity to this process that cannot be duplicated. As Weiss insists, a creation is a creation, while a copy is always a copy (*CV*, 9).

There is also something about the dynamis that resists complete determination, and that exceeds our self-determination. Weiss is no Nietzsche, but the aristocratic creativity that Nietzsche confined to the few Weiss sees as available as a promise in all selves in virtue of the powers of their non-duplicable privacy. Weiss sees "more" in the many, the singularized presence of the energy of transcendence, as it might be called, a "more" that Nietzsche denies to what he contemptuously calls "the many too many."

The second thinker I invoke is a strange bedfellow for Nietzsche: Thomas Aquinas. Aquinas and Weiss would have more to talk about as metaphysicians than either would have with Nietzsche as aesthetician. I name Aquinas because he has less an aristocratic concept of creativity than, so to say, a monarchical view. The privilege of being creative belongs to God alone. Aquinas is quite explicit about this, and one of the reasons is his mindfulness of the notion of creation *ex nihilo*. Creation names an unconditional origination, the real origination of the essentially other or new. To God alone belongs this radical act (*Summa Theologiae*, Q 45, art. 5).

Weiss is given to deprecating statements about anything smacking of creation *ex nihilo* (see *CV*, xiii). "There is no creation from nothing; each created work is the outcome of the utilization of available factors again and again in the effort to make an ideal excellence become a determinate unification" (*CV*, 74). Why not then just call the process one of production or making? There is in Weiss an insistence on *work*, on the effort to master a recalcitrance through one's concentrated effort. But is it simply within one's will or power to will to be a creator? One has to will and work, yes, but there is something *given* prior to will and work—the gift of being able to create, the promise of vocation of the creator. This gift is not democratically distributed. I do not find a strong sense of the giving of creative power, the sense that there is a gift in creation that is not to be described in terms of work simply, nor the product of work. There is an activist strenuousness to his account that does not pay attention enough to the divine lightness of origination, the gratuity of creation as given to us out of the generosity of being in its otherness.

Weiss also says: "If anyone could unite the various ultimates as they are in their full, independent majesty, he could produce a universe. Our finitude denies us that privilege" (*CV*, 7). Later I will ask about the possibility of such a "unity" of the ultimates and in terms not irrelevant to the notion of creation from nothing. But it seems to me that Aquinas would broadly agree with the Weiss's statement. This kind of creation is not the privilege of the human being. The qualification for Aquinas would be that the work that utilizes already-available conditions is not properly "creation" but "making." Creation proper is the privilege of God.

There is here a peculiar kind of mirroring between Aquinas and Nietzsche: God's being and act are one for Aquinas; and the meaning of that "unity" remains resistant to our conceptual analysis. One is reminded of the Nietzschean emphasis on being a creator rather than on the analysis of being creative, and the recalcitrance of that being creative to philosophical conceptualization. Aquinas, as it were, gives us an austere kingly limitation of creativity, Nietzsche an aristocratic privileging, and the question both raise is: in today's cultural climate should we speak more quietly, with more nuance, about creativity, now that its popularization and indiscriminate use have almost emptied the word of meaning? The point is not be to depreciate creativity but precisely to refresh our festive astonishment at its singular occurrence—astonishment that is paradoxically domesticated, even lost, because of our excessive facility with the familiar language of "creativity."

This question is not meant to implicate Weiss, for his work bears testimony to a delicate carefulness concerning the immanent intricacies of the different creative ventures. His attentiveness to their nuances is admirable. Nevertheless, he does dominantly stress the continuity of the creator with all humans, and hence would reject both the Nietzschean aristocracy of creation and the Aquinian monarchy.

## Is the Dynamis a Creative Source?

A second question takes us beyond the specification of creativity with respect to the human being. Turning from vulgar culture to philosophical ontology I ask in what sense, if any, is what Weiss calls the primary dynamis a creative source? The notion of the primary dynamis, conjures in my mind, perhaps against Weiss's intentions, the notion of primordial originative power that is not devoid of echoes of the notion of radical origination. In Weiss's account, the primary dynamis must intertwine with the conditions, the privacy, obdurate material and the perspective ideal before an instance of creation is to eventuate. The question this raises is how primary than is the primary dynamis. What weight are we to give to the term "primary"?

If the primary dynamis cannot be spoken of as creative without its coalescing with the conditions, the privacy, and so on, then it cannot be the unconditional origination just mentioned. "Creation" then would be the fabrication from the preexistent of a product with at best a conditional newness, rather than the bringing into being (*poiesis*) of an original without prior precedent. For if it were an unconditional origination, then the conditions might themselves be held to derive from the primary dynamis, and Weiss does not want to say this. If they are not derived from the primary dynamis, then any outcome will always be conditioned. This is significant because a crucial issue with respect to the notion of creativity is the implication of a radical newness, an emergence that cannot be accounted for fully in terms of a set of prior determinate conditions. If the primary dynamis were an absolute original, then the conditions would themselves be conditioned products, and the dynamis might be connected with the unconditioned condition of all finite creations. Alternatively, the dynamis would not be itself unconditional, but one of the conditions deriving from a more ultimate origin. I am treading close to the notion of creation *ex nihilo* again, and the reason I do so is not just theological (this is not negligible) but because of the metaphysical stress in the ideal of creativity itself.

Weiss does *not* want to speak of the primary dynamis as a creative source, for on occasion he compares it to Plato's receptacle (*khōra*) and Aristotle's prime matter (*protē hulē*). He speaks of it as simply ongoing. But these are comparisons to things that seem to be essentially passive, not dynamic; it is unclear if they *do* anything, undertake any work. To that extent they are significantly at odds with the implication of the primary dynamis as *dynamic*. Weiss *does* want to emphasize this latter aspect. Dynamis implies the presence of power, and hence, even if only potentially, some slumbering *activity*. The dynamic cannot but carry some trace of "creative activity." If Weiss's comparisons are well chosen, we risk suppressing these traces, I think; if they are not well chosen, then ought we not to radicalize the dynamic power, say, by unifying the primary dynamis and the conditions in one originative source, which then indeed might be said to be the primordial dynamis?

Suppose we bring my two questions together and ask: should we not be extremely cautious about ascribing creativity to human acts because of the implied radical nature of the ascription? The point is not simply with Aquinas to keep creativity in God's safe keeping, nor with the vulgarized Nietzscheans to throw the portals of creativity open to all. It is to ask (in relation to the human being, and indeed being as such) about the essential possibility of genuine newness, its character and its rareness. Or is there nothing really new under the sun? With the Nietzscheans we are tempted to be metaphysically conceited. With some theologians (I do not include Aquinas) we are inclined to be metaphysically abject. How does the primary dynamis help us avoid these two extremes of philosophical inflation and deflation?

Let me make one further remark. If we say that determinate rules are the outcome of a prior non-determinate source, and that the latter source is "creative," does not this mean that creativity cannot be completely intelligible in terms of determinate principles of explanation? Thus, the radical newness of the genuine creation always looks absurd, unintelligible when it first comes on the scene. It gives the rule, but is not itself generated univocally according to rules. Kant implied this about the genius: through genius nature gives the rule to art. Kant was wary of genius precisely because something about his or her originative activity could not be completely rule-bound. There is something anarchic here. There is a similar issue with the notion of productive imagination. After Kant the issue persists, for instance, in Schelling's idea of the unconscious, in Schopenhauer's view of the metaphysical will as a dark origin, in Nietzsche's affirmation of the creative chaos of the Dionysian will to power.

A similar consideration might be applied to Weiss's notion of the conditions and the primary dynamis: Is there not something about the primary dynamis that must be recalcitrant to rules of intelligibility, not because it is necessarily metaphysically absurd, but because we have to consider a source of principles of determinate intelligibility that is itself not one more determinate principle alongside others? If the primary dynamis is a principal, is it perhaps so in the sense of perhaps a *principium*—an originating power? As I understand Weiss, he does not want to go in this direction. But if we were to speak of such an originating power, this could not be absolutely determinate, I think.

In any case, do we not find in the democratic Weiss something similar to what we find in the aristocratic Nietzsche or the monarchical Aquinas: that something about creativity resists complete conceptualization? This does not mean we have to be resigned to an absurdist silence or celebration, but that our philosophical speech does reach a certain limit wherein it experiences a certain *aporia*: determinate categories no longer suffice; for creativity, while manifested through the determinate, can never be exhausted by determinacy.

I offer two illustrations of the point: first, the resistance of a great artwork to exhaustive analysis and the need for its ever-renewed interpretation and re-appropriation; second, the analogous recalcitrance of a great work of philosophy, e.g., Hegel's *Phenomenology of Spirit*. It is ironical, and to the chagrin of all our Cartesian propensities, that the great work of the philosophical concept seems to resist one definitive, finalized conceptualization. This re-raises the question about creativity in philosophy itself. There is a sense in which the really creative philosopher does not know what he or she is doing—and this is not a limitation or objection. Granting that our analytical tools have been sharpened a little over the last two millennia, granting that Weiss himself has given us an account of admirable intricacy and insight, when all is said and done, has anyone improved much on Plato when he spoke of divine madness?

## Creativity and the Eros of the Absolute

Let me make one final approach to the issue, this time by recalling some of Whitehead's views of creativity. Weiss claims that the dynamis, unlike Whitehead's creativity, does not make anything its creature (*CV*, 314). Nevertheless, there are some suggested affinities that help us think about the matter.

For Whitehead creativity is one category of the ultimate; it is the universal of universals by which the many enter into complex unity; it is also the principle of novelty; creativity introduces novelty into the content of the many such that there is creative advance from disjunction to conjunction; "the many become one and are increased by one."[5] Whitehead identifies creativity with Aristotelian "matter" or what he calls the modern "neutral stuff." Moreover, he indicates that creativity is without a character of its own in exactly the same way as Aristotle's matter. God Himself is a creature of the creativity and hence a determinate being. It is hard not to find some echoes of the dynamis: this too is indeterminate in itself, though it enters into the realization of determinate occurrences as a necessary constituent. Recall that the dynamis is described in terms of a kind of *prima materia*, albeit one that is *pulsating* in itself rather than a static stuff.

Is Whitehead's "creativity" really "creative" in the sense of radical origination? Is there a more ultimate sense of origination beyond "creativity" in Whitehead's sense? This is a question I have already put with respect to Weiss's dynamis in asking about the possibility of the original source of the plurality of "ultimates." In asking about "unity" of the plurality of ultimates, I ask about the nature of the ultimate of ultimates. I ask whether Whitehead's creativity and Weiss's dynamis remain tied to what

5. Whitehead, *Process and Reality*, 21.

elsewhere I have called an erotic absolute in distinction to an agapeic absolute.[6] I agree with Weiss that it makes sense to try to understand the divine creation once having tried to understand human creation (*CV*, 16). Even then we must be careful not to conflate differences. Let me briefly indicate what I mean.

An erotic absolute is modeled on the metaphor of desire as initially lacking in itself and driven beyond itself in the process of determinate self-becoming by which it concretely becomes and completes itself. I think of Hegel's absolute as erotic in that sense: in the origin in itself there is nothing but a lacking indetermination; the absolute as origin determinately becomes itself by externalizing itself in the world; but this creation is *itself* in its own otherness; it completes itself as an absolute whole by dialectically mediating with itself in the otherness of creation, which is really only its own self creation. There is no final otherness between the origin and creation; nor is there any radical creation in a sense that gives the created other its being as irreducibly for itself; everything is for the return of created things to the absolute. We end with a necessary dialectical monism of the whole, precisely because the origin *in itself* is thought of as a lack, an indefiniteness that *in itself* lacks actual determination.

By contrast, what I call an agapeic absolute—and I think of the absolute original in these terms—is modeled on the idea of being that is already a *plenitude for itself*, being that is overdetermined in the sense of being in excess of determinate being; it is not the indefinite as less than determinate being. Real, radical creation is the outcome of this excess of plenitude; it is the creation of the irreducibly plural. Moreover, it is the creation of the finite other, not for the sake of the agapeic original, but for the finite creation itself, which is let be in its genuine otherness. Any relation between the first origin and the creation is not that of the dialectical self-mediation of the monistic totality. There would be a sense in which human creativity, when it genuinely occurs, would also show forth the possibility of agapeic creation in finite being. That is, creation would be from an excess rather than from a lack; it would not simply be a movement from an initial indefiniteness to a final determination of an ideal excellence; there would be a prior plenitude of original being

6. I have treated of this contrast between an erotic and an agapeic absolute in *Desire, Dialectic and Otherness*, and other places; bringing the contrast to bear in criticism of Hegel, for instance, in *Beyond Hegel and Dialectic* and in *Hegel's God*; and seeking to articulate it in more substantive and not alone in contrastive terms, in connection with the question of God in books like *God and the Between*.

at work, making possible the creative venture of the human being. The erotic absolute tends to draw on too dominant a teleology of the *conatus* while shortchanging an archeology of the *passio,* which, agapeically understood, dovetails with a *compassio essendi* in which surplus generosity creates. The agapeic origin lets be and yet remains in companioning solidarity with the creation.

As I understand Whitehead, God in his primordial nature is himself the creature of creativity, understood as nothing determinate in itself, except as a dynamic nisus towards determination. Is this not close to what I mean by an erotic absolute? God's consequent nature completes the initial lack of determination in God's primordial nature. Whitehead describes God's immanence in the world in respect to his primordial nature as an urge towards the future based upon an appetite in the present. This appetition also refers to a principle of unrest, seeking the realization of what is not and may be. So it is not surprising that towards the end of *Process and Reality*, he echoes Hegel—wittingly or not I do not know—in suggesting that just as the world would not be what it is without God, God would not be God without the world. Is not all creativity reduced to self-creativity in this erotic view, self-creativity named especially in modernity in terms of God as *causa sui*? Indeed for Whitehead every entity is like God as *causa sui*. The universe is either a creative advance into novelty or a static morphological world. But is our choice exhausted by that between static being and dynamic origination (itself modeled after self-creation as erotic *causa sui*)? Where then is the genuine creation of the other as other for itself? This latter is what the idea of agapeic creation tries to think, beyond static morphology and circular *causa sui.*

Is not Weiss's view of creative ventures suggestive primarily of the above description of erotic becoming: from an initial indefiniteness, through a process of determination, to a final realization of an ideal excellence? But might we consider creativity—and again I do not mean just human creativity—as an excess of transcendence that allows for real otherness? As I say, some of his descriptions of the dynamis are not unlike Whitehead's "creativity." Moreover, he suggests a comparison of the dynamis with Schopenhauer's will. Yet Schopenhauer is explicit in comparing will as the ultimate source to a kind of blind erotic striving. Are all three—Schopenhauer, Whitehead, Weiss—within the circle of the erotic absolute that creates the determinate other in order for itself to be as determinate? Is there any real otherness here to the finite creation or is the latter only the ultimate in its own otherness?

For the difference of an erotic and agapeic origin concerns the nature of *relations* between a beginning and its creation; whether this relation is it going from one to the other that is for the other as other; whether this going towards the other is not amenable to articulation in terms of reciprocal mutuality or any logic of self-determination; whether there is a priority and excess to the beginning that is not defined by or exhausted in its relativity to its own creation.

The thrust of transcendence in Weiss is primarily a *going towards* perfection, not a *coming from*. He offers primarily a teleology of creativity, not an archaeology. Though he claims to return to ultimate sources, in the end the sources are understood in terms of the end. It is no accident that the title of one of his books is *The God We Seek*. The venture adventures towards, always seeking. There is a sense that perfection, the good, completion is always in the *end*, not in the beginning. We always work for and towards the end we perhaps will never absolutely reach.

At times one gets the sense of an infinite task, never quite reaching absolute perfection. This, I suggest, has some relation to Weiss's own tirelessness as a thinker. But what if they were a sense of the good of the beginning? Such a perfection of the origin would relate to creation as the generosity of being, the plenitude of the excessive good. Such a perfection would have to be conceived as in excess of any finite perfection, as more than perfection in the finite determinate sense, as a creative pluperfection. There is no sense of the absolute origin in this sense with Weiss. As always future oriented with respect to the good, the eros of creative becoming seems to be a self-mastery in overcoming otherness. There is no agapeic origin that creates the other as other.

The problem of the one in the many crops up here too. Is the many the self-pluralization of the one? Or is there another sense of the otherness of the plural to the original one itself? Does the one create the finite other in a manner that is not reducible to the originating one, and hence other in a stronger sense? Is the one nothing until it generates the many which are its own self-determinations? Or is there a creation of the finite other as for itself and as given its being for itself and not for the self-determination of the original one?

The dynamis, as Weiss describes this, is not the ultimate in the sense at issue. If we are not careful, and take our sights from his dynamis to talk about the ultimate of ultimates, we risk characterizing the latter in terms of the erotic absolute that really is nothing in itself except a nisus to self-externalization. As I suggested with Whitehead, the shadow of a kind of

"Hegelianism" hovers over this way of thinking. This is an outcome that Weiss certainly wants to avoid since he is a metaphysical pluralist, not an idealistic monist. This appears very clearly in his account of creative ventures. But just this account raises the question of an enigmatic "unity" that is more than a unity, a "one" that is more than a one, an "origin" that is more than "creativity," one that makes possible finite creation as other, real plurality and the irreducibility of non-duplicable privacy that we especially find in the magnificent singularity of the human being.

Weiss defends the latter against the encompassing embrace of any idealistic totality. To this end he offers us a vision of a sextuplicated universe. The vision brings to mind the pluralism of ultimates in Plato's *Timaeus*: demiurge, the intelligible paradigms, the receptacle, necessity, soul, the good. The question I have been pressing moves towards a view of ultimacy that is more "monotheistic," but not in any sense that conforms to the caricatures of "ontotheology," so prevalent today, and not in any sense opposed to the created pluralism of the genuinely new. The perplexities of metaphysics still remain before us. The ultimate of ultimates would have no other ultimate besides itself, on a par with itself, to limit its radical ultimacy. The ultimate of ultimates would generate "derivative ultimates" that, in turn, contribute to the conditions of the possibility of the intelligibility of given being as given, as other, and as plural. Nor must we let the word "ultimate" get in our way: the issue is the origin beyond "creativity" of the "ultimates," the unoriginated origin beyond origination that is the ultimate of ultimates.

Subsequent to *Creative Ventures* Weiss published *Being and Other Realities*.[7] Being is understood by him in a manner indicative of this source of the ultimates. Again I press the perplexing question: does Being do more than duplicate or pluralize itself? How does Being do more than duplicate itself?[8] Is the pluralizing of *itself* the same as the generation of a real plurality of beings as other to Being in itself? How does Being possibilize beings *other than itself*, genuinely other than itself, and not just as duplicates of itself? What must Being as source or ultimate origin be like for there to be beings as irreducibly plural and other to the origin itself?

7. Weiss, *Being and Other Realities* (1995). This book had not appeared when I originally wrote this reflection on creativity and the dynamis, but I did have conversations with Paul Weiss about some of these issues. For those interested in his reflections, see his "Response to William Desmond."

8. The caps on "Being" in this paragraph mirror Weiss's practice in *Being and Other Realities*.

It would require a further investigation into this latest creative venture of Weiss's philosophizing to hear and understand his answer. As we know, it is easier to raise questions than answer them, easier to start hares than catch them. But in dealing with "creativity" something more than the clearing job of Locke's under-laborer is appropriate for the philosopher. Weiss is no under-laborer, but a bold, risk-taking metaphysician. Indeed, the undergrowth of Paul Weiss's writings always teems with philosophical wildlife. And when all the conceptual bushes have been beaten, even when the soaring birds of thought have been downed and encased for analytic display, does not something about origin and "creativity" always remain wild?

# 7

# A Second Primavera: Stanley Cavell, German Philosophy, and the Redemption of Romanticism

## On Style of Thought

WHEN HEGEL BROUGHT ART, religion, and philosophy together in ultimate companionship in his understanding of Absolute *Geist*, he surely pointed to something of great importance. Stanley Cavell is not at all a Hegelian, and yet the companionship of these three is not entirely distant from his concerns. Very evident in his work is the companionship of philosophy (as practiced and understood by him) with literature and poetry generally. Religion, by contrast, is recessive. There is a certain cultural hesitancy with regard to explicit concern with religion, and yet we are made to ponder about it as a companion, given his engagement with redemption in Romanticism, and his striking claim that now the other has taken the place of God. If religion is recessive, is it entirely out of play? I think not, and one main aim of my thoughts here is to bring what is so recessed to some more explicit expression. His engagement with German philosophy and with Romanticism make this aim a worthy and a needed one.

Of course, Cavell is not one whose thought can be fixed easily with univocal determinacy. This is a thinking always on the move, and it moves more by perplexity and questioning than by arriving at assertoric claims, where finally rest at last offers itself. This is part of Cavell's great attraction and difficulty. *Attraction*: the subtlety of his interrogations lures one towards a moment of truth, less determined in conclusive propositions as in the question that now at last can be put, and that, in being put, gives us access to a light that, just in being stayed briefly, also as quickly passes. *Difficulty*: there seems no place to lay one's head, so to say, and one is left to wonder if, in fact, there was that brief access of light, which after all seems more now a new perplexity than any perplexity dissolved or problem solved. To anyone who insists on a more settled univocity in philosophical argumentation, there will be cause enough here for chewing the carpet. And yet there is nothing excessively studied in this, as if it were the *pose* of unsettling us that Cavell struck, rather than in fact offering us access to that place of unsettling where a different thinking might catch fire. There are rhythms in the writings of Cavell that duplicate a certain casting about for light, whose mimesis of perplexity is creative of an opening when, as if suddenly, after what seems like a fascinating fussing with detail, seemingly leading nowhere, there is this access of light, and something is communicated that is striking in its communication, without being domesticated in its elusiveness

To say more univocally what cannot quite be so said: there is something of art in the philosophical writing of Cavell, which draws water from a well whose secret spring still remains underground. This is the clue for my own opening relative to German philosophy and Romanticism. Cavell's concern with the first is, on first glance, less developed than his engagement with the second; and his engagement with both marked by resistance to the laundry list summary of themes beloved of certain univocalizers of thinking. The relation of art and philosophy, and more specifically the relation of literature and philosophy, as I said, is clearly central to Cavell; and indeed it is central to German philosophy and the great cultural movement so familial to it, called Romanticism. In Cavell's case there is also the ancestor Wittgenstein who said something to the effect: philosophy ought to be written as poetic composition.[1] Cavell's *The Claim of Reason*[2] ends just with the question of art and literature, and whether philosophy, were it to become literature, would still know itself. One could equally ask if it has managed to know itself after more than

1. Wittgenstein, *Culture and Value*, 24e.

2. Cavell, *The Claim of Reason* [hereinafter *CR*], 496.

two millennia of seeming to distance itself from the poets, most foundingly so in Plato's banishment of them from the philosophical republic. There is much at stake here, but it is central to the "problematic" given some articulation in classical German philosophy, its seemingly idealistic consummation, and its anti-idealistic dissolution, and not least in Romanticism.

The issue of the style of philosophizing, and with respect to the fruitfulness of the autobiographical,[3] also can be connected with the Romantic concern with "self," and with key elements of Cavell's own style of philosophizing. Of course, the challenge of the autobiographical is to avoid a kind of philosophical autism in the very act of speaking about oneself. Different readers will judge the success of Cavell differently, but some of the common reactions to his allegedly idiosyncrasy mirror reactions to Romanticism's so-called irrationalism. I think of Hegel's distaste for Romantic subjectivity, perhaps all the shriller because of his own proximity to it. Certain reactions to Cavell are quite Hegelian in that regard, and one might equally wonder if so out of an anxiety of proximity. One of the dimensions of philosophical naming I find in Cavell relates to what I call the *idiocy of being*: that intimacy of being that cannot be truly rendered in the language of the neutral, homogenous generality, for it concerns intimate singularities, that are yet redolent of a fuller, more radiant significance.[4] What cannot be so homogenized in terms of the neutral generality is itself more intimately involved in the articulation of language, in the sources of being as communicative: communication is made possible by what cannot be communicated in absolutely determinate terms. The idiocy is not unrelated to the idiom, and the idiosyncratic: philosophy has its idioms, as the philosopher has his or her idiosyncrasies; and neither finally is a neutral, homogeneous generality. Poetry and art are more often than philosophy subtler servants of this intimacy of being, this idiocy. To be true to it means that philosophy as a communication must go to school with, take time for, *skolē* for, the poets.

3. Cavell's *Little Did I Know* (2010) appeared after I wrote the first version of this exploration, and would require a study unto itself, but it confirms for me the importance of a consideration of styles of thought in connection with his work. I make some observations below—see notes 19 and 23.

4. See, for instance, Desmond, *Perplexity and Ultimacy*, chapter 3; also Desmond, *The Intimate Universal*, chapter 5. For Cavell, Emerson and Thoreau were "inheritors of Kant's transcendentalism" whose work reflected "a sense of the intimacy of words with the world, or of intimacy lost." Cavell, *In Quest of the Ordinary*, 170 [hereinafter *IQO*].

Philosophy has not always had that leisure enough to listen. We need to consent to the leisure of language to listen to Cavell. Part of the difficulty of Cavell's philosophical way is also this problem with the autobiographical, the confessional: to communicate oneself, and what is ontologically intimate to being, *without embarrassment*, not only to oneself but to the other who is being offered the confidence.[5]

Philosophers generally do not take this risk of the intimacy of being, which comes across as "too much." They are like the anorexics who like the leaner foods of perfections where less seems enough. They shun the "too muchness" of things and decamp to the neutral generality. Of course, if they are like such anorexics they have either begun to die, or perhaps something has not been born in them, or allowed to come to be. I think the later Wittgenstein was a kind of recovering anorexic in that sense: the younger was more under the spell of the austerer perfections of the logical ideal that would recreate or redeem, in an ideal language of univocity, the contaminating equivocities of the everyday. It turns out that the contaminating equivocal is the matrix of robust life, though the anorexic cannot taste this, for this robustness of healthy food is too much for it, too shockingly healthy. It has the smell of life, while the anorexic would prefer a world washed of smells, and alas too of its enchanting perfumes.

See Romanticism as a desire to return to the fragrant world, after the dead purity of the mechanical whole that Newtonianism gives us. But many Romantics were in the contagion of the anorexia of spirit; hence at times the spectral visitors, the nameless powers, the hidden hindrances of soul that still kept them back from the fragrant world. Sometimes they tried, so to say, to will themselves to wake from the mechanistic dream; but they still found themselves in a paralyzed state, even in willing to wake up from such a spell; they would move their legs, but they will not move, as if some ominous power had secreted a bewitchment to which they may have more than half succumbed. One cannot just will to wake up from such a bewitchment; for the character of one's willing is implicated in the bewitchment, and hence it too must undergo a *metanoia*; but from where is the saving power to come? The anorexic spirit, in trying to

5. Cavell witnesses to a sense of strain between philosophy as a practice of mindfulness and as an institutional practice; hence his touchiness about Emerson, and the professors at Harvard; and his touchiness at what he takes as Kuklick's claim that the transcendentalists were soundly whipped by the Harvard professionals: good (Christian) organization men (*IQO*, 13–14).

save itself, and with obeisance to what seem like the highest ideals of self-perfection, is in the grip of a spell cast on it, through itself, if not by itself. The spell is just itself as the bewitched prison it has made itself.

This sense of Romanticism is not unconnected with Cavell's engagement of skepticism. Think of a certain kind of skeptic as an anorexic mind: driven by an ideal of perfection, not always fully articulated; seeking a certain power over what initially presents itself as ambiguous and beyond; secretly desirous of its own sovereignty over what always threatens to disappoint it, or its secret ideal; more and more forced to close the circle of control over that which it believes it subdues; closing down the equivocal, but also closing down the "too muchness" of given life, and indeed the insurgent energies of itself that still come to surface unbidden (these are outlaw, hence outlawed); and at the end, mastery over its own "no," as it comes into its kingdom, where it inherits precisely nothing. Such a skeptic is driven to an extremity where a monstrous outcome awaits; as does the anorexic who will not accept and live the risk that comes with the ambiguous robustness of the food of life, and the tasting of its gift. Think of the inhumanity to which Cavell thinks philosophy can be driven. Why would you call that inhumanity "metaphysics"? Maybe truer "metaphysics" is concerned with being awoken to our being human? Of course, there are practices of "metaphysics" that answer more closely to the anorexic spirit. I do not mean only the bloodless scholasticism of some analytical approaches. Strangely enough, even what looks like the lush exuberance of deconstructions of metaphysics may be more anorexic than the victim of the deconstruction, say, Plato, whose dialogues are often fragrant with the "too muchness" of the so-called "ordinary."

How do we get our bearings in the muchness of Cavell's writings? The following citation from *In Quest of the Ordinary* might be taken as a helpful précis of some central themes to which Cavell gives expression and marking his affinities with major Romantic concerns. He tells us that the purpose of the Romantics was "to redeem genuine poetry from its detractors." This in turn was bound up with

> the preservation or redemption of genuine philosophy, where the preservation of poetry and philosophy by one another presents itself as the necessity of recovering or replacing religion. This contesting of philosophy and poetry and religion (and I guess of politics) with one another, for one another, together with the disreputable sense that the fate of the contest is bound

up with one's own writing, and moreover with the conviction that the autobiographical is a method of thought wherein such a contest can find a useful field, and in which the stakes appear sometimes as the loss or gain of our common human nature, sometimes as the loss or gain of nature itself, as if the world were no more than one's own—some such statement represents the general idea I have of what constitutes serious romanticism's self-appointed mission, the idea with which I seek its figures.[6]

In what is to follow I will focus on the concerns here named, forming my remarks around the relations of art, religion, and philosophy (with a bow again to Hegel's triad of absolute spirit). I will also touch on central themes like philosophical migration and inheritance; the death of nature, with some special reference to Coleridge; the equivocal displacement of religious redemption from religion to art with Romanticism; what the redemption of Romanticism betokens; and what this asks of the transcendence of thought and its sanity. But first the issue of inheritance allows us to offer some more general points of orientation.

## Inheritances between Worlds

The issue of *philosophical inheritance* is hard to avoid in any consideration of Cavell's relation to German philosophy and Romanticism. We find many references to Kant, to Hegel, to Nietzsche, a few to Heidegger. Perhaps Kant garners most attention in *The Claim of Reason*, given his "enormous prestige" with Hume in "recent philosophizing" (*CR*, 248), and certainly given Kant's concern with skepticism. Interesting for our theme, Kant himself speaks of the skeptic as a "species of nomads" of which fortunately (for Kant) there are few. Something of this nomadic spirit clearly has infected Cavell in his own affinities with a variety of skepticisms, and indeed his skepticism about certain skepticisms. Clearly also Cavell's interest exceeds skepticism as the problem is often formulated in modern, post-Cartesian epistemology. I will return to Kant in relation to Cavell's reading of Coleridge's *Ancient Mariner*, but here I want to note certain parallels. In the Anglo-Saxon tradition, Kant was primarily received as an epistemologist in the tradition of classical epistemology, and especially with respect to what was taken as a major outcome of this in Humean skepticism. Of course, there are other faces of Kant: the Kant

6. *IQO*, 43.

for whom freedom is the heart and soul of the transcendental philosophy, and for whom, arguably, the *Critique of Practical Reason* was decisive, decisive in making a space for human freedom in a world under the iron domination of deterministic mechanism; the power of freedom is from the outset prefigured, haunting in advance the theory of transcendental knowing in *Critique of Pure Reason*. There is the Kant of the *Critique of Judgment*, the Kant with perhaps most influence on the Romantic generation. This Kant would, in his own tortured scholastic way, want to bind up the wounds of dualism lacerating the first and second Critiques; more than anywhere else in his system, this Kant wanted to think the otherness of nature as not fully figured forth in the mechanism of the Newtonian paradigm. We might see intimations of Romantic and Cavellian themes: bringing nature back to life; bringing the human back to itself in a nature not its dead mechanical opposite but an other to be acknowledged in a significant, expressive relation, be it, say, the accordance of beauty or the discordance of the sublime. These themes are there in *The Claim of Reason*.

Of course, there is the perceived difficulty with Kant that has some parallel: *transcendental solipsism*. This brings up the problem of the other, central to Cavell's own movement from knowledge to acknowledgment. This is not entirely unlike the problem of recognition central to Kant's heirs. Thus Fichte: notoriously transcendental; yet intriguingly obsessed with the other; and perhaps obsessed so, because notorious thus. Thus Hegel too and the place of recognition. Think of the *Phenomenology of Spirit*: the early parts deal, it seems, with very classical problems in epistemology; and then about half way through the discussion, the human other makes an unceremonious entrance, through desire and the struggle for recognition, and the master and slave dialectic (mentioned in *CR*); and then the later parts of the *Phenomenology* offers an obscure dialectical trawl through the seas of history, in search of absolute knowing, or its historical conditions of possibility. The dialectical trawl culminates with philosophical knowing: the point where supposedly knowing no longer needs to go beyond itself. I would say Cavell inverts this: acknowledging is just the point where knowing knows it must go beyond itself. And there is something more absolved in that going beyond of acknowledgment than the putative self-certainty of knowing that knows *itself* as the certainty of truth. Cavell is not thus Hegelian.[7] There is a knowing that

7. Indeed, there is an echo of one of his great guides here. This is the older Wittgenstein, walking in the Phoenix Park, Autumn 1948, in conversation with Drury,

in acknowledging the other learns of differences, differences it perhaps had already *known from* others. It has perhaps forgotten this "knowing from," though still it is carried by the words of others, words themselves the treasuries of differences carried across time, as if in secret caches. One witnesses something of this treasury of differences being brought to the surface, as one is sometimes stunned to attention and to pause at Cavell's extraordinary wordings of ordinary English.

One of the complications in approaching Cavell's relation to German philosophy and Romanticism is the way Thoreau and Emerson exert a strong influence in the foreground, pushing back the European side into a more recessive shade. I sense that first and foremost Cavell wants to follow where his philosophical muse leads, but his muse keeps wanting to sing in an idiom that is distinctively American. Hence there is a tension from the outset. The muse must be wooed, and wooed in relation to genius, and genius is not just my genius as this singular thinker or poet or artist, but also the genius of a place or locale, which too is the genius of a people. One is located; and this is a great thing for Cavell, as for Thoreau. Where is he located? But much of his work is to come to terms with a sense of dislocation; where does the dislocation come from? From the very vocation of philosophy itself. But what if this is located in a place that is not always hospitable to the slower leisures of ruminative reflection, indispensable to philosophical thinking? Any ruminative thought must return again and again to what it believed it had digested or exhausted, only to find reserves hidden there still, perhaps reserves that hint finally at an inexhaustibility that will never be done with, that will always haunt all final claims on it. For these reserves claim us, we do not claim them. In some ways America is a name for the condition, or

---

who asks: What about Hegel? Wittgenstein: "No, I don't think I would get on with Hegel. Hegel seems to me to be always wanting to say that things that look different are really the same. Whereas my interest is in showing that things which look the same are really different. I was thinking of using as a motto for my book a quotation from *King Lear* 'I'll teach you differences.' [Then laughing:] The remark 'You'd be surprised' wouldn't be a bad motto either." In Drury, *The Danger of Words and Writings on Wittgenstein*, 157. I have found my own interest in Wittgenstein sometimes heightened less by Wittgenstein's own texts as by the voices of others who have directed me back to him, Cavell being one such other, and especially Richard Eldridge, who has done so much to elaborate the relations and affinities between Wittgenstein and Romanticism, particularly in *Leading A Human Life*. Eldridge also has very good things to say about such themes as inheritance, being between, the philosophical importance of poets like Hölderlin and Wordsworth. See Eldridge, "Internal Transcendentalism" and Eldridge, "Kant, Hölderlin and the Experience of Longing."

perhaps hope, that claims him with this promise of inexhaustibility, and that never leaves him alone.

Note the stress: rumination returns to what is hidden in the there; while America, mostly, is never quite there, it is always on the way, always to come. By contrast, Europe might seem, so to say, more there; and this is perhaps more true of England, relative to the extraordinary long time of inner stability its ways of life have generally enjoyed. Europe, the continent of war; England, an island place with its sanctioned way of life; its island race were yet great seafarers, not nomads, at the height of their world-historical significance. But where is America for Cavell? In many places, but philosophically in the forgotten or repressed. Thus, those thinkers who sometimes seem to look over him like gods of an Easter Island: Emerson and Thoreau—founders, but not now so acknowledged by the regnant caste of contemporary professors of philosophers. The caste shows its diffidence about giving them entry to the now respectable guild: they are genteel, they write literature, and it is edifying . . . but it is not philosophy. A different act of piety informs Cavell's work in relation to these two. To give a local habitation and a name requires a new philosophical imagination: to bring back to life those dead founders.[8]

What has this to do with Romanticism? One might say that a major theme of Romanticism, in its opposition to the allegedly neutral universalism of the Enlightenment, is its concern with a people, in the singularity of its traditions, and its cultural inheritance (think of Herder). Cavell's relation to Emerson and Thoreau can be seen in this light. So for him, their senses of the "common" serve to underwrite the ordinary language philosophy of Austin and Wittgenstein (*IQO*, 4). That Emerson and Thoreau haunted some of the places of Cavell's life (Harvard) is not insignificant. Their presence lives on in their absence, in the words they can no longer speak, words they need not speak now because they wrote them, and which we must learn perhaps to speak for them, from them. Thus, we bring them back to life, bring them back from the dead; we ourselves enter into converse with the dead. Seen in a certain light there is a kind of horror in speaking to and with the dead, something macabre. Why should one be obsessed with those dead? Or is it a love that impels a philosophical Orpheus to seek in the underworld?

8. See *CR*, 189 on language as a bequest, not just acquirement; on poetry as the second inheritance of language; on Thoreau on the mother and father tongues. "Poetry thereby celebrates its language by making it a return on its birth, by reciprocating."

One might compare Cavell and Heidegger relative to such a Romantic sense of inheritance. Cavell seems intrigued by some things in Heidegger but equally non-plussed or repulsed by other things. America getting in the way of Germany?[9] And yet it is the extremity of a certain Romanticism in Heidegger that both attracts and repulses: just as the problematic twinning of poetry and philosophy also draws. Heidegger wanted to be the voice of Germany, philosophically, as he claimed Hölderlin was poetically, and Hitler then was politically. Cavell: not quite the philosophical voice of America, but one voice seeking to be true to America. Since that voice seeks to be true to a more democratic impulse, there can be no arrogation of voice. Can a voice reach towards its own singularity, if it does not arrogate authority at some point? If not, will it not be like Emerson's scholar (so beloved of citation) who cannot, dare not, say "I think, I am." One might say this is very close to the predicament of Romanticism: community of source, singularity of voice. The first may be deeper than the second, and yet it is mute without the second, and hence it is a depth lost to itself without the boldness of singulars who say "I am, I say," the boldness to arrogate voice. Cavell is working towards this: To speak less *for* the other as *to* the other; and perhaps to find that others already have been speaking *in* one, and in one's words, and so what one must do is give heed to what is already communicated; and so then to *speak from* the other, out of our knowing from the other. Is this not why we must then return to the "common," for the muse that calls the singular genius there drowses incognito?

There is a very amusing passage in *In Quest of the Ordinary* that, were it offered by a Heidegger, would entail his summary conviction of haughty snobbishness relative to "Americanism." American philosophy is compared to *company scrip*. Cavell wonders: does the scrip, can it, have any currency outside the company or its holdings? One might add: What if the company scrip is becoming a reserve currency of the world? Would this be a very heavy thought to bear: that the currency of philosophy standardized by a company, like the American Philosophical Association, the APA, were to be universally exported? Would this be arrogation with a vengeance, and perhaps entail a devaluation of other currencies? (The British will hold on to sterling; the Continentals hope for a strong euro.) Cavell is worried whether the standard currency is really worthless

9. See in Cavell, *Philosophical Passages*, 39–41 the revealing remarks on Emerson and Heidegger, on slavery and Nazism, on Heidegger's unknowing mention of Nietzsche's mention of Emerson, on being philosophically compromised.

outside certain exchanges, perhaps even counterfeit—perhaps even partly counterfeit relative to the common and the community it seems to ostensibly serve (in this case, America). Hence the claim: Emerson and Thoreau were more true to the common in their seemingly uncommonness; perhaps truer to the treasury of differences that is the inheritance of a people, albeit marked by or held together by striking sameness. But one may not hear them, or hear from them, if one only stays at home; for staying at home, may not be to be at home; and perhaps one must learn not to be at home in order again to come home: being at home in not being at home; not being at home in being at home.

There are places where Cavell hints at some points of continuity with German idealism, but hesitates in his commitment to it, especially in regard to something about its philosophy of consciousness: "the concept takes in train a philosophical machinery of self-consciousness, subjectivity, and imagination, of post-Kantianism in general, that for me runs out of control" (*IQO*, 45). He could not follow. What is a philosophy that comes to be "out of control"? How important is it to be in control (see, *IQO*, 58)? As a philosopher? What are the "ordinary controls"? Why ask? Surely one of the effects of Cavell's writing is to remind us of how less in control of importances we are than we think; and not least in relation to what is tacit in words, in language itself. The poet brings something of this taciturnity to our attention; letting it be tacit while bringing it to speech; respecting the reserve of the true word itself. Resistance to being "out of control" suggests, to some degree, that Cavell is more heir to certain modern notions of self-determining humanity than is always evident. What then of what I called "knowing from," "speaking from"? I mean: the deeper message of Cavell's writing is to show us how little we determine through ourselves alone, not so as to make us powerless, but so as to let us partake of sources of empowerment that are as much other, as our own. What is most our own is not our own; and yet it is ours, or is to become ours, in being let live itself, as much from within out, as in its gift to us from those sources of speaking in whose endowment we have our share. What is the endowment in which we share; and which as given, is certainly not in our complete control, or perhaps ever ours to command? We have to give up certain modes of commandment, of thus being in control. I will return to the theme of "being beside oneself" in thought.

And perhaps it is not that the German idealists were epistemologically "out of control" but rather too much the opposite. They insisted more radically than ever on a knowing that would just be in its own control;

absolutely self-determining thought; absolutely autonomous. This is the monster of the self-empowering knower, the self-absolutizing, self-absolving thinker. There will be nothing given to it that (it claims) it does not give to itself. In fact, we cannot so absolve ourselves of something given. One might say: to be absolved is to be acknowledged by another, perhaps as the incarnation of forgiveness. The monster of self-determination is not far from an ontological tyrant: being in control thus is perhaps what it means not to be in control at all. (The tyrant and anorexic are, as it were, brother bullies, or sister.) For such a knowing perhaps least does justice to what Cavell calls "acknowledgment." There is no acknowledgment there, for finally there is no other to acknowledge.

If Emerson and Thoreau are often in the foreground, how do we see beyond this foreground to German philosophy (especially in work after *The Claim of Reason*).[10] Cavell wants to inherit Emerson and Thoreau and stake a claim to American philosophy; but this means to be in a somewhat different register to either "England" or the "Continent." One travels to England or the Continent, but one is always drawn back through them, hoping to come drawn back differently to the American scene (Henry James). This he always loves, and which always in some way also disappoints. Is this not that kind of knowing, Cavell mentions, the attainment of which brings with it disappointment? And yet, in that disappointment, acknowledgment as something other to that knowing, may eventuate.

One might then say that Cavell's voice begins to find its place somewhere *between* a number of different sources of philosophical inheritance.[11] Being *between worlds* is itself identified by Cavell with the Romantic response to Kant's two worlds. Look here at Cavell's non-American forbears. Was there not something quintessentially English about Austin? I do not think of him as marked by a plurivocal identity,

10. He is happy to discover Emerson as a forerunner of Nietzsche: especially with respect to the theme of not finding humans, but fragments of men. See Cavell, *Pitch*, 76, on his claim about Nietzsche's "transcription" of Emerson's passage about "walking monsters" of "The American Scholar" in *Zarathustra* and in *Ecce Homo*; this in a discussion of Derrida. See Ratner-Rosenhagen, *American Nietzsche*, 4–21 on Emerson; 295–305 Cavell on Nietzsche and Emerson and related matters.

11. See *CR* foreword, xviii: he speaks of the "connection of writing and the problem of the other, and the connection of both with my interest in a tradition, anyway an idea, of philosophizing opposed to the tradition in English, as that tradition is represented in the best English-speaking departments." He is and has been concerned with the link and loss of link of English and Continental traditions, and "to realign these traditions," . . . at least to write witnessing the loss in that separation. This "has been a formative aspiration of mine from the earliest of the work I refer to here."

as *between* different communities, and different stresses and demands; yet he does explore a rich vein of plurivocity in regard to language and the philosophical suggestiveness of the English language; but one feels he does it as an insider, not as one stressed between being inside and outside.[12] Wittgenstein is different: already in the German world, and in the English; stressed between these two; always perhaps, because of stresses both singular and inherited, more an outsider than an insider; a onetime professor, seemingly the *nec plus ultra* of being an insider, and yet, as we know, the ethos of academic life *then* was hospitable to the singularity of the eccentric, homegrown or imported. Wittgenstein: The professor of philosophy who would not thus profess philosophy, and yet who would profess philosophy.[13] (Did Wittgenstein, who read Kierkegaard, read what Kierkegaard said about the assistant professors producing their readings? *Not* to be learned from Kierkegaard: how to philosophize without suffering.) Wittgenstein preaches to us about the ordinary, but I wonder if this is just what Wittgenstein never knew: being too much on the outside. An outsider who would be an insider? I almost think of celibate priests who romanticize marriage, just because they have not really smelled it from close up. They might recoil from woman, neither virgin nor mother, as Cavell suggests Othello recoils from just the fleshed humanness of Desdemona: that she was human, this was Othello's horror.

So also with the ordinary: we can make it intellectually, as already suggested, into a world washed of smells. We hate the head-turning fragrances, we want a disinfected world. A Romantic theme, a Cavellian

12. Is the praise of Austin in Cavell, *A Pitch of Philosophy* a bit extravagant? Does Cavell protest too much the importances of Austin. He is gallant, almost pious, in places; but if one's love has not been awakened there, one is left colder by the gallantry. Though again, there are places where Cavell delicately suggests his reticent reservation, and perhaps even hints about the risk of turning the ordinary into a philosophy of the proper, of propriety. But who can canonize the proprieties of the English don? Ernest Gellner, *Words and Things*, early made us uneasy on this score: another middle European, inside, outside, and yet as outside-inside extremely perceptive about the customs of the native academics; even unto the threat of review boycott by Ryle; true, Russell came to the defense, but he did not much regard the later Wittgenstein. Cavell mentions Gellner in *This New Yet Unapproachable America*, 43, and while he grants that Wittgenstein allows himself to be open to a charge of petit bourgeois fear of change, he insists on the transfiguration, revolution, or conversion called for by *Philosophical Investigations*. I cannot hear that call in Austin.

13. See *CR*, xvi, on the difficulty of institutionalizing Wittgenstein. The issue of the esoteric—insiders, outsiders—is noted. See (*CR*, xvii–xviii) the worry of the philosopher about being "in the right place," about there being any "workable field of philosophy," about "the wrong ground."

theme: to give new fragrance to the world. What would it be like to be in a world without smells, without fragrances? A world so washed clean would perhaps be a dead world; since new life germinates in the compost heap of the humus. Washing life, purifying life, can also means killing it. And yet we must be washed, purified, to be alive after this death. If Wittgenstein is stressed between, Cavell communicates his distinctive stress as neither English nor Continental, and yet having blood that is indebted to both. Between the new world, the old world, and the island of analysis, this stress of "being between" breeds perhaps a new mutation of philosophical genes. Or a new plurivocity: a voice of voices. In some way, it turns out that we are all, in our own way, a voice of voices. Some voices come to mindfulness by entry into the quarrel and persuading of many voices; they speak in this Babel as more than dinned over echoes. One voice rises above the din, is heard above it, though it is in the midst of it. Another voice finds itself in a return to being in the midst of other voices, and ceases to claim the prerogative of being above. It does not "sublime," but finds the sublime, as in the blessing of the common: blessing it, being blessed in it, blessed by it.

## The Death of the World

Suppose we further consider this theme, touched on in the *The Claim of Reason*, central to the Romantic problematic, and also important in *In Search of the Ordinary*, where we find some of the most important pointers concerning Cavell's relation to German philosophy and Romanticism. In *In Search of the Ordinary* we are offered an extended discussion of Coleridge and Wordsworth, and some brief discussion of Heidegger. The discussion of Coleridge and Wordsworth is fascinating, taking up themes clearly evident in *The Claim of Reason*, as well as elsewhere, and in a manner that more fully releases them from the terms of more standard epistemological concerns.

It is worth remembering that Coleridge is kind of a double here. Coleridge is the figure from whom American transcendentalism would have learned much about German philosophy, Kant included (*IQO*, 40). In Coleridge's *Biographia Literaria*, Cavell recognizes something of a forerunner of his own interests in linking transcendentalism and ordinary language philosophy (*IQO*, 41). We might say Coleridge instantiates the problem of plural allegiances of intellect, of spirit. An Englishman, who will become canonical in the tradition of English poetry, and yet an honorary German, both in relation to his strenuous efforts to assimilate the new philosophy coming with Kant and his aftermath, and in relation to his importation of the spirit of the new Romanticism, not quite Kantian, but in the line of inheritance of a cultural ethos within which Kant was a crucial influence. In his way, Coleridge was between England and Germany, as he explicitly acknowledges in his *Biographia Literaria*. One sees here also soundings and resoundings, doublings, doublings back, redoublings, of the relation of poetry and philosophy. There is Coleridge's conceded, albeit qualified, debt to Schelling as philosopher. Perhaps this is too euphemistic a way of talking of his debt. Coleridge plagiarized Schelling, something known by Schelling, and indeed acknowledged by him with generous acceptance, so high a regard he had for Coleridge his friend, "such a truly congenial man."[14] There is the hint of a Cavellian theme in this: acknowledgement. For what might plagiarism be? An act of taking from another, without proper acknowledgement, and yet honoring the other in this taking, and hence secretly acknowledging this other.

Schelling, of course, was considered the "dark prince of Romanticism," and this was one reason he never received a proper and serious attention in the tradition of English philosophy. How "Hegelian" that reception was in treating his thought as mere Romantic irrationalism! Ostensibly Schelling might seem "out of control." Given Hegel's apotheosis of reason, he seems most "in control" philosophically; but given what I said above about being in control, perhaps he was epistemologically out of control, even though the surface says the exact opposite: being out of control is falsely doubled as being absolutely in control. And so perhaps Schelling was truer to the familial intimacy of art and philosophy than Hegel. Philosophy is no king on top of the dialectical pile; were it to claim this monarchy, it would have to usurp the artist, who, for Schelling, is more immediately at the absolute standpoint, hence can offer philosophy its organon; if not fed from there, or the sources shown there, and if it claims only to feed on itself, philosophy will end up wasted, for of itself its thinking can butter no parsnips.

I will shortly turn more fully to Cavell on Coleridge, but it is worth pointing out a question I think Schelling represents for German idealism: Is there any light of self-consciousness without the darkness of what is on

14. Schelling, *Historical-critical Introduction to the Philosophy of Mythology*, 187.

the other side of self-consciousness? Does this light come from darkness and never completely dispel it? Is this light as much given to be out of darkness, as that it illuminates that on which it sheds its radiance? This is to touch on the tender Achilles heel of self-determining knowing. I could put it thus: is all knowing, finally, *knowing from*: from a source not itself knowing; or perhaps fully knowable? One expression of this might be what Cavell calls the seam already there in any project of projection (*CR*, 424–25). The seam is not first projected; projection (if this is a good word, which I doubt) is already enacted in what is seamed, or already given over to difference that cannot be completely accounted for in terms of projection. That is one problem. It is not outside of consideration of transcendental solipsism. Schelling was more acutely aware of this than Fichte; and to his credit strongly insisted that nature in its otherness could not be slighted. Transcendental philosophy must be complemented, if not completed by a new system of the whole in which self and other, human and nature, subject and object, are together and known as together. I cannot go into the complications of this system, and the influence of Spinoza, among others, but it worth dwelling a little on nature, as revealing something of the *ethos* within which both transcendental philosophy and *Naturphilosophie* function.

Remember again: modern science, supposedly grounded in its overcoming of epistemological skepticism, goes to work with its new mathematical and geometrical tools, and produces a world conformed to formula, and indeed radically determined so in its deterministic outlines; but alas, nature so conceived seems to have little place for the human being who first conceived nature so. Thus, for instance, the difference of the inanimate and animated seems undercut by a certain principle of homogeneous intelligibility. If so, the place of the scientist or human who uses the homogeneous principle becomes deeply perplexing. We are not at home in the mathematical machine, nor can we be. Nature as machine, with the extrinsic God of Deism, seems a little like the estranged human dualistically opposed to an other with which it has no inherent rapport. With nature devalued, dedivinized, any deistic god perpetually on the verge of vanishing, the human wakes to itself as lost in an immense indifference. The Romantics rebelled against the fear Pascal felt, seeking neither nature as machine, nor God beyond that nature, but nature as an organism, and perhaps the immanent God such as someone like Spinoza seemed to promise. Thus, in German idealism, Spinozism becomes the balancing complement to Kant's transcendental solipsism: substance to subject. Hegel picked up on that, but the issue is very elemental and the Romantic poets knew this along the pulses. In fact, Spinoza is as much a "mechanist" as an "organicist," but it is the second image that prevails in Novalis's description of him as no atheist but as the *Gott-vertrunkene mann*. The generation of Romanticism and transcendental philosophy often saw what they needed and wanted to see, whether in Kant or in Spinoza. Spinoza's god may be a counterfeit double of God, yet the sense of the organic whole here intimated seemed to offer a way to a renewed rapport with the earth.

Different directions open up here. We might go the way of genius: an immanent "inner" pathway of originality prepared by transcendental philosophy. Genius is the favorite of nature through whom nature gives the rule to art, as Kant puts it. Yet here you have something beyond autonomous self-determination, since it arises from a source on the other side of our own self-legislation. The genius is a creative middle, an original medium through whom a more original power comes to articulation: nature beyond the law that yet brings the law to expression. Kant hesitated here; but he let this genie out of the bottle, and it could not be put back in terms of the education of taste. A source of exceeding otherness even in the innerness of genius, in its intimacy with the secret powers of nature, comes through. This means: no transcendental solipsism in transcendental selfhood itself.

This still leaves the problem of how, even if those immanent powers of self-transcending are released, we are released to nature as other. What will give it back to itself, or how will we be released to its otherness as other, and as not the deadened world that mechanism seems to produce. Coleridge went the first way, and realized, with Schelling, that this was not enough. Hence the famous lines: "O lady, we receive but what we give,/ And in our life alone does Nature live:/Ours is her wedding garment, ours her shroud!" ("Dejection: An Ode"). We are too much there, and the otherness of nature not enough there. The ancient mariner's journey below the line: Is this an entry into the inner otherness, and a transgression in that immanence? Consequence? The world of ice, dead nature. And when we have deadened ourselves, how is any renewed rapport possible? With the mariner, it is renewed in its blessing when he learns to bless—slimy creatures as well as beautiful. But how to bless? How be released? This is a suddenness, an *exaiphnēs* (ἐξαίφνης: remember Plato and the good, and the vision of beauty [*Symposium*, 210e], as well as Plotinus and the One). It is more like a grace than anything we could do; it comes *to* us, and does not first come *from* us; and we come to ourselves, and can go from ourselves again towards what is other as other. But these are *religious pathways of redemption*. I will return to this theme.

What here is at issue is hard to map entirely in terms of the inner otherness of self, since this is at stake, in question; nor indeed on to nature in its otherness, for how comes that transformation by which it is restored to its qualitative value. How comes it about that it is seen as blessed, such that we might murmur: it is good? We do not do this, it does not do it. What power below or beyond or above the line restores? And is not this death of the world inseparable from bewitchment, indeed from *eros* and religion? Bewitchments are what we are enchanted by, what we are infatuated by, or perhaps love. There is no chant without enchantment, no singing of being without seduction by a love beyond us. All of this is assaulted in early modernity: no more witches means no more bewitchment; means a world washed of dangers and fragrances, hence a dead place for love, no place, nothing to woo or overcome one. Yeats sought to reverse this and claimed: Newton gave us excrement but Berkeley restored the world. Berkeley may not be the restorer, but this too is Cavell's problem, our problem.

I could put it in pedestrian way: in modernity we find a certain objectification of being, itself inseparable from a certain subjectification, and both inseparable from a devaluation, neutering of being as other to us. As the neuter grows indifferent, we come to hate the indifferent, and hence the neuter grows hateful, for we cannot love it; and when we hate the neutralized world, we do not so much kill it as show rather that it has already been deadened. Have we perhaps deadened it? Are we ourselves perhaps as dead? And is our hatred the spasm of a life that has fallen into a seizure in which the energies of life have uncomprehendingly gone astray, even as they frantically or randomly course through our spastic flesh? And so we come to the felt need to restore the world. This is something both hyperbolic and yet common and ordinary. Image: A child awakes as if out of a nightmare: it screams at the shadow, but there is no shadow there; there is nothing there, the parent says, "shush, shush," nothing there; and the gesture of comfort restores the world. Who now will say "shush, shush" and restore the world? What if we are all that child? It is well to acknowledge that Cavell is very much engaged with the child, not least in how we come first to speech.[15] Child: you do

15. See *CR*, xxii, with reference to his daughter, learning words, and so on and the three-year child; also 124–25, on children, and their elemental questions: "In the face

not like that affront to your dignity as an autonomous self-determining adult, come of age? Very well, suppose we are all grown up, but strangely a condition of deadness, as we say, being dead and alive, mimics the child terrified at nothing? How be terrified at nothing? Who will restore the world, or restore the trust needed to restore the world?

Cavell will suggest: Now the other must bear the weight previously borne by God.[16] This reminds one of Levinas—but without God. What weight was that, and what weight will that now be, as borne by the other? Can the human other bear that weight? Think but of *Job's lament*: "Oh that my grief were thoroughly weighed, and my calamity laid in the balances together! For now it would be heavier than all the sands of the sea." Who has the measure to weigh such things? The human being tries to be the measure of all things, but can one be the measure of Job's outcry? Were one to say yes, would one add to the already-far-too-long list of Job's comforters, a vocation of special attraction to many philosophers? Can the human other be the measure? But what if the human other is less a measure than also in the scales, also in the balance? The other whose destiny is in the balance may not be able to give us the balance and ballast suggested by the weight of that other other, God. You still do not like the question? Very well, it is the question of the extremity of loss, or being at a loss that the tragic communicates to us: something in excess of the measure of finite recuperation is communicated in tragic loss. If no human can be the source of the recovery, and if all we have is the human, does loss then have the last word? And what becomes of such a loss, if there is nothing at all of finding or being found?

---

of the questions posed in Augustine, Luther, Rousseau, Thoreau . . . we are children; we do not know how to go on with them, what ground we may occupy." Philosophy is as an education for grown-ups—asking for change, conversion, symbolized by rebirth. In *IQO* Cavell is a little irritated with Coleridge's condescension to Wordsworth's view of the child as a philosopher. I would like to say more about Cavell's insightful remarks on Wordsworth, but space does not permit. In *IQO* (42) Cavell draws attention to a kind doubleness in Coleridge towards Wordsworth: generous and withholding; demanding a philosophical poem, but not seeing it already offered by the "Prelude," and "Ode to Intimations." There is something grudging about Coleridge's attitude.

16. Cavell, *The Claim of Reason*, 470. The words "the other as replacement for God" are used in the table of contents of *The Claim of Reason* (ix): replacement is a strong word. In how strong a sense is one to take it?

## On Crossing the Line and Coleridge

But let us look a little closer at Cavell's reading of Coleridge in *In Quest of the Ordinary*. A connection is made with Emerson and Kant, and with Wordsworth's desire to speak of the low and the rustic: the glory of and in the common. We taste the Kantian flavor:

> . . . in philosophy the task is associated with the overcoming, say critique of metaphysics, and in literature with the domestication of the fantastic, or the transcendentalizing of the domestic, call these movements the internalizing or subjectivizing, or democratizing of philosophy; and that this communication between philosophy and literature, or the refusal of communication, is something that causes romanticism. (*IQO*, 27)

We are on now relatively familiar territory: the turn to self characterizing the longer arc of modern philosophy; philosophy as a question to itself. With respect to self-repression and self-liberation, Thoreau and Emerson "first of all teach us that self-liberation is what we require of ourselves" (*IQO*, 28). In the more general outlook, how we see Romanticism is a function of how we view the philosophical settlement proposed in Kant's achievement (*IQO*, 29). This depends on how we conceive that achievement. Cavell's suggestion: Here we come across an "attacking [of] philosophy in the name of redeeming it." "It is true that philosophy habitually presents itself as redeeming itself, hence struggling for its name, famously in the modern period, since Bacon, Locke, and Descartes. But can philosophy be redeemed *this way*, this romantic way?" (*IQO*, 30).

In its relations with its others, the "identity" of philosophy and its call are at stake: to make philosophy other by engagement with these others, and so to help it survive its crisis, and perhaps come to itself again with these others. This is a great concern of the Romantics, expressed as a desire for reconstituted harmony in a time of human fragmentation. If a desire to transfigure life brings philosophy into relation with poetry and art, so also does it in relation to the religious. Hegel, for instance, might address this is terms of absolute spirit, but Cavell enacts the issue in the register of the ordinary. But there is nothing more ordinary than the religious: this is the ordinary extraordinariness. But Cavell is more often than not, not overt.

One might ask: Is not Cavell concerned with what one might call a "saving knowing"? Is he a practitioner of a new poverty of philosophy in post-secular form? What might be entailed by a saving knowing, and in connection with Romanticism? Saving knowing: not determinate cognition of new facts or theory; we are saturated with these, their richness is not to be added to; rather a knowing that lets a new light shine on what is granted as there. With certain kinds of knowing, the more we know the more we seem lost, and know we are lost: for instance, Romanticism's sense of being lost in the bright, machine world of Newtonianism. We need a different knowing to save us from being lost, by dwelling with lostness differently. Indeed, there might be a losing oneself differently that is more like a condition of poetry or being religious. Is this what Keats is getting at with his "negative capability"? Not a new theory or new system; but a release towards what is there and a new rumination. Is this what Cavell suggests in reading redemptively?

Whether redemption, philosophical or other, is a matter of self-redemption is central to the issue, I would say. For self-redemption may not be quite equal to the redemption of self. Cavell gives an economical resume of Kant by reference to the *Prolegomena*. Kant plots the limits of knowledge, relative to phenomena and the thing itself. Though we must grant the existence of the thing in itself, and though it cannot be known, nevertheless, the point is not entirely negative: "In discovering the limitation of reason, reason proves its power to itself, over itself . . . ." It is as if, within the limit Kant claims to determine transcendentally, reason is at home with itself, and in its own way master of itself, and this despite Kant's famously saying the he limited knowing in order to make room for faith. In truth of course, this faith will be a moral faith in the power of the moral subject to be self-governing or autonomous. Does self-redemption resound with some overtones of "being in control"?

A reoriented questioning of limit, or line, will be central to Romanticism and, with qualifications, to Cavell himself. For him Romanticism serves to monitor Kant's philosophical settlement, apparently the most stable in the modern period (*IQO*, 31). Nevertheless, settling the line between nature and freedom, the appearance and the thing itself is hard to keep entirely unmoving, if not least because the human being, as having to do with both sides, also seems to be a power moving *between* the two. Cavell considers the Romantic relation to Kant's notion of the two worlds, or two ways of seeing. This is to witness to the human being's dissatisfaction with itself, but also to an appreciation of a certain ambivalence in Kant's sense of limitation. One might add that Kant often seems to give us a kind of two-way seeing: now dare to know, now respect the limit; now no God, now God necessary; now restriction to appearances, now necessary reference to the thing in itself; now the law seems given, now it seems we must give ourselves the law. Such a two-way seeing might make us quite crossed eyed, even cross; especially if we have no protocols for negotiating the crossing or transition from one to the other; or no embrace that seems able to hold together the two. Where is the one that sees in and through the double, and with perhaps redoubled eyes?[17]

Another Romantic surmise might arise: perhaps we live in neither of these worlds, or as Cavell puts it, "that we are, as it is said, between worlds"(*IQO*, 32). I have alluded to such a condition of being between relative to philosophical inheritance, but here it must also mean being able to move between one and the other, mean that the human being is one and the other, or neither one nor the other, or both together. Such an intermediate condition could not be reduced to univocal homogeneity. Cavell underscores the centrality of the issue here. "Of course, all such notions of worlds and being between them, and dead to them, and living in them, seeing them but not knowing them . . . To test this is a purpose of the texts under discussion here" (*IQO*, 33). Nor is his outlook exclusionary: Wittgenstein and Heidegger can be said to share "this romantic perception of human doubleness."[18] If we have, on one extreme, the feeling of our "worldlessness, or homelessness," on the other, we have someone like Wordsworth seeking to arouse men from a "torpor" by making "the incidents of common life interesting," and so bring them home, give them a world. The extremity of the situation is not to be understated: as if the human race had suffered a calamity and we now were in the phase

17. On this doubleness, this being between, see Eldridge, "Cavell and Hölderlin on Human Immigrancy."

18. The theme of limit might be connected with inheritances. The Continental, Romantic sublime can seem a "subliming" that is grandiose, perhaps bombastic, to a sometimes primmer English sense of the "ordinary." Is there any "subliming" beyond bombastic aestheticism, that has also seen beyond the don's stiff upper lip, or the scholastic's squeezed lips? As I noted with inheritances, Cavell is between, and more than between the Continent and England. America is the open space of this other between, where sometimes an empty sublime strikes terror into the lone individual, or gives rise to the free-lance predatory self; where sometimes there is a sublime between of a creative opening up, which the constraining limits of Europe, and England, keeps damped down. One of the struggles there: to find form, the find a voice in this opening up that seems to lack a *measure* in process itself. Is this not part of Romanticism: the condition of exceeding measure and seeking the measure of such exceeding? Can the human be that measure, even if we are the exceeding? To be at the limit of the ordinary and the marvel: this is a between at the extremes. Cavell speaks of the *philosophical fantastic* as somewhere between the everyday and the supernatural (see IQO, 181ff.); and of the doubleness of the ordinary, with reference to Poe (*IQO*, 120ff.).

of a convalescence. The calamity is linked to the French revolution, and to Nietzsche's death of God (*IQO*, 33). With such extremities, thoughts of redemption are not far away. Cavell does not focus directly on the Romantic interest in the redemptive possibilities of politics, or in religion or in poetry, but on how such an interest pressures philosophy to "think about its own redemption."

And the ancient mariner? The ancient mariner, Cavell thinks, knows something of Kant's two worlds (*IQO*, 45). Perhaps he knows something more than Kant. The ship on which he travels passes below the line, drives to a cold country toward the south pole. We have to be attentive to the virtual figuration of much of German idealism here. Coleridge himself in quite explicit in *Biographia Literaria*, where his reference to the two polar sciences recalls, I believe, Schelling's efforts to overcome transcendental solipsism by a science that moves from object to subject as well a science that moves from subject to object. Again the recovery of self is inseparable from the recovery of nature. In Spinozist/Hegelian terms, we must move from substance to subject, but also from subject to substance. Thus Coleridge: "The result of both the sciences, or their equatorial point, would be the principle of a total and undivided philosophy." And yet, we must add, such a total and undivided philosophy remains more dream than achievement. Is there something about the desire that frustrates the achievement?

While Cavell speaks of being below the line as having to do with the repressed (*IQO*, 47), one might add that it also has ontological significance and not just psychological. Yet the temptation to knowledge is central here. "The explicit temptation of Eden is to knowledge, which above all means: to a denial that, as we stand, we know." Cavell offers us interesting remarks on the Fall (*IQO*, 48–49). If Hegel is mentioned, it is Kant's "extraordinarily interesting document" that is given more attention (*IQO*, 50). In fact, Kant's discussion of the Fall is not qualitatively different to Hegel's: both are quite faithful sons of rational enlightenment, in seeing the Fall as telling of our finally laudable transition from animal innocence to what constitutes and will save the human: autonomous reason. Clap your hands, reason, it is all a *felix culpa*. Job's comforter's find new friends, though it is less God who guarantees felicity, as nature or history, and that son of the serpent, the cunning of reason. Cavell does not dwell on the coils of that serpent, but insists there is no Hegelian recovery. He finds himself "winding up differently," and yet he only winds up, to further navigate what he calls "texts of recovery" (*IQO*, chapter 3). Recovery of what?

Kant had the sense that breaching the line creates fanaticism and skepticism; it would be to try to experience what cannot be humanly experienced (*IQO*, 50). Coleridge's poem shows that what is beyond the line can be experienced (*IQO*, 51). The problem of skepticism is not a question of ignorance, but of a repression of knowledge, a denial, a killing. This is what creates the line, hence also want and desire. True to one of his origins, Austin is cited for his version of the original Fall: this is the insistence of philosophers on an epistemologically favored class of sense statements; this is the original sin by which they cast themselves from the garden of the world. And Job's comforters? One can hear them murmuring: If only Job the philosopher had not insisted, if only in his heart, for such epistemologically favored statements, his crops and children would not have been blighted. I jest, I jest not. Something more urgent and hyperbolic than the domesticities of donnish life is here at stake. The theme comes back, like the doom of the ancient mariner. What is finally at stake is bringing the world back to life: a new habitation, a new dwelling (*IQO*, 52–53).

*Life-in-death*: How kill the world? Is the deadened world under a spell, bewitched? And not bewitched as in animistic spells? Does Newtonianism, so to say, cast the mathematical spell? For the Romantics the machine world was this deadened world, from which they wanted resurrection. Reborn: to come to a second mindfulness of creation as gloriously granted. We are nothing but something more or less; dead and alive; half-true, half-lie; half-and-half. How can we be more than half-and-half, one again, whole? How can we come alive again? How can we be as one, as whole? If creation is gloriously granted, we take it for granted, but not *as* granted. In taking it, we do not have it anymore; we have its dying double. What of projection? Projection seems to imply that we can breathe life again into what is lifeless. But what if we, those who breathe, too are under the spell; we too need to come to life again; but we cannot do it ourselves; the dead may be left to bury themselves but the dead do not resurrect themselves. Part of the dubious danger of any Romantic project of projection is that it becomes a will to reanimate the world through one's own projection: but in this case, it must be doomed to defeat, since self-projection would be again the spreading of the death-in-life.

What of Cavell's previously mentioned remark: "I want to understand how the other now bears the weight of God, shows me I am not alone in the universe."[19] Can the other bear that weight; resurrect the world; perhaps not create as perhaps God did, but re-create the world? Can the other bear this weight? How so, if the other is also under the same spell as I, in the chiaroscuro of the dead and alive, the half-and-half. Can two such half-and-halves make a true whole, be truly one, or at one? Or will their being at one rather be the multiplication of the half-and-half life, be the marriage of narcissisms that seems to be intimated in Cavell's discussion of marriage in the *Ancient Mariner*? But having knowledge of this death of the world, and perhaps of the God that dies with that half-and-half world, who or what could succeed God? What succession could be a success here? Would *our* success as successors be a more radical failure? What if only God could succeed in being his own successor? All others are disproportionate to life and death, and death in life. The human other is *beneath* God, so to say; even if miraculously freed from the spell. Beneath: but there need be no contempt in this order of *superiority*. Is not this order of otherness at issue and not just the human other?

Cavell had glanced off the theme of animism and the pathetic fallacy in *The Claim of Reason*, but here (*IQO*, 54) it comes more to the fore with its fuller force. (Encounter something or someone sublime. Speak to me then of a pathetic fallacy. I would rather think that this talk then was the real conceit—in betraying what it had just encountered.) "For an intellect such as Coleridge's, for which objects are now dead, they will not be enlivened by the infusion of some kind of animation from the outside" (*IQO*, 55). The issue, or specter, of animism makes a momentary, somewhat disguised or frightened appearance in a late speculation in the final part of *The Claim of Reason*. As does the theme of the Outsider. In considering Othello, he considers the claim that material-object skepticism derives from other-minds skepticism. Cavell is honest enough to acknowledge that these specters bring their horror and fright and one is not always prepared to endure or face it. Perhaps one may have to grow or be dragged into a deeper desperation. "It is understandable that I shrank from that anticipation. It invites the thought that skeptical doubt is to be interpreted as jealousy and that our relation to the world that remains is as to something that has died at our hands. . . . [W]e have killed the world,

19. This is offered on p. 470 of Cavell, *The Claim of Reason*. Twelve pages later on p. 482 he says: "When I said just now that I wished 'to understand how the other . . . ,' one cannot but smile at the deferral, or loop of connection! 'Just now . . .'—what specious present is this that holds us with this style of coming and going, sounding and resounding?

and specifically out of revenge." The death of the world has to do with obsessive love or hate, and finding oneself in a bewitchment or spell that one has both conjured and yet not lucidly instigated. Hence the puzzle of the fatal happening in the *Ancient Mariner* (*IQO*, 56). The Albatross: the bird loved the man; and yet the mariner killed the thing that loved him. Cavell sees the moral (*IQO*, 57) as bearing on one's letting oneself *be loved* (reversing somewhat the usual way). Drifting into the cold country is a consequence of a transgression rather than an original transgression.

Cavell is attentive to the fact that the poem might be seen as about *itself*, about the process of making poems: the old problem that seemed so new with the Romantic's obsession with self-reflection and self-reflexive art. I like what I take as Cavell's disclaimers of what pass too easily as the pieties of our claims to poetic power. The word can kill as well as heal: curse as well as bless. Words also are as transgressions: we murder to connect; we stuff nature into words, make points of it (*IQO*, 60). Well said. It is also true that we can murder to connect by making points about the process of making poems, making points about poetic point. Cavell is tempted to think of the redemptive powers of writing itself. When speaking about the Hermit as "shrieving" the Mariner, he connects "shrieve" to script (*schrift*, in Dutch): "Writing is accordingly a kind of self-redemption" ( *IQO*, 62).

He does not deny entirely the view of such as Robert Penn Warren for whom the poem cannot be sundered from a sense of the sacramental universe, and most strikingly in relation to blessing the sea snakes and the slimy things (*IQO*, 61). The Mariner "accepts animals of the slime as also his others—that is, accepts the fact, or you may say, the gift of life. This begins his recovery from the death-in-life of inexpressible guilt." Are some hesitations about the religious to be detected? After all, in more than one place he seems to endorse Austin's denial of the "sacramental" view of language. Here the stress is on the wedding at the end as having its sacramental character "problematized." (I am not on good terms with that word: some "problems" are not "problems"—there is no "problem" of the sacramental universe, for our perplexity, or astonishment, here does not concern a "problem.") The Mariner is not seen as reconciled with society (*IQO*, 62); he is a disturber of its peace, which is no peace. His endless repetition of the agony, puts me in mind of Pascal: Christ will be in agony till the end of the world; we must not sleep till then.

And then too for Cavell: "the Mariner wanders between Apostleship and Sagehood, as though it is too late for religion, because nothing is any longer common to our gods, and it is too soon for philosophy, because human beings are not interested in their new lives. (No wonder the writer's explicit autobiography will be written in continuous digressions.)" (*IQO*, 63).[20] I ask: might this mean that *philosophy is the original sin*; that it is the departure from the common, and that true religion is the true commons, the consummate commons, and that the reason why we are not interested in our new lives is because they have become dead without the commons with the divine; and that philosophy, no more than art, can stem the hemorrhage of spirit; though the patient has been bled many times and will say chirpily, I am fine, I feel fine; but it will be the fineness of feebleness; and that philosophy will continue the sickness because it can only name self-redemption, even though fitfully, as if in a dream or a fever, images seem to come to it, insurgently of *being redeemed*, as of *being loved*; and that now these fevers are to be treated as temptations from the new enfeebled commons we have created for ourselves, behind the line? And why the digressions? What is the line from which we digress? But if we do not know the thread of the story, while we seem to digress, we are not digressing; for we cling to ourselves as the thread running through a story that is none; and we do not need digressions so much as abandonments, more or less like the Mariner's. By contrast, such digressions are ways of satisfying a "craving for experience" (see *IQO*, 52) while seeming to remain contented with, or clinging to, the main line. An autobiography in "continuous digression" means there is no digression because there is no main line. In that sense, Cavell is right to tell us that the Mariner is "more a patient than a doctor, more a symptom than a cure." But then what "promise of redemption" can be here, since it seems evident that this ailment of the human cannot heal itself; it can only betray its symptoms; and many ways of betraying these symptoms are themselves betrayals of the promise of redemption. A hypochondria it may then be, but it is not a "holy hypochondria" as Hamman, Kant's friend and antagonist, put it.

Does marriage bring some solace? The question is posed by the end of the *Ancient Mariner* (*IQO*, 64) No more marriages? The mariner is one who stuns: one who is "permanently, one may say, awaiting redemption. No doubt this can be justified—say, as preparation for philosophy. But it is not philosophy's progress, and neither, I think, is it poetry's or religion's" (*IQO*, 64). Marriage is no longer a sacrament, for Cavell, as for Austin

20. I would not describe Cavell's own "autobiography" *(Little Did I Know: Excerpts from Memory)* as simply written in a series of digressions. See note 22 below.

language is not (see *Pitch*). And yet Cavell would have more (but how can he have *more*?): marriage "a new mystery . . . to which outsiders are irrelevant"; "a further adventure of aloneness, without solitude but also without society; . . . a further investment of our narcissism, as children so typically are. If marriage is the name of our only present alternative to the desert-sea of skepticism, then for that very reason this intimacy cannot be celebrated, or sanctified; there is no outside to it. You may describe it as lacking in poetry; as if intimacy itself, or the new pressure on it, lacked expression" (*IQO*, 64–65). Perhaps I misunderstand, but I fear that this marriage, if without enchantment or loving bewitchment, is too dreary to be true! The specter of being eternally trapped within a Woody Allen movie arises to shake my manhood. The secular heaven of this would be infinite penance: to have to hear, or worse partake, of the chatting of such irritated souls, endlessly, without *parole*. By such chatter we cling to our warm solitudes, intimate in our half-and-half lives, warmed against the darkness or indifference by our self-absorbed togetherness. Rather be stunned by the mariner. While Cavell goes on to suggest that "there is such an intimacy at large, and that poetry is responsible for giving it expression" (*IQO*, 65), such marriages without feasts make one wonder if we are still drifting towards the cold country. (I can say nothing of Hollywood marriages.)

A last remark on crossing the line: Are there lines that keep Cavell in, that he cannot or will not cross? That he cannot see? Ask this with respect to redemption as religious. Are there occasions when he keeps himself behind the line, withholding himself from crossing over? For some philosophers: how intolerable if the philosopher crosses the line over to poetry or art. But is it philosophy, then, they ask? But how much more intolerable would it be to cross the line between itself and *religion*? I anticipate an even more offended apoplexy: But surely it is not philosophy at all then? Has not philosophy in modernity forged its own identity mostly in crossing the road when it sees religion on the same side? (Religion sometimes crosses over too, and sometimes the two do not well anticipate their mutual avoidances and they bump in the middle embarrassed.) And yet: look at the practice of philosophy in terms of the longer heritage that we may inherit (one can refuse an inheritance): philosophy was always crossing the line, which did not preclude it from crossing the street to the other side also—(the line might be a marker of freedom, remember). Do I rightly detect a hesitation on Cavell's part on this line: he feints, as if crossing a line; or feints, as if not having crossed, but in fact having done so? More (of) the second I would say. See Cavell crossing this line from philosophy to literature, to opera, to film; though, necessarily, he also crosses back: this is not prohibited, be it applauded, or unapproved. Again these lines are not lines but definitions of the spaces of spiritual freedom. But can one say the same, as it were, *out loud*, with regard to the *religious*? Is this an intimacy that remains intimate: communicated and yet unsaid: unstated, or understated? Is philosophy in hiding here: as if shy of saying certain things: or shying off (away) from them? How hard here it would be to confess without embarrassment, to confide philosophically, to come clean.

## Bowing to Hegel without Bowing

This brings me to the theme of *art, philosophy, and religion*. I bow once more to Hegel, a third time in this text, though again I will not bow. Revisit the comparison I made between Cavell and Hegel on absolute knowing. If you protest this as too odd, remember also a contrast previously suggested: *absolute knowing*—attained for Hegel when knowledge no longer needs to go beyond itself; *acknowledgment*: where there is a going beyond, or something like it, though it remains wrapped in enigma; we are not locked in the circle of self. (Incidentally, this bears also on the argument against the *merely* private.) If there is no circle, in a sense we are outside always, though also always needing more full release to what is outside. By contrast with the circle of Hegel's absolute knowing, one thinks of Cavell's endorsement of Thoreau: to be by oneself, in the sense of a certain wholeness; and to be beside oneself.[21] You say: but is this not reminiscent of Hegel when he speaks of being at home with self (*bei sich*) in one's other? (Rewrite this, if you will, as being at home with oneself in one's other—Hegel's famous phrase: self-recognition in absolute otherness.) And yet the stress falls differently in Cavell. Or perhaps he wants it to fall a bit *more differently*. Does he put enough into the "being beside oneself"? I leave this open for now. Acknowledgment is a kind of absolved knowing, in the sense of being freed from obsessions that, in casting a spell on one, keep one imprisoned, imprisoned indeed in oneself.

Let us take the issue relative to the relation of art and philosophy, and a little further relative to religion. I mean: the relation to the other, who takes the place of God, or assumes the burden of God, might be

21. See *CR*, 367; he is referring to Cavell, *The Senses of Walden*, 100–104.

said to be mediated through a turn to literature, as offering us the imagined occasions in which we are released or absolved to acknowledge the others, even to Lear's extreme of exposing ourselves to feel as wretches and divinities feel. Very well: what of the divinities? I underscore that the community of art and philosophy is not at all denied by Hegel, who is here a follower of Schelling, hence a companion along the way with Coleridge. Art too is concerned with absolute knowing. I say follower but also mean dissident in that Hegel's dialectical concepts are said to do justice to both the form and content of the absolute, while the sensuous form of art binds us to, enchants us with, an otherness beyond which thought frees us into the purest form, at one, with the concept, by itself. For Hegel there seems too much of "being beside oneself" in the image of art. This is an old complaint against the artist going back at least to the *Ion*, and perhaps further. What if this "being beside oneself" (*mania*) is just the way "being oneself" comes into the needful openness wherein the access of light is made available for acknowledging. And what if philosophy too entailed "being beside oneself"? Suppose it often conceals this need and instead presents itself as purely being by itself? For were it to confess this, it too would look like madness. Give Plato some at least partial credit for being willing to grant this: the best of the philosophers need to be singled out by a divine madness; otherwise they are competent technicians, or experts, perhaps endowed professors. Nietzsche falls in the same line of inheritance as Plato's antagonist, thought he presents himself as the black sheep in that family, turning over the traces with a mixture of divine madness and mad madness. This is Hegel's claim and perhaps the Hegelian fraud: that it hides the truth of "being beside itself," and calls the concealment reason, or the counterfeit knowing of self called absolute knowing. I think Cavell might agree, though perhaps not quite with the brutality of the charge. In fact, the brutality requires a form of subtlety, since what is most at issue here is what I will call *discerning knowing*: knowing that can tell something of the difference between released knowing, genuine acknowledgment of the other as other, and its false doubles that slyly, with great show of argument, actually coil back on themselves, and thus remain in the end by themselves also counterfeit self-knowing.

Does the great power of art call Cavell here? Is not the great power of great art just in its actually calling us out of ourselves: out of ourselves to ourselves, and also to being besides ourselves as beyond ourselves, there out in the glory of creation where we were, strangely, but not as strangers simply, always already. I think of efforts to connect *to kalon* with the call. I think of the figures in the uncut rock that called out to Michelangelo. Suppose we are the still-formless figures in that rock, and we cannot call ourselves out of that stony existence, and another must begin to batter that stony existence to loose us, but batter the stone with a love, for otherwise the promise of the rock is betrayed and it shatters. Who is the outsider that hits the rock in love and brings forth life? Not the rock; not us. For we are not hitting the rock; we are the rock being hit.

This power of art or great poetry to stun thought into a different mindfulness names the intimation of the great Romantics. But Hegel, so close, yet so far, came to hate the Romanticism he loved while younger, and hate because he felt it dissolved in feeling and formlessness; and he could not quite give himself over to the formlessness that, like a return to zero, offered a new interface with creation, in which we are called out of the rock by a mysterious artist other than ourselves, and such that we are not as masters who hammer the world into our mold. Hegel finally wanted an epistemology absolutely in control of itself, if not now, then later, though he could not wait, and even here constructed a historicist monument to his own metaphysical impatience, which at last seemed to allow him to rest in his present. But it is a fraud, if the sources of this being by self are a deeper being beside oneself. Indirect witness to this is the impatience that will not let itself be receptive to the strike that comes from beyond the frozen stone of the unachieved self.[22]

22. Clearly Romanticism is more than a cult of narcissistic feeling, though Cavell is cognizant of this as one of its major dangers. One must wonder if Hegel's claim to escape this danger merely reinstates eternal or world-historical narcissism on the heights of absolute knowing: thought thinking itself; Aristotle's old god now historically coming back to itself, itself that it never really left, all appearances notwithstanding. Some recent commentators have trawled through the seas of Hegel's texts to find a few sentences in thousands and thousands where Hegel uses the word "*lassen*." And with this prize catch, Hegel is proclaimed a philosopher of "letting be," or released knowing. If one is struck by the happening of release, it would also strike one as odd that the truth of "being let" be would be named less than a half dozen time in an ocean of silence. I fear the embarrassed admirers have seized upon the specks in the wind and tell us that the absolute releases itself, is really released beyond itself. Even suppose Hegel thought this once, or twice, what it means is not at all clear. Perhaps it is a slip of being beside oneself that restores sanity; but then sanity immediately is overcome by the dialectical dream of a different madness. Of course, there is the crucial point also: whether it is the release of the absolute, or the absolute as releasing a genuine other into its own otherness or being for itself. The second would be genuine creation; the first might still be only the self-creation of the absolute that again remains by itself in its own other. For the end of (Hegelian) release towards otherness, in any case, will

Does this seem rather far from Cavell? Seem yes, but in truth no. Remember a third who walks beside us as if unseen, as if unnamed. This is religion. Where is this, this nothing? Present and not present as present. The answer here for Cavell must mimic the answer given for Shakespeare: the religious is nowhere because it is everywhere. Religion's importance for Romanticism is not in doubt, even if we want to say here we are concerned with "secular mysteries." But is this to beg the question, while nodding in the right direction? "Secular mystery" is finally just as incomprehensible as sacred mystery. Why omit to say this? Does our silence make it less offensive, as offensive as sacred mystery, to secular reason? Why not openly admit what is offensive to secular (scientific?) reason, offensive be it secular or sacred? What better protection does the word "secular" give us from the mockery of secular reason that will follow? Either way, sacred or secular, we are exposed. Suppose religion can be a way of *living the exposure*? It can also be a concealment of the exposure from oneself, from others—a way to go to sleep again. But the word "secular," like the sacred word "science"—is it not one of our great magic words with supernal dormative power? A *vis dormitiva* greater than which religion barely can dream?

What is a redemptive reading? Wittgenstein talked of bringing words home to their ordinary usage, but what would it be to bring the word "redemption" back to its *ordinary* meaning? There is something odd here, something out of the ordinary. Redemption entails being transfigured beyond ordinary ordering. Is this too much for any ordinary ordering home? Foxes have holes, but is this homeless in the world? And what would a *saving knowing or acknowledging be?* If one does not come clean on the religious, is it hard to have anything other than an equivocal suggestion here? Who needs redeeming? The text, the reader, the writer? And who redeems or what? The text or the author or the reader? I do not know who the redeemer is. I do not know if this redeemer lives. Should we say: redemption—either absurd or a miracle; or perhaps both?

The matter of being beside oneself is clearly at issue in Hegel's philosophizing about religion, when an analogous appropriation is performed, as with the ecstasis of art. The issue again is the recalcitrance of

---

always point to a truer last act in which the self will always be *by itself* in its other. If this is Hegelian letting, the absolute otherness is still absolved from its otherness and this otherness taken back into a final *self-recognition* by itself absolutely. The give and take is *within the one* absolute. There is no radical giving for the other as other, what I would call agapeic giving.

an otherness that will not be included within a more embracing thought at home with itself. Religion is beside itself; it shows something of the manic, in the Greek sense, as inspiration, as revelation, as coming from a source that exceeds our self-control, and yet makes ultimate demands on our "mastery" and "self-mastery." Religion as beside itself points to an acknowledging that is a knowing from.

What of that notable feature of post-Kantian culture, namely its granting of a certain autonomy to art, and not least with regard to the religious? There are many complex elements in this. One can understand the granting against the background of a miserable religiosity that fell out of praise of the glory of creation. This is another aspect of the deadening of the earth. And of course, the issue is not confined to the religious: where is the deep resource for such praise in modern science, then and indeed now? A fidelity to the voices of the earth is needed, you might say. But equally noticeable in post-Kantian culture is that the artistic assumes a metaphysical weight not so strongly accentuated earlier: as a possible revealer or medium of some transcendence even more ultimate than our own self-transcending. In some places, Cavell seems more Kantian than Hegelian; but if he shares companionship with Coleridge, he perhaps should be more Schellingian: art and religious are inseparable; they pass over into each other; it hard to disentangle the art of a people from the myth; and both from the inheritance of that people; the words a people treasures are the endowment of its sense of ultimacy, and this endowment the true poet keeps and guards; for there is a reticence or reserve about the religious.

Concern about bewitchment cannot be here avoided. Some place Pascal speaks about a powerful bewitchment cast over us, as if by the force of some supernatural spell. Cavell toys with something almost the same in *The Claim of Reason*.[23] I am inclined to think Pascal (as Cavell) understood far more profoundly what might be at issue in Descartes's supposition of the *malign genie*. These may be metaphorical ways of speaking, but if so there are no mere metaphors. If they were, all art would be a colorful baroque surrogate (a merely fantastic double) for what scientific psychology would render in unvarnished truth. But the point is: there is no such unvarnished truth; for always we are in the bewitchment. And the science that claims to dispel the bewitchment is also

23. See *CR*, 143, where he speaks of epistemology and "some power large enough either to keep us in a kind of hypnotic spell, or to arrange the world for our actions as a kind of endless stage-set, whose workings we can never get behind . . . ."

in the bewitchment; and perhaps even more lost in bewitchment, for it is convinced that it is free of bewitchment and the way out of these bewitchment; the shadow that looms over it is the spell cast by the heat of its own self-intoxication, though as always looking away from itself it can neither see shadow nor feel the heat (which takes itself as cold).

The witch is one caught in the mania of religion, be it hot mania or cold: but there is mad madness as much as divine madness; and the issue between the witch and her executioner is the discernment of the difference. How teach, or learn, these differences? This also bears on our waking from the spell. The executioner may also be beside himself in a bewitchment. The one claiming to dispel the bewitchment may be just as spellbound. We do not escape by saying: I am only concerned with art; these deliriums of religion I leave behind. Think here of the catharsis of tragedy as also a kind of exorcism. My point: Is not the home of the extreme equivocalities of our being human very nearby the religious, more intimate with the religious than with any other concern? We have to deal here with all the darkness of the religious, as much as the light; and hence have to deal more honestly than Hegel's idealistic apotheosis of reason did with this dark equivocality. Can we come clean on it? Not by conceptual anorexia, not by conceptual hubris. We seem to need some kind of philosophical confession. But here confession is the hardest. I do note what I take as Cavell's words of admiration for these most capable of confession: those most capable of going into themselves and the recesses of intimacy, or the idiocy of being, and without sacrifice of speaking for what is beyond them, and so besides themselves in a truer sense. Their own voice and the voices of the others somehow are matched.[24] Can this match happen without some source more ultimate than I and the others? Is this too not the question of God?

Even for Hegel some kind of confession and religious forgiveness seems to be the ante-chamber before final entry into absolute knowing. But Hegel gives us a counterfeit double of forgiveness also: the one divides itself into its own two extremities, and its yes, yes, is the return of the divide to unity with itself; forgiveness is its yes, yes to itself; and if

24. See *CR*, 109, where he speaks of confession, mentioning Augustine, Luther, Rousseau, Thoreau, Kierkegaard: they "were most convinced they were speaking from the most hidden knowledge of others," as from the most hidden knowledge of themselves, when to themselves they became a question. See Cavell, *Little Did I Know*. This is a marvelous (philosophical) memoir. The heart is catheterized. Lovely use of the cathar metaphor. Katharsis. Purging the heart. Making it though memory porous to its long-life and forgotten (familial) intimacies.

so, there is really no *being forgiven* by another genuinely other. Can you forgive yourself without being forgiven; can you be the two sides and both as one; the no, no that sunders and the yes, yes that reunites; but why play such a wicked, silly game with oneself; and what bewitches one to play that silly game? Do you say God plays it with himself? So God is redeeming himself in all of this? I let that God to itself, if its absolute concern is with itself finally. All we will get here is a counterfeit double of the ultimate amen.

Cavell knows that forgiveness and comedy are espoused (see *Pitch*, 87). Comedy is also a way of exposure and perhaps also of absolving sin. He also says: "Philosophy cannot say sin." Might this mean it cannot *laugh*? Is philosophy as a therapy really a catharsis, a purgatory? "Philosophy cannot say sin":[25] but perhaps that is just the laughless sin of philosophy; when it, so to say, withholds itself from its familial attunement with these extraordinary others. Worse sin (this is not Cavell's): philosophy goes on to self-exculpation by accusing the others of not managing to be as it claims to be: autonomous, self-determining knowing. If to be is to be beside oneself, this preaching of philosophy is a fraud form of being beside itself. Nietzsche may have fallen into this, now and then; but now we are significantly more feeble in spiritual passion, so if we seem to show less of being beside ourselves, this may not be an unequivocal sign of superior sobriety.

## Being Beside Oneself: Music, Madness, Thought

Is this to make too much of "being beside oneself"? Yet having written the above, I noticed, as if by accident, the epigraph to *A Pitch of Philosophy*. It is from Thoreau: "With thinking we may be beside ourselves in a sane sense. *Next* to us the grandest laws are continually being executed."

I am impelled further to ask. Beside oneself: what is there besides oneself? What also is it to be "by oneself"? What does "by" mean? "By" whom or what is one effected, affected? Could being by oneself also mean being besides oneself? And what is this *sane sense* of being beside oneself? Is this the temptation: to have one's cake and eat it too? I mean: is to be by oneself a kind of counterfeit of divine madness that cannot let

25. S. Mulhall devotes an interesting chapter to this in *Stanley Cavell's Recounting of the Ordinary*.

go, though it looks abandoned to what is outside, what is besides, what is other, what is next? And then next: What is this *next*, this nearby, this *nabij*, this *nachbahr*, this neighbor? Who is this neighbor? What other? And why are there *laws* being executed? Who executes? *Moira* or fate or some other power of the grandest execution? Who is the grand executer (not a grand inquisitor, I take it)? What is being executed? What, if anything, is being granted by the executing grandee? Only laws; and in relation to the neighbor, the ones who are besides one? Given that some *frenzy* is suggested by being beside oneself, how can one be or stay sane? Is this being beside oneself in a sane sense a kind of *grace*? If so, while there might be laws being continually executed, is there more being executed than law can fully express, and is this then the grandest thing?

One wonders also: Is Cavell's own form of being beside oneself, but in a sane sense, connected to *music*? Might one not acknowledge music to have intimate bearing on the happening of being beside oneself, but in a sane sense? I find it intriguing to think of a certain Romantic intonation in *A Pitch of Philosophy*. The idea of voice is central there, obviously, and in a number of senses, the most overt there being the finding of a philosophical voice out of philosophical peregrinations, or being on the road.[26] Obviously also there is the power of voice in opera, especially the female voice, and not out of hearing of his own mother. But consider this crucial turning point in Cavell's own becoming. This is his beginning to find himself differently in turning from his ambition to be a composer, turning towards philosophy. He recalls the influence of classes on music taught by Ernest Bloch. (How many echoes of Nietzsche are there muffled in these diverse destinies?) I am taken by Cavell's recounting of his being struck by what he calls the "transcendence of culture" (*Pitch*, 50). It is clear from the story that he is close to being struck speechless, not with lack of thought, but with excess, so much so that at the close of each class he would retreat to guard his thought in the solitude of adjacent rooms. What strikes one here is some echo of the view that music is the Romantic art par excellence (a view we find in Hegel, but not unique to him). One thinks of the religion of art in the nineteenth century and the absolute importance invested in musical culture, and not only by the musicians themselves. I mean just this sense of the "transcendence of culture," concentrated in music, as most epitomizing that communication from a creative origin on the other side of domesticated determinacy, and

26. See, Gould, *Hearing Things*.

passing through genius as the medium in which this other, surpassing source found its voice or articulated release.

Can we speak of music as a *sane ecstasy*? If so, this sane ecstasy of music has been heard too by philosophers before. I mention Schopenhauer, deeply formed in the culture of the Romantics at Jena, the Schlegels, and so on: music is the direct embodiment of the will itself; and objectifying it such as to release us from the vehement urgency otherwise marking its tyrannical *eros:* to be blessed with the voice of music, as singer, player, hearer, was to be blessed with release: redemption. Could we say: *eros* as tyrannical is saved from its insane frenzy, its mad bewitchments; music puts us beside ourselves, but in a sane sense? And Nietzsche: without music one might even think life to be intolerable, unbearable; music redeems life, brings us back to life. In the twentieth century, Adorno (close to the Benjamin who holds Cavell's fascination) holds to something of this hope for redemptive promise in music. And Cavell? Cavell finds himself displaced; speechless first, but besides himself, as he would be by himself; and then his musical hopes turned about in the direction of a philosophical quest that only took slow form in the years to follow, and the struggle for voice. There is nothing overt in Cavell: none of the young enthusiasm, the unguarded ardor, marking something of the religion of music, the religion of art in the nineteenth century. Nevertheless, one is made to wonder if there is here an older, perhaps more calm, passion for a not-dissimilar redemption. His story recollects his being besides himself in some tranquility, and so seeks sanity.

I cannot again avoid wondering about a religious displacement. For here we have again a theme most intimate to the Romantics: not just *Kunstreligion*, as in Hegel; but the religion of *Kunst*. Question: if the place falls to art to be the bearer of communicating transcendence, are we not witnessing a migration into art of what previously was religiously named? This is analogous to the point Cavell makes about theater replacing religion: the sacred drama of the ritual is overtaken by a secular, and perhaps no-less cathartic or reconciling, ritual. Again, I name tragedy and comedy. And again, one cannot forget the origins of tragedy and comedy in religious ritual in the ancient world: the great feasts, festivals of Dionysus; or forget Elizabethan drama inheriting something of the medieval mystery plays. Should one say that there is a replacement in the displacement, or that the redemptive power becomes more incognito, more hidden, the more it claims to be less hidden, less mysterious, in a human(istic) sense? But is there too much of ultimate equivocation here? I see this as a great question put to the culture of post-Kantian aestheticism. The displacement or replacement does not change the fact that what we want—want as lacking, want as needing, and needing urgently—is purgation and reconciliation, that is, redemption. Displacing sacred mystery to secular mystery does not elide mystery, surface appearances notwithstanding. When we are stunned by the mystery, we are also made to limp along more in terms of our humanistic confidences: we cannot do it, we do not do it; we participate in the festival. Art alone cannot bear the impossible burden of transcendence, as I argue elsewhere. This point is analogous to the point about the other as replacement or bearing the weight of God. Can art bear the burden of transcendence alone?[27]

If we recall the Dionysian festivals, we invariably today call back Nietzsche. The Dionysian festivals were the religious rituals in which Greek society sought to order its being beside itself, but in a sane social sense. Redemption seems to ask madness and sanity together. Can one think of that togetherness in terms of Nietzsche's claim: only as a work of art is the world justified; the only theodicy is an aesthetic theodicy? If so, art can no longer be just art. Was Nietzsche up to the redemptive togetherness of madness and sanity? Can Cavell bear the same question? And Nietzsche does figure very much as a companion in his *A Pitch of Philosophy*, and not least because of the autobiographical exercises of *Ecce Homo*. *Queritur* (as Nietzsche might say): Is Nietzsche's not a poet-philosophy for the *young*? Cavell seems to acknowledge as much (*Pitch*, 122). But is there not a different youth of *age*—another spring, a further primavera? Queritur. And Nietzsche was never quite born to this second primavera. One hears Cavell's praise for what is named as the moral perfectionism of Emerson (*Pitch*, 50). Is there too much of the *conatus essendi* in moral perfectionism and not enough of the *passio essendi*? Have we here too much of the earnestness of the young and not enough of the mad abandon of age? I love the bitter question of Yeats's poem: "Why should not old men be mad?"[28] And moral perfectionism? But this is not what the mad Lear (*Pitch*, 51), sane now beyond youth, sought, or saw. And Cavell, if I am not mistaken, would write beyond Nietzsche and Lear. But that beyond cannot be written as "moral perfectionism." Nietzsche: the child who cannot, will not, hear the father. Lear: the father who cannot, will not, hear the child. Are both brought to some hearing?

27. Desmond, *Art, Origins, Otherness*, chapter 8: "Art and the Impossible Burden of Transcendence."

28. Yeats, *The Poems*, 370.

Both go differently mad. But to be beyond their different madnesses—or lack of listening—may well seem to be also mad, differently—or to listen and hear, differently. But is it not here that one will find the second primavera, the second spring, and begin to find being beside oneself—but in a sane sense?

# 8

# The Theater of the Metaxu: Staging the Between

## Curtains Up: Opening a Space

Human life is defined between diverse extremes: birth and death, nothing and infinity, abysses of abjectness and superlatives of heights, interiorities of secret intensity and exteriorities of vast extension. Human being is a between-being, but more often than not these extremes are recessed in the domestications of everyday life. Theater tries to stage something of this between-being and bring it out of its recess in everyday life. The notion of the between is central to the philosophy I have been developing, and I want to explore whether theatrical space might be said to stage the between. I speak of a metaxological philosophy, and while "metaxological" initially sounds barbarous, once explained, it can take on more tender tones. *Metaxu* is the Greek word for "between," while *logos* can mean "an accounting," or "reasoning," or "wording." A metaxological philosophy is concerned with a *logos* of the *metaxu*, or a wording of the between. Such a philosophy is concerned with life itself as a between-space, a *metaxu*, and with the fact that this between is an articulated middle or intermedium. A metaxological philosophy is concerned with wording the between. Can we say that the theatrical stage, as an intermedium of human communication, is a distinctive wording of the between? Can a metaxological philosophy throw some light on what is staged on it, in and through it?

The relations of philosophy and theater are not commonly treated topics. When we think of theater we tend to light on two great periods, namely, Elizabethan England and ancient Athens. The latter we associate with philosophy, of course, but it is a very one-sided perception to think of the Greeks as philosophers. We should really think of them as a *people of art—ein Reich der Kunst* as Hölderlin calls Greece, and Hegel speaks of Greek religion as a *Kunstreligion*, religion in the form of art.[1] We do not think of Elizabethan England as a high period of philosophical reflection, and yet anyone who thinks Shakespeare's work is not saturated with philosophical significance surely has a very narrow sense of what it means to be philosophical.[2] His dramas are, so to say, philosophy in performatives.

It is worth remembering that the origin of these forms of powerful theater has something to do with a more religious or sacred occasion. This has been noted, of course, and it is important. The ancient tragedies and comedies were performed at the Dionysian festivals, and something of the significance of this goes into Nietzsche's view of the birth, and hope for the re-birth, of tragedy from the spirit of music.[3] There has been significant conjecture about the emergence of Elizabethan drama from medieval miracle plays and their displacement and transformation outside the context of a church.[4] This point is not lacking in importance concerning the connection of drama and the sacred, and their connection with philosophy. After all, it is a well-noted theme that philosophy as giving a *logos* emerges from an ethos in which the significance of life was expressed through *mythos*—a sacred story of origins and ends. *Mythos*

1. Hegel, *Phenomenology of Spirit*, §§699–747.

2. For two quite different approaches, see Cavell, *Disowning Knowledge*, and Nuttall, *Shakespeare the Thinker*.

3. Nietzsche's *Birth of Tragedy* is, in part, cultural propaganda for the opera of Wagner, which, relevantly, sought to approach the condition of a kind of aesthetic *liturgy*, and not incidentally Wagner thought of *Parsifal* not simply as opera but as "a festival play for the consecration of the stage (*ein Bühnenweihfestspiel*)."

4. We sometimes think of Catholicism as aesthetically porous to creation steeped in a sacramental sense of signs, dramatized in liturgical form, especially of the Mass, while Protestantism strips away the aesthetic, that is, pagan excess, and without accretions restores the supposedly unadorned original—unadorned, that is, unaesthetic original word—unaesthetic, even anaesthetic. For instance, Calvinism is seen as austere, if not hostile, towards aesthetic flourishing; but it is worth remembering that for John Calvin himself the whole world is the *theatrum gloriae dei*. For a recent reconsideration, see Taylor, *The Theater of God's Glory*.

makes sense of the between of life by connecting it with transhuman origins and transfinite purposes. The word translated as "plot" in Aristotle's *Poetics* is *mythos*, and it is, he says (VI, 19–20), the *archē* and soul (*psychē*) of tragedy, but we should not forget the sacred significance of this word. Drama and the sacred are bound together in the figurative expressions of mythic articulations.

There is also the fact that perhaps the great place where philosophy emerges is simply in conversation. People, having words with each other, exchanging *logoi*, enter into a dialogue, a "speaking between" two persons or more, where issues of great moment are in question. What is drama without the having of words, our having words with each other? I am thinking, needless to say, of Socratic-Platonic dialogue. Here we find a dialectic of question and answer, but this also requires multiple silences, and indeed a togetherness of saying and silence. It is in the interplay of saying and silence that the emergence of thinking shows itself to be dramatically embodied. The intermediate space between one speaker and another is transformed. If I question you, you must be silent to hear me, and I must again be silent to listen to your answer. The interchange of address and reply are framed by silence, silence that also qualifies the space of communication between us. In theater we often pay less attention to the silences than to the speaking, but they are no less important. Without multiple silences there would be no speaking and no communication. There are also silences that keep open, and strain against every wording of the between, and intimate what seems almost impossible for human beings to word at all. This point will bear not only on the origin of drama and philosophy but also on the end in relation to what exceeds them, and towards which, even in the defeat of human words, they point.

In seeking fidelity to this between and its wording, I contrast the metaxological sense of being with three other senses, respectively, the univocal, equivocal, and dialectical.[5] These latter senses have their role to play in wording the between, but none does justice to the full play that happens there. I name them now baldly because they offer some structure, in a broad sense, to the reflections to follow. Univocity puts the stress on something or someone *determinate*, this or that character or thing. Equivocity puts the stress on something more *indeterminate*, something neither this nor that, something ambiguous, especially in the heart of acting human beings. Dialectic puts the stress on a togetherness

5. See, for instance, Desmond, *Being and the Between*.

of oneself and others, on a mediation of our differences in the exchange with each other. Metaxology does not dispose of these three senses, but aligns them more truly with what in the between is *more than determinable* and *beyond our self-determination*. It is attentive to many-meaninged inter-play, bringing more to the fore the plurivocity of inter-mediations between oneself and others, between selving and othering. It opens us beyond every self-contained whole to what still is more: the companioning, mostly *incognito* mystery in all being and acting. This is beyond all determinations, all self-determinations, and it is not an indeterminate lack but a "too muchness," a surplus *overdeterminacy*. These four senses help us understand something of what staging the between brings to effect.

To round off: I am talking about a space opening up in which a diversity of articulations becomes possible. These articulations can put different stresses on what is showing itself in the between. There might be a stress on sacred significance with religion, an artistic stress in a more aesthetic orientation, or a stress on precisions of thought in a philosophical consideration. But without the opening of this space there is no wording of significance between humans and each other, and indeed between humans and the ethos of being wherein we wake up to ourselves and the world other to us. This opening is an ultimate between space. To consider drama as metaxological is not to conflate it with philosophy. Rather it offers a powerful expression of human being as metaxological, and in an aesthetic form that itself is metaxological, and thus as open to what is other to itself. The practice of philosophy and the art of drama are each responsive to the promise of metaxological being, and when true to it, when at their truest, they themselves richly exemplify what it means to be metaxological. The between offers itself for wording, words itself. Both drama and philosophy can be in the service of this wording of the between.

## The Stage as Porous Between

How can we see the stage as a between? As we know, there are different spaces of staging, but many of us think of the proscenium: before this stage the audience sits and the proscenium frames an arched space through which the audience, in the house, views what transpires on the other side of the framed space. Space is separated, but there are no walls, and it is communication that takes place through the appropriate separations: directly between players, it seems, and between players and audience, and indirectly between playwright and all the others. There are other modes of staging, such as theater in the round, but there too the arrangement of spaces serves a multi-layered happening of communication. Off-stage much may be going on that need not enter directly into the staging of the between on the theatrical space, and yet the framing itself, while delimiting a space, does not entirely close off the intimation of what is beyond this stage. The stage is a porous between.

Sometimes the curtain rises, or the theatrical lighting comes on, and sometimes the stage is empty, or already it is peopled and there is something going on. As the ocular origin of the word "theater" suggests, there is a looking, an onlooking going on (theater comes from the Greek *theatron*—a place of looking). We in the house are there *to behold* (*theasthai*: to behold). But "beholding" here is not just optical, since in hearing what is said, or listening for the unsaid, the whole of the seeing listener is called forth. The one who beholds is never a mere *tabula rasa*, for beholding is a released engagement. Something is communicated from what is other to us, and beholding is thus a beholding from. In an analogous sense, the stage is never an empty stage. Even when it is empty, it is a space wherein anticipations of possibilities come forth, some of which in due course come to pass. The emptiness is not empty.[6] It is more true to say that it is "a porous between" since it allows entrances and exits, enabling openings outwards with exposure to the gaze of spectators, while also being ringed round with recesses where actors retreat and regroup or emerge to take a bow, or remerge to the applause of an encore, or hide from the hissing or silence of an unappreciative audience.

The stage in that regard seems to be a kind of nothing, but as a nothing it is not merely indefinite. It is a milieu of possible happening and action. Even before any action takes place, it is what enables the possibility of exchange and interaction. As a porous between one might look on the stage as a space through which comes to flow an energy, embodied in the different characters, who themselves are brought to embodiment by the actors, in an action that sometimes has a strong narrative togetherness, sometimes a structure more loosely structured, should we think according to the Aristotelian unities of time, place, and action. The flow of energy on the staged between communicates a field that reaches beyond the dividing verge towards those who watch. Those who behold come

6. Peter Brook's *The Empty Space*, while reflecting its time, is still fresh and engaging.

over the threshold, from their side, even as the energies enacted on the other side of the verge are exchanged enigmatically with those watching the action.

In a word, there is nothing static about the stage as an empty space. It is entirely dynamic or the promise of such dynamism. It is not the actors, it is not the characters, it is not their actions, it is not their interactions, it is not the communication and exchange between them, and between them and those who participate by watching. It is rather *the enabling intermedium* that possibilizes all of these things, while itself not being any one of these things. The stage as porous between is less than and more than all of them. Less than, since without the actors and the characters, the interactions and exchanges, there is nothing determinate going on there—there is no play. More than, since while almost nothing, it enfolds them in an embrace whose presence retreats into absence as it enables what takes place in and through it. It is more like an *ethos of enabling* than any definite action or event that occurs in the space or on the stage.

In the language I use, the stage is both indeterminate and overdeterminate. Indeterminate, in that it is nothing definite till it is peopled; overdeterminate, since as the enabling intermedium it is more than every determinate event or exchange that comes to pass on the stage itself. I think this double character is also what makes the stage always a threshold in which the separability of life and art can never be absolutely fixed. Something is always escaping fixation, something is always going on in the wings. And what happens in the brief hours of theatrical staging seeps beyond these short hours of intense engagement, even as sometimes a lifetime of preparation might have gone into the performed instant of concentration which, at best, draws together a secret multiplicity into a kind of open whole. It is for such reasons that the stage itself offers a metaphor for life itself, and we do not know which comes first: lived staging of the between, or the beholding of the image of that lived staging in the theatrical *metaxu*.

## On Stage: Presencing beyond Univocalization

The stage offers a space, but howsoever we interpret its emptiness, it is not empty for long. "When we are born we cry that we are come/ to this great stage of fools," said Lear (*King Lear*, IV, vi, 176–77). We do not have to bawl for communication to be effected. An actor comes onstage, a determinate person makes an entrance, but this is not the neutral insertion of an object in a space itself entirely neutral. This space, as we saw, even before an entrance, is not neutral, and even less so is it neutral when a determinate being has made an entrance. There is someone there, though who it is initially we may not know, nor initially may we know why there is someone there, and why in particular this present person serves an unfolding. The entrance on the stage of someone reconfigures the between space of the stage. Once a space of possibility, even promise, the actual presence of someone reassembles the field of energy and the seemingly empty space itself begins to communicate. The space becomes alive with presence.

It is interesting to think of this as ingredient in the wording of the between, though it is a wording that may be wordless. Wordings need not be confined to vocalized utterances. Nothing need be said for something to be said. An actor stands there and simply by being there is a transformation of the space of the between in the direction of communicative possibility. An accomplished actor will know how to hold the silence, and hold it not so much as silence but as a way of being in communication, both with other players and those who watch. There is a kind of timing in silence—a way of being poised in the passage of time that holds the attention of others, just in its arousal of an anticipation of something more in the sheer presence of someone simply being there.

In a broad philosophical sense, I would say that there are determinate beings there, but they are never simply neutral objects or even persons. They are always saturated with a texture of worth or value. (The text even as read communicates texture of worth.) Worth is communicated even in the absence of overt communication—simply to be there is already to be in communication, and these communications can never be "value-free." Quite the opposite, to communicate on the stage as between is always to embody the worthy or unworthy, what arouses attraction or repulsion, what draws us and what pushes us away. Sometimes we talk about the "body language" and the commanding presence of the actor, and this is not wrong. But body language is not just body language. The embodied one who is there is more than himself or herself. She or he is as a wording of the between simply by being there. The presence of the actor is physically there, but what is there is always a passage of energy in the field of the between. The energy that is determinate there is not just determinately there; it communicated beyond itself by being there. A great actor can be both the servant and director of this energy of being in communication in the between. Some have an intuitive finesse for this, others become masters through years of disciplined training. Their bodily movement, their control of voice, their supple mastery of facial gesture and so on, are all put into the service of this energy. It seems to originate in them yet goes beyond them always in communication. It is never theirs alone, since it is what it is by being in communication. Great art gets out of the way of the release and communication of this energy. The stage as a between is a place of its porous passage. Again, a person has only to walk on stage properly and the stage swarms—wording the between by being there.

Thus, the determination of presence is univocal, but more than univocal. And so staging the between can never be reduced to the monologue of one. There is always more than one in staging the between. For instance, if an actor delivers a soliloquy he or she is alone, alone with his or her own thought, but he or she speaks in the company of an audience and hence is not alone. Every monologue is more than a monologue. No dramatist writes simply for herself or himself alone. And without the performance and the audience there is still something incomplete about the work. The performance before an audience somehow is the thing itself that reveals the work most fully. There can be bad or unprepared or unreceptive audiences, of course, but even these contribute something to bringing the play to effect. The multiplicity involved in staging the play on the between cannot be denied. When an actor is playing a role for himself or herself, she or he is only practicing, we say; but the practicing is with the view to performing before others. To perform for oneself somehow makes an autism of staging the between and in that sense collapses the between space into an uncommunicative block and hence seems diametrically opposed to the communication called forth by the stage as such. We might speak of a private performance, but usually this is one before an audience of a selected few, and so still the others enter into the staging of the between.

An actor is a singular person, but as acting he is other than any simple univocal identity. One might say that he others himself. Actors speak of finding the character, indeed of being that character. In an important regard, this othering of self makes the actor a no-self. He must be a kind of fertile nothing for the character to come to be and become embodied. Some actors speak of staying in character, and if the character is a malign one like Iago it can create effects in real life surplus to what transpires on the stage. I know an actor whose wife was spooked when he remained too much in the character of Iago. The actor seems to have no univocal identity, but what flows positively from this is that he may bring multiple identities to be. Socrates lamented this in the *Republic* (394d9ff.) where his thinking is governed by this law: one person, one job (370b-c). He does not consider the fertile promise of being nothing—being nothing as enabling the condition of a creative pluralization. This pluralizing of selving in acting is not easily reconciled with a too-fixed sense of univocal identity. It is entirely too equivocal for Socrates, but we can see something more affirmative in the plurivocity.

## Inter-action: Enmeshed in Equivocity

There is plurivocity in that on the stage there is a many—many actors bringing to life many different characters, actors interfacing accord to a plot that holds them in its embrace. Even a one-man show has a manyness in it. One voice speaking is more than one voice speaking. The voice that is one's own is the plurivocity of many voices that have entered into what one is, and that continue to resonate, most often involuntarily, in what seems entirely idiosyncratic to oneself. Think of the voices of parents resonating in the voices of their children. Each of us is the inheritance of other singular voicings of the between, each carrying aspects of an *incognito* legacy of wordings in passage through the between.

One voice speaking cannot confine the wording to one voice and many voices are re-voiced in the one voice. The plurivocity in staging the between is very important in telling us something beyond the univocalization of a fixed identity, namely, the subtler import of differences. "I'll teach you differences," uttered gruff Kent in *King Lear* (I, iv, 91), and Wittgenstein, as I recalled earlier, considered using this as a motto for his *Philosophical Investigations*.[7] Here I speak of the equivocal. The space of the between is inexorably qualified by equivocity. Actors enact characters in inter-action, but the inter-action exposes every act to equivocity, since it can be taken differently, reacted to otherwise, by all those other to the actor. Inter-acting entangles characters in a web of differentials, relations, in which each is defined by intermediations with others, and this web of relations can bind us to the others as well as put us in binds in relation

7. Wittgenstein in conversation with his friend Maurice O'C. Drury in the Phoenix Park, Dublin: in Drury, *The Danger of Words and Writings on Wittgenstein*, 157.

to others. The releasing power of relations co-exists with the restraining. Bonds of inter-action make free, they also create bondage.[8]

Of course, in the word "equivocity" is present a doubleness wherein lurks the possibility of duplicity. Equivocity is on the verge of possible deceit—or as the ancients tended to put it "saying the thing that is not." It also bears on the interplay of the true and the false, the seductiveness of the half-truth that draws us on to disaster by its secret deceit. One of the great examples of this is the way Macbeth is led on, lets himself be led on, by the equivocal prophecies of the Weird Sisters.[9] One thinks of the irony of the doubling of perspectives, say, when Oedipus understands his own words one way, those who hear him quite another way. One thinks also of the way some comedies turn on mistaken identity, turn on disguise in the form of being the opposite of what one truly is. Shakespeare again offers many examples. The character must hide his or her identity, even seem the opposite of what they are. Duplicity serves the advancement of the overall action. The equivocity serves something more than equivocity. One thinks of how in tragedy there may come about the revelation of truer identity, but if there is a moment of such recognition it is won out of and crystallized from the equivocity of the between. The great playwright is the servant of the equivocal, which, in being courted, is brought to serve a revelation. The dramaturge is like a demiurge, or perhaps even a theurge of the equivocal differences—an agent of magic mutations in which differences are shown in truth to make a difference. In the *Tempest*, Shakespeare hints at such Prospero-like theurgy of redeeming the equivocal differences.

Staging the between also courts the failure of communication, for communication is always stressed by the suffering of our dubious equivocation. There is something about staging the between that is on the verge of acknowledging both the need and the danger of exposure. For instance, if I am too direct about myself, I might expose myself to the hostility of others rather than their hospitality. There is no eradication of this double-edged character of exchanges between characters. Total exposure seems impossible, and total retraction seems the death of communication. Communication happens between exposure and retraction.

8. In this regard, it is interesting to note how in the *Poetics* (XVIII, 1) Aristotle says "In every tragedy there is a complication and a dénouement" (Loeb translation), but the words in Greek are simply a "tying" (*desis*) and a "loosing" (*lysis*)—one might say a knot and an unknotting, a twist and an unraveling, a binding and unbinding.

9. See my "Sticky Evil."

Dramatic revelation is also concealment in this middle space. There the intimate recesses and secrets of the character can hide. It is not just that the hidden can be shown and the concealed comes to light, but the event of hiding is itself not just hidden. The equivocal insinuosities of concealing are themselves exposed.

Drama is an interplay between the recessed and the expressed, the secret and the exposed. But the equivocity between those two is more subtle than one would expect, since it is often the expressed that itself is the recessed, and the exposed that is the secret that communicates to deflect attention from itself. A dramatist allows us to behold what avoids beholding, wording the between even when those in the play of its interplay would silence true wording. There is a kind of *companioning karma* at work in this. This was called fate in ancient drama. It seems to disappear in modern drama with the sense of the inwardization of the person, as well as the stress on the autonomy of the immanent. I will say that, nevertheless, the companioning power is not absent. Absent it and drama dies the bland death of slice-of-life naturalism—flat life wording flat life. Then drama is no longer a wording of the between that recedes inwards to terrifying abysses of self, that extends outwards to exteriorities that mock us, that plunges downwards into places of desolation where the soul overturns itself into infernal desolation, that throws us upwards into exaltations when it seems, like Lear, we have already died and we wonder if we see before us a beautiful spirit, though in truth it is our still living child.

There is danger in all drama. There is pain in all drama. There is suffering in exposure. There is exaltation in being in communication. There is laughter when absurdity is exploded. There is compassion when exposure is made receptive to forgiving of our failure. These are all dimensions of the equivocity of the staged between. On the stage, the moments of revelation are not univocal fixations. They occur in passing. They come to light in transit. There are passings in the between. There can be passages in a great play where a consecration of our mindfulness can come to pass, passages where the concentration of revelation is more intense. We have always to be attentive to the ambiguities of passage itself in order to do justice to the drama, attending well at what is unfolding before us.

It is the passing of the whole of the action that asks of us a certain finesse for the equivocal. This reveals a doubleness, to be sure, but it is not devoid of a secret "holding together" of the many differences that come to light. The stage itself functions, in one of its potencies, as a kind of holding area. This holding area is never a corral or closed circle. The play as a whole is a holding together, even when the edges are frayed, as in some more postmodern forms or deformations. It is a revealing fact that often one has to *work* at producing a deformation. Artistic deforming must be held together by a certain discipline intent on not letting things be held together. Such a studied not letting things hold shows its indirect complement to the power of holding together by just its will to subvert the form that holds us on the stage. One is reminded of those who study to have a two-day beard—as if they had no time to shave. Of course, it asks far more work to appear unshaved so, requiring far more studied intention to create the impression that you are uninterested in making an impression. The intention is to counterfeit the appearance that it is all unintentional anyway.

Perhaps this is a postmodern rebirth of the ancient sagacity, attributed to Ovid: *ars est celare artem*, it is art to conceal art. In any case, the staging of the between cannot be a fixed univocity, nor a dissolving equivocity; it requires rather the interplay of the two—of one and many, of the expressed and the recessed, of the shown and the secret, and these in light of a holding together of many in communication in the midst of passage. It is not that dissolving equivocity is not part of all this. But to absolutize this is to renege on the communicative vocation of wording the between. And even the evacuation of the stage of the between that we get, say, in the later Beckett does not contradict this, for the evacuation makes no sense without communication, even if we know not what is communicated. To stage absurdity is not itself absurd. Writer, director, actors enter into the interplay of these two, the univocal and the equivocal—not just at this moment or that but in the passage of the unfolding whole. Great art serves to discern something more plurivocally integral in the process qua process. It is not mere process, not mere integrity, but somehow a dynamic integrity in the process qua passage in the between. In this regard, this interplay points to more *dialectical* features involved in the staging of the between.

## Plotting: Storied Togetherness and Dialectic

We know that Aristotle considered plot the most important thing in tragedy, and as I already mentioned his word for plot is *mythos*. The *mythos* is the story that holds the whole together. A certain wholeness, with beginning, middle, and end, he also considers central to the excellence of tragedy (*Poetics*, VII, 2–11). I connect this with a dialectical sense of staging the between. Dialectic has much to do with a holding together into a kind of whole of an unfolding process. I would rather speak of an open whole than a self-enclosed totality. There is something dialectical about staging the between, but not in a closed sense.

People talk to each other, they converse; they speak together in a shared space, and this is even true of soliloquy, as I remarked before. So much of drama is carried by these words between one and another. We might call this "dialogue," but take this in a more extended sense. This is not a simple face-to-face talking but a communication in which is uttered the *logoi* of at least two: *dia-legein*.[10] The word *dia* contains the notion of the twoness, though *dia* can also mean a space of carrying between. *Dia-logos:* the carrying of *logos* across a *dia*. Think of something similar when we think of the carrying of light through a *dia-phanous* medium. Implicit in all this is the *porosity* of the between as presupposed by this *dia* of passage. There is no dialogue without this medium of porosity. We put a face on it; we front the other; we confront the other; we face the other; the other fronts and confronts us. We are persons in this fronting, and indeed here the connection of persona with the theatrical mask is overt. In the Greek, the word for mask, *prosopon*, brings the visual dimension more to the fore, while the Latin word *persona* reminds us of the auditory or sonorous dimension. *Per-sonans:* something is sounding through (*per*). The face, the surface, resonates with what is not just surface. The face of the person is an intermedium through which the intimate source of selving sounds and resounds—the ensouled being that communicates to and in the between.

Of course, with dialectic the connection of drama with philosophy intrudes on reflection, and one thinks of the masked Plato. Could one say that his dramatic dialogues are his plurivocal *prosopon*? He never appears in first person, in *propria persona*, nor can he be unambiguously identified with any of the dramatic personae that appear in the dialogue, not even with Socrates. Like Shakespeare, we can never be entirely sure what he thinks, though he is both nowhere and everywhere in his works. With Plato the dramatic nature of his dialogues have an indispensable role in the showing and communication of truth. The dialogues offer images of philosophical conversation as a living dialectic between singular human

10. See Nikulin, *Dialectic and Dialogue*.

beings, each of whom voices his understanding or misunderstanding of what is true. Though none possesses truth entirely, each offers something to the search for it in the interplay of voices. Dialogue is, as it were, a plurivocal mimesis of different possible pathways to our comprehension of the true in the intermedium of conversation, as indeed also of possible departures from true paths. Dialogue stages a middle of plurivocal *logoi*, each seeking to be true to what is coming to articulation in the spaces of questioning and answering between thinking human beings.

Relevant to our interest in staging the between, dramatic dialogue asks us to pay subtle attention to *surfaces*. Surfaces are the interfaces of communication. Surfaces are places of showing, thresholds where intimacies of being come to sur-face. Wordings are sur-facings. Surfaces word the between. A play stages such surfacings. Plato gives us a philosophy of surfaces by staging the drama of inter-human showing in our seeking the true in and through words. Voiced wordings can be the richest showings: surfaces that can be the communication of the deepest hiddenness. In a general sense, one might venture that art is an aesthetic happening where surface and depth coincide. In the sensible the hypersensible shows itself. The Platonic dialogue is a drama of surfaces, of words as the surfacing of souls in the between and in communication with each other.

In this *dia-legein*, there is a turn in, a turn out, a turn down, and a turn up. In the end, all the significance of dialogue is revealed and hidden in these various crossings of the between, crossings in and out, crossings up and down. One might say that in the crossing of the horizontal and vertical axes of the between the plot or *mythos* of the play is unfolded. Moderns totally shaped by a secular outlook will bridle at the thought of what is "up." And yet what is at stake, what's up in plot is what is *more* than ourselves, the equivocity of that "more," how we are in communication with it, or it with us, even when we think we are communicating only without ourselves. All living play is secretly porous to an intimate god. Of course, plot is not univocally evident. It often unfolds by means of surprising equivocations, such as mistaken identities or counterfeiting one's character or hiding one's name and so on. Oedipus did not know what he was doing when he met his father Laius at the crossroad (itself an intersection in a between), and yet the encounter was fateful. One thinks of how this notion is of importance to Aristotle, for without the secret of identity or a hidden otherness to the character, there is no moment of reversal and recognition, no *peripéteia* and no *anagnórisis* (*Poetics*, XI 1–8). The unfolding of the whole brings us to the secret significance—a significance that cannot be confined to this one episode or that, and that yet finally does not disseminate itself in a tissue of equivocations.

In the unfolding there is this "holding together," sometimes of opposites that otherwise threaten simply to break apart. The stage as a between holds them together. Certain characters may hate each other, but they cannot get away from each other. One thinks of George and Martha in Edward Albee's *Who's Afraid of Virginia Wolf?* Their love is their hatred, their hatred their love, their hatred prevents them from escaping each other. It is in the equivocal tension of hatred-love that a storied communication comes to unfold. A communication brings to be a community, though a community does not necessarily mean a reconciled togetherness. Often, in fact, war, undeclared or announced, is a significant engine of movements that bring the antagonists or protagonists to the moment of truth. They are enmeshed in something that is more than themselves and never more so than when they think they were achieving something thorough themselves alone.

There are different ways to understand this "holding together." I will mention Hegel's treatment of tragic drama.[11] Here we find the clash of ethical powers, he holds, and the two powers are equally right, equally wrong. His favorite example is that of Antigone and Creon. In the clash of the two, both are right yet one-sided, thus each must go under, but in that going under a more inclusive sense of a togetherness comes to the fore. The opposition that is emergent from the equivocity of the situation is overcome in a more reconciled end where the antagonists must each yield their one-sidedness under the pressure of the emergent and more embracing whole.

Hegel is not entirely wrong, but not entirely right. He is guided by a dialectical sense of the plot which is always teleologically oriented to a reconciled end—reconciled in his sense of the more inclusive whole. Staging the between, in this Hegelian wise, closes the middle between beginning and end back into a circle related to itself. Any such closure, I think, can only be relative, otherwise it does not do justice to the porosity of the between, not only in the middle, but also at the extremes. The origin remains in excess of the circle that closes on itself. The end seeps beyond the closed whole into the mystery of transfinite darkness and perhaps the promise of redemption. Hegel's wants closure, but the porosity of the between, while not inhospitable to visits of consolation,

11. Hegel, *Hegel's Aesthetics: Lectures on Fine Art*, 2:1217–18. Hegel's discussion of Antigone in his *Phenomenology of Spirit*, §§446–76 is also important.

cannot offer that kind of final closure. The close is always a new opening of the porosity—into the mystery of what exceeds closure. If we must use the language of the whole, to be true to staging the between it must be an open whole that releases beyond the whole.

I do not think we have to think reconciliation quite in the Hegelian way. This is undergirded by polemos and the struggle for recognition. It is silent about the secret surplus that enables the given intermedium of being to be a between at all. This is a way of talking about the companioning of the divine. Hegel is attentive to the manner the protagonists come across limits where they are confronted with something that is not of their own self-determination. But his understanding of the "holding together" is itself modeled on a more inclusive self-determination of the whole or *Geist*. It is not true to the open porosity of the between. His dialectic does not do justice to the mystery of the companioning power. His dialectic congratulates itself on being the measure of all mystery. But all dialectic is measured by this mystery of the between, and of the mystery of the many voices of otherness that are at play in the between. The togetherness is not an inclusive whole but rather calls for a more intensive dwelling with the between as communicative of the overdeterminate. The plot of storied togetherness calls out for mythic wording of the between.

## The Theater of the Metaxu and the Companioning Power

How are we to remain true to this intimation of the "more" in the between and its staging? I would say that metaxology remains true to it in its porosity to *mythos*. The companioning power can be communicated in the horizontal dimensions of out and in, but also in the vertical dimensions of above and below. In ancient tragedy the companioning role of fate refers to a power always reserved and finally always ruling, even though the characters in the plot are the agents of their own acts. We confront the equivocity of those who are guiltless and in guilt, at one and the same time. This doubleness refers to their being in unknowing companionship with more, much more than they can determine through themselves alone. There is a recessed relation to what is beyond their self-determination, in their own knowing/unknowing enactments of self-determination. No act is ever just a matter of self-determination if fate is the companioning power. There is always a secret and reserved "with." Providence, in the monotheistic world, reframes this companioning power in terms of an origin solicitous to the end rather than an implacable necessity to a doom. There is an intimacy to the companioning power all along all passing in the between, and more in *incognito* communication with the inward idiocy of the human selving. Of course, this secret intimacy might be taken to mean that there is *nothing* at work except our self-determination. If that is all it were, there would be no tragedy of the between. The power of fate recedes into the background and the companioning power is more internalized in modern tragedy with the advent and influence of Christianity. Hegel understood this, but his sense of the companioning power and the freedom of the human is rendered in terms of a logic of self-determination, and hence it is not true to the soliciting othering involved in staging the between, in excess of self-determination, in excess of selving, even in the intimacy of selving itself.

The relation of human freedom and the more-than-human is at issue. When Hegel sees this in light of a logic of self-determination, he concedes too much to the modern logic of autonomy. This in turn is actually to concede the drawn-out death of drama, understand as an exchange between the human and the more-than-human. The reputed death of tragedy in bourgeois culture is no problem for Hegel. Whether from the side of the human or the more-than-human, for Hegel it is the more inclusive self-determination of *Geist* that finally overcomes all otherness that resists incorporation. This is to make the between circle around the overarching logic of self-determination, to the betrayal of the more primordial and more ultimate porosity of being. This has to do with the great question in drama—the strange doubleness of the freedom of the characters who yet remain enmeshed in what is beyond freedom. The great question concerns the hostility of what is beyond, the hospitality of what is beyond. The great question concerns their interplay and interrelation, whether out of hostility a new hospitality can come, whether there is a hospitality before hostility, whether there must be the promise of a hospitality at work *incognito* even in the conditions of hostility.

I would say that staging the between indicates that we can only dramatize hostility in a between-space whose hospitality is such that it enables the enactment and even the overcoming of hostility. There is an agapeic promise in this play. There is something of the promise of festive reconciliation. I would say this is even true of Beckett's evacuation of the stage. It purges the porosity, and we are left to wonder what then might pour through that purged porosity. Joyce is not a dramatist (though he had one unsuccessful play), and seems the opposite of Beckett in stressing the fullness rather than the emptiness. But extremes meet—minimum and maximum, porosity and overdeterminacy, nothing much and what is always too much.

A *self*-mediating dialectic is not entirely true to this dialectical togetherness. It is not true to the sense of excess appearing in the interplay of the many in the staging of the between. This excess to self-mediation comes before us in tragic form and in comic. In tragic drama there can be an excess of suffering and evil, turning our bones to liquid, as happens when the disconsolate "howl, howl, howl" of Lear pierces our deepest defenses. Such suffering blasts open all the passageways of our self-protected porosity. Lear's "never, never, never, never" strips away all protections and we are as nothing again, suffering the extremity of exposure.[12] In comic drama, there is also a dissolving nothing against which our voluntary self-determination proves ineffective, and in this nothing the festive energy of the "to be" that resurrects itself again and again. We are actors and act, but we do not *do* this energy. It is not self-determined, it is a "yes" of life to life that exceeds self-determination.

That excess is always secretly in waiting on the wings of the stage, or even there on the stage, but mostly no one knows it, and only sometimes does it get acknowledged. The great dramaturge is the artist who woos it, and makes a work whose essence is a loving plea that this too muchness shows itself to us—through all that transpires on the stage. The stage as a between consecrates this transpiration to the sacred show.

One is reminded again of the question as to whether bourgeois culture has destroyed the theater, a question sung out in the poetic heyday of Simon and Garfunkel's "dangling conversation": "Can analysis be worthwhile? Is the theater really dead?" I would rather speak of a humanization of the between such that our own porosity to what exceeds us, to what is more than the human, is closed off. We live in secular, not to say, anti-sacred times, and the struggle against the closure of the human into its own self-circling encirclement produces tortured results. I am thinking, for instance, of the theater of cruelty, the theater of the absurd. These are expressions of the torment that wants to break out of humanistic encirclement, and allow a breakthrough onto the stage of the between of what exceeds us. Is this a theater of the sublime rather than the beautiful?

12. See Desmond, *Perplexity and Ultimacy*, chapter 2, "Being at a Loss: Reflections on Philosophy and the Tragic."

I ask it thus since supposedly we in modern and postmodern times have again and again tried to break out of the frame—breaking the frame in pictorial art, breaking out of the closed stage and allowing novel arrangements between actors and audience, breaking out of harmony and melody into cacophonous dissonances that structurally seem to give intellectual pleasure on paper but from which the listening body has difficulty getting pleasure—unless assault on the senses be one's pleasure. Apart from pleasure in pain, be it inflicted or inflicting, the problem with the postmodern sublime is that it is still created in predominantly man-made conditions, and hence in the end continues to reflect the human back to itself. We still are in decampment from creation as other, and the mirrors with which we surround ourselves reflect only our own faces. If the encirclement still goes on its yield can only be a kind of autism of the human, without release into the truly sublime.

Death always shadows the question of the companioning power. It is interesting how Aristotle in his discussion of *eudaimonia* in his *Nichomachean Ethics* (I, x) invokes Solon, though in the wings is Sophocles: Count no one happy till dead. Of course, we cannot but think of an archetypal tragic plot or *mythos*, namely that of Oedipus.[13] *Eudaimonia* is poorly rendered as "happiness," if this makes us forget the *daimon*, the companioning power. The *daimon* is between mortals and divinities and Aristotle in the *Poetics* (VI, 12) speaks of *eudaimonia* and *kakodaimonia* in connection with the action of a tragedy. There is no coming to full term without the *daimon* as the companioning power. If we are companioned by, or we invite with us along the way, a *daimon* that is *kakos*, evil, we are in trouble. It will come to no good. The equivocity between the good and the evil is not eradicated with the companioning power. Again I see this as relevant to the self-mediating dialectic of Hegel where there is a kind of between but in such a way that difference is turned into opposition and taken hold of as a moment of an immanent process of self-determination. This is not staging the between as daimonically porous.

Staging the between can bring us to hell again, and the infernal places. It can also bring to light a more benign, forgiving togetherness, but there is something porous about it to what exceeds determination,

13. The Chorus at the end of *Oedipus Tyrranos* (1678–84): "People of Thebes, my countrymen, look on Oedipus. He solved the famous riddle with his brilliance, he rose to power, a man beyond all power. Who could behold his greatness without envy? Now what a black sea of terror has overwhelmed him. Now as we keep our watch and wait the final day, count no man happy till he dies, free of pain at last."

our self-determination and any self-inclusive whole. A more fully metaxological sense of staging the between allows the granting of the descent into hell, but also the granting of a presiding otherness that now comes forward, now retreats from the stage. A finesse for this arriving and departing otherness marks great theater.

Remember again we cannot fix finally the between that is staged. It is all in passing between. It is all in transition, in transits, in being beyond self. The between is trans-objective, and trans-subjective, and yet it is enabling of objects and subjects to come to be themselves. It is true that certain stabilizations take place. There come to be more or less constant patterns of interaction—or a more or less constant character of this or that kind—or a relatively stabilized relation between different characters. The constancy is itself a "standing with"—*con-stans*. Something comes to a stand, but there is a "with-ness" in the coming, and hence a relation to what is other than self. The truly constant cannot be circled or encircled, since it is a fundamental reliability in the becoming of the between. Even in the expectation of doom, there is always the possibility of being surprised. We cannot determine the surprise of what comes in advance of its coming.

When we repeat a good play, this element of surprise surprises us again. It has a freshness about it that is not dimmed with repetition. Quite the opposite: repetition may itself be the activity that puts a shine of surprise on what comes to outing. "Repetition" is a word for rehearsal, but the actual performance which has been gone over many times can still shine with an unanticipated surprise. It is impossible to project, impossible to determine surprise in advance. It is always more than our self-determination. It upends our autonomy. An element of readiness for the coming of this otherness into the play is essential to a more metaxological understanding of staging the between. This dramatic surprise is more than self-mediation which, we know, retreats into an inward otherness. It is more than social intermediation, for the surprising hits a community. There is always an enabling power that is other to the relations between us and others. It is beyond selving, beyond othering, beyond even the relation between them. Art woos the companioning power of this enabling otherness. It is there and not there in the porous between that is the stage, the between on which the drama is being staged.

In terms of passing in the between, one thinks not simply of the physical space of entrances and exits, not only of characters coming and going, but a more metaphysical sense of entry and exit, and this not on the stage, or into the theater, but in terms of the companioning power that appears and disappears, and even though our wooing and disciplined attention may coax it closer, there is always something metaphysically gypsy about it. In the receding and the coming forward, we may try to gird it round in the time of the play but that is not enough. The girding round must offer itself more like a sacred space set apart than a self-encircled enclosure. The staging between prepares a ground for the coming of this companioning otherness, whether immanent in this character or the other, or in the equivocal intermediation of the many characters, and in their coming together beyond their singular expectation, and in the dialectical togetherness exceeding all dialectic.

While the porous between is evident in dialogue, since something other exceeds the final enclosing grasp of those who talk to each other, there is sometimes a truer image of it in our failure or frustration. Perhaps this is what Beckett saw—we fail, but we must fail better, fail gloriously. In this glory of failure something arises that is as releasing of the participants to something more than themselves. Failure stages one of the great questions for theater—the more-than-us, appearing in our efforts to be ourselves and more than ourselves. If so, there is a humanization of the between-space of the stage that ends up as a dehumanization if it turns out to be without this porosity to what exceeds humanity.

Worth bearing in mind here by philosophers is how many Platonic dialogues end in *aporia*, or a kind of failure. The effort to word the between brings us to an ending in significant silence. The dialogues repeatedly dramatize our not being able now to go further. We can't go on, yet we must go on. *Logos* emerges from silence and reaches towards silence, but in this second silence *logos* gives itself over to a different saying, the poetic saying of myth. Myth is itself the bearer of a silence that exceeds univocal conceptualization and yet it is addressed to philosophical thought. Plurivocal saying is wedded with plural silences: the silence out of which speaking together comes, the silence of each speaker and between speakers, the silence of the between itself as a space charged with the elicitation of response, the silence beyond univocal conceptualization edging us towards the sacred wordings of myth, the humble silence of true myth which knows it does not know absolutely. Failure is not mere failure, and silence is not beaten down but elevated into reverence.

## Curtains: On a Threshold

A theater of the *metaxu* must return us, in the end, to the connection of art and the sacred mentioned at the outset. The *metaxu* is the between space of the human and divine. What is at issue is not just a *deus ex machina*—though again we have to remember that this was a device that did serve its function to communicate something of the interruption and rupture of the divine in human affairs. That we are now more pickled in a secular humanism does not in any way make us superior on this score. True, there is the *deus ex machina* that is a merely extrinsic superimposition on the action (see, for instance, *Poetics*, XV, 10) when the sacred is pulled out of nowhere. Of course, we are sometimes guilty of the *humanitas ex machina*—the valueless thereness of the mechanical world, *mirabile dictu*, gives rise to the amazing human being as of some unconditional worth. Pulled out of nowhere, we cannot explain this arising on mechanical terms and we dull ourselves to its mystery. Without finesse for the mystery of the human, there would be no seeking of the more-than-human. If I am right, the between-space, even when empty, already communicates of the more. Extremes again can touch: nothing and everything, less than something and more than all things, the seemingly indeterminate and the surplus overdeterminate, the minimum and the maximum. It enters the pores of the characters. It companions their interaction. It outlives their loves and hatreds. And in all that, it still remains so intimate that it is almost an entirely *incognito* companion.

In the *metaxu* we find ourselves on the threshold of the sacred. When Aristotle (*Poetics*, VI, 2–3) spoke of *phobos* and *eleos*, horror and compassion, he was closer than Hegel to the porosity of the between, though I am unsure if he understood what that porosity signified, and perhaps wasted an opportunity when he touches on the element of pathos (*Poetics*, XI, 9–10). Exposure to the horror of the monstrous draws us into the space of the sacred. Even an art that seems more to desecrate than to consecrate is in that space, even if there is at work a secret hatred of everything sacred. Desecration would mutilate a sacredness that it would were not there at all, and thus shows itself enmeshed in what it would nullify. Beckett spoke about "the mess," and some artists are not loathe to stir the excrements lest we Polyannas have overlooked the stink. But what true artist—or philosopher—forgets (in Yeats's words) "the foul rag and bone shop of the heart"?[14]

14. Yeats, *The Poems*, "The Circus Animals' Desertion," 394–95.

Exposure on the threshold is differently accented in great tragedy and comedy. We are on a porous boundary where finitude cannot close itself off from an exposure to horror and compassion. This threshold is a frontier of the ultimate between. One thinks of the extremities of a kind of sacred idiocy. There is the idiocy Macbeth came to in the ruin of his sovereign will to power. He has let himself be led to destruction by the evil equivocity of the companioning powers for whom he chooses, the Wicked Sisters. "Out, out, brief candle!/Life's but a walking shadow, a poor player,/That struts and frets his hour upon the stage,/And then is heard no more. It is a tale/Told by an idiot, full of sound and fury,/ Signifying nothing" (*Macbeth*, V, v, 23–28). By contrast, one thinks again of King Lear, now stripped of regal sovereignty, and passing through madness to learn the wisdom of being nothing. He comes to a painful patience on the boundary and becomes porous to those who are as nothing. He learns compassion. He becomes, with Cordelia, one of "God's spies," who take upon themselves "the mystery of things," who "wear out, in a walled prison, packs and sets of great ones that ebb and flow by the moon" (see *King Lear*, V, iii, 9–19). Racked on the between, a life posthumous to life and death opens.[15] There may be almost nothing of what we normally deem consolation in this, yet there is consolation in truthfulness to the extremities of exposure, and a love beyond life and death.

In comedy, in its lowliness, we can see something of sacred idiocy in the irrepressible resurrection of life affirming itself, again and again, even in absurdity. Such comic irrepressibility, it is true, can be overtaken by a spirit of mockery that does not love, and the affirmative energy is curdled into sour negation. Nevertheless, there is comic laughter that breaks out in the mode of a forgiving release. It may debunk the risible pretensions of false finitude, but there is the festive energy of laughter that releases again, even in absurdity, something of the intimate joy in being at all. Such laughter, often loud in its outburst, is like the applause of life itself. There is an idiot wisdom which is the earthy double of divine comedy.

The curtain falls at the end, even if only a metaphorical curtain.The spell that has held us is broken but we wake to ourselves differently after the between is staged. It is not quite that the play rends the veil of Maya; or rends the curtain in the holy of holies for us only to find it empty. We have been brought to a threshold, and it is not only that we have crossed a threshold but something more has crossed it and crossed us. We do

15. On posthumous mindfulness, see for instance Desmond, *Philosophy and Its Others*, 278–82; also Desmond, *Being and the Between*, 36–37.

not depart the between. We live in it again with thought and with our ontological porosity purged.[16]

In the poem "What then?" (already heard in our earlier séance with hell) Yeats asks about what comes after a whole is completed, indeed successfully complete. This question is the repeated refrain in this song of Plato's ghost: What then?[17] When then is the finish? Endings are hugely important, but the porous between suggests there is no univocal end, for where can we definitely put the word *finis*? When someone dies we say "It is curtains." But there is no absolute finality—the finitude of the *finis* is porous. A metaxological sense of the between is hospitable to the sense that endings are all relative in the end. There is the ending of the play, but there is something beyond this. There is the return to life. There may be the next performance, there will be a new play. There is, within some plays, the beyond of posthumous mind. There is, when we go home, after the ball is over, another kind of posthumous mindfulness if the play has seared into the hyperspace of what is hyperbolic to immanent finitude. This entry into the space of the hyperbolic is part of the dramatics of the stage of the *metaxu*. The "too muchness," the "more," the "above" has been communicated. Great dramatic art kills us and brings us to death as an end, but it also resurrects us with the porosity purged. And outside too—there is the companioning power that goes before or behind us, above us and below us, by our right side or our left side, though we see nothing there. The companioning power is there, crossing the between, in a kind of sacred idiocy. The liturgy of a consecrated between has occurred in a place where, least of all, we have come to think of as sacred.

16. This suggests a way to rethink Aristotle's *katharsis* (*Poetics*, V, 2–3).

17. Yeats, *The Poems*, 349.

# 9

## Redeeming Laughter[1]: On the Body Beside Itself and the Passion of Being

### Prelude

TRAGEDY HAS OFTEN BEEN awarded a higher status in the spiritual hierarchy by thinkers dealing with high and noble things, while comedy has been less appreciated in the spiritual order, dealing as it does with lower things, with ridiculous and risible things.[2] Yet it is worth

1. This chapter had already been written and this book was advanced in the production process when I became aware that a book of the same title had appeared: Berger, *Redeeming Laughter* (2014). This came to my attention reading Ola Sigurdson's engaging "Emancipation as a Matter of Style." Sigurdson is currently completing a three-volume work, *Divine Comedies: Humour, Subjectivity, Transcendence*.

2. Aristotle's book on comedy we do not have, but given the things he has to say on comedy, the high nobility of tragedy comes through. One thinks of Heraclitus the weeping philosopher, of Democritus the laughing. Epictetus (*Enchiridion*): "Do not laugh much, or at many things, or without restraint." Giordano Bruno's motto exhibits a saturated equivocity: *In tristitia hilaris, in hilaritate tristis.* One thinks of Nietzsche's early work on tragedy as redemptive in a Dionysian way: this high place for tragedy makes the point, though there is much of laughter in Nietzsche and his later work can be viewed through the eyes of the comic. Strangely to some, Hegel appreciates comedy, especially that of Aristophanes, and while one might endorse his approval, his reasons for it one might not endorse (see my *Beyond Hegel and Dialectic*, chapter 6). One thinks too of Socrates at the end of *Symposium* and the encomia of eros and the drunken intoxication following: the same artist could write the tragic and the comic. Who would that artist be? One suspects Plato is indirectly and deviously talking about himself. There is something questionable in a thinker deficient in laughter. One thinks

recalling that in the ancient world, the festivals of Dionysus had *agōnes* for comedy as well as tragedy. Dionysus is the god of theater, and the complex religious character of the Dionysia is not to be forgotten. This character is intertwined with the political life of the city, of course, though in so far as tragedy is the "goat song" we are on a threshold between "nature" and "culture" (to use a later idiom). One thinks too of that same threshold in terms of the satyr play: satyr—half animal, half human, along with the Silenus, companions of Dionysus. Satire too is a kind of comedy. In these ancient comedies, and here we are thinking of Aristophanes, Dionysus is a frequently present figure. One thinks of his "Frogs": frogs singing in the underworld, for Dionysus is also Hades (remember Heraclitus, Fr.B 15), and here Dionysus is mistaken for his servant, Xanthias, and subject to a beating. Dionysus feels the pain, just like his servant—the god, mis-identified, suffers as a human slave. Bringing low the god, there is something of a participatory character to comedy, a kind of democracy of the low. As with Dionysus the wine god, there is also revelry and drinking, and it has been suggested that comedy comes from *comos*, meaning revel/riot, and *ode*, meaning song: *kōmōidía*—song of revelry. It has also been suggested and disputed that comedy has to do with Comus, spirit of harvests. Dionysus is a suffering god of renewal, but Comus, said to be his son, is sometimes his companion, along with Gelos (laughter). We are dealing with the spirit of fertility and harvests, perhaps somehow more full than Dionysus, if one could be more full than full.[3] These suggestions are to be thought about seriously, and yet not with deadly seriousness.

My question is: If we do affirm the low things, is this a low thing? Is there a noble laughter that in affirming the low things is indeed affirmative of the low things—without a lowering of spiritual nobility, indeed rather with a surprising elevation? Is there the promise of agapeic affirmation? Too true, there is so much of absurdity in human life, so much so that without it human life would not be human at all. To affirm the human is to affirm this absurdity. But how affirm, what affirm? For there are different ways of affirmation.[4] Some of these I will explore in relation

---

of Heidegger, a deadly serious thinker, totally devoid of a sense of humor, excepting a few streaks of sarcasm against inauthenticity, and episodic diatribes against the darkening of the world (if one could only find an element of black humor in these).

3. I speak of the pagan, but we should not forget the miracle of an impossible birth to Abraham and Sarah, who laughs: Isaac—*Yitskhaq*—"he will laugh" (see Genesis 21:6).

4. We need to heed the wisdom in Nietzsche's claim that the Greeks were superficial out of profundity, a profound statement uttered as if superficially. What happens

to what I call redeeming laughter. Redeeming laughter in a double sense: redeeming laughter from the imputation of the "merely" trivial or base because trivially dealing with the base; redeeming laughter as communicating laughter as itself redemptive—an elemental power of festive affirmation of deep ontological significance, one in radical intimacy with the absurdity and its transformation from a malign absurdity into a benign surd. I will not deny another double sense, namely, the saturated equivocity of laughter wherein we find violence and festive affirmation.[5] What does the festive affirmation do to the violence? Laughing at or with the absurdity does absurd things with the absurdity: turns it towards festive, ontological affirmation, without avoidance of the absurdity.

I am not avoiding the fact that some laughter can be violence, say, towards unapproved others, people of a different skin color, or facial contours. Bergson speaks of the comic "demanding something like a momentary anaesthesia of the heart. Its appeal is to intelligence, pure and simple."[6] But think of when we laugh, perhaps nervously, when a villain is hit on the head, or the gruesome scene, when a body is disposed of in a wood chipper (in the film *Fargo*, 1996). An energy other than that of the intellect is at play. I would say that laughter brings us back to something elemental: the (aesthetic) body beside itself. I will come to the body beside itself, whether in weeping or in laughing, but what is our sense of the ethos of being wherein this body finds itself? Thinkers have spoken of *homo ridens*, and yet when we try to give a univocal definition of the human or of laughter the results are themselves risible, such as Plato's joke, the featherless biped (*Statesman*, 266e). Diogenes the Cynic had his own joke in response when he plucked a chicken and brought it to the lecture room with the words: "Here is Plato's man" (Diogenes Laertius, *Lives of the Eminent Philosophers*, Bk VI, ch. 2, 40).

---

in the Nietzschean depths and on the surface is not now the issue. He too was attracted to the tale of the Bull of Phalaris, but also horrified at it. But is there a laughter not only superficial out of profundity but profound in its superficiality?

5. The doubleness of the saturated equivocity, comically inflected, is evident in the contrast of Aristophanes's *Birds* which takes us into the *upper world*, the other world, though it is cloud-cuckoo land, with 24 kinds of birds, played by men, and *Frogs* which takes us into the impossible-to-avoid *underworld*, with a chorus of singing frogs, played by men, and Dionysus, seeking to bring Euripides back from Hades, but misidentified as his own slave Xanthias, because they have exchanged clothes and no longer are easily separable as god and man.

6. Bergson, *Laughter*, 3.

What "propositions" does laughter affirm or deny? There is a trans-propositional energy at work in it. In our time we often encounter a pervasive sense of the absurdity of being. What has laughter to say of this absurdity, to this absurdity? I will be concerned with what to me is an incongruous juxtaposition: the stress of this ethos of absurdity with an equal stress on our freedom as autonomy, especially as moral beings. Not infrequently, in this ethos of absurdity we sing hymns to our autonomy and its power to "create" its own "values" in the face of absurdity. But does radical absurdity make autonomy also absurd? Do we, the autonomous ones, squint at it with one eye open, one eye shut? We say: we recuperate "meaning" through the "values" that our ethical and aesthetic self-determination "create." Has laughter something to do with puncturing the pretensions of claims to such self-determining power? How do the passion of being and our absurd endeavor appear in light of these questions? We stumble again and again on Macbeth's desolate outcry that life comes to nothing, being nothing but a tale told by an idiot, full of sound and fury, signifying nothing. Who would deny that there are some idiocies signifying nothing, but are some tales told with redeeming laughter and idiot wisdom?

## The Release of Laughter and Virtue

I begin high up and descend lower: high up with virtue, lower down later with the (aesthetic) body. Such a descent is not far from the spirit of laughter, what I will call the release of laughter.

Can we speak of *humor and virtue*, perhaps humor as itself witnessing to a kind of virtue? I take it that we need to acknowledge the source of "virtue" in *vir*, in *vis*, in *virtus*—matters dealing with power, given in the ancient usage the connotation of manly power, not connected with the woman or with the child. One might connect this ancient usage with a formation of a masculine *conatus*. A tie with courage and the excellences of the warrior are certainly present in the ancient usage. In due course, the range of virtue extends to women also, but the connection with our endeavor and power to be continues. It was something of this sense that Machiavelli expresses with his praise of *virtù*, a praise echoed by Nietzsche. It includes reference to sovereign power and the performance of mighty deeds. In my usage, *virtù* and erotic sovereignty would go together. One can see how tragedy concerns itself with high nobility in the relevant sense.[7] We stop in our tracks should we be tempted to laugh at the virtue of the erotic sovereign. One relevant instance (as recounted by Mary Beard): the story goes of how in imperial Rome the senator Cassio Dio tells of how he had to suppress his laughter at the ridiculousness of Emperor Commodus playing gladiator in the games. He stifles his laughter by chewing on laurel leaves. He is not quite biting his lips, but he is forcing the appearances away from an outburst of laughter. Laughter in the face of such a tyrannical Caesar was too dangerous, mortally dangerous.[8]

Of course, we can think of virtue in less extreme, more moderate or middling forms. We can think of virtue in Aristotelian terms with reference to the full self-actualization of our powers; or in Kantian terms, with reference to the proper moral activation of our rational autonomy. In both cases, we deal again with power, our powers, powers over ourselves, and proper actualization of those powers. Virtue invokes not least the rational mastery over ourselves and our own powers. It is not passive, even if it might contain passive dimensions. It deals with the (self-) actualization of our powers. We sometimes think of virtue in terms of a righteous person who stands by their dignity—a not un-Kantian way of speaking of being master of one's soul, even in the face of indignity and misfortune. At an extreme this can pass into a moral righteousness bordering on priggishness.

And laughter? Something about laughter dissolves our mastery over ourselves. There is an element of the involuntary that upends our endeavor to be (ourselves). Something other comes up in us, comes over us, and we are laughed at or we laugh, even laugh at ourselves. Something is released in laughter that robs us of full self-composure and mastery over ourselves. You could say: the moment a Stoic laughs, he or she is no longer a Stoic. Laughter makes evident that there is something "not up to us," over which we lose control, though the humiliation can be exhilarating. There is an involuntary side to this, though we may will not to laugh and short-circuit the energy it releases, say, in the name of standing on one's dignity. The wise man of ancient times was admonished not to laugh, at least not too much. Consult Aristotle, though interestingly there is much laughter and comedy in Socrates and Plato, the putative puritan

7. Something of the noble finesse of power is contained in our word: *virtuoso*

8. See Beard, *Laughter in Ancient Rome*, 1–8. One notices the language of the mouth, an opening of the body: biting one's lip, or keeping one's tongue in one's cheek—the mouth differently composed for different laughters.

philosopher of the pursed lips. If there is an involuntary side, what has this to do with the porosity of being and the *passio essendi* of our own being? Much, I would say. The will, *voluntas*, is not irrelevant, but I see a new willingness possible in laughter, a festive energy of affirmation that merits philosophical pondering.

I ask: is there a release of laughter that serves as an elemental overcoming of moral righteousness? The issue might be approached from a number of different perspectives. One might focus on the comic, but of course there are different forms of the comic, of which humor is one. One might speak of the contrast of humor, say, with irony, or satire, or sarcasm, or farce, or lampoon, and so on. But all forms of the comic require that we have a *sense of humor*. This sense of humor provides a kind of umbrella under which different kinds of laughter can gather. I will be less interested in a taxonomy of genres of the comic as in this embracing sense of humor, and (for now) the significance for virtue of the release of laughter.

In more ascetic traditions, whether philosophical or religious, laughter and the comic generally have been looked on with suspicion as detrimental to moral virtue, since they seems to focus on flawed human beings, with their various vices and follies, not least those associated with our "lower" nature, namely the body. To think of humor as a virtue seems counter to these traditions, for it is undoubtedly the case that comedy can be subversive of the high pretensions of the human being: it betrays our noble inspirations as having secret roots in baser origins. To give too much time and attention to this can seem to celebrate the base instead of to encourage the noble. Laughter can even be alarming to the political lords, the sovereigns of worldly power, if it implies that "nothing is sacred." A leader who becomes the butt of ridicule can quickly lose his or her authority. Laughter must be disciplined. I think of the German man who taught his chimpanzee to give the Nazi salute. He was quickly packed off to the concentration camp.[9]

9. Mary Beard's opening story was about the risible display of Commodus at the gladiatorial games in imperial Rome, but on the comic subversion of sovereignty in the former Soviet Union, Ben Lewis says in "Hammer & Tickle": Historian Roy Medvedev looked through the files of Stalin's political prisoners and concluded that 200,000 people were imprisoned for telling jokes, such as this: Three prisoners in the gulag get to talking about why they are there. "I am here because I always got to work five minutes late, and they charged me with sabotage," says the first. "I am here because I kept getting to work five minutes early, and they charged me with spying," says the second. "I am here because I got to work on time every day," says the third, "and they

There is something basic about laughter, basic though not necessarily base. There is also something celebratory about it without which life might be prudent, pinched, and prudish, but it would also be joyless. Humor may call the pretenses of certain views of virtue into question, but it may also contribute to a more finessed sense of virtue and human flourishing.

We usually associate moral virtue with the kind of person we determine ourselves to be. The stress falls on what lies within the power of self-determination. There may be differences between, say, the Aristotelian and the Kantian view, with acknowledgement of the role of good fortune in the former. Nevertheless, virtues are witnesses primarily of what lies within the power of the *acting self*. There is something about humor that cannot be simply determined by the acting self. There is an element of the involuntary. We cannot just will ourselves to laugh. (Equally, we cannot *tickle* ourselves into laughter that is self-produced. And kiss ourselves?[10]) This would be *forced laughter;* though interestingly, forcing ourselves to laugh may cause us to laugh truly, and others to laugh with us; we realize the absurdity of forced laughter, and then we truly laugh.) There is a dimension of *surprise* in a humorous situation.[11] Something funny manifests itself and we are *overcome* with laughter. Laughter releases something not fully in the voluntary power of the acting self. This is one of the reasons it cannot be entirely fitted with moral virtue as defined to fall within our powers of self-determination. A person with a keen sense of humor is someone with a certain finesse for this "something." She or he is a ludic virtuoso of what is beyond virtue

What is this "something"? I invoke here the *passio essendi*, the patience of being prior to our *conatus essendi*, our endeavor to be. Normally

---

charged me with owning a Western watch."

10. Researchers on the physiology of tickling and laughing distinguish between *gargalesis* and *knismesis:* the former, evoked by a pressure on parts of the body, cannot be self-induced, but it is laughter-producing; the latter type of tickle can be elicited by a light motion across the skin, but it is not associated with laughter. We can be tickled to the point of pleasurable helplessness, and the laughing turns into crying—the question is of knowing when to stop. See Phillips, *On Kissing, Tickling and Being Bored*, 9–11. Can we truly kiss ourselves? Shylock: "If you prick us do we not bleed? If you tickle us, do we not laugh. If you poison us, do we not die." (*Merchant of Venice*, 3, 1). Elemental humanness: neither Jewish nor Christian, neither male nor female, neither Muslim nor pagan.

11. Or witticism: Oscar Wilde on the death of Little Nell, surely a tear-jerker of Dickens—"One must have a heart of stone to read the death of Little Nell without laughing." Prompting the question: What kind of heart does one have if one laughs?

moral virtue is associated with what lies within the power (*virtus*) of the *conatus essendi* and its determination of itself. But there can be a discrepancy or discordance or disjunction between the *passio essendi* and how we give form to the *conatus essendi*. There can be forms of virtue, say moral righteousness, which are actually in denial of this *passio essendi*. The latter is beyond the full determination of the moral self, and hence the self-righteous person acts as if it had nothing to do with her or him. He or she lays claim to have overcome the *passio essendi*. In fact, there is no such overcoming of the *passio essendi*, since it is a constitutive dimension of the kinds of being we are: given to be before we give ourselves our own self-definition.

In the proverbial example: the pompous professor "standing on his dignity" holds his head aloft but fails to see the banana skin on the path before him—he slips, he is upended, he falls, we laugh. His dignity is bruised. His *gravitas* suffers from gravity. But this fall, when seen in the releasing light of laughter, shows the humanity of the professor in a truer light. The *passio essendi* is revealed as more primordial than the *conatus essendi*. The latter has become unfaithful to the former, and the humorous situation brings home to us the truth of this infidelity. The release of laughter can be the release of a joy in the very *passio essendi* itself, an affirming of something secretly worthy of affirmation, reserved in the energizing sources of our being fully alive as human. The affirming is not like a determinate yes to this or that, and yet it is a yes. I would say an overdeterminate yes, not an indeterminate one. We are yessed, so to say, rather than that we say yes. Joy, in one sense, affirms nothing; it is nothing but the gift of enjoyment. Enjoying is a being joyful, affirming nothing and yet nothing but affirming. There sounds a song that sings itself and we are in the song and sing along.

We need not deny that there are ways of laughing that are cruel, even vicious: they take joy in the humiliation of the human being. Much laughter may well be of that sort, when we delight to behold the involuntary return of the other to an unwilled patience of being. (*Schadenfreude*: delight in the sufferings of other.)[12] But there can be a release of laughter,

12. There is a set of theories about laughter that associate it with the delight in superiority over the (lower) other (Aristotle and Hobbes differently). In laughter there is a mixing of the involuntary and voluntary. In wit there is intelligence that in an almost unknowing way dips deep into something darker. Where Freud speaks of jokes and their relation to the unconsciousness, the suspension of the censor, and the springing up of the id, I would speak of the porosity, and its being surprised by odd turbulence between the *passio* and *conatus*. When Bergson speaks of the contrast of

and a return of and to the *passio essendi* whose character is a *compassio essendi*: we laugh not at but with the other. While forms of laughter like sarcasm laugh *at* the perhaps humiliated other, humor tends to laugh *with* the other, and so can be marked by a forgiving humility rather than a judging humiliation. This can suggest a shared affirmation of our finitude, even in its negative aspects, and in its tendencies to absurdity.

There is, however, a surd that is not just absurd: the idiocy of being, communicated in the *passio essendi*. The idiocy of being is intimately related to the release of laughter: the "that it is at all," beyond all systematic determination: a surd, there, and yet the elemental and primordial givenness allowing further all forms of self-determination—most of which are in flight from the idiocy of being—only to be later revealed as just as deeply entangled in laughable idiocy, just in their flight from idiocy. There is no escape.

The release of laughter returns us, more often than not involuntarily, to this *passio essendi*, by surprising ways that overcome, and overturn, the claimed self-sufficiency of moral righteousness. All of this calls into question any claims for absolute self-sufficiency on the part of moral virtue. This is not without its moral significance, and indeed there is something intimately related to human virtue about the sense of humor itself. The sense of humor in a person reflects a character marked by a more or less habitual attunement to the *passio essendi* and to the recurrent discordances between it and the overreaching claims of the *conatus essendi* in human life. The release of laughter may harbor the promise of overcoming moral righteousness, but if so, it does so in a manner revealing what

the mechanical and the living, the *elan vital*, he is on to something—laughter bears less on mechanical univocity as on, by contrast with this, becoming and the surprise of the emergent and unexpected. I would say we are surprised by a festive affirmation of life, even in its absurdity—laughter mysteriously can redeem the absurdity or mystery of life's energies, mad as the wind and rain. What of incongruity theories? (Yogi Berra about a particular restaurant: "No one goes there nowadays, it's too crowded.") These theories are not wrong, but not fully right, are right and not right. But strangely: what is laughable, just in incongruity, is what is most congruous with us. Superiority theories, such as those of Aristotle and Hobbes? They too are right and wrong: right in dealing with being above and being below; wrong in occluding the festive affirmation in stressing its shadow, namely, contempt for the inferior. True laughter is agapeic. It is not satanic or infernal (Baudelaire sees malice in the comic and shares the superiority view in the way he stresses the human as more than nature). Infernal laughter: See the story Beard (*Laughter in Ancient Rome*, 6) cites about Caligula: he forced a man to watch the killing of his son in the morning and in the afternoon "invited" him to dinner where he was forced to laugh and joke.

is more truly right concerning the *humanness* of moral virtue. Bringing us back to what we are, it can release us to what is beyond us. Its moral significance is transmoral.

## Humor beyond Self-righteousness

We can see the point relative to Aristotle's sense of virtue. Aristotelian virtue (*arête*) has to do with the ethical excellences that express the fullest flourishing of human powers, ingrained in the habitual character of a person, and his or her consistent acts. Virtues are connected to our powers, and their actualization through what we do habitually: what we do habitually comes to define the kinds of persons we make ourselves to be. Aristotle is clear that we are dealing with what lies within human power. Ethics does not deal with the necessary or the unchangeable, but with what might be otherwise and within our power to actualize. There are different ways of actualizing human power, of course, and not all of them are appropriate to human existence, nor to the kinds of being we are and are to be. It is importantly true that the *fullest flourishing* of human excellence does not lie completely without our own power. Circumstances of life play their role, the kind of political community we find ourselves in, as well as our native gifts and talents. The element of the unforeseen, of good or bad fortune, can play a significant role.[13]

There is the fact too that in the Greek notion of *eudaimonia* there is nested the granting of the *daimon*. Not enough is made of this usually, and certainly not if we use the word "happiness" to translate it. The *daimon* is between, *metaxu*, mortals and divinities, and thus refers our humanness to the transhuman: daimonic powers that ambiguously interplay with human powers and that in their otherness can have immense consequences for the way humans exercise their own powers. *Eudaimonia* also reminds us that the good daimon (*eu-daimon*) places us in an *ambiguous space between* the mortal and the divine. There are transhuman powers, above or below, that define our own intermediate character as between beings. Still I would say that, even given many qualifications that place certain constraints on human powers, virtue refers us primarily to the *conatus essendi*, our endeavor to be, and to be ourselves, and to be as

13. There is an important discussion of politics and music in Aristotle, *Politics*, Bk VIII, music in the encompassing Greek sense of *ta musika*, and connected with pedagogy (as is also the case with Plato in the *Republic* and the *Laws*).

self-actualizing of our immanent powers to the fullest extent possible for us.[14]

There is a certain satisfaction with self that can come out of a conviction that one has brought one's moral powers to their fullest expression. We speak of *moral righteousness*: I have done my duty—spoken with a certain pride that one has not deviated from the law, and that as observant thereof one is not to be judged lacking. Indeed, if anything, one's self-possession places one best in the position to judge—and perhaps to condemn. One might think of this more in a Kantian than Aristotelian register, in that one thinks of the Kantian moral agent, meeting the moral law, as confident in its own powers of self-determination, at home with itself, and filled with a certain self-respect: standing on his or her dignity. Bear in mind also that *virtus* in the Roman sense is related to the notion of *dignitas*. This sense of dignity is not quite the Christian or the Kantian sense, but it has to do with *one's standing*. I return below to laughter and "standing on one's dignity."[15]

Kantian dignity, of course, is inseparable from an understanding of the moral person as having worth but not a price. We respect and appreciate worth, we haggle about price. The moral person is an end in themselves, not a means to an end other than or beyond themselves. But is there a double edge to this nobility of moral worth? For one can so "stand on one's dignity" and be full of a self-respect that borders of "being full of oneself." The temptation is of the pride of righteousness that, thinking of itself as above reproach, looks down on others still sullied by the ungoverned passions, and the middle condition of muddle and undignified compromise. Standing on one's dignity: one is assured that one's power of

14. Obviously I am not using *conatus essendi* here in a specifically Spinozistic sense, though that is relevant in its own way (overcoming the passivity of the emotions and passions by the activity of the understanding and so on). Some forms of laughter can be gleeful malice—or glee bordering on blithe cruelty. I commented already in chapter 5 on Spinoza's glee in throwing flies to spiders, and Schopenhauer's revulsion to this (*Parerga and Paralipomena*, I, 73). One could not offer Spinoza the praise: "He would not hurt a fly." Compare Aquinas on flies: "Our knowledge is so weak that no philosopher was ever able to investigate properly the nature of a single fly. Hence we read that one philosopher passed thirty years in solitude in order that he might know the nature of the bee." See Ramos, ed., *Beauty, Art, and the Polis*, 109.

15. Roman *virtus* was connected to "outstanding deeds" (*egregia facinora*), great achievements which bring *gloria* and *fama* (the recognition of others). *Dignitas* thus was connected with public standing and office, *honos*, (we still speak of "dignitaries" in this respect). The connection of *gloria* with military excellence is evident in two exemplars of *virtus* recognized by the Romans: Cincinnatus and Pompey.

self-determination is and has been answerable to itself alone. One strives for the ideal condition of being not vulnerable, not exposed, not porous; not open to the *passio*, since one claims to be its successful master, hence also not open to the call of compassion—and this all in the name of the moral law of which righteousness claims to be the principled fulfillment. The pride of moral righteousness can show, paradoxically, a kind of moral corruption in the heights of ethical excellence. It is and knows itself to be in the right; how then could it possibly be in the wrong?

If there is possible a paradoxical corruption here, it is one that cannot be convinced of this in terms of its own (rational) self-determination—for this is the basis of its own superior self-possession. How could what is excellent be corrupting? How could virtue be the mask of vice? Yet we do sense intuitively that this pride of moral self-righteousness is not as much in the right as it claims for itself to be. Moreover, if it is thus, it cannot be released from its plight through itself alone. Its very power over itself is its own debilitation. For every move reasserts the dominion of its own self-determination, and it is just this dominion that has settled into corrupt self-satisfaction. One might think that there are many ways in which this circle might be broken up. Such forms of the release come from beyond self—in that breakdown may herald the breakthrough of something further than selving caught circling in the loop of itself. But what is at issue here must be a breakthrough that is not just an externally imposed release from self. It must be a release from beyond selving that makes its impact felt within selving—something transcendent striking within immanence—something transcendent emerging from within the immanence of the self-transcending of the *conatus essendi* itself. One might say that it would be all the more truly effective if it came from within—for this is just the terrain on which the self-closure of moral righteousness is erected, defended, and gloried in.

Humor, I hold, has something to do with this release of a kind of beyond that is also a within: a transcendence that emerges, erupts from the intimacies in immanence, that shows the limit of self-determination in self-determination, the limit of self-mastering virtue in the most human of things—a kind of forgiving release. And it may not even be known that there is a forgiveness offered again and again in this release—the self-righteousness may keep closing in on itself again and again—may not accept the eruption until at last it learns to laugh at itself.

## God Kisses the Mud

Turning now from virtue more directly to humor, significantly other considerations come before us.[16] In a number of passes I will offer some extended thoughts on these. Later I will come back to the person of humor as manifesting a kind of virtue that is indeed a human excellence but that is not an excellence simply the product of our self-determination. You must be kissed by another or kissed; you can't kiss yourself—not on the mouth anyway, not *ad-oro*.

First we might consider humor, as lying on the boundary of what is within the power of the endeavor to be, in connection with *the humors*: being in a good humor, for instance. In an earlier time, the humors were associated with the elements: fire, air, earth, water, but especially the fluid element.[17] We need not go into the details, but the connection with something elemental is significant. In the past a connection of humor with *humus* was proposed, but the etymology is disputed. Nevertheless, one can see why the connection, inaccurate as it may be, would come to mind. *Humus:* the earth, stuff (*stof*) into which the breath of the divine is said to be blown at the origin of our humanness. The humus becomes human because of this breath: inspired, inspirited. The humus becomes human through the spirit of the divine breathing in and through the stuff (*stof*).[18] There is no humanity without this humus. There is also a base, so to say, of this idiotic stuff, this matter, that is a kind of elemental surd of our being. A double givenness is basic, so to say: the stuff, and the breath of spirit.

16. These are related to the question I put about Moral Perfectionism to Cavell at the end of a previous reflection, "A Second Primavera."

17. The fluid element particularly is transient, passing, resistant to being determinately pinned down or fixed, and so runs the risk of flux-gibberish, and hence madness and laughter, though there is more to it all than this. The etymology of humor is said to be connected to the "fluid or juice of an animal or plant," from Anglo-Norman *humor*, from Old French *humor*, from Latin *umor* ("body fluid"), connected to *umere* (to be wet or moist). Ancient and medieval physiology dealt with the four fluids of the body, blood, phlegm, choler, and black bile (melancholy). One's state of mind and being were determined by balance or imbalance of these four. Heraclitus thought that dry souls are best. See my "Flux-gibberish."

18. An idiom in English for nonsense, for idiocy: "stuff and stuff." Our "*creativity*" and the breath: we are not "creating" the surge of air, but riding its surge—we are ourselves a surge. This is not just a second wind, but a wind that is sometimes at our back and we float, sometimes a headwind and we are lifted, running into its opposition.

Humor is intimately bound up with this double givenness, which qua doubleness is the basis of something equivocal about the human being: neither matter nor spirit but both, and yet neither, and yet again a unity in which the two are kneaded together into an unsteady, fertile, and flighty integrity. Humor has much to do with the stuff, but in its human character as both stuff and spirit. Is this what is funny: God adores the humus? *Ad-ora*: to the mouth, as in the kiss of the lover, breath quick and quickening. God kisses the mud: mouth to mud the divine breathes, and we come alive. (The intimacy of breathing: we don't notice it until we are choked up; released from the choke we breathe freely again.) In adoration of the creature, God creates a song-and-dance man. (Or perhaps God sings and we dance—or sulk.) We breathe, but we blow it, when we come to believe we breathe only through ourselves alone. Laughter happens when we come to recognize we have blown it. The blowing of the divine is compassionately more than our having blown it. That breath blows in us again, and we breathe freshly once more.[19]

One might wonder here about breath and the lack often associated with *eros:* breath, like the lack, almost nothing, yet not nothing. The lack is associated with *penia* (in the account of Socrates-Diotima), but less often is the "resource" of *poros* foregrounded. Is *poros* related to porosity? Is there a resource of *poros* intimately related to the porosity at the source of our being religious? Is there a resource in lacking itself that is not just a simple expression of power but intimately connected with porosity? *Poros* also has some connotation of a "way across." Porosity enables a passage through or across: something that is not any one thing, or an energy, an energy that seems like nothing, passes or is communicated from one to another. *Poros* names the making of a way: a transition that is no transition; since in making a way, it makes way and hence there is a withdrawal in the very opening of the way. The passage, or passing through, cannot be fixed as this or that; so it seems nothing, but in another sense it is not nothing: it is a way being made; a making way; an original coming to be. In some such wise I think of the between as constituted as a space of primal porosity. (One might put this in a somewhat different

19. To come down again to stuff: Piero Manzoni not only "created" *Merda d'Artista*, he also "created" "*Corpi d'Aria*" (Bodies of Air), an edition of forty-five balloons on tripods, with different prices, depending on whether the buyer blew them up or the artist. He also "created" "*Fiato d'Artista*" (*Artist's Breath*), a series of inflated balloons, red, white, or blue, on a wooden base, with the inscription "Piero Manzoni—Artist's Breath."

idiom: being created out of nothing, but as something, and as good, by the agapeic origin.) Porosity would itself be a kind of poverty, but a gifted poverty of being that is always rich beyond itself.

It would repay attention here to think upon the elemental human body: elemental because it partakes of the elements, hence is humorous. Humus: our body is not neutral stuff. Our body is, so to say, a laughing matter. I would connect matter with *mater*, the mother, the maternal element, and this is laughing matter in a benign sense. Something comes to birth in the matter, evident in *conatus*, as a *con-natus*, a being born with, but even more evident in the *passio* and the porosity. The body, or perhaps better, our being embodied, is the birth and coming to incarnation of "value," of worth, of an ontological affirmation of the good of the "to be." This is not moral worth in a Kantian sense. I use the term "worth" rather than "value," since value has too much the connotation of being primarily relative to us. Worth may well be what we value, but worth can be worthy *of itself*, rather than a function of our evaluation. We value the worthy; the worth is not simply the mirror of our evaluation. If value risks being subjectivistic, worth however is not objectivistic. There is something trans-subjective, trans-objective about this worth. This is a point I made about life in my reflection on the surface of things (chapter 2). The endeavor to be of our bodied being is already a self-affirmation that participates in this ontological affirmation of the good of the "to be." (Perhaps it might even be better to think of this wording of the mud as an ontological song.) To be embodied is to be the incarnation of such an ontological worth before one more mindfully participates in various "values," either shared with or communicated from the already-given world, or brought to form through one's own original contribution. This incarnation of "value," I think, has to be taken in an ontological sense, because it has to do with the good of the "to be" in which we live, before we live it. This sense of ontological worth is connected to the *passio essendi* as prior to the *conatus essendi*. Our being embodied as *passio essendi* incarnates ontological worth, lives the good of the "to be," in a sense that is prior to our efforts to be this or that, through our powers developed this way or that. The body, as it were, is *beside itself* before it determines itself: not beside itself just posterior to its own self-determination but *prior* to that. This other ontological sense of worth *precedes*, as well as *exceeds*, full expression in terms of our self-determining powers.[20]

20. It thus can never enter into full self-possession. Self-possession, such as it is, is nourished from sources that "possess" us rather than we possessing them. "Possession"

This preceding, as well as outliving excess, might be approached through a number of different manifestations,[21] but elemental happenings like laughing and weeping are very instructive: instructive because elemental, and because one might argue that with them the tension of the *passio essendi* and the *conatus essendi* is shown, though what is shown cannot be fitted into an exhaustive discursive conceptualization. We participate in what is shown, though what we participate in we do not, perhaps cannot, determinately know. We are made to be beside ourselves. And perhaps that is what we are made to be.

## On the Body Beside Itself

What does it mean to speak of the body beside itself? Obviously the body is an object that can be measured: it can be weighed, its features enumerated, its fat ratios calculated, it can be burned like wood and its energy output measured. Like any other physical object, it has determinate characteristics for which we can account more or less univocally. It is itself and nothing but itself, here and not there, now and not then, and so on. It seems to conform entirely to Bishop Butler's dictum: a thing is itself and not anything other. One might call this the univocal principle: a thing has one and only one determinate identity whose character is also fully determinable.

How then can we speak at all of the "body beside itself"? For this seems to transgress the univocal principle. It seems to imply the paradoxical position of both being itself and not being itself: in itself and outside itself: itself and not itself at one and the same time. This is surely an *equivocal*, if not outright contradictory position, if the univocal principle or Butler's dictum about identity is to be taken as the last word. The univocal mind finds this logically laughable, though it does not get the point

is not the right word if it is taken in a meaning too close to "property." Being embodied is not just a property. We are "possessed" of life, but we are never our own possession; nor are we the "property" of anything else either, when we are "possessed." Passion of being is a self-transcending energy, first gifted and in that sense "possessed," then capable of some self-possession, always qualified. All self-possession is dispossessed of itself by being given to itself more originally as "possessed"—but all of this is a *release*, not a *servitude*—though it may become a *service*.

21. The naked body of Job: "Naked I came out of my mother's womb, naked shall I go back to the earth. . . . Blessed be God for ever." The extremity of the *passio essendi: exposure to the extremes of blessing and curse, God and Satan.*

of the risibility. The human body as the incarnation of a kind of elemental equivocity is inseparable from our feel for the comic.[22]

We all know from experience something about the body being beside itself. Here are three examples. *Rage*: something surges up in us, a fire that overtakes us and we "lose it," as we put it in English. We say: I was beside myself with rage, incandescent with rage. The "red mist" came over me and I could not hold back. We say it *after* we have come back to ourselves and calmed down. *Erotic arousal:* the body, once cold and contained within itself, finds itself caressed first and then warmed and then it is no longer calm, but energies arise from who knows where and there it is outside itself, beyond itself beside itself. (*The mere touch of another* can also cause one to recoil in revulsion; in other situations, a mere touch can be strangely consoling. All witness to our bodies as immediately saturated with worth.) *Drunkenness:* first drink, the world of other-being is indifferent, even hostile; second drink, a softening, a release; third drink, the world is not an enemy but beginning to be rosy; another drink, and soon one is falling into the arms of being, and all is well with the world and all manner of things will be well. Ecstasy slept and now it wakens. The intoxicated body has forgotten itself as imprisoned in constraining determinacies and awakens to its drunkenness outside of itself beside itself.

We can seek to give determinate explanations for the mechanisms of what happens to the brain and body in the imbibing of drink, or in sexual arousal. Interestingly, rage is less specific, even though objective science can tell us of the flow of adrenaline and so on. But why be enraged with *this* rather than *that*? Why be beside oneself with *this* rather than *that*?[23]

22. The point is also relevant to any effort at reductive materialism or naturalism. Two instances worth thought: the naked body as saturated with equivocity: empty of covering, still full of communication; the dead human body, there is something uncanny even sacred about it, it is a crime to desecrate it.

23. There is something singular, perhaps even idiotic, about the precipitating occasion. It is interesting that one of the Greek words for rage, for fury, namely *orgē*, is the word from which derives "orgy," "urge," and one can see a perplexing porosity between raging urge and *eros*. Some recent studies suggest that most murders happen without anticipation: a stray word, an insult, a quarrel escalating and it gets out of hand: the rage awaiting its out—outcome? Rage *eros* and the urge to kill and destroy: we furiously desire and *thanatos* overtakes us. Wars: idiotic precipitating occasion, as in World War I, and the devastation takes over—the power of negation unloosed—the *nihil*. See the point about "great" wars in my *Is There a Sabbath for Thought?* chapter 9, "Enemies: On Hatred." Without the corruption of the idiotic intimacy there would be no wars, but the corruption takes place in darkness, out of the light of our rational

The mechanisms may be homogeneous; the being beside oneself is often bound up surprisingly with specific occasions or precipitating persons or events. This point is obvious with *eros:* this woman leaves me cold, and I can say she is pretty but to me only abstractly ravishing, so to say, nothing more; but this other woman, ugly as sin, does move me, and I do not know why. I am beside myself inexplicably, surprised by this other, surprised by myself as surprised. I have found myself beyond myself before I know why I am there. It is as if I have been stolen from myself before I realized I have been robbed of myself; and yet I am nothing but myself, and nothing has been taken from me, except perhaps my peace. There you have it again: the saturated equivocity of the body being beside itself. And while I am nothing, it is she, she of the ugly face, who is everything.

(An interlude as ludic interim: I remember when I was a teenager I had a friend who sometimes had to help in his family bar and serve, and I would wait for him while he finished work. But this was a bar into which ladies of the night and easy virtue came to mingle with visiting sailors. And one in particular I recall would sit on a bar stool and look around; but this lady was a cross-eyed prostitute and in my adolescent innocence or imbecility I could never make out who she was looking at, as she sat at the bar and looked around. Wandering eyes: her eyes crossed each other and crossed also the space between her and me, but since they simultaneously went in more directions than one, I was never sure if this Donna Dulcinea del Tobosa was looking at me or not. One eye mesmerized me, while the other cast around its cold indifference. This was discombobulating, an uncertain meeting of eyes of innocence and experience.)

I could multiply examples, but the point is especially interesting with regard to laughing and weeping. I use the present participle, in that I am less interested in "nouns" as in "verbs"—something either done or happening or a participating in something happening. Already in this being bodily as verb, and as adverbially qualified (being bodily *beside itself*), there is more than a static objectified body. It is the body as lived and living. But we find ourselves in an energy of life that lives us before we try to know it for what it is, or try to "stand back" from it and reflect. But how could one "stand back" from one's own body, since "standing back" would itself seem to be a bodily activity?

*Laughing* then: this too is the body beside itself. Something absurd happens or is said, something risible (but what is this?) and then before

---

self-consciousness. Unknowingly and yet by a kind of divine instinct, laughter dives into this darkness and surfaces again from its depths.

I realize it I am beside myself, mouth wide open, head thrown back, and this strange squealing or snorting or guffawing or sniggering or explosive sound is emerging from the body. My body may shake with laughter, I may try to repress it and then find myself exploding, I cannot stop. One can get a fit of the giggles: a fit—as if a kind of epilepsy were overcoming one. And this epilepsy of the body is happening all of the time, often unexpectedly. Strange explosions of energy. I break up with laughter. The breakdown of composure is a kind of breakthrough. (The analogy with erotic risibility is not far away: quickening of breath, opening of mouths, contorting of faces, squeals, grunts, groans, unanticipated outbursts without univocal vocabulary, faces in beaming serenity that seem also to be tortured beyond endurance, their wordless moans like pains, or prayers, and so on.)[24]

*Weeping*: the body is composed, and then something untoward happens and what is communicated pains one to the point where the composure is broken up. Pain: retraction of selving into the intimacy of the idiot. The face crumbles and a groan or a moan or a wail, or a howl may go forth and the body is beside itself in this dis-composition of itself. Look at the faces of those who weep: something is happening to them, and it is strange, and yet it is entirely intimate, for the stones do not weep, only a creature of flesh weeps.[25] It collapses in grief. It cannot stand it. It

24. Worth noting in the world of comedy is our pleasure in the fluidity and mixing of sexual identity: I am thinking of the masks and changes of sexual identity in Shakespeare's comedies, a masking heightened by the fact that the actors who played the female roles were themselves boys. Aristophanes's Lysistrata: the women threatening to withdraw sexual *sunousia* from their men till they give up war and make peace are played by men dressed as women. A low echo of such comedy is found in the (cross-dressing) Dame of the Pantomime. The film *Some Like It Hot* (1959) has been repeatedly voted as the top comedy movie (http://www.bbc.com/culture/story/20170817-why-some-like-it-hot-is-the-greatest-comedy-ever-made): two men Joe (Tony Curtis) and Jerry (Jack Lemmon) witness a murder by Chicago's most notorious gangster and his gang; they flee by disguising themselves as Josephine and Daphne ("I've never liked the name Geraldine," explains Jerry, though neither is a good drag queen), and join Sweet Sue's Society Syncopators in whose company they find Sugar Kane (Marlyn Monroe) and along the way, Osgood Fielding III (Joe E. Brown); much funniness and fun ensues in the lying, the cross-dressing, the faking of sexual identity, in the incongruous romances. The brilliant final exchange between Daphne and Osgood ("I'm a man" . . . "Nobody's perfect") puts one in mind of Lola not Lolita (with a wink to the Kinks: "Girls will be boys, and boys will be girls./It's a mixed up, muddled up, shook up world/Except for Lola . . .")

25. Niobe, all tears for her dead children, is said in the end to be turned into the "Weeping Rock" near Mount Sipylus. Stones weeping: What of the *statues of the*

is beyond standing on its dignity. It break down in tears that can deform the face, but in the deformity there is an impossible appeal.

Scientists have studied the mechanisms of laughter and weeping, though less than one would expect, given their universality in human cultures and their all-pervasiveness in everyday life. In the case of weeping, for instance, tears have been distinguished as basal, reflex, and psychic. *Basal tears* have to do with the continuous lubrication of the eye, and the composition of the liquid here has been studied (Darwin's views of weeping were focused on this). *Reflex tears* are such as those that can be induced by the use of an onion: this irritates the eye, tears follow as a reflex and as a determinate result of the irritating cause. *Psychic tears* are said to bear on certain emotions, and their chemical composition is not the same as the other two types.[26] But there are tears and tears: onion tears, crocodile tears, and there are tears. Crocodiles do not weep. As they eat their prey and as they swallow, the ducts are compressed and the tears are induced. It is we who attribute to the crocodile weeping in the metaphorical sense: those who enjoy their victims and seem to weep for them shed false tears. The crocodile does not weep false tears; it is *we* and we alone who shed crocodile tears.[27]

Weeping is an occurrence that is not exhausted by the mechanism of the tear ducts. It has everything to do with our being in certain meaningful, or meaningless, situations. This does not mean we know determinately what the meaning is. Most often we don't know at all. The shadow of a painful absurdity falls on us and we find ourselves helpless. The situation cannot be completely absurd, for absurdity as absolute could not even be recognized as such. We find ourselves in situations of saturated equivocity, marked by mixtures of some meaning and lack of meaning. We participate rather than know, and the saturated equivocity is shown

---

*Madonna*, the Mother of God, that are said to weep, or seen to weep? What does one think? A *pia fraus*, a miracle? *Lacrimae rerum*: the tears of things. Yet the things become tearful with humans. We are the *lacrimae rerum* become mindful—the stones become flesh. Tears are more often associated with women: tears as womanish. In addition to Niobe, Dido, Ruth "in tears amid the alien corn," "a cry is heard in Ramah" of Rachel refusing to dry her tears over her dead children (Melville's Ishmael was saved by the *Rachel*), Monica weeping for Augustine, Mary Magdalena, if she is the woman who washed the feet of Christ with her tears.

26. See Lutz, *Crying*, chapter 2 "The Crying Body."

27. I think of the Walrus in *Alice in Wonderland*. As he eats the oysters: "'I weep for you' the Walrus said:/'I deeply sympathize.'/Holding his pocket handkerchief/Before his streaming eyes."

in the body beside itself thus: as either weeping or laughing, and sometimes as both weeping and laughing. And this being beside itself of the body is not an optional exteriorization of a meaning or lack of meaning, otherwise inner. It is the incarnation of what cannot be fully objectified. In that sense, it is objective but not objective: there, and yet nothing is there, for what is there, when we begin to examine it? There is an ecstasis, entirely present, and entirely vanishing.

The meaning is in the happening. So it is not always easy to repeat occasions of laughter and weeping, though we may vary them. Thus, what people found funny ten years ago may now leave us cold. The jokes in Aristophanes are sometimes hard to get, because so much is dependent on the particularities of this culture and society at this one time (jokes at the expense of this politician, or general or sophist or farmer, and so on).[28] Of course, something of the energy outlasts the occasion, and this often has to do with the elementals of the flesh.[29] The evanescence of both laughing and weeping recalls too our being helpless, revealing the opposite of our self-sufficiency, something closer to the helplessness of the infant. Is the scream of laughter an echo of the scream of the *infans* communicating exposure and need, though also communicating something more: the appeal of self-affirming life reaching beyond itself, beyond lack?

This does not mean the matter is something that is subjective as opposed to objective. This is no laughing matter; this is laughing matter. Recall again my point about life as trans-objective and trans-subjective. In the present instance, we must recur to the elemental character of both laughing and weeping. They seem to be peculiar to the human being, since no other animal weeps or laughs. They are universal, to be found in all cultures, even though obviously each is shaped and formed differently in different cultures (just as there are rituals of mourning, there can be rituals of laughter).[30] There are different forms of weeping and laughing, as multitudinous as human reality itself. Not objective and not subjective, there is something *intimately universal* in this elemental character.

Perhaps a sign of this elemental character might be the common experience of laughter as *infectious*. What is this? Think of "canned"

28. See Ehrenberg, *The People of Aristophanes*.

29. Again see Desmond, *Beyond Hegel and Dialectic*, chapter 6 on this. I do not think Hegel gets it right in the *Phenomenology of Spirit* when he claims that the outcome of the Old Comedy is the realization that the Self is absolute essence (*Wesen*).

30. On how mourning is ritualized differently, see Lutz, *Crying*, chapter 5, entitled "Cultures of Mourning." See Ghose, *Shakespeare and Laughter*.

laughter. Are we laughing just at the joke? Or laughing with the cue to laugh? And yet we laugh. But is it just a mechanism? This is a macabre thought, but some of the canned laughter (on American TV) was "canned" in the 1950s. We are being infected with the laughter of the dead. Laughter: contagious beyond mortality, against mortality. Sorrow too is contagious. There is a porosity. Laughing and weeping find secret ways into our deepest porosity, even despite our most fortressed defenses. Do they not testify to an elemental porosity of being that defines us, showing in our incarnate being as beside itself, but beside itself with a passiveness deeper and wiser than all our activeness? (Perhaps Wordsworth was getting at some of this with his "wise passiveness," and Keats with his "negative capability?") But what is the porosity that allows the passage, the passing that is later expressed in the contagion. Passing from what to what? And what have laughing and weeping to do with this elemental porosity? Does not human self-transcendence, shown in the body beside itself in elementary laughing and weeping, reveal a more primal porosity of being?

The contagion reveals an intimately communal character. Only consider how laughing is often transgressive of social and moral conventions. Forms of laughter may have their conventions, but laughter is a threshold, one side of which is conventional, the other side unconventional. And yet in being on the threshold, energies in turbulence come out, breaking down one's sense of the conventional, breaking through into another sense of the conventional, on the other side of the accepted convention: a new, or renewed community of being when we break out in laughter together, beyond the constrictions of the normal conventions or already-domesticated community. This community, this convent: elemental humanity in its self-affirmation and porosity to the other, and not exhausted by any determinate human community. Something of this is, or was, ritualized in carnival, for instance: up is down, below is above, the ignoble are noble, the noble ignoble. One thinks of what was the Irish wake—the dead have become like stone, their flesh cold, but the living, warm in flesh, cry out for both the dead and the living, with a sometimes reckless playfulness, extending to young men leaping over graves (keening games: *cluichí caointe*). The festive is not the opposite of the sorrowful but its recognition and the disarming of its disablement, and release of a new enabling of affirming life.[31] ("A life-affirming titter": it is

31. See Ó Laoire, *On a Rock in the Middle of the Ocean*, 259–60. Ó Laoire witnesses (ibid., 272–76) to the dying of the wake, due to the more univocal enforcement of

true, we do not speak this way.) Recall that carnival as a religious festival is tied to Lent: fast and feast, preparation for death and resurrection of Easter. The carnival grotesqueries of Rabelais,[32] say, have roots not only in the medieval world but lost in pagan antiquity (think of the Saturnalia). We often have a univocalized view of religion in modernity as one autonomous space, often moralized without mystery, with not enough of a metaxology and its plurivocity between humans and the other powers. Comus, drunken companion of Dionysus, expresses a festive fullness, on the porous threshold of darkness, growing out of the ground, with laughter outering something above ground whose still-fertile seeds are below ground.

## Low Wisdom and the Elemental Body

We have come down from the heights of virtue to the low wisdom of the elemental body. Suppose we explore this further in relation to laughter. (Of course, we can turn up again from this low wisdom to the excellences of noble virtue.) The elemental body is not only a carrier of worth from the outside: it is the intimate living of a certain worthiness, not forgetting again the ontological dimension of all this. I develop this point in six considerations.

*First consideration*: the human body is an aesthetic incarnation of worth. "Aesthetic" here is taken in the broad sense: bearing on all that is sensuous and sensible. Aesthetic incarnation is a neutral materiality. At the most elemental, the worth at play here is ontological, since it has to do with being, with the value of simply being. The human body is a singularization of the good of the "to be." This incarnate affirmation of being: self-affirming thereness as singularly fleshed.

*Second consideration*: there is the *intimacy* of the human being, something that is always lived from within. And this living intimacy is impossible to reduce fully to objective terms. There is an idiocy to this intimacy: something not open to capture in neutral general terms. This

rules both by "civil Victorian Catholicism" (suspicious of "savage" paganism perhaps) and by modern regimes of power intent on the desacralization of life, and manifesting many forces not funny (science, technology, moralism, liberal and leftist ideology, and so on). As I said above in chapter 1, chapter 9 of this book ("Laughter and Tears") is worthy of note. He also draws attention to the connection of song and keening (*caoineadh*) (e.g., ibid., xv, 272–77).

32. As explored by Bakhtin, *Rabelais and His World*.

is so, even though the body as a material system may well be describable in such neutral general terms. For instance, a surgeon has to neutralize himself, make himself objective, in working on the flesh of another *as if* it were a machine. It is and is not a machine, and "neutralization" is itself an abstraction from his fuller human engagement with the fullness of *this* human being before him. It is not *the* body; but *my* body, *your* body: an intimately singularized *this*. This fuller human engagement surges up again when an emergency arises, or has passed (I mean after the surgery). The abstraction is itself motivated by concerns of what is valuable that do not appear *directly* in the neutralized action itself. The surgeon's mechanical work on the body as machine is not just mechanical: it is to help, to heal. The body is my own, but I do not own it; there is an intimacy of being more elemental than property. The intimate ownness of being embodied is my own, but not just owned as mine. I cannot completely objectify the bodied being I am, the "being embodied" I am. There is an intimacy of being prior to the objectifying distance that is, in some measure, needed for something to be my property. There is an *intimate propriety* prior to property, and which gives meaning to the relation of property, not the other way round.

*Third consideration*: this idiocy of the body is intimately rooted in darkness. I mean we know *surfaces*, but we know these surfaces as participating in sources that do not fully surface. The sources are on the other side of determinate cognition—but this does not mean they are not intimately known. We know them carnally. (The desire for carnal knowledge of the other has to do with the entry into, sometimes intrusion into, penetration of, the secrecy of this intimate idiotic source—in the body, on the other side of its objectification, but risking in carnal knowledge another objectification: the intimate otherness "had" rather than "tasted" in the tactile sense which shows tact for the reserved intimacy of the other.) The surface shows the recessed intimate: surfaces are the faces of the idiocy. Example: think of how an erotic caress, a touching of the skin of another, or being touched, tries to solicit to the surface sources of selving, of soul music, hidden otherwise in the idiocy of our darker intimacy.

Parenthesis with respect to the night of this darker intimacy: Think of the refreshing power of *sleep*. No one really comprehends what this is all about, though efforts at objective research into rapid eye movement (REM) and so on, have been attempted. Yet without sleep we would go mad. The consciousness that surfaces has to disappear into this intimate darkness every day. If it did not, it or we could not be resurrected as a fresh willingness and eagerness to face the day again. The self-affirmation of the day is rooted in an intimate darkness that it does not understand, though without it, we would weary and sicken and go mad. The torturer know and exploits this. A "good" torturer must have finesse: malign finesse bearing on our intimate vulnerability. A "good" torturer shares this with a seducer: finesse used to overcome or overtake (literally: take over) the other in that place of intimate vulnerability. Sleeplessness, sleep-deprivation is frequently used by torturers to *break down* the other under interrogation.

I mention an important point that binds sleep with weeping and laughing. Sleep is not only a restorative of sanity, as Macbeth knew. More deeply, it is restorative of a *native ontological faith*: lived trust and indeed pleasure in the good of the "to be." Sleep allows us a pause; and in the intimate darkness, the native ontological faith of the human being is more or less repaired and restored.

Thus Macbeth: "sleep that knits up the ravelled sleeve of care," "great nature's second course," and so on.[33] We wake to the day, and can *go on*. The self-affirming of the good of the "to be" is more or less resurrected. Lady Macbeth cannot go on. She cannot sleep, she goes mad, she kills herself. She has killed the good of the "to be," directly in complicity with the murder of Duncan, proximately in her own singularity, mediately for all by her murder of the good of the "to be" of Duncan.

We all know those days when this restoration seems not to have been effected; we can hardly get out of bed, and only an act of will gets us going, and an hour later one wants to crawl back in. The endeavor has to will itself forward, though the passion of being has dried up, and the original porosity is not a spring of energy but seems closed down. Our "yes," or our "no," to the first "yes" of the "to be"—the latter can be so battered, either through our own fault, or powers beyond us, that we find it hard to continue. Hard not just to continue to do this or that, but to *continue to be*. We may be on the verge of despair and weep. Or we may, contrariwise, learn to laugh at the absurdity.

This is an important point for laughing and weeping, I think, for both of these say something about the effect of that dark intimacy being registered in mindfulness, though what is registered is not understood. We participate in it as a happening. The darkness surfaces and yet does

33. What might the "*first course*" be? The *diurnal living* of the good of the "to be"? A course, as if were a *serving* at a feast, or a nourishing meal; or a *coursing* of energy; or the *course* of a river—marking the form of what the fluid is *in passing*.

not surface, since it is rather that the surface is cracked, either through sorrow, or the absurd. Weeping and laughing: responses to the impasse: how to go on. (Beckett: I can't go on, I must go on.)

*Fourth consideration*: nevertheless, this intimacy is not just an inwardness that is devoid of expression. The idiocy is aesthetic; the intimacy is sensuously outered, uttered in the body itself. The aesthetics of the body in this more express sense is crucial. The *passio essendi* is enfleshed.[34] When above I said the body was an aesthetic incarnation of worth, this givenness of worth is here extended—self-extending in the incarnate and communicative body. There is not only the happening of worth in our aesthetic being, but we give expression to ourselves aesthetically. Being given to be aesthetically, we give ourselves out aesthetically. And so we not only live our bodies but our bodies are our communication to what is other to ourselves. You might say that we begin more actively to shape the form of that communication, and a creative *conatus* can come to cooperate with the passion surging out of a now and newly unclosed porosity. This communication is also saturated with equivocity.

Given worth is a kind of ontological immediacy; communicated worth is a mediating of that given worth—taking form as self-mediating, and also as intermediating with others. Being embodied is beside itself in being an *outcry*. The outcry is directed to the other: I am here, and I am directed to you; but in fact, by being so directed, I am *already porous* to you, the other. Being beside ourselves, besides being ourselves, we are both already in a between. Words are the communication of that between, and of what one is, what we are. The cry, the outcry: not only crying, as in weeping, but crying as the spontaneous gesture of the body reaching out from itself to what is other—either out of need, or perhaps joy or astonishment, or care. The cry makes the body an *emphatic* communication.

The aesthetics of the body define communication as an outering sensuousness, but the outering sensuous is of the idiotic intimacy. There is a *stress of selving* in the sensuous communication. There is not just the body: the body is always already my body, your body—always singularly stressed, the aesthetic stress of a singular selving. This is the body as an emphatic: it qualifies itself as within a space between itself and others, and its emphatic presence there communicates in this space.[35] This emphatic stress is at play even when a person wants to "vanish into the woodwork," or be only "a fly on the wall."

34. See Desmond, *Ethics and the Between*, 370.

35. See Weiss, *Emphatics*.

*Fifth consideration:* if the expression is rooted in intimate darkness, it is important to see the expression as an outering that is also a self-transcending. The incarnate being is a singularized self-affirming but it is also an opening beyond itself. Remember that this opening is not only *later*. There is an opening from the origin, an opening not defined by us, but by which we are defined. I refer to the idiocy in the above sense: being given to be, before we begin to give ourselves to ourselves or to others. There is a primal givenness in the "to be" at all. No finite being determines this, since every finite being presupposes it as enabling its own power of determining. It is in excess as prior, and indeed its excess remains in all the determinations we achieve, both shadowing them as more, and outliving them as not thereby exhausted. This excess has much to do with the happenings of laughing and weeping. The opening beyond self places the embodied person in a more public world. In expressing itself in that world, it is also a recipient from others, and in an important sense here it is more recipient than determinant. If not first *spoken to* by the other, it is not clear it would be enabled to *speak to* the other; if not first "being encouraged," then no "having courage"; if not first welcomed, no exodus beyond itself; if not first given to itself, then no giving of itself to what is other to itself. So there is excess here too.

In the more public between, all the attractions and temptations of objectification emerge. Then we are overcome by forgetfulness of the intimacy at the root, and also the excess that shadows the whole process, and indeed the excess of giving others that enables us to be ourselves. For all these latter are participant in energies of transcending, and objectification deals with products or results of such energies, and so forgets the energies of transcending as beyond complete objectification.

This is especially important with respect to the living body. Being embodied is always a living of these energies of transcending. Hence a merely objective approach to it is again an abstraction from these living energies. Hence its truth, while true, is also always false.

*Sixth consideration*: there are more complex expressions of our bodily being, but I think the interpenetrating relation of the aesthetic and idiotic is important for the kind of being beside itself we find in laughter and weeping. One must remember a process of *transcending* from the idiot onwards: transcending rooted in the intimacy and aesthetic incarnated in the body. Laughing and weeping tend to happen, or respond to a stress, somewhere *between* the idiotic and the aesthetic. Something is precipitated by an occasion, often with an outerness that interrupts.

The outer stress of the occasion communicates something concerning the concordance or discordance between the outer and the intimate. Something befalls us, and we fall. Once again the grave professor, swaggering with his briefcase and his nose in the air, does not see the banana skin on the ground, and lands on his backside. We laugh. The brutality of the fall is a return to an elemental intimacy. Herr Doktor Professor is not his (socially) constructed self, he is not his social prestige and vanity. He is nothing: nothing but his vulnerable flesh and his sore backside. *He has been brought to nothing, yet there he is.* And we laugh. Or weep.

What we find here is a return to idiocy—and against the tendency of the *conatus essendi*—everything about us that strives to be for itself, to be its own master, to affirm itself and nothing but itself, to determine through itself and nothing but itself, to be master of self-determination. The *conatus* is interrupted by a contingent, innocent occasion that shows again the *passio essendi* that underlies it all, that refers us to the givenness of the beginning, and the excess that shadows all our constructed determinations, and that now exceeds them as never exhausted. *Conatus interruptus; passio essendi revivus.*

## Discordant Endeavor and the Passion of Being

Focusing on the relevant tension of the *passio essendi* and *conatus essendi*, I offer a few further reflections on weeping and laughing. The *conatus* drives itself beyond itself—to be itself. It affirms itself in order to affirm itself. This it might say about itself if it tried to give an account of itself. But there is more, when it ponders itself more. Return of, and to, the *passio essendi* (and this in weeping and laughter) is a negation of this affirmation of self, just as self-affirmation alone—even though the *passio essendi* itself is the gift of being as self-affirming. *Conatus* is a being beside self: but its temptation is to be beside itself, just to be with itself again. It seeks to be for self; in one sense rightly, but in another sense, not so rightly, for in this guise it is not quite the *ekstasis* beyond itself it might seem to be. The form of self-affirmation is such that the *passio essendi* is made hidden from view.

When there is a return to the *passio essendi*—or rather when the *passio essendi* reemerges, when it returns, for it cannot be done away with—there is a disturbing discordance between the *conatus* and the *passio essendi*. The result is remarkable, for we find then a *strange being beside oneself*: an *ekstasis* at odds with itself in seeking to be true to itself. We deal with an *ecstasy that is in passage against what looks like its native direction out of and beyond the* conatus essendi *itself*. The *ekstasis* seems to be: for itself and not for itself; not against itself and yet being just against itself in being for itself; something intimate and something strange.

We might say then that the selving is made intimately strange to itself. It is estranged from itself in becoming itself, in coming to itself, and in that estrangement more in return to strange intimacy with itself.

*Think of some forms of laughter in terms of this intimate strangeness.* Some forms of laughter can be both violent and loving. A joke at our own expense can make us strangers to ourselves; and yet this being strange shows us up more intimately. Think of a *caricature*, in this regard. To be true, it must be false to the original; but by being false to the original, it is being true to it; for something intimate about the original is being touched—by being touched up—by the caricature. Of course, this always risks a *betrayal* also. So there can be a laughter that destroys, as well as a laughter that debunks, in order to release something truer and hence differently to affirm (something not univocally true, but more truly in the spirit of truth).

Think of the way some teachers use sarcasm against students: it is a violence, a weapon, in a war of words. (We speak of a "put down": language of enforced descent, deflation, subjection, fall—direction low not high, not free lifting up.) Compare this to a releasing irony that disturbs the student into a truer affirmation of his or her proper powers. This is the *danger* of laughter as a saturated equivocal happening. Socratic irony was enacted in the constitutively ambiguous space between these extremes. Not surprisingly, it generated both hatred and love.

The teacher's sarcasm, built on the asymmetry of relation with the student, can reduce the student to helplessness: the superior power of the teacher (*conatus*) squashes the student on the receiving end (*passio*). This is what Hobbes and Freud(?) have eyes for: will to power.[36] Socratic

36. Hobbes is very one-sided in too univocally stressing laughing as expression our "superiority" in its "sudden glory." He sees things too much from the standpoint of the *conatus*: there is not enough of the discombobulation of the *passio*: his is not the best understanding of the *passio*. Freud is superior to Hobbes on this score. When Aristotle also stresses our laughing at those inferior to ourselves (he sees its origin in invective), he is like a good Greek aristocrat who does not see how in the idiocy of being the social disjunction of superior and inferior is not the last word or the first. There is an agapeic festivity in laughter beyond the superiority of the erotic sovereign or the *megalopsychos*—and this is not a matter of the abject passivity of the servile or

irony is also a kind of reduction to helplessness: almost a reduction of the interlocutor to the infant. It is a kind of return to zero: I know nothing. It is like being a baby, a child: becoming a child. *Infans*: without speech. But being without words can be the threshold of the recreation of our wording of things. And the return to childlikeness need not be infantilizing, can be more renewing of wonder and astonishment: purer passion of being as desiring to know.

To return to this strange being beside oneself and the tension of *conatus* and *passio essendi*: I would speak of a self-transcending, first beside itself in trying to be beyond itself, and then finding itself in a self-transcending return, and against itself, to the source of self-transcending: the *idiotic root*. Instead of being beyond itself, it finds something beyond itself, in itself. More, it finds itself as beyond itself, in its deepest intimacy. This is *the immanent otherness* that returns it to its elemental vulnerability and porosity: *passio essendi*.

But this idiotic root is beyond determinate reason: it is pre-objective and pre-subjective. It is reopened often by means of an occasion of *breakdown*. What we have become is not what we are, and in the coming to nothing, something is intimated of what we elementally are. In that breakdown, there is the possibility of a *breakthrough*: of the *passio essendi* in the *conatus*, and exceeding the willed determinations of the latter. Thus, both laughing and weeping are the happening of a kind of breakdown. They are also the possibility of a breakthrough of the trans-objective and the trans-subjective. What we seem to find then is a self-contradictory self-transcendence: *it is an ecstasy that is passive, or exposed to be so passive, to its own idiocy or intimacy.* Exposure of what? Exposure to what? Our self-transcending is shown up as at odds with itself, and its oddity is exposed, sometimes in its strange mysteriousness, sometimes just in its absurdity. In this self-contradictory self-transcending that is returned to itself, brought back into intimacy with its own root idiocy, there is communicated a more ultimate passivity that is always other to its own self-determining *conatus*.

Fascinating about laughter and weeping is that these seemingly *normal* happenings are fraught with immense ontological significance. The ordinary is extraordinary—even as it continues in the form of the ordinary. And what is communicated continues to be communicated, though we pay no notice. Each makes life bearable in its own way: but it is our

---

the slavish. It laughs beyond servility and sovereignty. Bataille does not quite get this when he associates laughter with his own sense of sovereignty.

kind of life they make bearable. Stones do not weep. Only flesh weeps. And so too with laughter. Only the suffering human being can laugh and weep. But this suffering is not the pain of this or that only, but, at the deepest, is in the undergoing of the *passio essendi*. This undergoing also indicates why the most redeeming laughter is compassionate. And why weeping is itself a kind of helpless appeal for compassion—an appeal that goes beyond even our crying out to compassionate humans, but reaches to the divine. For if the root of the undergoing goes all the way down into the abyss of the soul—the idiotic root—the breakdown we undergo, in the extremity it reveals, and the outcry, reach down or up to the ultimate itself. Laughing and weeping are porosities of being that have a secret affiliation with *prayer*, the ultimate religious porosity. *De profundis ad te Domini clamavi;* out of the depths, I have cried to thee, O Lord. Laughter and weeping are forms of the *clamor of intimacy*: the *clamavi* of the idiocy of being.

Clamor of intimacy: paradox or contradiction? Perhaps both. In any event, without the *equivocity of being*, there is no laughter and weeping, a point very evident with human being. The self-contradictory nature of our self-transcending could be seen to suggest something *constitutively equivocal* about human being. Our odd being, our being odd, is defined in an ambiguity between *passio essendi* and *conatus* that it cannot overcome through itself alone. For every effort to thus overcome it, repeats the ambiguity running to contradiction. Hence there is implicitly in this being beside self an openness to something beyond human self-transcending: transcendence itself.

We are the equivocal question to itself that can only partially answer for itself; and every answer we propose to our own equivocity repeats the equivocity in some other form. If there is any answer, it has to come from beyond ourselves. Though again, if so, it must also be communicated in the most intimate recesses of the idiot source. Hence the secret connection of laughter and weeping with being religious: the ultimate porosity.[37]

37. Our being religious is not necessarily linked to institutional expression and its official seriousness, though it can be in a kind of metaxological conversation with this. If we are talking about a between, it is not univocal and more equivocal; if it is dialectical, it is so as open to transcendence as other and hence metaxological, where the point is not dialectical totality but the opening of the whole to the beyond of wholeness. This beyond is beyond the institutional and yet is not without institution. To mention the Irish wake again as partaking of posthumous mind: inside and outside: linked to death, to mourning for the dead, the celebration of life, the continuation of living. It was connected to what in Irish was phrased as *caitheamh aimsire* (see Ó Laoire, *On*

Nothing is sacred to laughter, almost nothing, and yet there is something sacred too in this (almost) nothing. This world is fluid and full of transformation, on the threshold of the sacred—offering entry into the green world, where nothing is predictable according to the univocities of common sense. Yet the darkness of the saturated equivocities are saved in a double sense: saved as not being denied, and yet saved as mysteriously redeemed—a metaxological plurivocity. I am thinking of the late romantic comedies of Shakespeare—where frustration, multiple mistaken identities, crossings of sexual boundaries, end in a feast of marriages.

## Absurd Laughter: A Late Interlude

I am struck by a revealing analogy between "creativity" and "absurdity": once "creativity" (or "originality") was the preserve of a cultural elite, but now it seems to have become more and more democratized; similarly, the feeling of "absurdity," once confined as a retail luxury to an existentialist few, is now available wholesale to the many, to many too many. Being is at bottom absurd: this overall orientation has migrated outside of the sophisticated skepticism of a philosophical and aesthetic elite and found channels of communication to a larger audience through the mass media. In response, there are yea-sayers who urge us to "get on with it," "create" our own "meaning," and make the "best" of things. There are nay-sayers will urge various types of existential therapy or quarantine, ranging from bleak despair to groundless courage in this storm of our idiotic tale signifying nothing. The attitude is sometimes expressed, sometimes recessed, but that it is widely at work is hard to deny.[38]

There is something odd here. With the developments of modern science the astonishing intelligibility of the universe has been disclosed more and more, and not always with the dispelling of a sense of the mystery of being, but often with a deepening of it. Our curiosity about the determinacies of creation is resurrected as renewed astonishment before

---

*a Rock in the Middle of the Ocean*, 36–37, 268, for instance), "recreation," pastimes: passing the time; whiling it away, spending time. Life is passing time; our lives are in how we pass time. If time allows expenditure, what is spending time? Overspending? Underspending? Spending just the right amount of time? How can you pass the time when time itself is passing, regardless of how you pass it? Does something pass you by when you pass the time, are you passing something by?

38. This attitude is not unrelated to the turn against beauty we explored in our opening chapter.

its overdeterminacy. Here's the rub: as the universe shows to us more of its astonishing intelligibility, we seem to sink more into apprehension about our own absurdity. We make being more and more intelligible, and our own being seems to sink more and more into unintelligibility. Is there something absurd about this, something perhaps even risible? If being is absurd, are not we doubly absurd, especially in so far as we are enjoined, one way or another, to "make" it meaningful? Is this a cure that re-doubles the ailment: absurdity making itself "meaningful"? Are we then the absurdity raised to a second power? If being is absurd, are we too, as being, also absurd, in the beginning and in the end, as is all the "meaning" we make in the middle between beginning and end?

The more intelligible seems the world, the more absurd we seem. Has this something to do with our difference as humans? Nevertheless, this apprehension of absurdity is in the face of what is intelligible. Just because it is intelligible as *other* to us? But if we understand it, this otherness of intelligibility is in mysterious consonance with our intelligence, our power to understand it (however partial this is). Our difference cannot be the end of the matter: our difference is yet no difference, though still we tend to hug ourselves, ourselves alone. We are not released beyond ourselves, nor indeed receptive to what strikes us, comes to us from beyond ourselves. Laughter at the absurd happens, and yet in hitting us, making us crack up, it comes up in this crack from deeply intimate sources within us.

Generalized absurdity is itself absurd. Phrases like "It is absurd," "God is dead" are repeated like religious mantras, though intoned as if they were propositions with the certainty of Euclidean geometry. Mantras that stop thought rather than opening transcending put one in mind of narcissistic self-absorption. The ancients enjoined us to conform to the intelligibility of the cosmos, we want the world to conform to us, and it does not. Yet there is an accord—often mysterious. The discord of absurd laughter is a deeper accord. *Reductio ad absurdum* in the flesh: logos reaffirming, in the absurdity of the absurd, that the absurd is not absurd.

One asks too if in talk of our "making" of "meaning" there is not enough of the *passio essendi* for laughter to occur. There is not enough entry into the *passio*, granting it, giving oneself over to it, acknowledging it as absurd. There is too much of a certain *conatus* getting itself going, "working itself up" (in more senses than one) in the face of the absurd; a certain *conatus* whose endeavor to be anticipates the world to be hospitable to it on its own terms, and finds itself disappointed rather than relieved to discover that being is otherwise. We are hit with something more, and we are relieved of our false projections in affirming laughter. But if we think "meaning" is what we "make," then everything other that remains other must be a recalcitrance or resisting otherness to our "meaning" and the feeling for the absurd continues—without, however, our going through the magic door of the absurd itself—which is just indeed its absurdity. Absurdity is what gifts us with redeeming laughter on the other side of the threshold. "Making meaning" means, in an inverse sense, making the world (in its otherness) absurd.

There is pathos in laughter, but if we hug our own difference we end up with a kind of pathological erotics and we cry out: "Who loves me?" (Marion), rather than "Who do I love?" The *passio* is warped, but in the warp of the *passio* laughter breaks through. How warped? By a formation of the *conatus* that would deny or betray its own sources in the *passio* and the porosity. Pure endeavor turns into *conatus interruptus* and we take a hit: hit by something funny, struck by the absurdity of it; the joke is on us. "Making meaning": with not enough finesse for the *passio*, it takes itself too seriously. It misses out on something by not being receptive enough, not patient truly. Sometimes this is more a refusal of finitude than the ostensible granting of finitude it claims to be. Absurdity—emergent from the failure of a false god—and the erection of a new idol in its place—namely, ourselves? But can one not laugh at all of this? In light of the givenness of being, the gift of being? Is there a restorative laughter that comes to us as redeeming absurdity? My view here neighbors nihilism, but it is not nihilism. In my more nihilistic moods I give myself advice or am given: Get a life! The demotic expletion comes from something very deep. And then I realize I already have a life. What I get flows from what I am given. I get it and laugh at my (nihilistic) self.

We are ridiculous. This is an open secret. We do not need a philosophy of the absurd to tell us this. We are ridiculous and we laugh. We know it in our bones. We accept the ridiculous and we accept. We are freed of ourselves. Something is freed in us, has been freed in us. Laughter frees the ridiculous. It draws on an ontological nakedness. The poverty of this nakedness is a poor emissary of the endowing mystery (Charlie Chaplin, Comic Christ). Laughter is inseparable from the necessary failure of our freedom. Such failure is only possible if there is something great in our condition, either promised or secretly working.

In a way, are we not dealing with the sheer gratuity of existence: existence without a why? And yet are there not different "whys" and ways of "why-ings"? The "why" is not always just a determinate cause or our self-determining causing. There can be something overdeterminate in some "whys" and "ways of why-ing." Joy in existence as worthy for itself? Joy without a reason beyond itself? Joy its own reason for being. Not a means to an end, as enjoyment is not a means but affirmation of the gift: given for nothing—beyond itself. We are graced with being. As I pointed out on a previous occasion, even Schopenhauer granted a kind of atheistic grace. Camus's Sisyphus is, by contrast, plodding. Camus tells us we must imagine Sisyphus, plodding up and down, as happy. Is this a joke? One might laugh if it were intended as a joke, but in fact it is all rather moralistically serious. It might be funny if we thought of Sisyphus's going up and the going down as not unlike Wile E. Coyote's: recurrently he vanishes over the cliff and into the abyss as a puff of smoke, only to reappear, again chasing after the irrepressible Road Runner—Wily E. perennially resurrected, though never learning anything from being precipitiated into the abyss, again and again. Camus does not want us to laugh, but wants moralistically to stick us with absurdity, albeit with a hue of aesthetic existentialist cool, and happiness that can *only* be imagined, if that.[39]

We eat our bread and drink our wine each day—if we are lucky—and we do the same thing day in day out, to exist and to continue to exist. But we enjoy it, if we are lucky. We don't have to imagine our food and drink as happy things—they are happy things, and when we have them we count our blessings. I am reminded at every turn that I cannot enjoy my bread if my neighbor goes hungry, and this is true, and yet not entirely

39. It is interesting how Samuel Beckett is thought to epitomize the sense of existential absurdity in the middle of the twentieth century. Beckett is a poet of the absurd, and yet he makes us laugh at the absurdity; there are profoundly human moments in his work, tender to our helplessness. It is interesting that Beckett and Francis Bacon came from a not dissimilar social background marked by social and political diminishment, while Joyce passed through a kind of Saint Patrick's Purgatory, emerging a renegade priest of art and not religion. I see something Schopenhauerian in one, something anti-Schopenhauerian in the other. Beckett is an artist of disillusion, working towards the minimal and the releasing "no," Joyce an aesthetic priest consecrating the maximum of life and the reiterated "yes." A renegade priest might still have some consecrating favor from the companioning power. Joyce must be enjoyed as a great comic writer in which we find a redemption of the everyday, just in redeeming laughter (especially in *Ulysses*). In *Finnegan's Wake* there is journey into the saturated equivocity of the night-side of the dream world, with language broken down and cobbled together again, with the cobblers of mad punnings that sound and resound but that are less mad when they are spoken out loud. When flux-gibberish takes the form of fleshed human wording, then we overhear many stretches of singing in the dark, in the underworld of the human soul.

true. As a move to make one feel guilty, I acknowledge its power—but the enjoyment I have I would the other has too, and it is the enjoyment that is being affirmed, not the fact that I have it—or that the other has it not or perhaps has it too. Joy in being, not just enjoyment of this thing, or that—beyond the determinate cause, prior to the determinate cause, not due to our self-determination, not just indeterminate but overdeterminate. Secret agapeic surplus: the bread and the wine are good. My greed or guilt or sorrow when the other goes hungry or thirsty does not take away from this goodness. That very goodness asks intimately its extension to all the needy others.

## A Benign Surd

If we are dealing with something absurd, there is an absurdity that is just that. We cannot finally just laugh at that, for its effect is horror; nor weep either, for this absurdity would be a stone we could not digest, and we rather turn to stone than weep in the face of it. For weeping thus would itself be a furthering of the futility against which our tears appeal. One might think of the absurd as a *surd*: an excess that is elementally at work; that enables something other to itself, but that is not exhausted by these others; that is irrational only in the sense that it is not explained in our determinate systems of rational co-ordinates, but is at the boundary, or beyond, enabling such systems to function as a rational alleviation of perplexity. I would say that this second sense of the absurd betokens the surd in a hyperbolic sense: a "beyond" of surplus meaning; not a horror hostile to all meaning. God is absurd and a surd in that sense. Is this what the saying intends: God writes straight with crooked lines?[40]

Different senses of the absurd are to be noted. There is the ir-rational, the contradictory; there is the stupid; there is the horrifying absurd in what to us is senseless death; there is hostile absurdity that laughter can disarm; there is social absurdity that satire mocks; there is the absurd as the surplus surd that releases and enables without ever being containable in a determinate system of meaning. This last most concerns us. This surplus surd is not just with respect to an Ideal beyond. There are stylizations of the matter that might speak of a clash between immanence and transcendence as dualistic opposites. This is not the end of the matter.

40. From the Portuguese proverb "*Deus escreve direito por linhas tortas*," whose further origins are disputed.

Were we to speak of our own inward otherness, the surplus surd does not directly convert us to an Ideal beyond, but reverts us to the *root idiot beyond within our own self-being*. We are as much called into question by the "beyond" beyond us, as by the "beyond" within us.

Laughter and weeping are happenings in which this *double beyond* breaks through in the breakdown of the self-affirming pretensions of the *conatus essendi* that would be for itself alone (you are to be "on your own"). This latter is secretly hubris, but it is also both lamentable and comic.

Once again weeping and laughing reveal our embodied being as *pathological*. We often associate pathology with disease, and yes here, there is dis-ease. Being is pathological: but its disease is also its unease, and in the unease stirs something more than its own immanence can contain. It is empty of itself, and full in itself with more than it can contain itself, even were it to empty itself infinitely. Being is pathological: the pathos conditions the coming forth of the logos, but the pathos in us creatures is not commensurate with the logos. With finite creatures like us the pathos of the a-logical is not up to the serenity of the logos. Not being up to it, we are the suffering of the "It is nothing." The pathos of the a-logical can be sub-logical or sur-logical, hypo-logical or hyper-logical. I find it best to call it meta-logical, where "meta" means both "in the midst," and also "over and above," "beyond." The ontological pathos of our being as *passio essendi* comes to exposure in our suffering of the "It is nothing." *It comes to nothing*: we come to nothing. There is a tragic weeping: It comes to nothing and we weep. There is a comic nothing: then the "It is nothing" frees laughter: an energy of affirming being released is released in the coming to nothing. And so paradoxically, *joy* is released in this "coming to nothing." This is why laughter can be "life enhancing." It is life, the transcending energies of living, overcoming the "It is nothing" in our "coming to nothing." All this is like a *return to zero* in which we can refresh our interface with creation, and its original potencies of being. Return to zero is a breakdown, but in the breakdown something more original breaks through.[41]

41. "It is night." What is laughing during the day? It can well be the interruptions of the refreshing night. Laughter is the refreshing night, in the day itself. Interruption of the native ontological faith, and its renewal in the intermittences of our being: laughter especially comes as an intermittence—inter-mittence: sent in and to the between: communicated to the porosity as inter-ruptions of our lives. Inter-ruption: what does this say of the between (*inter*)?

If all this seems very high-flown, the point is really the puncturing of false high flying, of false self-transcendence in flighty self-intoxication. Here is something very elemental that the cultural sophisticates normally underestimate. Consider *slapstick comedy*. There is so much violence in this. A bottle is broken over a man's head; a person walks into a glass door; a head is unwittingly bashed by a swinging ladder (check out Laurel and Hardy, for instance). These are stock images, used again and again. They are stock violences, and yet we laugh. There is comic cruelty raised to high art: Malvolio (in *Twelfth Night*) "most notoriously abused." Not different to slapstick comedy, we witness the clash of the *conatus essendi* with the *passio essendi* and the humiliation of its ill-will (Malvolio). It is the violence of the patience to being that releases something more elemental in the patience of being, in the breakdown of the false flighty self-transcending of the *conatus essendi.*

In this light one might say that comedy as much as tragedy is a form of the *pathei mathos*, learning from suffering. The endeavor to be is brought to a limit where it runs against a wall. It tries to surmount it (hubris), and overreaching hits a limit—and then falls back—or falls forward, further beyond, and falls on its face . . . into nothing. And then? Nothing more? See tragedy as putting this *question* to us: Nothing—nothing more? Once, never more? See this as tragedy: a question to which we are impelled, which we cannot evade, but which we cannot answer through ourselves alone. Weeping is an appeal in the nothing, and through the coming to nothing—appeal to nothing? Or more?[42]

And comedy? The *conatus essendi* does not always reach a limit beyond itself. This can be true, of course, in the trivial occasions of falling and breakdown—the banana skin on which we slip. But the *conatus essendi* again hits a limit: the endeavor to be cannot go beyond itself in going beyond itself; but it hits in itself more deeply the *passio essendi.* Is it this that we see enacted in slapstick? *It slips on itself*, so to say: not just the *conatus essendi*, the whole human, the incarnate being. The clash of the *conatus essendi* and the *passio essendi*: we are that clash; it is not just imposed on us; we are the enactment of the disjunction of the two; and

42. And it is not just gentle weeping. We cannot forget the howl of Lear to the men of stones. The dead body of Cordelia: no longer the *passio essendi*, no longer the *conatus essendi*—the flesh is turned to stone through death, and the flesh of the living cry out. From the deepest intimacy of the idiocy comes the howl. From the place of absolute destitution on the border of nothing. And in that place of destitution—absolute porosity. Here we have the *pietà* of the father.

we come to the intimation, sometimes in the very crudity of the violence, that there is a more radical and *elemental and intimate "limit,"* always already at work in what we are: it is what we are—the patience, the passion of being. The *conatus essendi* is pretentious in forgetting this, in thinking it can always overcome it.

Thus the great heroic *conatus essendi* hits the limit, both beyond itself, in an order it cannot determine through itself; but also *in itself*, and in the givenness of the *passio essendi*, which secretly always made possible its own self-overcoming.[43] *What is most intimate to its own self-overcoming cannot be overcome by itself.* And the absurdity of thinking this to be possible, and of trying to be this overcoming, is secretly communicated in laughing and weeping, and more ritually dramatized in comedy and tragedy. Secretly communicated even though there it is, right out in the open. And we know and do not know what is there.

The clash of the *conatus essendi* and the *passio essendi* is not only with reference to an external limit to us. More elementally, it is with respect to our own being, and a limit internal to what we are. We are both sides, as it were, and in running from ourselves, we are only coming to ourselves again. But in all running from ourselves, we are coming to ourselves as lamentable or as laughable. The clash, that invisible glass door into which we walk head on, is our indisposed return to ourselves as false *conatus essendi*, and as *passio essendi* beyond our will to power.

This clash can be differently qualified, and you then have different forms of laughing and weeping; or comedy and tragedy. But both, not just tragedy, are forms of the *pathei mathos*. One might put it this way: everything here occurs in an equivocity that is constitutive of our being. But there is a kind of *karma of the equivocal* here also. More, the karma is one that is immanently enacted on us, and we are our own karma. Perhaps in premodern tragedy, the karma seemed to take a more "external" form,

43. The problem of Hamlet: internal vacillation, elusive inner unease that does not fit into the model of the heroic *conatus essendi:* quite the opposite. Hamlet is already infected with unease about this; passive to something he does not understand; passive to himself also in that he cannot be decisive and upbraids himself for this seeming lack; but perhaps what is deeper about him is just the equivocal dis-ease of the *passio* and the *conatus*: their unresolved inner discord; and perhaps this the image of the modern consciousness; the limit is not any externally determinable limit, but immanently equivocal and elusive: the immanently constitutive equivocity of the human being itself. When this breaks on mind, there is a loss of orientation, beneath which lies a bewilderment about what to be: to be or not to be: return to zero, and the interface between being (and the good of the "to be") and nothing (destined to die: "but what to me is this quintessence of dust?").

and I am not denying something transcendent at work. But I am saying that its immanence is far more intimate; such that we are ourselves both patients and actors; and both our patience and activity are each liable to the justice of this karma of the equivocal. The karma of the equivocal bears on an other measure that we meet in our own exceeding of measure, in our unavoidable, yet unavoidably false, exceeding of measure.[44] This other measure is beside the soul, but beside it as a strange intimate. When we are beside ourselves, this other is also beside us with us, though we may not know this.

And it is not only in the end that laughing and weeping lament, and are compassionate with, the counterfeit doubles of God. They seek blessing, not curse, and so aid redemption from these counterfeit doubles. Blessed are those who weep, for they shall laugh, and be comforted. But also blessed are those who laugh, for being beside themselves they too have suffered benignly beyond themselves.

## Black Humor

Black humor: André Breton says it is the "mortal enemy of sentimentality," but I would not put it in terms of enmity. I find it strange how the absurdity of it all can be felt as strangely redeeming, provisionally reconciling one with things absurd that then are not merely absurd. It is not unlike the forgiving of sin, which strangely makes it to be as if it were nothing, and the new release of life's festive energy comes. The music of life is made manifest in vile cacophony: away from *to kakos* (the evil), a way to *kalokagathia* (nobility, goodness). Releasing laughter and the passion of being: what is at stake is the defeat of despair. There is nonsense on the verge of affirming mystery in which shines the brightness of the dark. Is it all madness? Mad madness, not divine madness? Is there an idiot wisdom? If there is, is it a family relation to the ironic nescience of a Socrates, or an Augustine (*si comprehendis, non est deus*), or the *docta ignorantia* of Cusanus? We know nothing: a skepticism close to nihilism, but what does our sense of the nothing neighbor? Yeats: "Why should not old men be mad?" Wise foolishness? The body beside itself shows our bodies to be not our own but mysteriously incorporated in a body greater than our own: the archaic flesh of being. Does laughter reveal a

44. See Desmond, "Exceeding the Measure"; also Desmond, *Is There a Sabbath for Thought?* chapter 1, "The Sleep of Finitude"; Desmond, "Sticky Evil."

kind of *corpus mysticum*—intimate body returned to the idiotic body of the whole: returning not just to the mud, but to the kiss of the divine in the mud, perhaps in the mud returning the kiss?[45]

What might be mistaken for nihilism is rather joy in being at all, and enjoyment: affirming nothing, yet nothing but affirming. The body beside itself is not a unit of matter, dualistically opposed either to its own mind or to other bodies; it is embodiment as a crystallization of a between that is porous to the energy of the "to be," intimately universal in that all beings participate in it, a fleshed between that suffers the *passio essendi* in its joy and sorrow, its laughing and weeping, that surges beyond finite desire in its jubilating *conatus essendi* whose excessive endeavor to be also crashes, brought to earth again, whether as a tragic wreck or a comic comrade of Icarus. The road of excess does not always lead to the palace of wisdom—unless that wisdom be idiot wisdom. Perhaps we ought to amend Blake and say: the road of excess leads to the palace of idiot wisdom. Blake is wise in his own idiotic way: "Excess of sorrow laughs. Excess of joy weeps." This marriage of heaven and hell is not made in hell.

I have noted an analogy between laughter and eros, bearing on the body beside itself. The porosity in this means no mindless convulsion but laughing *matter*. We *are* (a) laughing matter. We can be choked with laughter, but often there is also great intelligence in laughter. If we were to speak of matter and mind, something happens in a passage between them. There is not dead matter and living mind as opposites, but an (aesthetic) transcending in the flesh itself: there are contortions in that transcending, there is the ridiculousness of, the idiocy of, madness of it. Laughing matter keeps the body in mind (especially the body's porosity, often literally its holes, the mouth, the anus). Absurdity is only intelligible against the background of some intelligibility. Absurdly we take absurdity to be intelligible. If I show you something absurd, you get the point (of the joke). Getting the point is not the same as being able to explain the point. Only human animals laugh because they are minded and mindful

45. From the sublime to the ridiculous, a Cork joke (though the animal is also participant in the archaic body of creation): "A prim and proper Cork lady had a number of prize cats and one of them was a little under the weather. So she called the vet and after a quick examination the vet said, 'There is nothing wrong with your cat—it's the most natural thing in the world. She's going to have kittens.' 'But that is impossible,' said the lady, 'she hasn't been out of my sight since the moment she was born, and she has never been near a tomcat.' 'What about him over there?' said the vet, pointing to a tomcat sitting on a couch smiling to himself. 'Don't be ridiculous,' said the lady, 'that's her brother.'" MacHale, *The Humour of Cork*, 9.

animals. Aristotle recognized this in the fineness of the human body as open to tickling. The body is formed in finesse for the absurd. Beside itself in laughing, the aesthetic body is an intelligence: minded and mindful, caught between *passio* and *conatus*, suffering and endeavor. Laughter, like sleep, is a restorative, as grief can also be.

A restorative, laughter can also break down. One thinks of Jonathan Swift's restorative: sheer festivity in hatred. Finally it is the festivity that moves us, not the hatred (this shocks us). Festivity in hatred carries its own concealed love. Beckett and Joyce come to mind again as two comic artists, though their laughter is not quite the same. There is the tug towards a kind of gnostic evil of being in the first, in the second there is a festive divine comedy.[46] Choked with laughter, tears streaming from the eyes, there can be a mockery of death in this, transforming our fear of it. It is not quite whistling in the dark but laughing in the dark. The laughter itself is a form of darkness that lightens things up. It is a strange and intimate lightening in the dark, by the dark. Laughing matter again: in the novel of Máirtín Ó Cadhain, *Cré na Cille* (translated as *The Dirty Dust*) there is laughter in the mud, laughter in the graveyard.[47] The dead continue to converse, talk on, complaining to and at each other, carping about the irritants of life above ground. This is a kind of black comedy of posthumous mind—the chattering dead are on the other side, but no passion spent—the passion of being is interned in nonbeing, but it is still the passion of being. Beckett's voices are often between life and death, or in the ditch, the voices of the dead, revenants going on and on, shades,

46. Beckett's interests are haunted by Schopenhauer; Joyce is omnivorous, but interests in, say, Aristotle/Aquinas and Vico mark a different orientation. One is a kind of atheistic Protestant, the other a kind of atheistic Catholic and the mixing of no and yes is different. It would be illuminating to compare these two female voices, Joyce's Molly Bloom, and the mouth of Beckett's "Not-I" in light of the *poros* and *penia* of *eros*.

47. Ó Cadhain, trans. Alan Titley. *The Dirty Dust: Cré Na Cille* (2015). Remarkably there is another translation in the same series and by the same publisher, dated 2016: *Graveyard Clay: Cré na Cille*, trans. Liam Mac Con Iomaire and Tim Robinson (2016). George Saunder's acclaimed *Lincoln in the Bardo* (2017) is a variation on the theme of conversations of the dead, with the dead. I hear echoes of what I call posthumous mind. The *Bardo Thodol* (*The Tibetan Book of the Dead)* deals perplexingly with the in-between state between death and being born again.

ghosts of beings, gone but not gone, not unlike Ó Cadhain![48] Without the black humor it would be hardly bearable. These dead do not shut up.[49]

## Applause

## Being of Good Humor: The Passion of Being Not Spent

Can we conclude by turning back with laughter towards the high ground of virtue? It is true that moralized laughter is no laughing matter. Laughter policed by political correctness, whether of left or right, is the death of joking. The release of laughter returns us, more often than not involuntarily, to the *passio essendi*, by surprising ways that overcome, and overturn, the claimed self-sufficiency of moral righteousness. Any claim for absolute self-sufficiency on the part of moral virtue is called into question. Our excellences are not any the less our excellences, but the release of laughter is not without its moral significance.[50] The person

48. I think of Yeats's late poem about Cúchulain entering the other world, and the shades there no longer have human voices but have taken on the voices of birds. "Cúchulain Comforted," *The Poems*, 379–80. These are not the birds of Aristophanes.

49. Vivian Mercier and Lillis Ó Laoire do not blink attention to the ugly and the macabre in the Irish comic tradition (Mercier, *The Irish Comic Tradition*). The connection of *eros* and death are mirrored sometimes in distaste for the ugliness of the sexual organs and act. Mercier recalls how the role of the poet at one time was not only in praising the noble but in cursing the ignoble and the enemies of his chieftain. Poetry was capable of dangerous imprecation. The poetic word not only affects us but, more radically, effects what it communicates. Swift (something of the Irish Aristophanes in him) is closer to being a great curser, pronouncing a curse perhaps on the entire human race in his picture of the Yahoos. Satire, sarcasm, hyperbole, invective, parody, comedy of scale are to found in his work. (Scale: reversal of big and small: Lilliput, Brobdingnag). Laputa is especially interesting concerning the disjunction of high and low, the soaring *conatus* and the *passio* with its feet on the ground. One thinks of the porosity of the women to the earth, even to wretched love on the earth, by comparison with the closure into abstraction of the cogitating men who float above it all.

50. Interestingly, Aristotle does maintain a middle position, true to the central ethical inspiration of his *Nichomachean Ethics*. He refers to two extremes relative to the ridiculous: the buffoons (*bōmolochoi*) "who itch to have their joke at all costs, and are more concerned to raise a laugh than to keep within the bounds of decorum and avoid giving pain to the object of their raillery" (Bk IV, viii: 1128a6–7), and the boorish (*agroikoi*) and morose, "who never by any chance say anything funny themselves and take offence at those who do" (1128a7–9). Between these two excesses, the middle is the witty (*eutrapeloi*) or versatile, "who jest with good taste" (1128a9–10), those who engage "only the sort of things that are suitable to a virtuous man and a gentleman" (1128a17–23).

of good humor can be one whose very character incarnates a feel for the stress between the *passio* and the *conatus* I have tried to sketch. Being of good humor may incarnate an excellence that is not defined by our self-determination since it is alert to the absurdities that accompany our effort to determine ourselves through ourselves alone.[51]

There is something intimately related to human virtue about the sense of humor itself. A person marked by a good sense of humor gives expression to a character marked by a more or less habitual attunement to the *passio essendi* and to the recurrent discordances between it and the overreaching claims of the *conatus essendi* in human life. The release of laughter for this person is profoundly humane. It is not a laughing *at* but a laughing *with*, and is so because this person witnesses in his or her laughter the wisdom of being able to laugh at themselves. This is something that is easily overlooked in the earnest seriousness of the day's business. Absent the feel for the humorous and human commerce becomes deadly serious: the word "deadly" is the entirely right word. A deadening seriousness falls on human commerce when we lack the lightness of touch that shows us to be intimate with the comedy of our own finiteness. Strangely again this intimacy is felt as lightening, as exhilarating even: the same things of importance can still be done, and their importance recognized, but they are carried differently now, indeed we may experience ourselves as being carried rather than have to be the carrier of the burden of serious things.

The release of laughter overcomes us: comes over us, and hence has an element of the surprising. We cannot project surprise, and yet it overcomes us with its shining newness. There is no project in the surprise of laughter. It is not something we do, it is something we receive. It takes us out of ourselves, though strangely it thrusts us back into ourselves more intimately. So also it may overcome moral righteousness, but it does so in a manner intimating what is more truly right concerning the more intimate *humanness* of moral virtue. Bringing us back to what we are intimately, it releases us to what is beyond us strangely. We are beside ourselves in the intimate strangeness. A good sense of humor is an excellence released from concern with its own excellence—and all the more excellent for living this kind of generous self-forgetting. The heart is lightened by it.

51. Remember too that humanists like Erasmus (*Laus Stultitiae*) and Thomas More were full of jest and wit and had a feel for absurdity; purging, perhaps redeeming laughter was ingredient in their humanistic mission and the reform of manners.

The point need not be confined to the so-called private individual. The matter can apply to a society at large, even to a whole culture, perhaps even epoch. The fact that the fool was a kind of ritualized figure in earlier cultures: the fool as the foil of the sovereign, but the sovereign was often a different kind of fool, as too full of the self-importance of his own power. I think of the great fools in Shakespeare. (Correct political incorrectness: Žižek—erstwhile clown of the post-Left "Left," now wanting to be taken more seriously.) If one lives in a society where the wisdom of the fool is acknowledged, one is living in the presence of a wisdom that can embrace the absurdities of the human condition, in a kind of idiot wisdom, as I call it. An age where humor is a matter of entertainment or distraction is not one of this idiot wisdom. It is too busy with the grand projects of the *conatus essendi* in hypertrophy to notice the banana skin that perhaps will bring a world historical fall. There is a fall that follows from forgetting that we are already fallen. A good sense of humor enables us to deal with the first fall, the forgetting, and the second fall. A society or epoch may have fallen into deadly seriousness, even on the heights of its moral excellences. Its heart can be lightened only with idiot wisdom, but alas, it is too wise to know that what it most needs is not itself. The absurdity that does not know it is absurd takes itself alone to make real sense. Equally, as we have the knowing that claims absurdity to be the truth of being is also absurd. Raising absurdity to the second power in an absurd way is a recipe for madness, though this madness presents itself as reason. It is counterfeit: everything is right about it, and in being right, everything about it is not right. This is a madness, but it is not divine. There is a laughter which is the true raising of absurdity to the second power. It saves the absurd, redeems the absurd. This release of laughter can be closer to the madness called divine.

How will this all end? The noises of laughter, think of them: titter, snigger, giggle, cackle, chortle, chuckle, snicker, snort, wheeze, guffaw, crow, roar, peal, roar, shout, shriek, bellow, tee-hee, hee-haw, ho-ho, ha-ha. . . . A plurivocity tending to the ridiculous! Is this just noise or logos in the incognito of the ludicrous? Perhaps not white noise, unless that leads us back to the origin of the universe. Perhaps idiotic logos? But what is being worded? A surd amen? If it begins with a benign outburst, how does it end? Perhaps with applause. Call to mind applause at the end of a musical performance. Think thus about it. The music offers, say, a melodious piece we appreciate—and then on ending comes the applause. Applause is amazing when you think of it: a gathering of human animals all banging one hand against the other, clapping we call it, sometimes accompanied by shouts of bravo or encore, with cheers and whistles and stamping of the feet on the ground. How loud, how ugly, how meaningless! We end almost like noisy monkeys in evening wear. But this senseless noise is totally significant—significant of our appreciation of the achieved excellence of the music. The end of the music is meaningless noise that itself qua gratitude for the beauty of the music fulfills the musical performance in thanks. The absurdity of the applause is entirely benign. The noise is itself a kind of music. Such applause, after all, is absurd thanks and pure affirmation.

APPENDIX

# "Intimate Intertwining": An Interview with William Desmond on Art and Religion

STEVEN KNEPPER

IN *PHILOSOPHY AND ITS Others*, William Desmond claims that both art and religion can "speak out of a shared sense of the mystery of being."[1] Both can reawaken our ontological astonishment at this mystery, can renew our wonder that *anything* exists. There are tensions between art and religion, Desmond realizes, but throughout his expansive body of work he returns again and again to their "intimate intertwining," as he puts it in this interview.

Desmond began elaborating an ambitious metaphysics at a time when, in many philosophical circles, calling someone a "metaphysician" was a slander and when few wrote with openness to God and religion. He has been a "consistently *untimely* thinker," Christopher Ben Simpson reflects, "addressing the times from a position of a certain outside."[2] Simpson here uses the kind of wordplay that is characteristic of Desmond's own style, though. (Desmond doesn't just write about poetry; he

1. Desmond, *Philosophy and Its Others*, 89.
2. Simpson, Introduction to *The William Desmond Reader*, xiv.

writes poetically, with a gift for metaphor and a keen ear for matching sound to sense. His study *God and the Between* contains a sequence of poetic "prayers" and "metaphysical cantos" that parallel the volume's prose explorations.[3]) Beyond being démodé for so long, Desmond's work is "untimely" in that it focuses on perennial concerns. It offers an incisive reading of the philosophical tradition, and it engages lasting questions in fresh ways. This means that Desmond's work has gained a large following regardless of intellectual fads. And given the recent metaphysical and "post-secular" turns in continental thought, his metaphysics of the between has suddenly become "timely" in disciplinary conversations.

Literary scholars have given Desmond's work less attention than philosophers and theologians, but it might be especially timely for us. Critique and a narrow historicism have become the dominant—indeed, nearly exclusive—methodologies in literary studies. Rita Felski, Russell Berman, Thomas Pfau, Lisa Ruddick, and others have shown why this is problematic. These methodologies shine little light on the experience of reading or on the way that literary works speak to us across time. They can be corrosive, alienating many students. Ruddick writes, "In the name of critique, anything except critique can be invaded or denatured."[4] Ultimately, these methodologies, which suggest that little of positive value can be learned from literary works, beg the question of why we should read literature at all. Desmond shares these qualms, and he also shows us possible paths forward. He has offered a suggestive account of literature's capacity to engage being in different ways. In addition to exploring the relationship between religion and art, he has written about tragedy and comedy, the origin of the work of art, the tension between autonomy and transcendence as artistic ideals, and literary depictions of radical evil and radical goodness. He has offered insightful readings of many literary works, from *King Lear* and *Moby-Dick* to the poetry of Yeats and the fiction of Joyce. Desmond does not shy away from bleakness or from critique, but as he says in this interview, "negativity must presuppose some more affirmative promise of thought if it is not to dissolve into a finally nihilistic outcome." Desmond can help literary studies be more attuned to this affirmative promise.

3. Cyril O'Regan, who has been one of the most insightful commentators on Desmond and literature, writes about these prayers and cantos in "What Theology Can Learn from a Philosophy Daring to Speak the Unspeakable," 251.

4. Ruddick, "When Nothing is Cool," 71.

Currently a professor at Villanova University, and until recently also at the Katholieke Universiteit Leuven, Desmond was born in 1951 in Cork, Ireland. After a brief time as a Dominican novice, he earned bachelor's and master's degrees from University College Cork and a doctorate in philosophy from Penn State University. His books include *Art and the Absolute* (SUNY, 1986), *Philosophy and its Others* (SUNY, 1990); *Being and the Between* (SUNY, 1995), *Ethics and the Between* (SUNY, 2001), *Art, Origins, Otherness: Between Philosophy and Art* (SUNY, 2003), *God and the Between* (Wiley-Blackwell, 2008), *Being Between: Conditions of Irish Thought* (NUI Galway, 2008), *The Intimate Strangeness of Being: Metaphysics after Dialectic* (Catholic, 2012), and *The Intimate Universal: The Hidden Porosity Among Religion, Art, Philosophy, and Politics* (Columbia, 2016). Christopher Ben Simpson has also edited *The William Desmond Reader* (SUNY, 2012), which serves as excellent introduction to Desmond's writings. This interview was conducted by email from November 2015 to August 2016. It has been lightly edited for clarity.

**Steven Knepper:** Kathleen Raine, the poet and scholar of Blake and Yeats, has a couplet that reminds me of your work:

> Incredible that anything exists—this hotch-potch
> World of marvels and trivia, and which is which?[5]

Raine seems to be getting at what you call the "intimate strangeness of being," the mystery that there is something rather than nothing. The couplet also seems to hint at another concern in your work—a concern with how easy it is, in part because we are intimately a part of the world, to lose track of this mystery, to see trivia instead of marvels. Does poetry have a significant role to play in helping us recover a sense of this mystery?

**William Desmond:** Many thanks for your well-put and probing questions. Large questions all, and not easy to address fully in a limited space. Here is a try.

The distinction between marvels and trivia is very interesting, and to the point, but one can ask how ultimate it finally is. What we often take to be trivial can reveal, from another perspective, marvelous newness. In *The Intimate Strangeness of Being*, I have written about different ways of wondering: wonder as astonishment, wonder as perplexity, and wonder

5. Raine, "Soliloquies," *The Collected Poems of Kathleen Raine*, 319.

as curiosity.[6] I think that what Raine is calling trivia is more connected with a certain banalized version of curiosity. Of course, curiosities engage our attention, sometimes through sheer surprise, sometimes in a more intrusive manner. If I'm not mistaken from around the end of the sixteenth century or the beginning of the seventeenth century there was a tremendous interest in the collection of curiosities. One worries, however, that "curiosities" in the sense here intended has to do with the dearth of a deeper ontological astonishment. Curiosity is absolutely central in the scientific quest for knowledge of the details of the world, but wonder as astonishment and wonder as perplexity have a more overall orientation and reflect a sense of the whole, a sense sometimes celebratory, sometimes troubled. When we talk of "curios," something of a contraction of original wonder is suggested. Think of "The Old Curiosity Shop"—a storehouse of oddities, full of bric-à-brac, odds and ends—though Dickens does weave a rich story about all of this that turns out to be fuller than mere curiosity can penetrate. Wonder as astonishment is not marked by a kind of intrusive curiosity, a kind of unhealthy curiosity, as we sometimes speak of this. That said, there is a continuum between wonder as astonishment and wonder in the form of a more determinate curiosity. I don't think that one can exclude the possibility of a reborn astonishment happening in the face of the wonder of trivia. One could make the case that true poetry is in the business of opening us to this rebirth, even in the midst of the seeming trivia that too often surround us.

**SK:** Could you say some more about how poetry can open us to this rebirth?

**WD:** One could write a book in answer to such a question; one would have to write a book to do justice to it! One thought strikes me here: we are born as humans, but we are more fully born as human when we begin to speak.

Before that we are human but infants: "*infans*" as without speech or language. Accession to language is a kind of *first poetic birth*, a birth soon forgotten once we are carried into the world of articulation by the gift of language itself and our access to the world that opens up. We are more awakened to the self of things, so to say, when we come into language in this first sense. We often forget that this first beginning is poetic, and

6. Desmond, *The Intimate Strangeness of Being*, 5–12 and 260–300.

instead stress the poetic as if it were only later and unconnected with this, as if it were a birth unto itself. But what we normally call the poetic is rather a *second birth* of those who are already born into language, or perhaps one should say, *already birthed* into language. There is continuity and a rupture involved in the second birth. It is seeded in the first, but what it brings forth would otherwise not receive a fresh and refreshed name without this second birth. It is a paradoxical thing to try to say, since once having been born, there seems no need to be born again; and yet the point here is that one has to be born again and again and again.

Think of it in this other paradoxical way: one awakens, one is awakened, and we go about our lives in consciousness of things, of others, and of ourselves. We are awake, and we are inclined to say "that is that." But suppose in being already awake one were to be awoken for a second time, awoken to a second degree, so to say. How can one be awakened being already awake? I think the rebirth of poetry is like this second awakening. It is an awakening to a second degree in our already being awake. We get a sense of this when we say: something *dawns* on me, on us. What is such a dawning? It is not easy to say, but one has the experience: things are as they are, and nothing changes, and yet there is a qualitative change, for there is now a new light shining on things, shining from them, shining for us. The second birth of the poetic is a dawning in our already being awake, and hence is both a return of something already given and the emergence of something given, as if for the first time. The second time we see is when we see things for the first time.

There is a deep *continuity* in this to our already being awakened to things, and so we find that the poetic word often *refreshes* words already in communication, though perhaps they have fallen asleep to themselves. But there is also a *discontinuity* in that now in the second awakening there can emerge a *fresh* attentiveness to things, and a fresh wording of things that brings them into the space of communication, as if for the first time. There is a renewal of what is as old as creation; there is new naming that offers creation as original for itself, and as new as on the first day of creation.

In the language I often use, this second birth of the poetic word opens again the original porosity of our being, waking us into new astonishment, for even though we are already awake we have fallen into the sleep of the world made too familiar by us, made untruly familiar. Dawning happens when the porosity is unclogged, and the true poetic word has the power to dissolve the untrue dreams that fixate us.

**SK:** In *Art, Origins, Otherness*, you claim that the West finds itself in a paradoxical position: ". . . too much has been asked of art, with the result that too little, or almost nothing, is now being asked of art. And too little is now asked, because too much was asked—asked in the wrong way."[7] Would you briefly explain what you mean by that? And would you comment too on what we can legitimately ask of art?

**WD:** In the statement I am thinking of a significant displacement of the sense of the sacred, a displacement of transcendence from its hitherto home in the religious towards the artistic. In *Art, Origins, Otherness,* I have tried to explore this displacement. It perhaps begins towards the end of the eighteenth century, notably with the Romantic movement, and in reaction to the more desacralized world of the Enlightenment. The latter with its neutralizing rationality, and well-meant ameliorative intention, tended to be reductive of the more extreme, that is, original and ultimate, possibilities of the human being, especially in connection with religion. I see the Romantic movement as being ambiguous between religion and art. In its own way it is not untouched by one inheritance of Enlightenment reason, which entails a leave-taking from a strong sense of transcendence as other to the human being. One result is a migration of the sense of transcendence into immanence itself, whether in a feel for a newly re-sacralized nature or in a discovery of a kind of inward otherness in the human being, the source of human creativity, one drawn upon especially by the great artist or poet. In this movement of displacement, the sense of the sacred is covered with an equivocity that in time becomes less and less named as the sacred. The result is that we lose what we have tried to hold onto in this very migration of transcendence. It is a complex picture, but this is part of the meaning of what I intended when I talked about asking too much of art: namely, asking for a kind of substitute for strong transcendence, but in terms that perhaps art alone cannot carry—cannot carry, especially if the mindfulness of the more richly sacred sense of the world and the human being is progressively being hollowed out.

Then there is the second part of the citation, namely, that now we ask too little of art as a consequence. This has to do with our having become more comfortable with the "aesthetic" than the religious; it is playful about possibilities rather than being demanding with unavoidable actualities and ultimate choices. All this is in a form that will not

7. Desmond, *Art, Origins, Otherness: Between Philosophy and Art*, 265.

come clean about the secret communication between those two in acts of genuine creativity. The weakening of spiritual seriousness occurs when that secret communication dries up, with the consequence that claims made by the "aesthetic" for complete autonomy reveal something hollow at the core of the claim. We see this in our own time in the way the genius has now become the celebrity, and the mark of worthiness of a work revolves around the mass of dollars it commands. I have to chuckle at the way André Breton tartly re-baptized Salvador Dalí with the name, old and new: Avida Dollars.

As to the last part of your question: I'm not sure what to say, since I don't think it is wise for the philosopher to dictate to art *ab extra* in a programmatic manner. But openness here to surprise does not mean "hands off." In my work I am metaxologically re-thinking the relation of art, religion, and philosophy. Hegel places these three at the apex of dialectical development in his philosophy of absolute spirit. What I mean by metaxologically is to word the between (*metaxu*) differently. There is an open communication between these three, in which their otherness and intermediation is given a different form other than, as in Hegel, an ascending dialectic in which philosophy as self-determining thought becomes the speculative Cheshire cat grinning on the top of the tree of knowledge.

The ethos within which art is created requires renewing, and philosophical thought can be involved in that. This also, in my view, asks for a resurrection of the sense of the sacred. Art is not to be equated with the religious univocally, but once again the porosity between the two needs to be (re-)opened, from both sides. Of course to speak of that porosity also suggests that neither art nor religion can be sealed into an autonomy that keeps them outside of each other by means of determinate borders. I think of art and religion as both being children of a more original porosity of being. Religion is the firstborn of that porosity; art is a slightly later child. Or perhaps in some ways the two are twins, with art the one that is born later. It is the renewal or reopening of this porosity that is the most essential. The obsession with an autonomy that closes off this porosity is part of the problem. Art, as second-born, can assert an autonomy that would take nothing from what is other to itself, but in thus asserting its life it is really giving itself over to its own lingering death. A second birth is needed but in a different sense. I am exploring this porosity between religion and art in a book that has just appeared: *The Intimate Universal: The Hidden Porosity among Religion, Art, Philosophy and Politics.*

**SK:** Who are some figures who have, to your mind, written out of a productive porosity?

**WD:** Again a large question not easy to answer. I can only speak of some of the voices that have struck me, and it is surely the case that there are many voices unheard by me, voices that ought to be heard. A selection of some: writers that I find invigorating on this score in the twentieth century include the American writers Saul Bellow and Flannery O'Connor. More might be said about these, but both have a festive feel for the comedy, often grotesque absurdity, of the human condition. I think this brings us to a threshold where the aesthetic borders on something that is trans-aesthetic.

There are other writers I find worthy, and again this is a mere sample from my own experience. I find myself reading and re-reading certain Irish poets, especially William Butler Yeats. Patrick Kavanagh is not as well-known as Seamus Heaney but both are true poets. Needless to say, I find James Joyce as a writer exhibiting something of the displacement I talked about above from religion to art, even to the degree of comparing his art to the act of priestly consecration. Is this a usurpation of the sacred? Can one consecrate daily life through human power alone? This is a question that I would put also to Heaney. Yeats is heterodox in his religious belief, but there is no doubting the genuineness of his quest for the sacred. Samuel Beckett moves more and more towards an apophatic silence, by contrast with Joyce, whose "yes" to immanent life adds more and more to what is already given. Apophatic silence can border on the sacred as can the festive "yes." A religious "yes" is directed not only on the fullness of the immanent world but on a fullness that exceeds the immanent world. The work of art shows signs of this excess. I am not sanctifying either of these writers, since there is much equivocal suggestion in the work that leaves perplexing this question of the relation of art and the sacred.

William Golding, the English writer best known for his *Lord of the Flies*, is also worthy of honor, especially in his contrariness to the latent hostilities to spiritual seriousness that were present in the reaction of some of the English critics to his work. His *Pincher Martin* is a daring exploration of the postmortem struggle of a drowned soul with itself. It grapples perhaps with the *infernal side* of what I have called "posthumous mindfulness"—though one does not know this till the end of the book. Golding's book *Darkness Visible*, borrowing for its title a pregnant phrase from Milton, is a courageous effort to write about redemptive goodness. This is a point perhaps with relevance to our feel for the goodness of being or the evil of being.

In the nineteenth century, of course, I think of Dostoevsky. Dickens is marvelously dark in many of his works, and yet he manages to say "yes" to a kind of ineradicable goodness of being. Gerard Manley Hopkins is an extraordinary poet. His contribution to the communication between the poetic and the religious can hardly be gainsaid. The Welsh poet R. S. Thomas wakes one up, although bleakly. I am invigorated by the hope in Czesław Miłosz (no stranger to the darkness of evil), and his desire to glorify.

Seán Ó Ríordáin is a poet from Cork, Ireland, who wrote in Irish and whom some consider the finest poet of the twentieth century to have done so. He has a richly suggestive poetics in which he speaks of the inseparability of the creative act and what he calls "prayer." I am writing a philosophical reflection in which my own notions of the porosity of being, the *passio essendi*, the sense of imagination as a threshold power, praise and prayer, and related ideas are brought into dialogue with Ó Ríordáin. What Heidegger does in dialogue with Hölderlin, a dialogue fraught with the sacral vocation of the poet, I would like analogously to do in dialogue with Ó Ríordáin.

One of the things that is worth mentioning here is that when it comes to the written word, in the long run it is very hard to counterfeit genuine artistic merit. I find it exhilarating to see how the word renews itself again and again. Perhaps there is much chatter and babbling, but out of the child's babble the communicative word emerges. It is perhaps easier to be a successful counterfeiter in the world of the visual arts where the commodification of art by consumer capitalism has led to the "corruption of consciousness," as R. G. Collingwood put it in his *The Principles of Art*. Interestingly he is referring to T. S. Eliot's "The Waste Land" (Collingwood was friendly with Eliot). Eliot was everywhere in my younger days, and while now he is not so to the fore, he will not go away. Incidentally, I wrote my MA thesis on Collingwood's concept of imagination in *The Principles of Art*, a sign perhaps even then of the crossing of the philosophical and the poetic for me. My first published article was on Collingwood and imagination.

**SK:** You mention Heidegger, who of course was also interested in poetry and the mystery of being. Could you say some more about how your views on poetry relate to those of Heidegger?

**WD:** I seem to have to repeat one more time: this again is a very large question! I have a long chapter in *Art, Origins, Otherness* on Heidegger and the origin of the artwork.[8] Heidegger mentions the between episodically, but does not undertake a systematic exploration of it in the way I do. The between remains still underexplored. In that chapter I speak of Heidegger and the "still unthought between."[9] The space between the philosopher and the poet is a concern to which Heidegger came later in his career, whereas from the beginning of my own itinerary in thought it has concerned me. One of the reasons I have admired Hegel, even while criticizing him, is the audacity he displays in putting art with religion and philosophy at the highest level of absolute spirit. He is right to remind us of their ultimacy, though how he construes their relation is something I question: for me there is a three-way conversation, rather than a dialectical subsumption of art and religion into philosophy. Heidegger's dialogue of the thinker and the poet, incarnated for him in his own dialogue as thinker with Hölderlin as the poet, is right to stress a non-reductive relation of the poet to the thinker. Yet this seems to be a *dyadic* intermediation (Heidegger often indeed thinks in terms of dyads). This dyadic intermediation is more equivocal, I find, than the *triadic* conversation suggested by Hegel and endorsed by me, though differently carried through. What I mean is that Heidegger is less forthright about the relation of the poetic and the sacred than I would like. In my view also, there are strategic silences that are not warranted by the paradigmatic interlocutor he engages, namely, Hölderlin. This has to do with the fact that in Hölderlin, and indeed in Hegel, the crucial role of Christianity cannot be underestimated. Put slightly differently, in Hölderlin (close friend of Hegel's youth) we do find not only a concern with the flight of the Greek gods, we find a longing for fraternal reconciliation between those gods and the One of Christianity. In this sought-for reconciliation Christ is (to be) the brother of Dionysus. While I have great sympathy for Heidegger's prolegomenon to the dialogue of poet and thinker, he does not come clean enough for me on the intimate intertwining of the aesthetic and the

8. Ibid., 209–63.

9. Ibid., 209.

religious. This would entail not only a different interpretation of the poetic, but also of biblical religion, and especially Christianity. Admittedly there is much more I could say, but this is an important point.

**SK:** You recently wrote the introduction for an issue of the journal *Political Theology* focused on evil. In it you claimed,

> We are quick to give expression to our fascination with evil, while the good comes across as bland. The banality of good makes many yawn. Our taste for radical good has been dulled. The thought of radical evil makes us sit up, as if here at last there will be some thrilling adventure in transgressive transcendence. The astonishing idea of radical good finds itself homeless. Radical: an original good at the roots of things—but can we be honest about radical evil without honestly addressing this promise of original good?[10]

Much of your work has sought to affirm, without being naïve or complacent, the elemental goodness of being. You have drawn on literature, philosophy, and religion in your effort to do so, recognizing the tensions and differences between them, but also dismissing the notion of intractable quarrels or hostilities. In her essay "Morality and Literature," though, Simone Weil claims that literary narrative is at least partly to blame for making goodness banal. She claims that "fictional good is boring and flat, while fictional evil is varied and intriguing, attractive, profound, and full of charm."[11] Only in great works of literature do "good and evil appear in their truth."[12] Weil said that from the late nineteenth century onward this has become a bigger issue. She claims that one of the ways we have asked too much of literature is in turning to it as a primary source of spiritual guidance. Do you think there is anything to Weil's claims?

**WD:** The last part of your question recalls the second question above, and I take it Weil's point turns on trying to make art or literature bear a burden that they cannot do alone. If that is what is intended, I am in agreement. On the question of good and evil, it is very hard to portray goodness in literature. People are often attracted to what they take to be the grandeur of Milton's Satan, even seduced by this counterfeit grandeur.

10. Desmond, "On Evil and Political Theology," 95.

11. Weil, "Morality and Literature," 290.

12. Ibid., 293.

I offer a doctoral seminar on "Radical Evil in German Philosophy," and students are eager to sign up for it, but on the first day I tease them by asking if they would turn up if the course was named "Radical Good in Philosophy." They do not always appreciate being teased. I think it was Tolstoy who said something to the effect that happy families do not make the basis for good literature. Hegel speaks about the pages of happiness in history being blank pages. All of these are quite right in their own way, but I think of Dostoevsky as someone who has tried to offer us images of goodness, whether successfully or not is another question. I am thinking of *The Idiot* in which Prince Myshkin seems to embody a kind of idiotic goodness about which Dostoevsky leaves us with an equivocal impression. One thinks also of his efforts to present goodness in figures like Alyosha in *The Brothers Karamazov*. What would Dostoevsky think of the "Piss Christ"? Or Sammler's question in Saul Bellow's *Sammler's Planet*: "Who had made shit a sacrament?"[13]

I plan a book entitled *Desecrations*, a philosophical nocturne on the evil of being. My hope is that it will be part of a trilogy, the other volumes being called *Purgations* and *Consecrations*. But it is very important that we grant the impossibility of avoiding the question of radical goodness. Radical evil would be impossible to talk about if there was not secretly at work some sense of the good that is mutilated or betrayed in the evil. The secrets of the good are powerful by being reticent. I suppose writers like Jane Austen and Emily Dickinson have attunements to this. There is something coarse about radical evil that easily excites us. There is something subtle and intimate about real goodness that we cannot pin down easily. This is not the fault of goodness.

You asked above about artists or writers who I thought got something of the balance right, and a writer whom I admire, another Irish writer as it turns out, William Trevor comes to mind: he is a master of the short story, and his stories show tremendous agapeic generosity towards his characters, even when these characters are mediocre, even when they are vile. Ultimately this agapeic generosity is perhaps not unconnected with what Keats calls negative capability, though perhaps it is more festive and fully affirming of the otherness of the other.

I find this agapeic generosity in Shakespeare, but to return to my remark about the blank page of the good, Dostoevsky's story "The Dream of a Ridiculous Man" is illuminating. The ridiculous man has a dream

13. Bellow, *Mr. Sammler's Planet*, 36.

about an earth that is the twin of our earth, the same and yet other. Our present earth has become so dreary to him as to make him want to kill himself, but the earth of his dream is inexpressibly good. Though living in our world of death, he dreams of the earth of inexpressible goodness, and deep down in the intimacy of his being he knows it as the true world. Alas, his evil eye introduces corruption into the dream earth and he confesses he is responsible. The corruption blossoms as the counterfeit world whose mingling of life and death mimics life—though it really serves death. Nevertheless, even then the ridiculous man refuses to betray his dream of primal goodness. There are ridiculous men everywhere, North, South, East, West, their dream often hidden in intimate silence. Of course, frequently we mock the ridiculous man, for we refuse the dream of the inexpressible goodness of the true life beyond the counterfeit. He is ridiculous because, though the corrupted life is inextricable from his (re-)configuration of being, he still yet dreamed. We refuse to be ridiculous in casting from us such a dream; we make our peace with the counterfeit creation and hardly realize we are truly ridiculous in another sense. This latter "higher" ridiculousness loves to talk about the struggle for existence in the showy, aggressive language of the street tough. The dream of the ridiculous man is sneered at as the feeble softness of the tenderized soul, the patient being, the porous being, the feminine man who cannot see the point of the war. Such manly swagger glories in cruelty to the porous and the patient. The glory, like its world of war, is counterfeit.

**SK:** We hear a lot of talk today about a crisis of the humanities. One concern is that the study of literature is dominated by negative critique, by an at times flat-footed or formulaic hermeneutics of suspicion. How might we rejuvenate the study of the humanities today?

**WD:** I wish we had or could have the elixir for such a rejuvenation!

In *The Intimate Strangeness of Being* there are two chapters dedicated to exploring this question in connection with philosophy and metaphysics, but some of the points I make there are relevant to your question also. In one chapter I ask "Is There Metaphysics after Critique?" Another chapter is entitled "Metaphysics and the Intimate Strangeness of Being: Neither Deconstruction Nor Reconstruction."[14] A central argument there traces our current hermeneutical situation back to the notion of think-

14. Desmond, *The Intimate Strangeness of Being*, 89–119 and 120–52.

ing as negation or negativity, an idea at the heart of Hegel's dialectic and inherited by many of his successors, even when they are his critics. I show how negativity must presuppose some more affirmative promise of thought if it is not to dissolve into a finally nihilistic outcome. The technical details of the arguments to one side, I think we see many bad consequences in the practice of reading and interpretation that follow.

I tell a story: some very talented students I know had gone to perhaps the most prestigious Liberal Arts college in the US where there were exposed to reading great literary texts by means of the deconstructive way, or other assorted "radical" hermeneutical methods. The end result was severe disappointment with "reading" in this way at all. On graduating, these very intelligent students simply wanted to be done with this whole manner of proceeding. They wanted simply to read good books intelligently and for pleasure. These students had no ideological axes to grind, but felt that, as I might put it, a more humanistic appreciation of literature was denied to them by teachers with ideological axes to grind. Interestingly, some colleagues now tell me that in some departments deconstruction is passé. The deconstructionists of the erstwhile heyday have become the senior members of the department, perhaps even on their way to being superannuated, a veritable kiss of death to those who want to be on the cutting edge of the current. In such an ethos the surest way to be unoriginal is to want to be nothing but original. I tell the story without further hermeneutical intervention.

For myself, perhaps the greater worry relative to humanistic studies is the bureaucratization of the university, and the transformation of the scholar and the thinker into a middle manager. One applies for funding for a "project," and if successful one manages one's career and that of others, controlling outputs, and making sure they match or exceed inputs, and so on and so on. Sometimes in making things more professional we end up making things less true to the profession of the humanities. Who can forget Jonathan Swift's black vision of "projects" in Gulliver's voyage to the land of Laputa?

I certainly worry about this question in relation to the current manner in which philosophical studies are organized. Young scholars hesitate to pursue what takes hold of them as worthy of dedicated research and investigation. They look ahead and see what will get them a project, what will get them funding for a project, and they reconstruct themselves accordingly. This is possibly a Trojan horse relative to the future of the humanities.

When I was a younger student I often came across older academics who spoke with a sigh about the end of philosophy or the destruction or overcoming of metaphysics. If I had taken them seriously, I would not have moved from the spot. I would have been paralyzed by the discouragements of the already-defeated. I know I am no longer young, but I would not like to speak the discouragements of one defeated. The human spirit is resurrected again and again. The death of the old is often the secret seed of the new. There are seeds that are neither old nor new, and they keep on germinating. Resurrection may not always occur within the universities. This has been true in significant instances in modern philosophy. Think of Descartes, Spinoza, Leibniz, Schopenhauer, Kierkegaard, and Nietzsche, to name a few. The glories of early Islamic culture were not the outcome of the bureaucratic organization of the scholar manager.

Similar points might be made, *mutatis mutandis*, in connection with literature. Being part of a writing program, and having to have a writing project, may not always be the most fertile ground for creative endeavors. In answer to your last question, I do not have any program for rejuvenation. I do feel that the Western tradition, just to speak of that, is extraordinarily rich, and without memory for the longer tradition, there are no true humanities. Our current ethos is dominated by what I call serviceable disposability: something must serve us, and when it has served its use for us, it is used and used up and then is disposable. Its value for itself is nothing. In this dominion of serviceable disposability the service of such a longer humanistic memory is not always appreciated. Those of us who are still in the Academy have to keep alive the spirit of that service. But rejuvenation may come from elsewhere also. Sometimes those who have endured exile come out the stronger from the desert and bring back into the more settled places fresh visions of the marvel of being and its intimate strangeness.

# Bibliography

Aristotle. *Nichomachean Ethics*. Loeb Classical Library XIX. With an English translation by H. Rackman. Cambridge: Harvard University Press, 1926.

———. *On the Soul, Parva Naturalia, On Breath*. Loeb Classical Library VIII. With an English translation by W. S. Hett. Cambridge: Harvard University Press, 1936.

———. *The Poetics*. Loeb Classical Library. With an English translation by W. Hamilton Fyfe. Cambridge: Harvard University Press, 1927.

———. *Politics*. Loeb Classical Library XXI. With an English translation by H. Rackman. Cambridge: Harvard University Press, 1933.

Augustine, Saint. *Confessions*. 2 vols. Loeb Classical Library VIII. With an English translation by William Watts. Cambridge: Harvard University Press, 1912

———. *De Doctina Christiana*. Edited and translated by R. P. H. Green. Oxford: Oxford University Press, 1995.

———. *The Trinity*. 2nd ed. Introduction and translated by Edmund Hill, O.P. Hyde Park, NY: New City Press, 2012.

Bakhtin, Mikhail. *Rabelais and his World*. Translated by Helene Iswolsky. Bloomington, IN: Indiana University Press, 1984.

Baldwin, James. *Sonny's Blues*. London: Penguin, 1995.

Balthasar, Hans Urs von. *The Glory of the Lord: A Theological Aesthetics. I: Seeing the Form*. Translated by Erasmo Leiva-Merikakis; edited by Joseph Fessio S.J. and John Riches. San Francisco: Ignatius, 1982.

Bartlett, Karen. *Dusty: An Intimate Portrait of a Musical Legend*. London: Robson, 2014.

Barrett, William. *Death of the Soul: From Descartes to the Computer*. Oxford: Oxford Paperbacks, 1987.

Battersby, Christine. *The Sublime, Terror and Human Difference*. London: Routledge, 2007.

Bayles, Martha. *Hole in our Soul: The Loss of Beauty and Meaning in American Popular Music*. Chicago: University of Chicago Press, 1995.

Beard, Mary. *Laughter in Ancient Rome: On Joking, Tickling, and Cracking Up (Sather Classical Lectures)*. Berkeley: University of California Press, 2015.

Bergson, Henri. *Laughter: An Essay on the Meaning of the Comic*. Translated by Cloudesley Shovell Henry Brereton. New York: Dover, 2005.

Bellow, Saul. *Mr. Sammler's Planet*. New York: Penguin, 2004.

Bernstein, Richard. *Radical Evil: A Philosophical Interrogation*. Oxford: Blackwell, 2002.

Berger, Peter L. *Redeeming Laughter: The Comic Dimension of Human Experience*. 2nd ed. Berlin: De Gruyter, 2014.

Breton, A. *Oeuvres completes*. Vol. I. Paris: Gallimard, 1988.

Brook, Peter. *The Empty Space*. Harmondsworth, UK: Penguin, 1968.

Burke, Edmund. *A Philosophical Inquiry into the Origin of our Ideas of the Beautiful and the Sublime*. Edited with an introduction by Adam Phillips. Oxford: Oxford University Press, 1990.

Cavell, Stanley. *The Claim of Reason: Wittgenstein, Morality, Skepticism and Tragedy*. Oxford: Oxford University Press, 1979 (2nd ed. 1999).

———. *Disowning Knowledge: In Seven Plays of Shakespeare*. Updated ed. Cambridge: Cambridge University Press, 2003.

———. *In Quest of the Ordinary: Lines of Skepticism and Romanticism*. Chicago: University of Chicago Press, 1998.

———. *Little Did I Know: Excerpts from Memory*. Stanford: Stanford University Press, 2010.

———. *Philosophical Passages: Wittgenstein, Emerson, Derrida, Austin*. Oxford: Wiley, Blackwell, 1995.

———. *A Pitch of Philosophy: Autobiographical Exercises*. Cambridge: Harvard University Press, 1994.

———. *The Senses of Walden*. San Francisco: North Point, 1980.

———. *This New Yet Unapproachable America: Lectures after Emerson after Wittgenstein*. Chicago: University of Chicago Press, 1989.

Chambers, Whittaker. *Witness*. Washington, D.C.: Regnery History, 2014.

Chrétien, Jean-Louis. *The Call and the Response*. Translated by Anne Davenport. New York: Fordham University Press, 2004.

Copjec, Joan, ed. *Radical Evil*. London: Verso, 1996.

Courtine, Jean-François, ed. *Of the Sublime: Presence in Question*. Albany, NY: SUNY Press, 1993.

Cousineau, Phil. *Soul: An Archaeology*. New York: HarperCollins, 1995.

Crowther, Paul. *The Kantian Sublime: From Morality to Art*. Oxford: Clarendon, 1991.

Davis, Michael. *The Soul of the Greeks*. Chicago: University of Chicago Press, 2011.

Dante Alighieri. *The Divine Comedy: Vol. I Inferno*. Translated by Mark Musa. New York: Penguin, 1984.

Danto, Arthur C. *The Abuse of Beauty: Aesthetics and the Concepts of Art*. La Salle, IL: Open Court, 2003.

Desmond, William. "Agapeic Selving and the Passion of Being: Subjectivity in the Light of Solidarity." In *Post-Subjectivity*, edited by Christoph Schmidt, Merav Mack, and Andy R. German, 77–102. Cambridge: Cambridge Scholars Press, 2014.

———. *Art and the Absolute: A Study of Hegel's Aesthetics*. Albany, NY: SUNY Press, 1986.

———. *Art, Origins, Otherness: Between Art and Philosophy*. Albany, NY: SUNY Press, 2003.

———. "*Autonomia Turranos*: On Some Dialectical Equivocities of Self-determination." *Ethical Perspectives* 5.4 (1998) 233–52.

———. *Being and the Between*. Albany, NY: SUNY, 1995.

———. *Beyond Hegel and Dialectic: Speculation, Cult and Comedy*. Albany, NY: SUNY Press, 1992.

———. "Creation and the Evil of Being." *To Discern Creation in a Scattering World*, edited by F. Depoortere and J. Haers, 171–206. Leuven: Peeters, 2013.

———. *Ethics and the Between*. Albany, NY: SUNY Press, 2001.

———. "Ethics and the Evil of Being." *What Happened in and to Moral Philosophy in the Twentieth Century: Philosophical Essays in Honor of Alasdair McIntyre*, edited by Fran O'Rourke, 423–59. Notre Dame, IN: University of Notre Dame Press, 2013.

———. "Exceeding the Measure: On Ethics and the Between." *Ethical Perspectives* 8.4 (2001) 319–31.

———. "Flux-gibberish: For and Against Heraclitus." *Review of Metaphysics* 70 (2017) 473–505.

———. *God and the Between.* Oxford: Blackwell, 2008.

———. *Hegel's God: A Counterfeit Double?* Aldershot, UK: Ashgate, 2003.

———. *The Intimate Strangeness of Being: Metaphysics after Dialectic.* Washington, DC: Catholic University of America Press, 2012.

———. *Is There a Sabbath for Thought? Between Religion and Philosophy.* Bronx, NY: Fordham University Press, 2005.

———. *The Intimate Universal: On the Hidden Porosity among Religion, Art, Philosophy, and Politics.* New York: Columbia University Press, 2016.

———. "It Is Nothing: Wording the Release of Forgiveness." Presidential Address, ACPA, *Proceedings of the American Catholic Philosophical Association* 82 (2008) 1–23.

———. "On Evil and Political Theology." *Political Theology* 16.2 (2015) 93–100.

———. "On Festival, Ecstasy, and Masquerade." In *Syndicate Theology*, March/April 2016, 41–45. Online:https://syndicatetheology.com/commentary/remarks-gifts-glittering-poisoned-spectacle-empire-metaphysics/.

———. *Perplexity and Ultimacy: Metaphysical Thoughts from the Middle.* Albany, NY: SUNY Press, 1995.

———. *Philosophy and its Others: Ways of Being and Mind.* Albany, NY: SUNY Press, 1990.

———. "The Porosity of Being: Towards an Agapeic Catholicity. In Response to Charles Taylor." *Renewing the Church in a Secular Age*, edited by Charles Taylor et al., 283–305. Washington, DC: The Council for Research in Values and Philosophy, 2016.

———. "Sticky Evil: On *Macbeth* and the Karma of the Equivocal." In *God, Literature and Process Thought*, edited by Darren Middleton, 133–55. Aldershot, UK: Ashgate, 2002.

———. "Tyranny and the Recess of Friendship." In *Amor Amicitiae: On the Love That Is Friendship*, edited by T. Kelly and P. Rosemann, 99–125. Leuven: Peeters 2004.

Dickens, Charles. *The Life and Adventures of Martin Chuzzlewit.* Harmondsworth, UK: Penguin, 1968.

Diogenes Laertius. *Live of the Eminent Philosophers.* 2 vols. Loeb Classical Library VIII. With an English translation by R. D. Hicks. Cambridge: Harvard University Press, 1925.

Dreyfus, Hubert, and Sean Dorrance Kelly. *All Things Shining: Reading the Western Classics to Find Meaning in a Secular Age.* New York: Free, 2011.

Drury, Maurice O'C. *The Danger of Words and Writings on Wittgenstein.* Edited by D. Berman, M. Fitzgerald, and J. Hayes. Bristol: Thoemmes, 1996.

Eco, Umberto, ed. *History of Beauty.* New York: Rizzoli, 2004.

———. *On Ugliness.* New York: Rizzoli, 2007.

Ehrenberg, Victor. *The People of Aristophanes: A Sociology of Old Attic Comedy.* 2nd ed. Oxford: Blackwell, 1951.

Eldridge, Richard. "Internal Transcendentalism: Wordsworth and 'A New Condition of Philosophy.'" *Philosophy and Literature* 18.1 (1994) 50–71.

———. "Cavell and Hölderlin on Human Immigrancy." In *The Persistence of Romanticism: Essays in Philosophy and Literature*, 229–45. New York: Cambridge University Press, 2001.

———. "Kant, Hölderlin and the Experience of Longing." In *The Persistence of Romanticism: Essays in Philosophy and Literature*, 31–51. New York: Cambridge University Press, 2001.

———. *Leading a Human Life: Wittgenstein, Intentionality and Romanticism*. Chicago: University of Chicago Press, 1997.

Emerson, Ralph Waldo. *Collected Works of Ralph Waldo Emerson*, Volume II: Essays: First Series. Cambridge: Belknap, 1980.

Fechner, Gustav Theodor. *Religion of a Scientist: Selections from Gustav Theodor Fechner*. Edited and translated by Walter Lowrie. 1946. Reprint. Whitefish, MT: Kessinger Legacy Reprints, 2007.

Foss, Hubert. "Schoenberg, 1874–1951." *Musical Times*, 92, no 1 (1951) 401–3.

Freud, Sigmund. *Civilization and Its Discontents*. Edited and translated by James Strachey. New York: Norton, 1961.

———. *Jokes and Their Relation to the Unconscious*. Edited and translated by James Strachey. New York: Norton, 1960.

Gellner, Ernest. *Words and Things*. 2nd ed. New York: Routledge, 2005.

Ghose, Indira. *Shakespeare and Laughter: A Cultural History*. Manchester: Manchester University Press, 2011.

Gould, Timothy. *Hearing Things: Voice and Method in the Writing of Stanley Cavell*. Chicago: Chicago University Press, 1998.

Harmon, A. M., trans. *Lucian*, Vol. 1. New York: Macmillan, 1913.

Henry, Michel. *I am the Truth: Towards a Philosophy of Christianity*. Translated by Susan Emanuel. Stanford: Stanford University Press, 2003.

Hegel, G. W. F. *Enzyklopädie der Philosophischen Wissenschaften im Grundrisse* (1830). Edited by Friedhelm Nicolin and Otto Pöggeler. Hamburg: Meiner, 1991.

———. *Hegel's Aesthetics: Lectures on Fine Art*. 2 vols. Translated by T. M. Knox. Oxford: Clarendon, 1975.

———. *Hegel's Lectures on the History of Philosophy*. Translated by E. S. Haldane and F. H. Simson. 3 vols. London: Routledge and Kegan Paul, 1892–96.

———. *Hegel's Philosophy of Mind: Being Part Three of the Encyclopedia of the Philosophical Sciences*. Translated by W. Wallace. Oxford: Oxford University Press, 1971.

———. *Lectures on the Philosophy of Religion: One Volume Edition, The Lectures of 1827*. Edited and translated by Peter Hodgson. Berkeley and Los Angeles: University of California Press, 1988.

———. *Lectures on the Philosophy of Spirit (1827–1828)*. Translated with an introduction by Robert R. Williams. Oxford: Oxford University Press, 2007.

———. *Outline of the Philosophy of Right*. Translated by T. M. Knox, revised and introduction by Stephen Houlgate. Oxford: Oxford University Press, 2008.

———. *Phänomenologie des Geistes*. Hamburg: Meiner, 1952.

———. *Phenomenology of Spirit*. Translated by A. V. Miller. Oxford: Clarendon, 1977.

———. *Science of Logic*. Translated by A. V. Miller. New York: Humanities, 1969.

———. *Werke in zwanzig Bänden*. Edited by E. Moldenhauer and K. M. Michel. Frankfurt: Suhrkamp, 1970.

Heidegger, Martin. *Being and Time*. Translated by Joan Stambaugh. Revised with a foreword by D. J. Schmidt. Albany, NY: SUNY Press, 2010.

Hone, J. M. *W. B. Yeats, 1865–1939*. London: Macmillan, 1942.

James, William. "Concerning Fechner." In *A Pluralistic Universe*, 133–77. Lincoln, NE: University of Nebraska Press, 1996.

Janaway, Christopher, ed. *Willing and Nothingness: Schopenhauer as Nietzsche's Educator*. Oxford: Clarendon, 1998.

Jonas, Hans. *The Phenomenon of Life: Toward a Philosophical Biology*. Evanston, IL: Northwestern University Press, 2001.

Kant, Immanuel. *Critique of the Power of Judgment*. Edited by Paul Guyer; translated by Eric Matthews. Cambridge: Cambridge University Press, 2000.

———. *Groundwork of the Metaphysics of Morals: A German-English Edition*. Edited and translated by Mary Gregor and Jens Timmerman. Cambridge: Cambridge University Press, 2011.

Kierkegaard, Søren, *The Journals of Kierkegaard, 1834–1854*. Edited and translated by Alexander Dru. London: Collins Fontana Books, 1958.

———. *The Last Years: Journals 1853–1855*. Edited and translated by Ronald Gregor Smith. London: Collins, Fontana Library, 1965.

Lara, María Pía, ed. *Rethinking Evil: Contemporary Perspectives*. Berkeley: University of California Press, 2001.

Levinas, E. *De l'existence à l'existant*. Paris: Fontaine, 1947. Translated by as *Existence and Existents* by A. Lingis. The Hague: Nijhof, 1978.

Lewis Ben. "Hammer & Tickle." *Prospect Magazine*, Issue 122, May 2006. http://www.prospect-magazine.co.uk/article_details.php?id=7412.

Lutz, Tom. *Crying: The Natural and Cultural History of Tears*. New York: Norton, 1999.

Lyotard, Jean-François. *The Inhuman: Reflections on Time*. Translated by Geoffrey Bennington and Rachel Bowlby. Cambridge: Polity, 1991.

———. *Lessons on the Analytic of the Sublime*. Translated by Elizabeth Rottenberg. Stanford, CA: Stanford University Press, 1994.

———. "Newman: The Instant." In *The Lyotard Reader*, edited by Andrew Benjamin, 240–49. Oxford: Blackwell, 1989.

———. "The Sublime and the Avant-Garde." In *The Lyotard Reader*, edited by Andrew Benjamin, 196–211. Oxford: Blackwell, 1989.

Marchenkov, Vladimir. *The Orpheus Myth and the Powers of Music*. Hillsdale, NY: Pendragon, 2009.

Miłosz, Czesław. *Czesław Miłosz: Conversations*. Edited by Cynthia L. Haven. Jackson, MS: University Press of Mississippi, 2006.

———. *New and Collected Poems 1931–2001*. London: Penguin, 2005.

MacHale, Des. *The Humour of Cork*. Cork: Mercier, 1995.

Marion, Jean-Luc. *The Idol and Distance: Five Studies*. 2nd ed. Translated by Thomas Carlson. Bronx, NY: Fordham University Press, 2001.

———. *In Excess: Studies of Saturated Phenomena*. Translated by Robyn Horner and Vincent Berraud. Bronx, NY: Fordham University Press, 2002.

Matuštík, Martin Beck. *Radical Evil and the Scarcity of Hope: Postsecular Meditations*. Indianapolis: Indiana University Press, 2008.

Mercier, Vivian. *The Irish Comic Tradition*. Oxford: Clarendon, 1962.

Melville, Herman. *Moby-Dick*. New York: Norton, 2002.

Morange, Michel. *Life Explained*. Translated by M. Cobb and M. DeBevoise. New Haven: Yale University Press, 2008.

Mulhall, Stephen. *Stanley Cavell's Recounting of the Ordinary*. Oxford: Clarendon, 1994.

Neill, A., and C. Janaway, eds. *Better Consciousness: Schopenhauer's Philosophy of Value*. Oxford: Wiley-Blackwell, 2009.

Neiman, Susan. *Evil in Modern Thought: An Alternative History of Modern Philosophy*. Princeton: Princeton University Press, 2002.

Newman, Barnett. "The Sublime is Now." In *Art in Theory 1900-2000: An Anthology of Changing Ideas*, 2nd ed., edited by Charles Harrison and Paul Wood, 580–82. Oxford: Blackwell, 1999.

Nietzsche, Friedrich. *Basic Writings of Nietzsche*. Translated by Walter Kaufman. New York: Modern Library, 1992.

———. *The Portable Nietzsche*. Edited and translated by Walter Kaufmann. New York: Penguin, 1977.

———. *Thus Spoke Zarathustra*. Translated and introduced by R. J. Hollingdale. London: Penguin, 1964.

———. *The Will to Power*. Translated by W. Kaufmann and R. J. Hollingdale. New York: Random House, 1969.

———. *Der Wille zur Macht*. Leipzig: Kröner, 1930.

Nikulin, Dmitri. *Dialectic and Dialogue*. Stanford, CA: Stanford University Press, 2010.

Nuttall, A. D. *Shakespeare the Thinker*. New Haven: Yale University Press, 2007.

Nye, David. *American Technological Sublime*. Cambridge: M.I.T. Press, 1994.

Ó Cadhain, Máirtín. *The Dirty Dust: Cré Na Cille*. Translated by Alan Titley. New Haven: Yale University Press, 2015.

———. *Graveyard Clay: Cré na Cille*. Translated by Liam Mac Con Iomaire and Tim Robinson. New Haven: Yale University press, 2016.

Ó Crualaoich, Gearóid. *The Book of the Cailleach: Stories of the Wise Woman Healer*. Cork: Cork University Press, 2006.

Ó Laoire, Lillis. *On a Rock in the Middle of the Ocean: Songs and Singers in Tory Island*. Indreabhán, Conamara: Cló Iar-Chonnachta, 2007.

O'Regan, Cyril. "What Theology Can Learn from a Philosophy Daring to Speak the Unspeakable." *Irish Theological Quarterly* 73 (2008) 243–62.

Pessoa, Fernando. *The Book of Disquiet*. Translated by Margaret Jull Costa, with an introduction by William Boyd. London: Serpent's Tail, 2010.

Pieper, Josef. *The Platonic Myths*. Translated by Dan Farrelly with an introduction by James V. Schall. South Bend, IN: St. Augustine's, 2011.

Plato, *Euthyphro, Apology, Crito, Phaedo, Phaedrus*. Loeb Classical Library I. With an English translation by Harold North Fowler. Cambridge: Harvard University Press, 1971.

———. *Laws*. 2 vols. Loeb Classical Library X and XI. With an English translation by R. G. Bury. Cambridge: Harvard University Press, 1968.

———. *Lysis, Symposium, Gorgias*. Loeb Classical Library III. With an English translation by W. R. M. Lamb. Cambridge: Harvard University Press, 1967.

———. *Republic*. 2 vols. Loeb Classical Library V and VI. With an English translation by Paul Shorey. Cambridge: Harvard University Press, 1969.

———. *Statesman, Philebus, Ion*. Loeb Classical Library VIII. With an English translation by Harold North Fowler. Cambridge: Harvard University Press, 1962.

———. *Timaeus*. Loeb Classical Library IX. With an English translation by Harold North Fowler. Cambridge: Harvard University Press, 1971.

Raine, Kathleen. "Soliloquies." In *The Collected Poems of Kathleen Raine*, 319. Washington, DC: Counterpoint, 2001.

Ramos, Alice, ed. *Beauty, Art, and the Polis*. Washington, DC: American Maritain Association, 2010.

Ross, Chanon. *Gifts Glittering and Poisoned: Spectacle, Empire, and Metaphysics*. Kalos. Eugene, OR: Cascade, 2014.

Ratner-Rosenhagen, Jennifer. *American Nietzsche: A History of an Icon and His Ideas*. Chicago: University of Chicago Press, 2011.

Ruddick, Lisa. "When Nothing Is Cool." In *The Future of Scholarly Writing: Critical Interventions*, edited by Angelika Bammer and Ruth-Ellen Boetcher Joeres, 71–86. New York: Palgrave Macmillan, 2015.

Saunders, George. *Lincoln in the Bardo*. New York: Random House, 2017.

Sachs, Joe. *Aristotle's On the Soul and On Memory and Recollection*. Santa Fe, NM: Green Lion, 2001.

Schelling, F. W. J. *Historical-critical Introduction to the Philosophy of Mythology*. Translated by M. Richey and M. Zisselsberger. Albany, NY: SUNY Press, 2007.

Schoenberg, Arnold, *Theory of Harmony*. Translated by R. E. Carter. Berkeley: University of California Press, 1978.

Schopenhauer, Arthur. *Manuscript Remains*, Vol. 1. Translated by E. F. J. Payne. Oxford: Berg, 1988.

———. *Parerga and Paralipomena*. 2 vols. Translated by E. F. J. Payne. Oxford: Oxford University Press, 1974.

———. *Sämtliche Werke*. Edited by Wolfgang Frhr. von Lohneysen. Darmstadt: Wissenschaftliche Buchgesellschaft, 1968.

———. *The World as Will and Representation*. 2 vols. Translated by E. F. J. Payne. New York: Dover, 1966.

Sigurdson, Ola. "Emancipation as a Matter of Style: Humour and Eschatology in Eagleton and Žižek." *Political Theology* 14.2 (2013) 235–51.

Simpson, Christopher Ben. "All Things Shining: Desmond's Metaxological Metaphysics and *The Thin Red Line*." In *Between System and Poetics: William Desmond and Philosophy After Dialectic*, edited by Thomas Kelly, 239–59. Aldershot, UK: Ashgate, 2007.

———. Introduction to *The William Desmond Reader*, edited by Christopher Ben Simpson, xiii–xvi. Albany, NY: SUNY Press, 2012.

Sterne, Laurence. *The Life and Opinions of Tristram Shandy, Gentleman*. Edited with an introduction by Ian Campbell Ross. Oxford: Oxford University Press, 2009.

Stone-Davis, Férdia J. "Music and Liminal Ethics: Facilitating a 'Soulful Reality.'" In *The Resounding Soul: Reflections on the Metaphysics and Vivacity of the Human Person*, edited by Eric Lee and Samuel Kimbriel, 285–306. Eugene, OR: Cascade, 2015.

Silverman, Hugh J., and Gary E. Aylesworth, eds. *The Textual Sublime: Deconstruction and Its Differences*. Albany, NY: SUNY Press, 1989.

Tabbi, Joseph. *Postmodern Sublime: Technology and American Writing from Mailer to Cyberpunk*. Ithaca, NY: Cornell University Press, 1995.

Taylor, Charles. *A Secular Age*. Cambridge: Harvard University Press, 2007.

Taylor, W. David O. *The Theater of God's Glory: Calvin, Creation and the Liturgical Arts*. Grand Rapids: Eerdmans, 2017.

Weil, Simone. "Morality and Literature." In *Simone Weil Reader*, edited by George A. Panichas, 290–95. Wakefield, RI: Moyer Bell, 1999.

Weiss, Paul. *Being and Other Realities*. La Salle, IL: Open Court, 1995.

———. *Cinematics*. Carbondale, IL: Southern Illinois University Press, 1975.

———. *Creative Ventures*. Carbondale, IL: Southern Illinois University Press, 1992.

———. "Dunamis." *Review of Metaphysics* 40.4 (1987) 657–74.

———. *Emphatics*. Nashville: Vanderbilt University Press, 2000.

———. *Nine Basic Arts*. Carbondale, IL: Southern Illinois University Press, 1966.

———. *The Philosophy of Paul Weiss: The Library of Living Philosophers, Volume XXIII*.

———. *Religion and Art*. Milwaukee: Marquette University Press, 1963.

———. "Response to William Desmond." *The Philosophy of Paul Weiss: The Library of Living Philosophers, Volume XXIII*, edited by Lewis Edwin Hahn, 558–64. La Salle, IL: Open Court, 1995.

———. *The World of Art*. Carbondale, IL: Southern Illinois University Press, 1961.

Whitehead, A. N. *Process and Reality: An Essay in Cosmology*. 1929. Corrected ed. Edited by David Ray Griffin and Donald W. Sherburne. New York: Free, 1978.

———. *Science and the Modern World*. New York: Macmillan, 1925.

Wittgenstein, Ludwig. *Culture and Value*. 2nd ed. Edited by G. H. von Wright with Heikki Nyman; translated by Peter Winch. Chicago: University of Chicago Press, 1980.

———. *Lectures and Conversations on Aesthetics, Psychology and Religious Belief*. Edited by Cyril Barrett. Oxford: Blackwell, 1966.

Wordsworth, William. *The Major Works*. Edited with an introduction by Stephen Gill. Oxford: Oxford University Press, 2008.

Yeats, W. B. *Explorations*. Selected by Mrs. W. B. Yeats. London: Macmillan, 1962.

———. *The Poems*. Edited by Daniel Albright. London: Dent, 1990.

William Desmond is David Cook Chair in Philosophy at Villanova University, Thomas A. F. Kelly Visiting Chair in Philosophy, Maynooth University, Ireland, and Professor of Philosophy Emeritus at the Institute of Philosophy, Katholieke Universiteit Leuven. His work is primarily in metaphysics, ethics, aesthetics, and the philosophy of religion. He is the author of many books, including the ground-breaking trilogy *Being and the Between* (1995), *Ethics and the Between* (2001), and *God and the Between* (2008). *Being and the Between* was winner of both the prestigious Prix Cardinal Mercier and the J. N. Findlay Award for best book in metaphysics. Other books include *Art and the Absolute* (1986); *Desire Dialectic and Otherness: An Essay on Origins* (1987; 2nd ed. 2014); *Philosophy and Its Others: Ways of Being and Mind* (1990); *Beyond Hegel and Dialectic* (1992); *Perplexity and Ultimacy* (1995); *Hegel's God* (2003); *Art, Origins, Otherness: Between Art and Philosophy* (2003); as well as *Is There a Sabbath for Thought? Between Religion and Philosophy* (2005). He has also edited five books and published more than 100 articles and book chapters. His book *The Intimate Strangeness of Being: Metaphysics after Dialectic* appeared in 2012, the same year in which the *William Desmond Reader* also appeared. His new book, *The Intimate Universal: The Hidden Porosity among Religion, Art, Philosophy and Politics* appeared with Columbia University Press 2016. He is Past President of the Hegel Society of America, the Metaphysical Society of America, and the American Catholic Philosophical Association.

# Index

www.ingramcontent.com/pod-product-compliance
Lightning Source LLC
LaVergne TN
LVHW041106080826
845145LV00007B/1708

* 9 7 8 1 5 3 2 6 1 7 1 0 2 *